Climate Change before International Courts

This book provides a comprehensive analysis of enviror climate change litigation within international courts, both : procedurally. Climate change litigation is an area of contin complexity, particularly within international courts and b uses a comparative approach, analysing case law from inter It focuses on three key areas, namely trends and features, litigation, and legal standing before courts. A concluding cor highlights the specific shortcomings and potential of each : with climate change problems, taking stock of fragmentat international law. The book presents instances in which int are applying procedural and substantive law to this disrupti and intergenerational legal problem. It addresses gaps in the and identifies systems which are not fit for purpose.

With international contributions from authors of diver this book will be of interest to researchers in the field o and environmental law, EU and international law, and in litigation.

Carla Amado Gomes is Associate Professor at University of Law, Portugal. She is also Guest Professor at the Facul Catholic University, Porto. She teaches in the area of Env Administrative Law, and Energy Law.

Heloísa Oliveira is Assistant Professor at the University of Law, Portugal. She is also a Research Fellow at Lis Research Center, where she is PI for the Climate Litigation Legal Roadmap for Sustainability project. Outside of acac Coordinator Consultant for Environmental Law at the Leg Portuguese Government.

Routledge Research in International Environmental Law

Implementing International Environmental Law and Policy
An Interactive Approach to Environmental Regulation
Joanna Miller Smallwood

Environmental Law and Policy in India
Sairam Bhat and Centre for Environmental Law, Education, Research, and Advocacy (CEERA)

Protection of the Environment under International Law during Occupation
International Humanitarian, Human Rights and Environmental Law
Waad Abualrob

State Accountability for Environmental Damage in International Armed Conflict
Aïda Tamer Chammas

Corporate Environmental Responsibility and Pollution Control Laws
The Case of Oil Spills in the Niger Delta
Millicent Ele

Corporate Criminal Liability in Environmental Jurisprudence
Indrajit Dube and Mia Mahmudur Rahim

Climate Change before International Courts
A Comparative Study
Carla Amado Gomes, Heloísa Oliveira, Armando Rocha and Matteo Fermeglia

https://www.routledge.com/Routledge-Research-in-International-Environmental-Law/book-series/INTENVLAW

Climate Change before International Courts

A Comparative Study

Edited by Carla Amado Gomes, Heloísa Oliveira, Armando Rocha and Matteo Fermeglia

Routledge
Taylor & Francis Group
LONDON AND NEW YORK

Fundação para a Ciência e a Tecnologia

First published 2026
by Routledge
4 Park Square, Milton Park, Abingdon, Oxon OX14 4RN

and by Routledge
605 Third Avenue, New York, NY 10158

Routledge is an imprint of the Taylor & Francis Group, an informa business

British Library Cataloguing-in-Publication Data
A catalogue record for this book is available from the British Library

ISBN: 978-1-032-86789-2 (hbk)
ISBN: 978-1-032-89048-7 (pbk)
ISBN: 978-1-003-54097-7 (ebk)

DOI: 10.4324/9781003540977

Typeset in Sabon
by Deanta Global Publishing Services, Chennai, India

Contents

List of Tables *ix*
Contributors *x*
Acknowledgements *xiv*

Introductory Note 1
CARLA AMADO GOMES, HELOÍSA OLIVEIRA, ARMANDO ROCHA, AND MATTEO FERMEGLIA

PART A
Legal Grounds in International Climate Litigation 3

1 The United Nations System – Legal Grounds in Climate Litigation 5
MARGARETHA WEWERINKE-SINGH, MANASA VENKATACHALAM, AND ARMANDO ROCHA

2 The Inter-American Human Rights System and Climate Litigation 41
MARIA ANTONIA TIGRE AND THALIA VIVEROS-UEHARA

3 In Search for the Content of States' Positive Obligations under the European Convention on Human Rights: *KlimaSeniorinnen* and Climate Change 75
VLADISLAVA STOYANOVA

4 The Protection of the Climate System in the African System of Human Rights – Possible Legal Grounds 105
WELENA DA SILVA AND ARMANDO ROCHA

5 Climate Litigation before the Court of Justice of the European Union: A Quantitative and Qualitative Review of Features and Legal Grounds 127
HELOÍSA OLIVEIRA, ANA RUIZ, AND PEDRO SAMPAIO MINASSA

PART B
Procedural Issues in International Climate Litigation 159

6 Climate Litigation within the United Nations System – Unity, Pluralism, and a Common Goal 161
JOSÉ ALBERTO AZEREDO LOPES AND MARIA ISABEL TAVARES

7 Climate Litigation in the Inter-American Human Rights System: Addressing Legal Standing 187
DÉLTON WINTER DE CARVALHO AND CAROLINA MERIDA

8 Climate Litigation before the European Court of Human Rights: A Catalyst for Reevaluating Prerequisites for Legal Standing 206
MAŁGORZATA KWIĘDACZ-PALOSZ

9 Climate Litigation in the African Human Rights System: Possibilities, Limits, and Constraints 224
WELENA DA SILVA

10 Environmental Litigation and the CJEU: Overcoming Barriers to Standing? 247
NIELS HOEK AND ARIANNA CROSERA

11 Climate Litigation before International Courts: Conclusive Remarks on a Comparative Study 266
CARLA AMADO GOMES, HELOÍSA OLIVEIRA, ARMANDO ROCHA, AND MATTEO FERMEGLIA

Index *275*

List of Tables

5.1 Climate Cases Brought Before the CJEU, According to Type of Proceedings, Core Theme, Originating Entity, and Type of Decision 131
5.2 ETS Cases Core Themes 134
5.3 Non-ETS Cases Core Themes 135
5.4 Climate Cases Brought Before the CJEU, According to Phase and Type of Proceedings 137
5.5 Climate Protection Impacts of all Cases and Cases Decided on Merits 138
5.6 Outcomes of Climate Cases and Pending Cases: All and by Subject 139
10.1 Avenues for Standing Reform in EU Climate and Environmental Litigation 263

Contributors

Arianna Crosera is a PhD Researcher at the European University Institute (EUI), where she coordinates the Information Society Working Group (InfoSoc). She has a background in European and international law and a specialisation in environmental law and energy law, which are also core to her PhD research. Since November 2024, she has acted as Assistant Editor at the *Transnational Environmental Law Journal* (*TEL*). She has coupled her work in academia with an active presence in EU non-governmental organisations, in particular in the area of intergenerational justice and the circular economy.

Matteo Fermeglia is an Assistant Professor of Climate Law and Governance at Amsterdam University, Faculty of Humanities. His main research interest lies in the interplay between international investment law and the climate change legal regime. He regularly (co-)authors internationally peer-reviewed journal articles in the field of environmental and climate law and was awarded the Raúl Estrada-Oyuela Award for Emerging Scholars in Climate Law in 2017 by Lexxion publishers. He was a visiting scholar at Columbia Law School, where he collaborated with the Sabin Center for Climate Change Law and the Columbia Centre for Sustainable Investments.

Carla Amado Gomes is an Associate Professor at the University of Lisbon School of Law, a Guest Professor at the Porto School of Law of Universidade Católica Portuguesa, and a Research Fellow at the Lisbon Public Law Research Centre. She has extensive teaching experience in master's and postgraduate courses in environmental law in Angola, Brazil, Cape Verde and Mozambique, and has published over 300 papers and books in several areas of public law, namely administrative law, administrative procedural law, environmental law, cultural heritage law, animal law, constitutional law, energy law, and parliamentary law.

Niels Hoek is a PhD researcher in law at the European University Institute (EUI), where he also coordinates the Environmental Law and Governance Working Group. His work focuses on EU environmental and biodiversity law. Niels is a senior editor at the *European Journal of Legal Studies* and a member of the legal working group of the Society for Ecological Restoration. He was a lecturer at Radboud University Nijmegen and active in environmental NGOs. He has published on topics including the Nature Restoration Law, Environmental Litigation, Rights of Nature, and EU Governance of Light Pollution.

Małgorzata Kwiędacz-Palosz is a Senior Fundamental Rights Lawyer at ClientEarth. She works at the nexus of human rights and environmental law. Before that, Malgorzata worked at the Polish Ministry of Foreign Affairs, the Ministry of Environment and the Ministry of Justice, and at the Registry of the European Court of Human Rights. She holds a law degree (M.A.) from the University of Łódź and a Master from the University François Rabelais of Tours. She graduated from the Polish National School of Public Administration. She is also Polish-qualified lawyer.

José Alberto Azeredo Lopes is an Associate Professor of International Law and the Coordinator of the International Studies Programme, masters in International and European Law, Oporto Law School, Catholic University of Portugal. Member of the Católica Research Centre for the Future of Law. Visiting Professor of Blanquerna Comunicació, Universitat Ramon Llul, Barcelona.

Carolina Merida holds a PhD in Law from Unisinos and completed a post-doctoral fellowship at the Universidad de Las Palmas de Gran Canaria. She is Municipal Attorney of Rio Verde. Coordinator of the Post-Graduate Program (Master's Degree) and professor of International Law at the Universidade de Rio Verde (UniRV). Member of the National Council for Research and Graduate Studies in Law (CONPEDI), and the Brazilian Academy of International Law (ABDI), both based in Brazil.

Pedro Sampaio Minassa is a PhD candidate at the University of Lisbon and pursuing a Master's in Environment and Development at UNIVATES (Brazil). He also holds a Master's degree in Legal-Environmental Sciences from the University of Lisbon and a postgraduate specialization in Public Law. He is a Collaborator Researcher at the Lisbon Public Law Research Centre (LPL).

Heloísa Oliveira is an Assistant Professor at the University of Lisbon School of Law. She is a Research Fellow at Lisbon Public Law Research Center – where she is the PI for the Climate Litigation Observatory project – and a Consultant for environmental law at the Legal Service of the Portuguese Government. Her research is on environmental law from an administrative, international, and European Union Law and fundamental rights perspectives, particularly on climate litigation, soil protection, and the transition to a circular economy. She has published over 30 papers and book chapters on her areas of research and coedited several books.

Armando Rocha is an Assistant Professor at Lisbon School of Law of Universidade Católica Portuguesa and a member of the Católica Research Centre for the Future of Law, where he has been responsible for conducting and reviewing legal research in the law of the sea and international climate change law. He is also a Guest Professor at the Catholic University of Lille (France) and the University of St. Joseph (Macao, China), and he was invited professor at Reichman University (Tel Aviv, Israel). Armando Rocha has published and coedited multiple books, book chapters, and journal articles.

Ana Ruiz is a Collaborator Researcher at the Lisbon Public Law Research Centre. She holds an LLM in Global Environmental Law and Governance from the University of Strathclyde. She was a policy Analyst at ERCST – European Roundtable on Climate Change and Sustainable Transition and a lawyer in public and corporate law.

Welena da Silva holds a law degree from the Faculty of Law of Bissau and a Master's degree in Legal-Environmental Sciences from the University of Lisbon School of Law. He is currently a PhD candidate in Legal-Political Sciences at the University of Lisbon. He is also a lecturer at the Faculty of Law of Bissau and a lawyer and legal consultant in the areas of environmental law, land law, human rights, and natural resources law.

Vladislava Stoyanova is Associate Professor of Public International Law at the Faculty of Law, Lund University. She holds the Wallenberg Academy Fellowship (2021–2026) and is the receiver of the 2023 Henrik Enderlein Prize for research excellence. Stoyanova's multiple high-level publications include the monograph Positive Obligations under the European Convention on Human Rights: Within and Beyond Boundaries (Oxford University Press, 2023). Stoyanova's research interests relate to public international law, human rights law, migration law, and EU law.

Maria Isabel Tavares is an Associate Professor of International Law at Oporto Law School, Catholic University of Portugal and a Member of the Católica Research Centre for the Future of Law. She was also a political Advisor on internal and external affairs of the Minister of National Defense of Portugal (2016–2018).

Maria Antónia Tigre holds a PhD from the Elisabeth Haub School of Law at Pace University (2022). Tigre is a Director of Global Climate Change Litigation at the Sabin Center for Climate Change Law at Columbia Law School, Deputy Director of the Global Network for Human Rights and the Environment (GNHRE), and Member of the IUCN World Commission on Environmental Law. Togre has done extensive high-level research on human rights and climate change.

Manasa Venkatachalam is a Legal Consultant at Blue Ocean Law. She holds an Advanced Master's Degree in Public International Law (Specialization in Peace, Justice, and Development) from Leiden University (cum laude) and a BA LLB (Hons.) from Gujarat National Law University. Her research and practice focus on international human rights in the context of climate change, emphasizing the impacts on the global majority.

Thalia Viveros-Uehara is a Senior Research Fellow at the Max Planck Institute for Comparative Public Law and International Law and a postdoctoral researcher in the Department of Public Law and Governance at Tilburg University. She is a lawyer with postgraduate studies at the London School of Economics and Political Science, where she earned a Master's degree in Environmental Policy and Regulation, and holds a Doctorate in Global Inclusion and Social Development from the University of Massachusetts Boston. Her work focuses on socio-legal approaches to human rights, environmental and climate change law, and their intersections with social development, emphasizing the human face of contemporary environmental and climate challenges.

Margaretha Wewerinke-Singh is an Associate Professor of Sustainability Law at the University of Amsterdam, Adjunct Professor of Law at the University of Fiji, Member of the Permanent Court of Arbitration, Barrister & Solicitor of the Supreme Court of Vanuatu and Of Counsel at Blue Ocean Law. She holds a PhD in Law from the European University Institute and has published widely on human rights, climate change, and international law.

Délton Winter de Carvalho is an attorney and legal expert in environmental law, climate law and disaster law. Professor and researcher in the Post-Graduate Program at Unisinos. Délton holds an LLM and a PhD Guest Lecturer of the LLM Program at Berkeley School of Law. Visiting Scholar at University of California and Loyola University. He has also been a member of the Environmental Law Commission of the Brazilian Bar Association's Environmental Law Committee and a Consulting Member of the Special Commission on Climate Change and Environmental Disasters of the Brazilian National Bar Association.

Acknowledgements

This book is an output of the Climate Litigation Observatory project of the Lisbon Environmental Law cluster, part of the Lisbon Public Law Research Centre. The editors acknowledge support from FCT – Fundação para a Ciência e a Tecnologia, I.P. through national funds under references UIDB/04310/2020 and UIDP/04310/2020.

Heloísa Oliveira acknowledges support from FCT – Fundação para a Ciência e a Tecnologia, I.P. through national funds under references UIDB/04310/2020 and UIDP/04310/2020.

Pedro Sampaio Minassa acknowledges support from FCT – Fundação para a Ciência e a Tecnologia, I.P. through national funds under reference UIDB&P/04310/2020/LRS.

Thalia Viveros-Uehara acknowledges support from the TransLitigate project (ERC-2021-STG 101039648), funded by the European Union. Views and opinions expressed are, however, those of the author(s) only and do not necessarily reflect those of the European Union or European Research Council. Neither the European Union nor the granting authority can be held responsible for them.

Niels Hoek and Arianna Crosera would like to thank Dr. Mario Pagano, Saverio Della Corte, and Dr. Heloísa Oliveira for their tremendous help and feedback on earlier drafts of this manuscript.

Introductory Note

Carla Amado Gomes, Heloísa Oliveira, Armando Rocha, and Matteo Fermeglia

Global databases show that climate litigation is a worldwide phenomenon. Despite its global nature, most climate cases have been brought before domestic courts, where non-governmental organisations, companies, and citizens have been able to file cases and contribute to the development of international and domestic climate-related laws through judicial reasoning. Consequently, a significant amount of legal research has focused on domestic climate litigation, examining its features, challenges, and outcomes.

This scenario is changing. International cases are on the rise, and, due to the particular nature of international law, legal research is essential to understand how courts and other adjudicative bodies have addressed climate cases and to anticipate how they might do so in the near future. This book represents an effort to combine in-depth research on adjudicated cases with prospective analyses of how international climate case law may develop in the near future, both substantively and procedurally.

In this framework, the task at hand proved to be herculean, requiring negative delimitations, namely, choosing which legal systems were to be the object of study. The notable fragmentation of international law and the coexistence of a myriad of legal systems and bodies in the international realm is fertile ground for a comparative study. Human rights regional systems (American, European, and African) are usual suspects for comparative analysis, but the UN System[1] itself includes a varied set of treaties and institutions, each with jurisdiction for applying a variable set of legal norms. How are materially similar topics being addressed, and how are apparently common legal doctrines being applied by these bodies? Is there consistency of uniformity in legal reasoning or in the interpretation of the same legal acts?

1 For the purpose of this edited book, the UN System includes treaties that were adopted under the aegis of the UN as well as judicial courts, tribunals, and para-judicial bodies that are responsible for the centralised interpretation and enforcement of these treaties. These treaties and these institutions are usually not labelled as "UN System"—except for the purposes of human rights law. Still, empirical observation shows that, apart from sharing the same genetic fabric, there is a certain coordination of efforts and approaches justifying the use of the noun "system" to describe the treaties and institutions that operate in this context.

DOI: 10.4324/9781003540977-1

In addition to this list of international courts and adjudicative bodies, we also decided to venture into the consideration of the Court of Justice of the European Union in this comparative exercise. While it is formally an international court, due to its creation by international treaties, it possesses a unique nature stemming from the specificities of European Union law. This led us to question how its case law might be similar to or radically different from that of other international bodies. This book is, therefore, structured to consider five legal systems, one of which is a compound system: the UN system, the Inter-American Human Rights system, the European Human Rights system, the African Human and Peoples' Rights system, and European Union law, limited to the jurisdiction of the Court of Justice of the European Union.

Moreover, identifying existing and potential legal grounds for climate cases was an obvious part of this book. However, it also became clear that procedural hurdles are crucial to understanding the context and content of many cases and could, therefore, not be excluded, particularly in relation to standing. It should be noted, however, that rules on access often depend on, and intertwine with, substantive issues, such as those concerning the legal positions invoked. This division between substance and procedure is therefore a defeasible rule, not rigid, as these areas often intersect.

This has resulted in a work with two parts: the first dedicated to legal grounds (Part A) and the second to procedural issues (Part B), with one chapter focused on each of the chosen legal systems, totalling ten chapters. The chapters offer diverse perspectives and structures, reflecting the diversity of international climate litigation itself. Together, however, they provide a comprehensive understanding of what climate litigation is today and how it might develop in the short term, presenting possibilities for overcoming challenges to the role of courts in the context of climate change.

Part A

Legal Grounds in International Climate Litigation

1 The United Nations System – Legal Grounds in Climate Litigation*

Margaretha Wewerinke-Singh, Manasa Venkatachalam, and Armando Rocha

1.1 Introduction

Addressing climate change is inherently a global effort, requiring the coordination of all States to ensure that the actions taken are effective and equitable. A treaty-based framework for such coordination was established through the UN Framework Convention on Climate Change,[1] supplemented by the Kyoto Protocol,[2] and, more recently, the Paris Agreement[3] – treaties that aspire to "stabilis[e] greenhouse gas [GHG] concentrations in the atmosphere at a level that would prevent dangerous anthropogenic interference with the climate system",[4] in line with the principle of common but differentiated responsibilities and respective capabilities.[5] At the same time, however, dangerous anthropogenic interference with the climate system has already manifested, with losses and damages being suffered around the world.[6] However, global GHG emissions, largely from fossil fuels, continue to rise and reach record levels.[7]

In this situation, it is no surprise that States, organisations, and individuals have turned to international judicial and quasi-judicial bodies to seek a course correction and to obtain reparations for climate harm. Such bodies can provide critical guidance or interventions by clarifying the limits of States' discretion,

* This chapter was submitted in January 2025, before the advisory opinions from the ICJ and the IACtHR were delivered.

1 UN Framework Convention on Climate Change (adopted 9 May 1992, entered into force 21 March 1994) 1771 UNTS 107 ("UNFCCC").

2 Kyoto Protocol to the UNFCCC (adopted 10 December 1997, entered into force 16 February 2005) 2303 UNTS 162, Article 3(5).

3 Paris Agreement (adopted 12 December 2015, entered into force 4 November 2016) 3156 UNTS 79.

4 UNFCCC, Article 2; Kyoto Protocol, Article 10, Paris Agreement, Article 2(1)(b) and (c).

5 UNFCCC, Article 3; Kyoto Protocol, Article 2, Paris Agreement, Article 2(2).

6 Obligations of States in relation to Climate Change. UNGA Res 77/276 (29 March 2023) UN Doc A/RES/77/276, Preamble, para. 9; IPCC, Summary for Policymakers. Climate Change 2023: Synthesis Report. Contribution of Working Groups I, II and III to the Sixth Assessment Report of the Intergovernmental Panel on Climate Change. (IPCC 2023) 20.

7 Conference of the Parties serving as the meeting of the Parties to the Paris Agreement. Draft decision -/CMA.5. Outcome of the First Global Stocktake. FCCC/PA/CMA/2023/L.17 (13 December 2023) ("First Global Stocktake").

DOI: 10.4324/9781003540977-3

setting out the legal consequences of breaches of obligations, and providing redress to victims.[8] In practice, resorting to judicial and quasi-judicial bodies has become an important strategy for addressing climate change at the domestic level and, increasingly so, at the international level, too.[9]

In this light, this chapter assesses what are the *features* of dispute settlement mechanisms within the UN system that could be used to address climate change and the *trends* in the actual use of such mechanisms to date. In light of space limitations, our analysis is confined to a few particularly prominent bodies and mechanisms: the International Court of Justice (ICJ), the dispute settlement procedures mentioned in the UNFCCC (applicable to the Paris Agreement), the International Tribunal on the Law of the Sea (ITLOS), the International Criminal Court (ICC), and UN human rights treaty bodies. In the subsections referring to features and trends, this chapter relies on the findings of Chapter 6, by Lopes and Tavares, who develop in more detail the legal standing before these courts, tribunals, and quasi-judicial bodies. The purpose of this chapter is to present how concerned States, individuals, and civil society movements may look to the multiple *fora* as an opportunity for bringing climate change into the international judiciary docket, and what cases have actually been presented. Section 2 focuses on the International Court of Justice (ICJ) and the dispute settlement options under the UNFCCC and the Paris Agreement. Section 3 addresses the International Tribunal for the Law of the Sea (ITLOS), and section 4 explores international human rights treaty-based bodies. Section 5 then considers the International Criminal Court (ICC). Each section discusses both the overarching characteristics and the developments within each forum, as well as the legal arguments that have been raised or could be made in the future. Section 6 concludes.

1.2 The International Court of Justice and the Arbitral Tribunal Mentioned in the UNFCCC and the Paris Agreement

1.2.1 Features and Trends

International dispute settlement is inherently consensual, since the competence of a court or tribunal to settle an inter-State dispute depends on the consent of both States in that dispute – although consent may be provided in advance, often under a condition of reciprocity, such as pursuant to Article 36(2) of the ICJ Statute (the "optional clause").[10] Often, however, treaties set out a system of centralised interpretation and enforcement, by conferring

8 Strauss A. Climate Change Litigation: Opening the Door of the International Court of Justice. In: Burns WCG, Osofsky HM, eds. Adjudicating Climate Change – State, National, and International Approaches. Cambridge University Press; 2009. pp. 334, 337.

9 Rocha A. Suing States – The Role of Courts in Promoting States' Responsibility for Climate Change. In: Garcia MG, Cortês A, eds. Blue Planet Law. Springer; 2023. p. 99.

10 See, *inter alia*, Collier J, Lowe V. The Settlement of Disputes in International Law – Institutions and Procedures. Reprint. Oxford University Press; 2010. pp. 140 ff.

jurisdiction to one or more courts and/or tribunals. This latter is the system followed under the UNFCCC and the Paris Agreement.

In fact, according to Articles 14 UNFCCC and 24 Paris Agreement, States may declare in advance that, in relation to disputes on the interpretation or application of these treaties, they recognise the mandatory jurisdiction of the ICJ and/or an arbitral tribunal, *ipso facto* and without special agreement, provided that the other State in the dispute has submitted the same declaration (i.e., under a condition of reciprocity).[11] Being a form of advanced consent, these provisions imply that the ICJ and the arbitral tribunal are the only *fora* for ruling on State-to-State claims arising from the interpretation or application of the UNFCCC or the Paris Agreement (although they are not the only *fora* competent to adjudicate in climate change–related cases), and therefore they are the most authoritative *fora* for the development of the international law on climate change also.

1.2.1.1 The Mandatory Jurisdiction Clause under the UNFCCC

The prospect for State-to-State litigation under the UNFCCC legal complex is short: as of 31 January 2025, only the Netherlands declared to accept both the mandatory jurisdiction of the ICJ and the option of arbitration pursuant to Articles 14 UNFCCC and 24 Paris Agreement, whilst the Solomon Islands and Tuvalu declared to accept only the option of arbitration – and only for the purposes of the UNFCCC.[12] Accordingly, as of 31 January, no dispute was brought before the ICJ or an arbitral tribunal regarding the interpretation or application of the UNFCCC or the Paris Agreement.

The limited scope of the dispute settlement system under the UNFCCC legal complex is a design flaw but also a design choice. This type of treaty clause is prevalent in multilateral environmental treaties, where judicial or adversarial proceedings are uncommon.[13] In general, States are often reluctant to institute judicial proceedings against other States, since they fear damaging their diplomatic relations or triggering retaliation in future proceedings.[14] In the case of climate change, it is not a figment of imagination that GHG emitting States might fear contributing to the creation of an informal precedent

11 UNFCCC, Article 14(2), also applicable *ex vi* Paris Agreement, Article 24.

12 See Declaration by Parties. UNFCCC. [Accessed 31 January 2025]. Available from: https://unfccc.int/process-and-meetings/the-convention/status-of-ratification/declarations-by-parties; and Paris Agreement. United Nations Treaty Collection. [Accessed 31 January 2025]. Available from: https://treaties.un.org/Pages/ViewDetails.aspx?src=TREATY&mtdsg_no=XXVII-7-d&chapter=27&clang=_en.

13 Bodansky D, Brunnée J, Rajamani L. International Climate Change Law. 1st ed. Oxford University Press; 2017. p. 155.

14 E.g. Shelton D. The Participation of Nongovernmental Organizations in International Judicial Proceedings. American Journal of International Law. 1994;88:611, 615; or Stephan P. Privatizing International Law. Virginia Law Review. 2011;97:1573, 1641–1642.

that may be invoked in the future in the context of diplomatic negotiations or judicial proceedings.[15] The largest GHG emitting States are key players in the course of negotiations that take place in the COPs – bearing in mind that their position as "largest emitters" implies they hold a more pronounced responsibility (*ex ante* and *ex post facto*) for climate mitigation.

1.2.1.2 The Contentious Jurisdiction of the ICJ

The fact that Article 14 of the UNFCCC or Article 24 of the Paris Agreement are unlikely to be used as a basis for inter-state dispute resolution in the near future does not mean that dispute settlement regarding these treaties or their subject matter is impossible. As seen with the *COSIS Opinion*[16] and the *KlimaSeniorinnen* judgment,[17] climate change impacts virtually all social domains, and thus renders a wide range of international legal norms relevant and applicable. The interpretation and enforcement of these norms can take place before different *fora* – including fora with specialised jurisdiction and, indeed, the ICJ.

Article 36(2) of the ICJ Statute allows States to make optional declarations accepting the Court's compulsory jurisdiction (but with various reservations allowed) – the 74 States that have done so to date include Australia, Canada, Germany, India, Japan, Mexico, the Netherlands, Norway, Poland, and the United Kingdom, among others.[18] Climate change *per se* can be viewed as a "question of international law" for the purposes of Article 36(2)(b) ICJ Statute; as a "fact which, if established, would constitute a breach of an international obligation" for the purposes of Article 36(2)(c) ICJ Statute; and climate change–related harm can be brought before the ICJ as a matter related to "the nature or extent of the reparation to be made for the breach of an international obligation" for the purposes of Article 36(2)(d) ICJ Statute.[19]

Article 36(2) provides a realistic avenue for States that have already recognised the Court's compulsory jurisdiction to pursue contentious proceedings concerning climate change.[20]

15 Mayer B. The International Law on Climate Change. Cambridge University Press; 2018. pp. 240–241.

16 *Request for an Advisory Opinion submitted by the Commission of Small Island States on Climate Change and International Law* (Advisory Opinion, 21 May 2024) Case No. 31, paras. 47 ff (*COSIS Opinion*).

17 *Verein KlimaSeniorinnen Schweiz et al. v Switzerland* (App. No. 53600/20) ECtHR [GC] 9 April 2024.

18 Declarations recognising the jurisdiction of the Court as compulsory. [Accessed 27 January 2025]. Available from: https://www.icj-cij.org/en/declarations.

19 *Ibid*, 240.

20 See Wewerinke-Singh M, Aguon J, Hunter J. Bringing Climate Change before the International Court of Justice: Prospects for Contentious Cases and Advisory Opinions. In: Alogna I, Bakker C, Gauci J-P, eds. Climate Change Litigation: Global Perspectives. Brill; 2021. p. 401.

Several Small Island Developing States (SIDS) – including Barbados, Dominica, the Dominican Republic, Haiti, Mauritius, Suriname, and Timor-Leste – have lodged such declarations.[21] The advisory proceedings in *Obligations of States in respect of Climate Change* ("*Climate Change Opinion*") at the ICJ have been a clear indicator that it is not only SIDS but also numerous other States and organisations – particularly from the Global South – that strongly argue for stringent climate protection and legal consequences for failing to meet climate obligations.[22] Taken together, these developments signal that recourse to the Court's compulsory jurisdiction remains a tangible option for advancing climate litigation.

By contrast, for States that have not yet recognised the ICJ's compulsory jurisdiction, certain carve-outs in existing compulsory jurisdiction declarations may pose additional hurdles. Several States with declarations – such as Australia, Germany, Japan, and the United Kingdom – exclude from their acceptance any dispute in which another party accepted the Court's jurisdiction solely for that dispute or did so less than 12 months before filing.[23] Consequently, a State newly recognising the ICJ's compulsory jurisdiction must wait a year before instituting proceedings, and it might still face an argument that it accepted jurisdiction only for the matter in question.[24]

Notwithstanding these constraints, the ICJ emerges as a forum that is particularly well-suited for adjudicating climate change cases. Should the forthcoming outcome of the advisory proceedings on climate change fail to prompt adequate State action with respect to both mitigation and reparations for loss and damage, affected States may consider embarking on a contentious case to compel such action and secure further legal remedies.

1.2.1.3 The Advisory Jurisdiction of the ICJ

Climate change as a topic has already arrived at the ICJ and ITLOS dockets through two requests for an advisory opinion. Since opinions are dispute-detached, seeking an advisory opinion may be perceived as a politically less sensitive move than instigating contentious litigation. Moreover, the authority of a court or tribunal to clarify a question of law stems from the sociological perception of the quality and independence of that court or tribunal, which means that the impact of opinions is not necessarily less than that of a

21 Declarations recognising the jurisdiction of the Court as compulsory: Australia. March 2002. [Accessed 27 January 2025]. Available from: https://www.icj-cij.org/en/declarations/au.

22 And several of these States have made Declarations recognising the Court's jurisdiction. Declarations recognising the jurisdiction of the Court as compulsory: Australia. March 2002. [Accessed 27 January 2025]. Available from: https://www.icj-cij.org/en/declarations/au.

23 See, for example, Declarations recognising the jurisdiction of the Court as compulsory: Australia. March 2002. [Accessed 27 January 2025]. Available from: https://www.icj-cij.org/en/declarations/au. See Wewerinke-Singh M, Aguon J, Hunter J, (n 20) p. 400.

24 Wewerinke-Singh M, Aguon J, Hunter J, (n 20) p. 401.

binding judgment, and could even exceed it given its potentially wider reach. This is clear from past ICJ's opinions, which have had a tremendous impact in shaping international law and spurring State action.[25]

Between December 2022 and March 2023, three advisory opinions on States' obligations in relation to climate change were requested from ITLOS, the Inter-American Court of Human Rights (IACtHR), and the ICJ. This subsection analyses the opinion requested to the ICJ more specifically, whilst in the next section 3 the opinion requested from ITLOS is assessed.

The advisory jurisdiction of the ICJ is established in the Charter of the United Nations and in the ICJ Statute,[26] which states that an opinion from the ICJ can be requested by the UN General Assembly (UNGA), the UN Security Council, or by a UN organ or specialised agency – provided that this body or agency is authorised by UNGA and that the question submitted falls within the scope of activities of the said organ or agency.[27] Hence, States cannot request an advisory opinion from the ICJ, although they can propose, campaign, and vote in UNGA a proposal for the submission of a request for an advisory opinion to the ICJ.[28] In this framework, on 29 March 2023, UNGA approved a request to the ICJ for an opinion in relation to States' obligations under general international law, environmental law, the United Nations Convention on the Law of the Sea (UNCLOS),[29] and human rights law, including the consequences in case of significant harm.[30]

According to the UN Charter and the ICJ Statute, the ICJ can receive a request on any "legal question" of "international law", which implies that it cannot receive a request regarding a question of domestic law or a purely political nature. Implied is also the idea that the ICJ cannot receive a question related to a treaty whose interpretation and enforcement are attributed exclusively to another international body. Looking at most submissions to the ICJ in the *Climate Change Opinion,* none of these hindrances seem to

25 For example, the *Chagos Advisory Opinion* has spurred the United Kingdom to cede sovereignty over the Chagos Archipelago. See *Legal Consequences of the Separation of the Chagos Archipelago from Mauritius in 1965* (Advisory Opinion) [2019] ICJ Rep 95 ("*Chagos Opinion*"); "UK and Mauritius joint statement, 3 October 2024" (3 October 2024). Available from: https://www.gov.uk/government/news/joint-statement-between-uk-and-mauritius-3-october-2024#:~:text=The%20Prime%20Minister%20of%20the,sovereignty%20over%20the%20Chagos%20Archipelago.

26 Charter of the United Nations, Article 96 (adopted 26 June 1945, entered into force 24 October 1945) 892 *UNTS* 119 (UN Charter), and Statute of the International Court of Justice, Articles 65–68 (adopted 26 June 1945, entered into force 24 October 1945) 892 UNTS 119 (ICJ Statute).

27 UN Charter, Article 96.

28 *Ibid*, para. 1. See Wewerinke-Singh M, Viñuales J, Aguon J. The Role of Advocates in the Conception of Advisory Opinion Requests. American Journal of International Law Unbound. 2023;117:277.

29 United Nations Convention on the Law of the Sea (adopted 10 December 1982, entered into force 16 November 1994) 1833 UNTS 3.

30 UNGA Res 77/276, (n 6).

manifest in the current case. All submissions accept that the ICJ has jurisdiction.[31] Although some argued for the ICJ to apply its discretion in limiting the question,[32] other States countered this position specifically.[33]

1.2.2 Legal Arguments before the ICJ

At the time of writing, all written and oral submissions to the ICJ in the *Climate Change Opinion* have been made publicly accessible. Thus, this section assesses the legal arguments explored before the ICJ. In this regard, the request for an advisory opinion from the ICJ included legal questions related to UNCLOS and general human rights law. However, arguments based on the law of the sea and human rights law are explored in Sections 3 and 4, which are equally applicable to the ICJ. Other legal arguments may, of course, be used in future disputes or requests for advisory opinions, but the purpose of this section is to provide a bird's-eye view and assess the legal backing of the major arguments advanced in the *Climate Change Opinion.*

1.2.2.1 Non-compliance with Provisions of the Climate Treaty Framework

Given the relevance of the UNFCCC and the Paris Agreement, more than a few obligations can be discerned from the same. However, this section will be restricted to arguments on the temperature goal of the Paris Agreement, mitigation obligations, and the overall reading of provisions under the climate treaty framework. This has no bearing on the importance of adaptation, support, and loss and damage under these treaties.[34]

At the outset, it is of note that a large number of high-emitting States emphasise the non-binding nature of the temperature goal per Article 2 Paris Agreement.[35] However, most other States submit otherwise.[36] Moreover, several States upheld that while Article 2 Paris Agreement provides a long-term temperature goal of "holding the increase in the global average temperature to well below 2°C above pre-industrial levels and pursuing efforts to limit the temperature increase to 1.5°C above pre-industrial levels", in subsequent decisions, States have decisively shifted the focus of the international community's efforts towards 1.5°C.[37] This decision, arrived at through consensus,

31 *Climate Change Opinion,* Written Comments of Vanuatu, p. 11, Fig. 1.
32 *Ibid*, paras. 13–14.
33 *Ibid*, paras. 14–28.
34 For these arguments, see *ibid*, paras. 419–427, 431–434.
35 For example, *Climate Change Opinion,* Written Comments of USA, para. 6.6; Saudi Arabia, para. 4.23; Japan, para. 54; United Kingdom, para. 17.2; Australia, para. 2.24.
36 For example, *Climate Change Opinion*, Written Statement of Vanuatu, paras. 400–405; Seychelles, para. 38; Latvia, para. 13; Gambia, para. 3.17; Mauritius, paras. 15, 19.
37 *Ibid.* See also Written Statement of Colombia, para. 3.34; IUCN, paras. 34, 111–113; Singapore, para. 3.30; Seychelles, paras. 91; Kenya, paras. 5.41; Sierra Leone, paras. 91.

represents subsequent agreement of the Parties to the Paris Agreement in relation to its article 2(1)(a).[38] Such an understanding is strengthened by the international community's consensus, as discernible from UNFCCC and the Paris Agreement, that States' responses must be guided by the best available scientific knowledge.[39]

In terms of mitigation, some States have argued that Articles 4(1) and (2) UNFCCC and Article 4(2) Paris Agreement only set out a "soft" obligation to reduce GHG emissions, as they establish an obligation of conduct (i.e., to prepare, communicate, and maintain successive NDCs, and to align their domestic policies with their submitted NDCs).[40] However, there is more than meets the eye and, in fact, standard treaty interpretation will reveal such provisions to contain binding mitigation obligations. *First*, because an obligation of conduct is always goals-oriented, States are bound to act in a manner consistent with this goal. For instance, Article 2 Paris Agreement is clear in requiring States to limit the temperature increase to 1.5°C above pre-industrial levels.[41] Moreover, Article 4(1) Paris Agreement establishes that "in order to achieve the long-term temperature goal set out in Article 2, Parties aim to reach global peaking of [GHG] emissions as soon as possible".[42] Therefore, although Article 4 Paris Agreement does not write in stone what is the mitigation effort for each State, it is clear (and binding) in stating what is the goal for States to achieve in drafting and submitting their NDC. *Second*, Article 4(2) Paris Agreement is also clear in stating that States must adopt domestic policies with a view to achieve the goals of their NDCs (i.e., it also sets an obligation of result). And *third*, Article 4(3) looks to a State's "highest possible ambition" as a benchmark in determining what effort can be asked from States.[43] Implicit, thus, is at least an obligation of due diligence, which further implies that the mitigation effort of each State can be reviewed by international bodies, and that the observance of States' obligations at the domestic level is also a matter of international law. This is confirmed by the recent *COSIS Opinion,* per which the standard of due diligence is "stringent".[44] Thus, Article 4 Paris Agreement can be read to indicate that States must undertake mitigation measures that are in line with the

38 Glasgow Climate Pact, Decision 1/CMA.3, FCCC/ PA/CMA/2021/10/Add.1, para. 21; Decision 1/CP.27, Sharm-el-Sheik Implementation Plan, FCCC/CP/2022/10/Add.1 (17 March 2023), para. 4; Draft decision -/CMA.5, "First Global Stocktake", (n 7) para. 49.

39 See UNFCCC, Preamble, para. 16; Paris Agreement, Preamble, para. 4. Also see Glasgow Climate Pact, *ult. loc. cit.*, para. 23; "First Global Stocktake" (n 7) para. 6.

40 Rajamani L. The 2015 Paris Agreement: Interplay between Hard, Soft and Non-obligations. Journal of Environmental Law. 2016;28:337.

41 Paris Agreement, Article 2(1).

42 *Ibid*, Article 4(1).

43 Mayer B. The "Highest Possible Ambition" on Climate Change Mitigation as a Legal Standard. International & Comparative Law Quarterly. 2024;73:225.

44 *COSIS Opinion*, (n 16) para. 241.

1.5°C temperature goal and reaching "net zero" by or around mid-century, and that reflect their "highest possible ambition".

1.2.2.2 *State Sovereignty and Territorial Integrity*

Sovereignty and territorial integrity are foundational principles of international law that guide relations among States.[45] However, this principle implies more than a mere prohibition of non-interference in domestic affairs or the prohibitions of the use of force in the territory of another State: it also includes the adoption of harmful conduct that leads to the partial or full loss of a State's territory, or the partial or full loss of the capacity to sustain human life in that territory. Such an interpretation is supported by the submissions to the ICJ in the *Climate Change Opinion*.[46] Some States submitted in these proceedings that climate change is the prime example of conduct that has constituted, and will continue to amount to, the infringement of such an obligation.[47]

In fact, according to the observations and projections of the IPCC, the disruption of the climate system implies a varied set of effects (including sea level rise, changes in rain patterns, more intense and more prolonged periods of drought, desertification, or flooding of coastal and riparian areas) that can affect the survival or territorial integrity of a State.[48] These effects include the partial or full erosion of a State's territory; the increased salinity of the soils; the loss of ecosystems, biodiversity, natural services, and resources; or the loss of forms of life (which also means the loss or harm to freshwater and food sources). Thus, even if a State's territory is preserved, the fact that it is less capable of sustaining human life can be qualified, under the lenses of international law, as damage to the sovereignty and territorial integrity of a State.

It is important to note that the principle of State sovereignty requires that activities within a State's jurisdiction or control do not cause damage to the environment of other States or areas beyond the limits of national jurisdiction.[49] Still, despite the importance of the human element in the definition of a State, a traditional interpretation suggests that the "territory" is the ultimate, necessary substrate for its subsistence – meaning that the loss of it implies the non-existence of a State. Thus, given the scientific realities that several States are already losing significant portions of their territories (with

45 UN Charter, Article 1(2) and Article 2(2) and (4).

46 For instance, see *Climate Change Opinion*, Written Comments of Tuvalu, para. 7.

47 See oral submissions of participants in *Climate Change Opinion* at CR 2024/35, p. 105, para. 6 (Vanuatu and MSG); CR 2024/36, p. 55, para. 13 (Bahamas); CR 2024/48, p. 25, para. 15 (Dominican Republic); CR 2024/49, p. 39, para. 48 (Senegal).

48 Crawford E, Rayfuse R. Climate Change and Statehood. In Rayfuse R, Scott SV, eds. International Law in the Era of Climate Change. Elgar; 2012. p. 243.

49 UNFCCC, Preamble, para. 8.

scientific evidence indicating that this will eventually lead to entire States being submerged),[50] which has a downstream impact on related resources such as maritime entitlements, there is a strong call from affected parties to preserve sovereignty – mainly via recognition of unchanged original borders and freezing maritime entitlements.[51] Such arguments find support in related principles of permanent sovereignty over natural resources, State continuity, and legal certainty and stability,[52] the foundational principles of maritime delimitation per the UNCLOS.[53]

1.2.2.3 Customary International Environmental Law Principles

1.2.2.3.1 APPLICATION

Although some argue that the UNFCCC and the Paris Agreement work as *lex specialis* in the international legal system,[54] the general principles of international environmental law apply to climate change. Several reasons for this have been put forward by submissions in the *Climate Change Opinion.*

50 NASA Analysis Shows Irreversible Sea Level Rise for Pacific Islands. NASA. 25 September 2024. Available from: https://www.nasa.gov/science-research/earth-science/nasa-analysis-shows-irreversible-sea-level-rise-for-pacific-islands/#:~:text=Climate%20change%20is%20rapidly%20reshaping,sea%20level%20change%20science%20team.

51 *Climate Change Opinion*, Written Comments of Vanuatu, paras. 604–605. Also see oral submissions of parties in *Climate Change Opinion*, namely: pp. 69–71, paras. 4–16 (El Salvador); CR2024/44, p. 10, para. 10 (Latvia); CR 2024/48, pp. 19–20, p. 2 and p. 25, para. 15 (Dominican Republic); CR 2024/48, p. 41 para. 76–78 (Romania). Also see International Law Association. "International Law and Sea Level Rise," Interim Report from Sydney Conference, 2018. Available from: http://www.ilahq.org/images/ILA/DraftReports/DraftReport_SeaLevelRise.pdf; Frost R et al. Redrawing the Map of the Pacific. Marine Policy. 2018;95:302; Rayfuse R. Sea Level Rise and Maritime Zones: Preserving the Maritime Entitlements of "Disappearing" States. In: Gerrard MB, Wannier GE, eds. Threatened Island Nations: Legal Implications of Rising Seas and a Changing Climate. CUP; 2013. pp. 167–194.

52 Mendenhall E. Interpreting the Law of the Sea "Regime of Islands": An Opportunity for Productive US Leadership. Marine Policy. 2019;99:213–215; Final Report of the SLR Committee, International Law Association Report of the Seventy-Eight Conference (Sydney 2018) 29.

53 Final Report of the SLR Committee, International Law Association Report of the Seventy-Eight Conference (Sydney 2018) 13, 21; Also see ILA, Report of the Seventy-Sixth Conference, 880–881 (interventions by the Committee Member, Professor David Caron and the Committee Chair, Professor Davor Vidas); Interim Report of the Committee on International Law and Sea Level Rise, presented at the 77th ILA Conference, Johannesburg, South Africa, August 2016, at 17. For international jurisprudence in this regard, see *The Bay of Bengal Maritime Boundary Arbitration (Bangladesh v India)*, PCA Case 2010-16 (Award, 7 July 2014) para. 216. In general, see *Temple of Preah Vihear (Cambodia v Thailand)* (Merits) [1962] ICJ Rep 6, at 34.

54 See in *Climate Change Opinion*, Written Statement of Japan, para. 11; Kuwait, para. 3; OPEC, paras. 17, 64 ff; Saudi Arabia, paras. 1.9, 1.15; South Africa, paras. 14–15; USA, paras. 3.1–3.4, 4.1.

First, the UNFCCC, the Kyoto Protocol, and the Paris Agreement specifically acknowledged, even reserved, the application of other rules of international law to anthropogenic emissions of GHG, and such rules have been effectively applied, *inter alia*, by various courts and interpretative bodies. Recently, thus, ITLOS confirmed that there is no primacy, centrality, or pivotal character of the Paris Agreement with respect to the pollution of the marine environment resulting from anthropogenic emissions of GHG.[55] *Second*, there is a temporal mismatch between the activities that have caused climate change and the application of the climate treaty framework. As an illustration, the IPCC's 2021 Report on the Physical Science Basis of Climate Change covers the period 1750 to current times,[56] while there is clear evidence that captures States' awareness of climate change and the conduct that caused it since as early as the 1960s.[57] Yet, the UNFCCC only entered into force on 21 March 1994, the Kyoto Protocol on 16 February 2005, and the Paris Agreement on 4 November 2016. At best, by singularly considering the matter *ratione temporis*, the *lex specialis* rule would lead to the sole application of the climate treaties post-1994. *Third*, the *lex specialis* arguments fail post-1994 *ratione materiae*. In order for the UNFCCC and the Paris Agreement to apply *lex specialis* and fully displace any other more general rules, they would have to comprehensively govern the conduct under question. However, the treaties simply do not capture all the impacts of climate change and the various obligations that apply to States in this regard. For example, human rights obligations (which are both customary and treaty-based) or those obligations governing the law of the sea have been recognised by the relevant bodies to apply to climate change.[58] Yet, the climate treaty framework fails to capture any of these nuances.

Considering the customary environmental principles (the principle of prevention and the precautionary principles), they are not identical to the provisions of the climate treaty framework. While mitigation obligations (as found in Articles 4(1)-(2) UNFCCC or Articles 3 and 4(2) Paris Agreement) focus on reducing the impact of potentially harmful activities, in contrast, the duty of prevention aims to halt or prevent activities that cause significant harm.[59] Moreover, the climate treaties do not posit any derogation per se. In fact, the

55 *COSIS Opinion*, (n 16) para. 224.

56 IPCC, "Summary for Policymakers", in Climate Change 2021: The Physical Science Basis. Contribution of Working Group I to the Sixth Assessment Report of the Intergovernmental Panel on Climate Change (IPCC 2021), 80.

57 Expert Report of Professor Naomi Oreskes on Historical Knowledge and Awareness, in Government Circles, of the Effects of Fossil Fuel Combustion as the Cause of Climate Change (dated 29 January 2024). See *Climate Change Opinion*, Written Statement of Vanuatu, Exhibit D, para. 4.

58 *Daniel Billy et al. v Australia*, Communication No CCPR/C/135/D/3624/2019, 21 July 2022 ("*Billy*"); *COSIS Opinion*, (n 16).

59 *Climate Change Opinion*, Written Comments of Vanuatu, para. 106.

preamble of the UNFCCC "recall[s]" both the "pertinent provisions" of the Stockholm Declaration and the prevention principle itself.[60] This suggests that the principles stated in the preamble are recalled because they are and continue to be applicable. Since there is no normative conflict between the general international principles and these conventions, the main prerequisite for the operation of the *lex specialis* maxim fails to be met. This follows that the *lex specialis* argument is not applicable to the conduct responsible for climate change.

1.2.3.3.2 CONTENT

The principle of prevention is mentioned in the UNFCCC Preamble but was first developed in the *Trail Smelter* arbitration.[61] In its most basic formulation, it means that "no State has the right to use or permit the use of its territory in such a manner as to cause injury by fumes in or to the territory of another or the properties or persons therein when the case is of serious consequence, and the injury is established by clear and convincing evidence".[62] Accordingly, the principle of prevention results in a negative and a positive obligation for States: on the one hand, an obligation not to adopt conducts that may cause serious detrimental injuries to other States, their territory, citizens, and property; on the other hand, an obligation to monitor and control private conducts that may create the same serious detrimental injuries.[63] Moreover, the ICJ established the binding and customary law nature of the principle of prevention and the resulting due diligence obligations.[64] The framing of the principle of prevention by the ICJ in *Nuclear Weapons* makes it abundantly clear that there is room for this principle to apply in the climate change context, which is also a part of the environment.[65]

Given the broad framing of the principle of prevention, questions arise as to what is a "serious" injury or what is the standard of due diligence. In this regard, it is helpful to turn to the *COSIS Opinion*, where the tribunal

60 UNFCCC, Preamble, paras. 7–8.

61 *Trail Smelter (USA v Canada)* Arbitral Award of 11 March 1941 (1949) III *UNRIAA* 1938. See also *Legality of the Threat or Use of Nuclear Weapons* [Advisory Opinion, 8 July 1996] ICJ Rep 226, para. 29; *Gabčikovo-Nagymaros Project (Hungary v Slovakia)* [Judgment, 25 September 1997] ICJ Rep 7, para. 53. *Responsibilities and Obligations of States Sponsoring Persons and Entities with Respect to Activities in the Area* (Advisory Opinion, 1 February 2011) ITLOS Rep 10, Case No. 17, paras. 110–150 ("*Sponsoring States*").

62 *Trail Smelter, ult. loc. cit.*, 1965.

63 Sands P et al. Principles of International Environmental Law. 4th ed. Cambridge University Press; 2018. p. 206.

64 *Pulp Mills on the River Uruguay (Argentina v Uruguay)*[Judgment, 20 April 2010] ICJ Rep 14, para. 101; *Certain Activities Carried Out by Nicaragua in the Border Area (Costa Rica v Nicaragua) and Construction of a Road in Costa Rica along the San Juan River (Nicaragua v Costa Rica)* [Judgment, 16 December 2015] ICJ Rep 665, para. 104.

65 *Nuclear Weapons*, (n 61) para. 29.

interpreted the similarly broadly worded obligations under Article 194 UNCLOS.[66] The ITLOS held that per Article 194(1) "States Parties to the Convention have the specific obligations to take all necessary measures to prevent, reduce and control marine pollution from anthropogenic GHG emissions and to endeavour to harmonise their policies in this connection".[67] The obligation to take all necessary measures is a "due diligence" obligation,[68] the exact content of which is influenced by several factors, including "scientific and technological information, relevant international rules and standards, the risk of harm and the urgency involved".[69] In the context of GHG emissions, the ITLOS found the due diligence standard "is stringent, given the high risks of serious and irreversible harm to the marine environment from such emissions"[70] and governed by the CBDR-RC principle.[71] In previous jurisprudence, it has been established that Articles 192 and 194 codify the customary international law principle of prevention.[72] This approach stands in contrast with arguments that the fulfillment of obligations under the climate treaties satisfies the level of due diligence as required by this principle.[73] Such arguments do not consider the nuances of the due diligence standard and misrepresent the relationship between customary international law and the UNFCCC regime. In its forthcoming opinion, the ICJ could offer further clarity by underscoring the independent nature of the prevention principle and clarifying the content of States' obligations resulting from the principle.[74]

Finally, Article 3(3) UNFCCC provides that States "should take precautionary measures to anticipate, prevent or minimise the causes of climate change and mitigate its adverse effects", whilst the Paris Agreement is completely silent on this matter. The reason for such a minimal reference is simple: the precautionary principle applies to cases of uncertainty in scientific knowledge.[75] Furthermore, the precautionary principle applies more at the level of public policies, as it requires policymakers to design domestic mitigation policies according to a standard of care that takes into account the scientific uncertainty regarding not only the causes but also the effects of climate change. More importantly is the fact that, if the precautionary principle establishes a standard of care in the adoption of domestic policies, then it may operate in the *ex post* assessment of States conduct, namely in relation

66 *COSIS Opinion*, (n 16).
67 *Ibid*, para. 243.
68 *Ibid*, para. 235.
69 *Ibid*, para. 239.
70 *Ibid*, para. 243.
71 *Ibid*, para. 241.
72 *South China Sea Arbitration (Republic of the Philippines v People's Republic of China)*, PCA Case No. 2013-19 (Award, 12 July 2016) paras. 941, 944.
73 *Climate Change Opinion*, Written Statement of USA, para. 4.28.
74 de Sadeleer N. Environmental Principles – From Political Slogans to Legal Rules. 2nd ed. Oxford University Press; 2020. p. 87.
75 *Ibid*.

to their international responsibility for past GHG emissions: if States knew (and ought to have known) that GHG emissions could lead to a disruption of the climate system, keeping a rhythm of emissions and downplaying the risk of these emissions in the design and implementation of their domestic policies is *not* appropriate diligence under the precautionary principle.[76] Not observing this standard of conduct, therefore, is an infringement of the precautionary principle and, accordingly, of an international obligation binding upon States.

1.3 The International Tribunal for the Law of the Sea

1.3.1 Features and Trends

1.3.1.1 The Contentious Jurisdiction of ITLOS

The reports produced by the IPCC[77] have highlighted the impact of GHG emissions and global warming on the state of the marine environment. In the same vein, in the advisory opinion recently rendered by ITLOS, this tribunal not only endorsed the science produced by the IPCC as "authoritative" and "established",[78] but also elaborated on the legal implications, from a law of the sea perspective, stemming from GHG emissions and global warming. In particular, ITLOS stated that the introduction in the marine environment of GHG (as a form of "substance") and heat (as a form of "energy") qualify as pollution for the purposes of Article 1(1)(4) UNCLOS.[79] Such qualification entails the application of Part XII of UNCLOS, which is premised on the obligation of States to protect and preserve the marine environment.[80] Hence, it establishes a comprehensive set of rules and obligations related to the protection and preservation of the marine environment, which also includes the full gamut of marine pollution sources.

Furthermore, UNCLOS also establishes a complex dispute settlement system, based on the jurisdiction of the ICJ, ITLOS, an arbitral tribunal, and a special arbitral tribunal.[81] When ratifying or acceding to UNCLOS, or at any time thereafter, a State is free to indicate what is its preferred means of dispute settlement.[82] Unless States' preferred body of adjudication coincides, by default the jurisdiction to settle disputes is assigned to the arbitral tribunal.[83]

76 *Ibid*, p. 261.
77 E.g. Pörtner H-O, et al., eds. IPCC Special Report on the Ocean and Cryosphere in a Changing Climate. Cambridge University Press; 2019.
78 *COSIS Opinion*, (n 16) paras. 47 ff.
79 *Ibid*, paras. 159–179. See also Mayer, (n 15) p. 242.
80 UNCLOS, Articles 192–194.
81 UNCLOS, Article 287.
82 UNCLOS, Article 287(1).
83 UNCLOS, Article 287(5).

In this sense, the courts and tribunals mentioned in UNCLOS can also be asked to settle a climate change–related dispute – although the object of such dispute cannot be the interpretation or application of the UNFCCC or the Paris Agreement, but the interpretation and/or application of UNCLOS and other law of the sea rules.[84] This is the very meaning of ITLOS's idea that "[UNCLOS] and the Paris Agreement are separate agreements, with separate sets of obligations. While the Paris Agreement complements [UNCLOS] in relation to the obligation to regulate marine pollution from anthropogenic GHG emissions, the former does not supersede the latter".[85] Yet, ITLOS (as other dispute settlement bodies mentioned in Article 287 UNCLOS) can clarify and develop the international law on climate change, namely by clarifying what are States' obligations to protect, preserve, and ameliorate the marine environment in relation to GHG emissions and the resulting effects – which entails reading UNCLOS and other law of the sea conventions in conjunction with the UNFCCC and the Paris Agreement, as indicated in Articles 237 and 311 UNCLOS and Article 31(3) of the 1969 Vienna Convention on the Law of Treaties (VCLT).[86] Plus, ITLOS's contentious jurisdiction also includes the settlement of disputes related to an "agreement which confers jurisdiction on the Tribunal",[87] having in mind that the object of this special treaty might be related to the protection and preservation of the marine environment against the detrimental impacts of GHG emissions and climate change.

Nonetheless, the vexed question is what would encourage States to institute proceedings under UNCLOS, if they did not consent in advance to the mandatory jurisdiction of the ICJ and an arbitral tribunal under the UNFCCC and the Paris Agreement? Here, one cannot ignore that all States that ratified UNCLOS (including some of the major GHG emitting States) have accepted in advance the jurisdiction of at least one of the dispute settlement bodies listed in Part XV of UNCLOS. Therefore, the reason cannot be the fact that emitting States shield behind the lack of consent, but perhaps the enhanced complexity of such a case (which needs to reconcile climate change and law of the sea regimes), hand in hand with the same concerns with damaging diplomatic relations and creating a precedent that could be used against them.

84 UNCLOS, Article 288(1)–(2), and Annex VI (Statute of the International Tribunal for the Law of the Sea), Article 21 ("ITLOS Statute").

85 *COSIS Opinion*, (n 16) para. 223.

86 1969 Vienna Convention on the Law of Treaties (adopted 23 May 1969, entered into force 27 January 1980) 1155 UNTS 331.

87 ITLOS Statute, Article 21.

1.3.1.2 *The Advisory Jurisdiction of ITLOS*

As seen, the lack of disputes under Part XV of UNCLOS is suggestive of the political sensitivity of climate change, but did not refrain States from campaigning for requesting an opinion from ITLOS.[88]

The basis for ITLOS's advisory jurisdiction requires a brief explanation. Part XV of UNCLOS only establishes ITLOS's contentious jurisdiction, in contrast with Part XI, Section 5, whose Article 191 explicitly confers upon the Seabed Disputes Chamber the competence to render advisory opinions regarding the legal regime of the area. Yet, Article 21 of the ITLOS Statute[89] sets out that the jurisdiction of ITLOS comprises "all matters specifically provided for in any other agreement which confers jurisdiction on the Tribunal". If Article 21 of the ITLOS Statute includes only the conferral of contentious jurisdiction, or whether it also comprises the advisory jurisdiction, was the crux of the issue in the *Request for Advisory Opinion submitted by the Sub-Regional Fisheries Commission*,[90] where ITLOS concluded that any matter, contentious or advisory, may be conferred to it by an ad hoc treaty related to UNCLOS's purposes.[91] The criteria laid down in the *SRFC Opinion* are: there must be a treaty related to the purposes of UNCLOS expressly providing for the submission to ITLOS of a request for an advisory opinion; the request must be transmitted to ITLOS by the body authorised by or following that treaty; and the opinion requested must relate to a legal question.[92]

Using this opportunity, on 31 October 2021, the Government of Antigua and Barbuda and the Government of Tuvalu adopted the Agreement for the Establishment of the Commission of Small Island States on Climate Change and International Law,[93] whose only object is to institute and mandate the Commission to request an advisory opinion from ITLOS in relation to States' obligations, under UNCLOS, to protect, preserve, and ameliorate the marine environment.[94] It is not clear whether the COSIS Agreement is completely in line with the requirements set out in the *SRFC Opinion* and Article 138(1) ITLOS Rules, but, on 21 May 2024, ITLOS rendered the requested advisory opinion, acknowledging that it holds advisory jurisdiction under the COSIS Agreement.[95]

88 *COSIS Opinion*, (n 16).

89 Annex VI of UNCLOS, which forms an integral part of UNCLOS and holds the same legal status in international law. UNCLOS, Article 318.

90 *Request for Advisory Opinion submitted by the Sub-Regional Fisheries Commission* (Advisory Opinion, 2 April 2015) ITLOS Rep 4, Case No. 21 ("*SRFC Opinion*").

91 *Ibid*, paras. 56, 58.

92 *Ibid*, para. 60. See also Article 138(1) ITLOS Rules.

93 Agreement for the Establishment of the Commission of Small Island States on Climate Change and International Law (adopted 31 October 2021, entry into force 31 October 2021) 3444 UNTS 1 ("COSIS Agreement").

94 COSIS Agreement, Article 2(2).

95 *COSIS Opinion*, (n 16) paras. 84–109.

1.3.2 *Legal Arguments before ITLOS*

Since ITLOS has already rendered the *COSIS Opinion*, one can find a line of arguments that may be used in future litigation before, or requests for opinions from, ITLOS. However, the *COSIS Opinion* does not aim to be an end game: by answering those specific questions posed, ITLOS left open other legal arguments and questions, such as the ambulatory nature of maritime boundaries or the need for their adjustment.

In any case, ITLOS clarified, in the *COSIS Opinion*, that GHG emissions are a form of marine pollution under Article 1(1)(4) UNCLOS.[96] Hence, Part XII of UNCLOS is *also* relevant in the regulation of GHG emissions, in addition to the UNFCCC and the Paris Agreement, as had already been pointed out by scholars.[97] ITLOS relied on Article 194 UNCLOS, "which requires States [...] to take all necessary measures to prevent, reduce and control pollution of the marine environment from "any source". Thus, this article lays down an obligation common to all sources of pollution with which States must comply".[98] Moreover, ITLOS also clarified that the obligation under Article 194 UNCLOS "is complemented and elaborated upon by [other] provisions", including Articles 207 to 212 UNCLOS (on States' obligations with respect to the adoption of domestic and international measures to regulate marine pollution),[99] Articles 213 to 222 UNCLOS (on States' obligations to enforce national legislation and to implement international rules and standards),[100] and provisions regarding global and regional cooperation, technical assistance, and monitoring and environmental assessment.[101]

In particular, ITLOS stated that three major obligations stem from Article 194 UNCLOS: an obligation to take necessary measures to prevent, reduce, and control marine pollution; to ensure that certain situations relating to pollution do not occur; and to take necessary measures to protect and preserve rare or fragile ecosystems as well as the habitat of depleted, threatened, or endangered species and other forms of marine life.[102] The reading of these obligations must be informed by the UNFCCC and the Paris Agreement, even though the obligations under Article 194 UNCLOS cannot be discharged by mere compliance with those treaties.[103]

The first obligation was particularly developed by ITLOS. On this matter, it clarified that the "necessary measures" must be taken individually or jointly "as appropriate", meaning that the choice for "individual or joint

96 *Ibid*, paras. 159–179.
97 Boyle A. Law of the Sea Perspectives on Climate Change. The International Journal of Marine and Coastal Law. 2012;27:831.
98 *COSIS Opinion*, (n 16) paras. 189, 192, 193 ff.
99 *Ibid*, para. 190.
100 *Ibid*.
101 *Ibid*, para. 191.
102 *Ibid*, para. 195.
103 *Ibid*, paras. 222–223.

action depends on the particular circumstances in which measures are taken".[104] ITLOS did not explain the meaning of "necessary measures", in order to preserve a State's margin of discretion in the adoption of domestic policies. However, ITLOS highlighted, *first*, that States do not hold a complete margin of discretion in the choice or design of mitigation policies, as these latter should be determined objectively, informed by science, inspired by the precautionary approach, and take into account a State's capabilities.[105] *Second*, ITLOS clarified that these "necessary measures" include "not only measures which are indispensable to prevent, reduce and control marine pollution but also other measures which make it possible to achieve that objective",[106] although they do not require the immediate cessation of all GHG emissions.[107] In this regard, ITLOS resorted to the concept of "continuous obligations" under UNCLOS,[108] with a view of mirroring the evolving nature of a State's obligation under Article 4 Paris Agreement. *Third*, ITLOS clarified also that some obligations stem directly from Part XII of UNCLOS, such as the adoption and enforcement of a regulatory framework aimed at reducing GHG emissions from the State's territory or jurisdiction, conducting environmental impact assessment studies, monitoring private conduct, or implementing international rules and standards at the domestic level. And *fourth*, ITLOS elaborated on the doctrine of States' due diligence obligations, based on its own prior case law.[109] The major implication of such qualification is that, if there is a pattern of appropriate diligence in the observance of an international obligation, the manner in which this obligation is performed, even if at the level of domestic law, is subject to international judicial oversight. Unsurprisingly, ITLOS said that "an obligation of due diligence can be highly demanding".[110]

On a different level, ITLOS also pointed out that States have different responsibilities and capabilities in addressing marine pollution resulting from GHG emissions. At this point, ITLOS was aware of the difficult use of the "common but differentiated responsibilities" principle under the UNFCCC and the Paris Agreement, but implied the principle from Article 194 UNCLOS, whilst adopting a capacity-based reading of this provision.[111] In particular, ITLOS took into account each State's specific technological and available resources.[112] Thus, "States with greater means and capabili-

104 *Ibid*, para. 201. However, considering that climate change results from the global concentration of GHG, "joint actions should be actively pursued". *Ibid*, para. 202.
105 *Ibid*, paras. 206 ff.
106 *Ibid*, para. 203.
107 *Ibid*, para. 199.
108 *Ibid*, paras. 273, 311, 319, 346.
109 *Sponsoring States*, (n 61) and *SRFC*, (n 90).
110 *COSIS Opinion*, (n 16) para. 257.
111 *Ibid*, para. 229.
112 *Ibid*, paras. 205 ff.

ties" "must do more" in order to reduce GHG emissions.[113] Taking the lead also implies providing assistance to States with lesser capabilities and directly affected by the adverse effects of climate change.[114] Nonetheless, in a message directed to *all* States, ITLOS also clarified that "the reference to available means and capabilities should not be used as an excuse to unduly postpone, or even exempt from, the implementation to take all necessary measures" under UNCLOS.[115]

1.4 International Human Rights Treaty Bodies

1.4.1 Features and Trends

Global warming and climate change – which result from GHG emissions – rank among the major environmental challenges we face. However, climate change is not just an environmental problem: it also poses severe stress to the enjoyment of human rights.[116] The rights to life, physical integrity, health, access to food and freshwater, to enjoy one's domicile and private life, and to private property are the most apparent human rights whose enjoyment can be affected by climate change–related events, although the entire catalogue of human rights and freedoms can easily be argued to be affected by such events.[117]

In this light, human rights bodies are increasingly becoming essential venues for standard-setting and adjudication of climate change–related matters. While these bodies' primary mandates concern the implementation or application of human rights law, doing so in the context of climate change also requires having regard to the broader normative context of international law, including the UNFCCC and the Paris Agreement where these treaties are relevant. Particularly significant is the role of human rights bodies in providing redress to those who are themselves affected by climate change, including individuals and communities. Some bodies may also hear complaints from public interest organisations or States.[118] For most bodies, filing a complaint

113 *Ibid*, para. 227.
114 *Ibid*, paras. 326, 330.
115 *Ibid*, para. 226.
116 See Human Rights Council Resolution No. 7/23 (*Human Rights and Climate Change*) UN Doc A/HRC/7/78, 14 July 2008, where the link between human rights and climate change was first established. Afterwards, the Human Rights Council and the Special Rapporteurs on Human Rights and the Environments have repeatedly highlighted how human rights' enjoyment are likely to be affected by climate change–related events.
117 E.g., Humphreys S. Human Rights and Climate Change. CUP; 2010; Wewerinke-Singh M. State Responsibility, Climate Change and Human Rights under International Law. Hart; 2019.
118 See, among others, American Convention on Human Rights (adopted 22 November 1969, entered into force 18 July 1978) OASTS No 36 ("ACHR"), Article 44; European Convention on Human Rights (adopted 4 November 1950, entered into force 3 September 1953) ETS No. 5 ("ECHR"), Article 34; Protocol on the Establishment of an African Court of

requires that the complainant qualifies as a victim of a human rights infringement – though exceptions exist, e.g., for inter-State complaint mechanisms under most human rights bodies.

In the United Nations system, human rights treaty bodies have already started to receive communications related to the effects of climate change on the enjoyment of human rights. The Human Rights Committee (HRC), responsible for interpreting and applying the International Covenant on Civil and Political Rights,[119] received and decided on two communications. The first is the *Ioane Teitiota v New Zealand* case,[120] where the author of the communications claimed that his right to life was violated by an order from the New Zealand authorities to remove him to Kiribati (i.e., his State of nationality, but also a low-lying Pacific island State expected to disappear as a result of sea level rise). The second case is *Daniel Billy et al. v Australia* (Torres Strait Islanders Petition),[121] where a group of Torres Strait Islanders – Australian nationals – claimed that Australia's failure to adapt to and mitigate climate change had violated their human rights under Articles 6, 17, 24, and 27 ICCPR. Whilst the *Teitiota* case was dismissed on the merits,[122] in *Billy*, the HRC found a violation of Articles 17 and 27 ICCPR and highlighted the respondent State's obligation to provide an effective remedy. This obligation entailed, at least: providing adequate compensation; engaging in meaningful consultations with the authors' communities in order to conduct needs assessments; continuing its implementation of measures necessary to secure the communities' continued safe existence on their respective islands; and monitoring and reviewing the effectiveness of the measures implemented and resolve any deficiencies as soon as practicable.[123]

The Committee on the Rights of the Child also received a set of related communications regarding the enjoyment of the human rights of the child and climate change, namely in *Sacchi et al. v Argentina et al.*[124]. The authors of these communications alleged that their rights under Articles 3, 6(1)

Human and Peoples' Rights (adopted 9 June 1998, entered into force 25 January 2004), Article 5(3); (First) Optional Protocol to the International Covenant on Civil and Political Rights (adopted on 16 December 1966, entered into force 23 March 1976), Article 1; Optional Protocol to the International Covenant on Economic, Social and Cultural Rights (adopted on 10 December 2008, entered into force 5 May 2013), Article 2; or Optional Protocol to the UN Convention on the Rights of the Child on a Communications Procedure (adopted 19 December 2011, entered into force 14 April 2014, 2983 UNTS 135), Article 5.

119 Adopted 16 December 1966, entered into force 23 March 1976 (999 UNTS 171).

120 *Ioane Teitiota v New Zealand*, Communication No. CPR/C/127/D/2728/2016, 24 October 2019 (*Teitiota*).

121 *Billy*, (n 58).

122 *Teitiota*, (n 120) para. 10.

123 *Billy*, (n 58) paras. 9–12.

124 *Chiara Sacchi et al. v Argentina et al.*, Communications Nos. 104/2019 (Argentina), 105/2019 (Brazil), 106/2019 (France), 107/2019 (Germany), and 108/2019 (Turkey) 23 September 2021 ("*Sacchi*").

and (2), 24, and 30 Convention on the Rights of the Child[125] (which secure the protection of the best interest of the child, the right to life, the right to enjoy the highest attainable standard of health, and the right to enjoy one's culture) were infringed by States' continued GHG emissions. Although the communications were declared inadmissible for failure to exhaust domestic remedies,[126] the Committee on the Rights of the Child (CRC) confirmed that it has jurisdiction to consider communications regarding alleged violations of children's rights resulting from climate change and took the opportunity to uphold a conception of States' extraterritorial jurisdiction as "control over the source" of the polluting factor.[127]

The last matter of note is a submission made to the ten United Nations Special Rapporteurs of the UN Human Rights Council titled the *Rights of Indigenous People in Addressing Climate-Forced Displacement* ("*Rights of Indigenous People*").[128] The communication, authored by five Indigenous communities in the United States, claims that the US government, by failing to address climate displacement, has violated their human rights. The case demands action against the ongoing extraction of oil and gas and emphasises the need for material resources to safeguard against worsening climate impacts.[129] The complaint stands out for several reasons, two interesting ones being that: *first*, it urges the Special Rapporteurs to recommend that the Louisiana state government hold oil and gas corporations responsible for damages to the Louisiana coast and compensate the victims.[130] By doing so, it lays much-needed focus on corporate responsibility within the international human rights framework, specifically for climate loss and damage. *Second*, and more broadly, by addressing ten of the UN Special Rapporteurs, it emphasises the intersectionality of the human rights impact climate change has on the authors.[131]

Yet, human rights bodies have been grossly underused to spearhead climate litigation. With the HRC and the CRC having received climate change–related complaints, there is yet to be a direct submission on this issue. Moreover, it is only the HRC that has actually provided a ruling on the substantive matter of the complaints. Other than three mentioned avenues in this section, there are several other human rights bodies which are yet to be engaged, such as the Committee on the Elimination of Racial Discrimination (CERD), the Committee on the Rights of Persons with Disabilities, and the

125 United Nations Convention on the Rights of the Child (adopted 20 November 1989, entered into force 2 September 1990) 1577 UNTS 3 ("Rights of the Child Convention").

126 *Sacchi*, (n 124) para. 10.21.

127 *Ibid*, para. 10.12.

128 Complaint filed in *Rights of Indigenous People in Addressing Climate-Forced Displacement*, UN, USA 16/2020, 15 January 2020.

129 *Ibid*, at 10–11.

130 *Ibid*, at 11.

131 *Ibid*, at 3.

Committee on the Elimination of Discrimination against Women, to name a few.

1.4.2 *Legal Arguments before International Human Rights Treaty Bodies*

This subsection delves into the various international human rights that are potentially impacted by climate change and how they have been argued in various instances. Given the lack of a large range of material at the human rights bodies, this section draws from various human rights arguments made in the *Climate Change Opinion,* as well as the cases mentioned above.

1.4.2.1 *The Right to Life*

The right to life concerns the entitlement of individuals to be free from acts and omissions that are intended or may be expected to cause their unnatural or premature death, as well as to enjoy a life with dignity.[132] It is a "supreme right from which no derogation is permitted",[133] protected as a principle of customary international law.[134] Its fundamentality is derived not only from its own nature but also since its protection is the prerequisite for the enjoyment of all other human rights.[135] Parties who engaged in the *Climate Change Opinion* also recognised the fundamentality of this right and alluded either directly or indirectly to the violation of the right to life in their submissions.[136]

The right to life imposes negative and positive obligations on States: to refrain from violating the right to life and arbitrarily depriving a person of life, as well as to adopt measures to protect human life.[137] To ensure their

132 HRC, *General Comment No. 36 (Article 6),* 3 September 2019, CCPR/C/GC/36, para. 3. See also African Commission on Human and Peoples' Rights ("AfrCmHPR"), *General Comment No. 3 on the African Charter of Human and Peoples' Rights: The Right to Life (Article 4),* 12 December 2015, paras. 3, 6.

133 HRC, *General Comment No. 36,* (n 132) para. 3.

134 William Schabas, *The Customary International Law of Human Rights* (OUP 2021) 111–112; *Mario Alfredo Lares-Reyes et al. v United States,* Inter-American Commission of Human Rights Case 12.379, Report No. 19/ 02, 27 February 2002, para. 46; AfrCmHPR, *General Comment No. 3,* (n 132) paras. 5, 14.

135 AfrCmHPR, *General Comment No. 3,* (n 132) paras. 3, 6; see *Billy,* (n 58) para. 8.3.

136 In *Climate Change Opinion,* for example, see Written Statement of Vanuatu, para. 346; Portugal, para. 74; IUCN, para. 473; Singapore, para. 3.77; Solomon Islands, para. 165; Kenya, para. 145; MSG, para. 265.

137 HRC, *General Comment No. 36,* (n 132) para. 4; AfrCmHPR, *General Comment No. 3,* (n 132) para. 7; *Baldeón García v Peru* (Merits, Reparations and Costs) IACtHR Series C No. 147 (6 April 2006) para. 84; HRC, *Toussaint v Canada,* Communication No. 2348/2014, 24 July 2018, para. 11.3; *Advisory Opinion OC-23/17 on the Environment and Human Rights,* IACtHR Series A No. 23, 15 November 2017, paras. 117, 121("*OC-23/17*"); *Budayeva and Others v Russia* (App. No. 15339/02) ECtHR 20 March 2008, paras. 128, 133, 137; *Brincat and Others v Malta* (App. No. 60908/11) ECtHR 24 July 2014, para. 102. Also see in *Climate Change Opinion,* Written Statement of MSG, paras. 265–267.

respect of the right, States must refrain from "engaging in conduct resulting in arbitrary deprivation of life".[138] Consequently, States must exercise due diligence to protect the lives of individuals against deprivations attributable to the State and persons/entities whose conduct is not attributable to the State.[139] Such due diligence obligations extend to reasonably foreseeable threats and life-threatening situations that can result in loss of life.[140] Thus, States must take positive obligations to protect against life-threatening situations, even if they do not result in the loss of life occurring. Otherwise, they violate their obligation to respect, protect, and fulfil the right to life.[141]

Although the right to life seems the most relevant normative lens through which to address climate change, given the severity and scale of escalating climate impacts,[142] human rights mechanisms have been reluctant to find a violation of the right to life in climate change–linked cases. For instance, in *Billy*, the HRC found an infringement of the right to privacy and home life, but it could not find the same conduct to have met the severity required to find it violative of the right to life. Similarly, in *Teitiota*, the author relied on the ICCPR as a protection against the right against involuntary return to his State of origin (Kiribati) wherein this return would violate his rights under Article 6 (right to life).[143] The HRC did not find a violation of the right to life in this case, reasoning that a 10 to 15 years timeline before Kiribati would be uninhabitable allowed for "intervening acts" to prevent a violation.[144] While this interpretation of Article 6 has been criticised for being unduly restrictive and inconsistent with the Committee's own practice,[145] the HRC took care to stress that a different set of facts could have produced a different outcome: it expressly affirmed that States could, in principle, incur international responsibility for returning individuals to States where they face life-threatening conditions due to the impacts of climate change.[146] This opens a new avenue

138 HRC, *General Comment No. 36*, (n 132) para. 8.

139 *Ibid*; HRC, *General Comment No 31 (2004) on the nature of the general legal obligation imposed on States parties to the Covenant*, 26 May 2004, CCPR/C/21/Rev.1/Add.13, para. 8. See also *Osman v United Kingdom* (App. No. 23452/94) ECtHR 28 October 1998, para. 116.

140 HRC, *General Comment No. 36*, (n 132) para. 8.

141 *Ibid*, para. 7.

142 *Teitiota*, (n 120), "Dissenting Opinion of Vasilka Sancin", para. 1; *Teitiota,* (n 120), "Dissenting Opinion of Duncan Laki Muhumuza", para. 1. See also Wewerinke-Singh M and Antoniadis M. Vessel for Drowning Persons?: The Standard-Setting Potential of International Human Rights Litigation in Addressing Climate Displacement. Yearbook of International Disaster Law. 2022;3:238, 255–257; Rocha A, Sampaio R. Climate Change before the European and the Inter-American Court of Human Rights: Comparing Possible Avenues before Human Rights Bodies. Review of European, Comparative & International Environmental Law. 2023;32(2):279, 283.

143 *Teitiota*, (n 120).

144 *Ibid*, para. 9.12.

145 *Ibid*, para. 9.12.

146 *Ibid*, paras. 9.4, 9.14.

for climate litigation, where litigants can couple the right of non-refoulement with the right to life.

Moreover, multiple human rights bodies have recognised that States' acts and omissions that have caused climate change may constitute violations of their obligations arising under the right to life;[147] a conclusion that has been reinforced by domestic courts.[148] The HRC, for example, has clarified that States' failure to take adequate mitigation and adaptation measures "may expose individuals to a violation of their rights under article 6".[149] The IPCC has made it clear that climate change has resulted in the loss of life and, more so, life-threatening conditions. This is derived from the increased intensity and frequency of extreme weather incidents.[150] Such conditions, especially when exacerbated by social and economic inequalities, have resulted in huge losses of life and disastrous life conditions.[151] Clearly, these constitute violations of the right to life and States' failure to respect, protect, and fulfil the same.

1.4.2.2 The Right to Self-Determination

The right to self-determination refers to the rights of all peoples to pursue their economic, social, and cultural development freely without outside interference.[152] It is enshrined in the UN Charter and it has been recognised as a *jus cogens* norm[153] and as a rule entailing obligations *erga omnes*.[154]

147 HRC, *General Comment No. 36*, (n 132) para. 62; *OC-23/17*, (n 137) para. 66.

148 *Urgenda Foundation v State of the Netherlands, Supreme Court of the Netherlands*, ECLI:NL:HR, 20 December 2019 (Netherlands) para. 5.3.2, see also paras. 5.6.2, 5.8; *Neubauer et al. v Germany*, 1 BvR 2656/18 2020, Decision of 24 March 2021 (Germany) para. 144, see also paras. 120, 177–181; *Generaciones Futuras v Ministerios de Ambiente y Desarrollo Sostenible*, República de Colombia Corte Suprema de Justicia STC4360-2018 (5 April 2018) para. 11.

149 *Teitiota*, (n 120) para. 9.9; *Billy*, (n 58) para. 8.7.

150 IPCC, *Climate Change 2022: Impacts, Adaptation and Vulnerability. Contribution of Working Group II to the Sixth Assessment Report of the Intergovernmental Panel on Climate Change* (IPCC 2022) 18, 50.

151 "Chapter 8: Poverty, Livelihoods and Sustainable Development", in IPCC, *ult. loc. cit.*, Executive Summary.

152 CERD, *General Recommendation No 21: Right to self-determination*, CERD/48/Misc.7/Rev.3, para. 4; ICCPR, Article 1; ICESR, Article 1.

153 See also *Chagos Opinion* (n 25) Separate Opinion of Judge Robinson, para. 71(a); Tladi D. Fourth Report of the Special Rapporteur on Peremptory Norms of General International Law (*Jus Cogens*). 31 January 2019, UN Doc A/CN.4/727, paras. 108–115.

154 *East Timor (Portugal v Australia)*(Merits) [1995] ICJ Rep 90, para. 29; *Chagos Opinion*, (n 25) para. 180; *Legal Consequences of the Construction of a Wall in the Occupied Palestinian Territory* (Advisory Opinion) [2004] ICJ Rep 136, paras. 88, 155–156. See also HRC, *General Comment No 12: Article 1 (Right to Self-Determination)*, 13 March 1984, HRI/GEN/1/Rev.9, para. 5.

The right to self-determination belongs to "all peoples",[155] which includes peoples who make up the entire population of a State,[156] as well as minority groups within the State, including Indigenous peoples.[157] The right has a wide ambit, guaranteeing the right to permanent sovereignty over natural resources,[158] the right to cultural integrity and development,[159] and the right to economic and social development.[160] In the climate context, collective self-determination also ensures that communities are empowered to make the critical decisions related to climate adaptation, including relocation.[161] In summary, the right to self-determination can be regarded as protecting the right to exist demographically as a people, covering all aspects of conditions that underpin the political, economic, social, and cultural aspects of peoples' existence, in the face of climate change.[162]

Given that the right to self-determination goes hand in hand with permanent sovereignty over natural resources, it is safe to say that the right is intimately connected to territorial integrity.[163] This connection is especially important for groups whose fundamental lifestyles and existence are intimately tied to their natural surroundings, namely, Indigenous peoples. For Indigenous peoples, their close ties to their land are "the fundamental basis of their cultures, their spiritual life, their integrity, and their economic survival".[164] This truth is echoed in the context of climate-forced displacement

155 "Declaration on the Granting of Independence to Colonia Countries and Peoples", UNGA Res 1514 (XV) (14 December 1960) UN Doc A/RES/1514(XV) para. 2; ICCPR, Article 1(1) and International Covenant on Economic, Social and Cultural Rights (adopted 16 December 1966, entry into force 3 January 1976) 993 UNTS 3 ("ICESCR"), Article 1(1).

156 Kohen M. Self-Determination. In: Viñuales JE, ed. The UN Friendly Relations Declaration at 50 An Assessment of the Fundamental Principles of International Law. Cambridge University Press; 2020.

157 "Declaration on the Rights of Indigenous Peoples" UNGA Res 61/295 (2 October 2007) UN Doc A/RES/61/295, recitals 15–16 and Articles 3–4.

158 "Recommendations concerning international respect for the right of peoples and nations to self-determination", UNGA Res 1314 (XIII) (12 December 1958); "Permanent Sovereignty over Natural Resources", UNGA Res 1803 (XVII) (14 December 1962) para. 1.

159 Xanthaki A. Indigenous Rights and United Nations Standards: Self-Determination, Culture and Land. CUP; 2007. International Convention on the Elimination of All Forms of Racial Discrimination (adopted 21 December 1965, entered into force 4 January 1969) 660 UNTS 195 (ICERD); CERD, *General Recommendation No 21* (n 152) para. 5.

160 ICCPR, Article 1; ICESR, Article 1.

161 *Rights of Indigenous People in Addressing Climate-Forced Displacement*, (n 126) at 13.

162 In *Climate Change Opinion*, see, for example, Written Statement of Vanuatu, para. 294.

163 UNGA Res 1514 (XV) (n 155) paras. 6, 7; *Climate Change Opinion*, Written Statement of Vanuatu, paras. 292 (also see Expert Report of Professor Martin Scheinin on International Human Rights Law Obligations of States in Respect of Climate Change (dated 31 December 2023) (Exhibit C) para. 32).

164 *Mayagna (Sumo) Awas Tingni Community v Nicaragua* (Merits, Reparations and Costs) IACtHR Series C No. 79 (31 August 2001) para. 149. See also *Yakye Indigenous Community v Paraguay* (Merits, Reparations and Costs) IACtHR Series C No 125 (17 June 2005)

in the complaint initiating *Rights of Indigenous People*,[165] can be similarly be extended to other peoples, such as those belonging to the Pacific island States, who also share an intimate connection to nature.[166]

The majority of Indigenous peoples depend on lands and natural resources for their livelihoods, employment, and subsistence.[167] As recognised by the HRC in *Billy*, the lives and cultures of Indigenous peoples depend on the availability of the limited natural resources to which they have access, and on the predictability of the natural phenomena that surround them.[168] It is therefore surprising that the right to self-determination was neither invoked by the authors nor considered *proprio motu* by the HRC. Indeed, the HRC's jurisprudence suggests that the factual context that led to the finding of violations under the ICCPR (i.e., of Articles 17 and 27) might also have supported the finding of a violation of the Torres Strait Islanders' right to self-determination.[169]

Submergence of land, increased flooding and storm surges, stronger tropical cyclones, and the destruction of freshwater resources and cultivable land violate the right to economic development as well as sovereignty over natural resources as assured by the right to self-determination. Similarly, the environmental degradation posed by climate change resulting in a peoples' inability to carry out traditional fishing and farming, as well as cultural ceremonies,[170] violates the social and cultural aspects of the right to self-determination. In fact, the HRC's finding that the State's failure to adopt the required measures to allow the community to maintain their traditional way of life, as well as transmit to their children and future generations their culture and traditions and use of land and sea resources, violates the State's positive obligation to protect the authors' right to enjoy their minority culture[171] can squarely apply

para. 135; *Saramaka People v Suriname* (Merits, Reparations and Costs) IACtHR Series C No 172 (28 November 2007) para. 90.

165 Complaint filed in *Rights of Indigenous People in Addressing Climate-Forced Displacement*, UN, USA 16/2020, 15 January 2020, 12.

166 *Climate Change Opinion*, Written Statement of Vanuatu, paras. 291–301.

167 See UN, State of the World's Indigenous Peoples (2009); See Goal 15: "Sustainably manage forests, combat desertification, halt and reverse land degradation, halt biodiversity loss", UN, n.d., <http://www.un.org/sustainabledevelopment/biodiversity/>.

168 *Billy*, (n 58) para. 7.10.

169 HRC, *General Comment No 23: Article 27 (Rights of Minorities)*, 8 April 1994, CCPR/C/21/Rev.1/Add.5, paras. 2–3.2; CRC, *M.E. V et al. v Finland*, Communication No. 172/2022, 13 September 2024, para. 9.12; Committee on Economic, Social and Cultural Rights (CESR), *J.T. et al. v Finland*, Communications Nos. 251/2022 and 289/2022, 27 September 2024, para. 14.5; HRC, *Wunna Nyiyaparli Indigenous People v Australia*, Communication No. 3585/2019, 15 March 2023, paras. 7.2–3.

170 *Billy*, (n 58) paras. 8.12, 14.

171 *Billy*, (n 58) para. 8.14.

to their right to self-determination. Indeed, the latter point was advanced by several parties at the ICJ in the proceedings in the *Climate Change Opinion*.[172]

These developments illustrate the importance of the right to self-determination for peoples who, by virtue of strong and fundamental ties to their natural environment, are specially affected by the impacts of climate change.

1.4.2.3 The Right to Privacy, Family, and Home Life

Article 17 of the ICCPR guarantees that "[n]o one shall be subjected to arbitrary or unlawful interference with his privacy, family, home or correspondence, nor to unlawful attacks on his honour and reputation".[173] This human right is also recognised by the UDHR, the ICESCR, and in other human rights treaties,[174] and it is relevant in the context of climate change, since subsistence of ways of life (which depend on crops, livestock, fruit trees, hunting, foraging, fishing, and water resources) are elements of a relationship with territory that fall within the scope of this right.[175]

As noted above, the HRC in *Billy* affirmed that States' inadequate responses to climate change may constitute violations of the right to privacy, family, and home life. It held that

> when climate change impacts – including environmental degradation on traditional [indigenous] lands in communities where subsistence is highly dependent on available natural resources and where alternative means of subsistence and humanitarian aid are unavailable – have direct repercussions on the right to one's home; and the adverse consequences of those impacts are serious because of their intensity or duration and the physical or mental harm that they cause, then the degradation of the environment may adversely affect the well-being of individuals and

172 See, for example, *Climate Change Opinion*: Written Statement of Vanuatu, paras. 291-301; Singapore, para. 3.81; Solomon Islands, paras. 2172–2173; Cook Islands, paras. 342–354; Kenya, paras. 5.65–5.68; MSG, paras. 236–237; Philippines, para. 106; Albania, para. 196.

173 ICCPR, Article 17.

174 "Universal Declaration of Human Rights", UNGA Res 217A (III) (10 December 1948) ("UDHR"), Article 12; ICESCR, Article 10(1); Rights of the Child Convention, preamble, para. 5; International Convention on the Protection of the Rights of All Migrant Workers and Members of their Families (adopted 18 December 1990, entered into force 1 July 2003) 2220 UNTS 3 ("Migrant Workers Convention"), para. 44(1); ECHR, Article 8; ACHR, Article 17; "American Declaration of the Rights and Duties of Man", OAS Res XXX, adopted by the Ninth International Conference of American States (1948), Article VI; African Charter on Human and Peoples' Rights (adopted 27 June 1981, entered into force 21 October 1986) 1520 UNTS 363 ("AfrCHPR"), Article 18.

175 See *Billy*, (n 58) para. 8.10; HRC, *Francis Hopu and Tepoaitu Bessert v France*, Communication No. 549/1993, 29 December 1997, para. 10.3; HRC, *Portillo Cáceres and Others v Paraguay*, Communication No. 2751/2016, 20 September 2019, para. 7.8.

> constitute foreseeable and serious violations of private and family life and the home.[176]

This finding illustrates how climate change undermines or negates the protected elements of private, home, and family life – including the destruction of homes and livelihoods, endangerment of significant flora and fauna, and destruction of ancestral burial sites and sacred artefacts – in violation of States' obligations to respect and ensure this right.

1.4.2.4 Cultural Rights

Cultural rights refer broadly to the set of human rights that seek to safeguard an aspect of a community's cultural life in its own way. Article 27 of the ICCPR confers a right in relation to "ethnic, religious or linguistic minorities", namely that "persons belonging to such minorities shall not be denied the right, in community with the other members of their group, to enjoy their own culture, to profess and practise their own religion, or to use their own language".[177] Article 15(1)(a) of the ICESCR protects the right of everyone to "take part in cultural life".[178] The right protects participation, access, and contribution to cultural life.[179]

Cultural rights are impacted by climate change. As an illustration, in 2020, the Special Rapporteur in the field of cultural rights dedicated her annual thematic report to addressing the cultural rights dimensions of the current climate emergency.[180] Here, the Special Rapporteur observes how climate change can violate cultural rights, especially for Indigenous communities.[181]

The report provides tangible examples to indicate the impact of climate change on human rights. It refers to several sites and buildings of cultural heritage – spanning sites of religious value, traditional burial groups, and natural wonders – which are being destroyed by climate change.[182] Similarly, the report draws on examples of climate change's erosion of intangible aspects of culture, namely, traditional knowledge and ways of life, such as fishing traditions, agrifood traditions, traditional medicine, and even wine production.[183]

176 See para. 8.12.
177 *Billy*, (n 58) para. 8.13. See also HRC, *General Comment No. 23* (n 171) paras. 1 and 6.1.
178 ICESCR, Article 15.
179 CESCR, *General Comment No. 21: Right of everyone to take part in cultural life*, 21 December 2009, E/C.12/GC/21, para. 15.
180 Special Rapporteur in the field of cultural rights, *Report on climate change, culture and cultural rights*, 10 August 2020, UN Doc A/75/298.
181 *Ibid*, para. 34.
182 *Ibid*, para. 37.
183 *Ibid*, para. 41

Linguistic diversity and Indigenous languages may also be eroded, impacting the very identity of a people.[184]

The HRC's views in *Billy* illustrate how a State's failure to adequately address climate change may violate Article 27 ICCPR. This provision, interpreted in the light of the United Nations Declaration on the Rights of Indigenous Peoples (UNDRIP), enshrines "the inalienable right of Indigenous peoples to enjoy the territories and natural resources that they have traditionally used for their subsistence and cultural identity".[185] Subsequently, especially given that the climate impacts experienced by the Torres Strait Islanders could have reasonably been foreseen by the State party, owing to knowledge of these issues as late as the 1990s, the HRC found that Australia violated the cultural rights guaranteed by Article 27 ICCPR.[186]

Of course, cultural rights are not necessarily attached to a claimant's minority status, although that is frequently so in the case of Indigenous communities. Violations of cultural rights may also occur where climate change impacts entail harm to the cultural heritage and identity of peoples who form the majority of a State's population.[187] The right to self-determination is particularly relevant for understanding States' obligations arising from cultural rights in this context.[188]

1.4.2.5 Right to Equality and Non-discrimination

Non-discrimination and the prohibition on racial discrimination are *jus cogens* norms,[189] constituting a basic and general principle relating to the protection of human rights.[190] This right is enshrined in all major human rights treaties,[191] and guarantees equality before the law; equal protection of the law; and protection against discrimination on the grounds of race,

184 *Ibid*, para. 46.
185 *Billy*, (n 58) para. 8.13.
186 *Ibid*, para. 8.14.
187 *Report on climate change, culture and cultural rights*,(n 180) para. 42.
188 HRC, *General Comment No 23*, (n 171) paras. 2–3.2; CRC, *M.E.V et al. v Finland*, (n 169) para. 9.12; CESCR, *J.T. et al. v Finland*, (n 169) para. 14.5.
189 Special Rapporteur on Contemporary Forms of Racism, Racial Discrimination, Xenophobia and Related Intolerance, "Ecological crisis, climate justice and racial justice", 25 October 2022, UN Doc A/77/549, para. 41; *Barcelona Traction, Light and Power Company, Limited* (Merits) [1970] ICJ Rep 3; *Legal Consequences for States of the Continued Presence of South Africa in Namibia (South West Africa) notwithstanding Security Council Resolution 276 (1970)* (Advisory Opinion) [1971] ICJ Rep 16. In the context of regional human rights bodies, see, e.g., AfrCmHPR, Communication No. 245/2002, para. 169; *Juridical Condition and Rights of Undocumented Migrants*, Advisory Opinion OC-18/03, IACtHR Series A No. 18 (17 September 2003) para. 101.
190 HRC, *General Comment No. 18: Non-discrimination Adopted at the Thirty-seventh Session of the Human Rights Committee*, 10 November 1989, para. 1.
191 ICCPR, Article 26; ICESCR, Article 3.

colour, sex, language, religion, political or other opinion, national or social origin, property, birth, or other status.[192]

The impacts of human-induced climate change are felt unequally, with overlapping discriminatory impacts being felt along the lines of gender, race, colour, and national origin.[193] As the UN Special Rapporteur on contemporary forms of racism, racial discrimination, xenophobia, and related intolerance notes, "The global ecological crisis is simultaneously a racial justice crisis. As countless studies and submissions received show, the devastating effects of ecological crisis are disproportionately borne by racially, ethnically and nationally marginalised groups – those who face discrimination, exclusion and conditions of systemic inequality because of their race, ethnicity or national origin".[194]

Similarly, as women play important roles in rural and agricultural life, they are typically on the frontline of environmental and climate-related human rights violations. A study by the World Bank finds climate change–induced weather shocks to have a three-pronged gendered impact: endowments (health and education), economic opportunities (combining access to jobs and assets as well as a broader view on aspects that affect economic opportunities), and agency (gender-based violence and early marriage).[195] Furthermore, the Special Rapporteur on violence against women and girls has reported that climate change–induced violence against women is a distinct phenomenon caused by the feminisation of intersecting vulnerabilities.[196] This is all to show just how intersectional an issue the human rights impact of climate change is and the importance that this intersectionality be recognised.[197]

States have committed to guaranteeing equality and non-discrimination. They have an obligation to respect, protect, and fulfil all human rights for all persons without discrimination. Consequently, efforts to address climate change should not exacerbate inequalities within or between States. For example, Indigenous peoples' rights should be fully reflected in line with the UNDRIP, and actions likely to impact their rights should not be taken without their free, prior, and informed consent. Care should also be taken to ensure that a gender perspective, including efforts to ensure gender equality,

192 *Ibid.*

193 See *Climate Change Opinion*, Written Statement of the OACPS, paras. 83-9; Cook Islands, para. 64; Expert Report of Professor E Tendayi Achiume, *Racial Equality and Racial Non-Discrimination Obligations of State in Respect of Climate Change*, March 2024 (Appendix B to *Climate Change Opinion*, Written Statement of the OACPS) paras. 10-2.

194 "Report", (n 189) para. 1.

195 Fruttero A et al. Gendered Impacts of Climate Change Evidence from Weather Shock. World Bank Policy Research Paper No. 10442. 2023. p. 3.

196 Alsalem R. "Violence against Women and Girls, Its Causes and Consequences" (Special Rapporteur on Violence against Women and Girls, Its Causes and Consequences) 11 July 2022, UN Doc A/77/136, paras. 11-2, 16-7.

197 *Climate Change Opinion*, Cook Islands, para. 66; Vanuatu, para. 342.

is included in all planning for climate change mitigation and adaptation. Similarly, the rights of children, elder persons, minorities, migrants, and others in vulnerable situations must be effectively protected.[198]

As human rights becomes increasingly used as a tool in climate litigation, what comes to the forefront is the differential impacts of climate change. This has already begun, with the HRC (*Billy*) pronouncing the specific impact of climate change on Indigenous peoples and the CRC (*Sacchi*) discussing similar impacts on children. Such actions are encouraging for climate justice and, as different peoples seek redress for the harms caused by anthropogenic climate change, the tapestry of impacts considered will continue to grow.

1.4.2.6 Right to Health

The right of everyone to the enjoyment of the highest attainable standard of physical and mental health is guaranteed by the ICESCR[199] and other treaties.[200] The right to health goes beyond the mere absence of disease or infirmity – it guarantees a state of complete physical, mental, and social well-being, as well as the underlying determinants of such well-being (such as access to freshwater and adequate sanitation, adequate supply of safe food, nutrition and housing, and healthy environmental conditions).[201]

The impacts of climate change have interfered with the provision of health and medical services in many States in vulnerable situations, and they have amplified other problems.[202] For example, the health effects of extreme heat include death, heat stroke, heat cramps, hyperthermia, and exacerbation of

198 HRC. Human Rights and Climate Change: Key Messages. Available from: https://www.ohchr.org/sites/default/files/Documents/Issues/ClimateChange/materials/KMClimateChange.pdf.

199 ICESCR, Article 12(2).

200 UDHR, Article 25(1); ICERD, Article 5(e)(iv); Convention on the Elimination of All Forms of Discrimination against Women (adopted 18 December 1979, entered into force 3 September 1981) 1249 UNTS 13, Article 12(1); Rights of the Child Convention, Article 24; Convention on the Rights of Persons with Disabilities (adopted 13 December 2006, entered into force 3 May 2008) 2515 UNTS 3, Article 25; Migrant Workers Convention, Article 28; Maputo Protocol to the African Charter on Human and Peoples' Rights on the Rights of Women in Africa (adopted 1 July 2003, entry into force 25 November 2005), 3268 UNTS 1, Article 14(2); Revised European Social Charter (adopted 3 May 1996, entered into force 1 July 1999) ETS No 163, Article 11; ACHR, Article 26; Additional Protocol to the American Convention on Human Rights in the Area of Economic, Social and Cultural Rights (adopted 17 November 1988, entered into force on 16 November 1999) OASTS No 69, Article 10(1); Arab Charter on Human Rights (2004), Article 39(1); AfrCHPR, Article 16(1).

201 CESCR, *General Comment No 14: The right to the highest attainable standard of health (Article 12)*, 11 August 2000, E/C.12/2000/4, paras. 11, 15; *OC-23/17*, (n 137) para. 110.

202 For instance, see Leal Filho W, et al. Climate Change, Extreme Events and Mental Health in the Pacific Region. International Journal of Climate Change Strategies and Management. 2023;15(1):20.

existing illnesses. Similarly, climate change–induced rainfall patterns and humidity create conditions for increased vector-borne diseases. Just as an example, the IPCC has made it very clear that the intensity and frequency of daily temperature extremes, as well as heat waves, are *very likely* caused by the anthropogenic interference in the climate system,[203] and such extremes will continue to increase in the future.[204]

1.4.3 *Conclusion*

International human rights law can be used to discuss States' obligations to mitigate and adapt to climate change, namely, in the framework of States' positive obligations thereunder. Accordingly, one can expect that more communications will be submitted in the future, not only before the HRC or the CRC, but also before other human rights treaty bodies. Nonetheless, considering the rules of *lis pendens* and *res judicata* – which precludes the examination of a communication which "has been or is being examined under another procedure of international investigation or settlement"[205] – one can expect that cases from concerned individuals in America, Europe, and Africa may be submitted to regional human rights courts, since these latter can issue binding judgments, contrary to the non-binding views espoused by the human rights treaty bodies in the United Nations system.

1.5 The International Criminal Court

Another important judicial body to consider is the ICC, established under the Rome Statute as a permanent institution empowered to exercise its jurisdiction over natural persons for "the most serious crimes of international concern".[206] International criminal law targets human rights abuses practised by individuals (not States), but it only operates in face of extreme circumstances. In the case of the ICC, Articles 5 to 8 ICC Statute limit its subject matter jurisdiction to the crimes of genocide, the crimes against humanity, war crimes, and the crime of aggression. No provision is specifically devised for dealing with environmental or climate harm, although Article 8(2)(b)(iv) qualifies as a war crime as the intentional attack that knowingly causes "widespread, long-term and severe damage to the natural environment which would be clearly excessive in relation to the concrete and direct overall military advantage anticipated". Moreover, where environmental degradation

203 Adnan M et al. Chapter 11: Weather and Climate Extreme Events in a Changing Climate. In: IPCC. Climate Change 2021: The Physical Science Basis. IPCC; 2021. p. 1552.

204 *Ibid*, p. 1158.

205 (First) Optional Protocol to the ICCPR, Article 5(2)(a); Optional Protocol to the ICESCR, Article 3(2)(c); Optional Protocol to the Rights of the Child Convention, Article 7(d).

206 Rome Statute of the International Criminal Court (adopted 17 July 1998, entered into force 1 July 2002) 2187 *UNTS* 3 ("ICC Statute").

or the disruption of the climate system amounts to such immense threat and damage to the enjoyment of life, physical integrity, or other human rights, it might amount to a crime against humanity pursuant to the ICC Statute.[207]

Two recent communications highlight the possibility of framing severe climate harm as crimes against humanity. First, in *The Planet v Bolsonaro*,[208] it was argued that the policies adopted during the term of the former Brazilian president Bolsonaro (namely, deforestation and excessive exploitation of natural resources in the Amazon) are punishable under Article 7(1)(a), (h), and (k) ICC Statute. Moreover, *NZ Students for Climate Solutions and UK Youth Climate Coalition v Board of BP*[209] alleges that the senior executives of BP's knowingly and intentionally contributing to GHG emissions amounts to a crime against humanity under Article 7(1)(k) ICC Statute. Both communications appear not to have triggered any action on the part of the Office of the Prosecutor.

Thus, the Rome Statute may provide a basis for climate change–related investigations and prosecutions, but its potential for addressing climate change remains uncertain in the absence of explicit provisions addressing environmental harm. The inclusion of ecocide in the Rome Statute through an amendment, as advocated by civil society organisations and formally proposed by three State Parties in 2024, points to a possible future evolution of the ICC's mandate. If adopted, such an amendment would widen the Court's reach to encompass grave acts of environmental destruction – and could thus help reinforcing accountability for the most serious harms caused by climate change.

1.6 Conclusion

Climate litigation under the aegis of the UN system is, in its various forms, an increasingly central mechanism for clarifying and enforcing States' obligations on climate change. Recent and ongoing developments – whether before the ICJ, ITLOS, or UN human rights treaty bodies – highlight the reality that climate impacts pervade nearly every aspect of international law. They also show how litigants are engaging different legal vocabularies (environmental,

207 Notably, the Office of the Prosecutor is currently developing a new policy on environmental crimes under the Rome Statute. [Accessed 2 January 2025]. Available from: https://www.icc-cpi.int/news/office-prosecutor-launches-public-consultation-new-policy-initiative-advance-accountability-0.

208 See *The Planet v Bolsonaro*. [Accessed 2 January 2025]. Available from: https://climatecasechart.com/non-us-case/the-planet-v-bolsonaro/.

209 See Request to open investigations & Request for reparations regarding the crimes against humanity of climate change. [Accessed 2 January 2025]. Available from: https://climatecasechart.com/wp-content/uploads/non-us-case-documents/2022/20221208_19343_points-of-claim.pdf.

human rights, law of the sea, even international criminal law) to clarify and test the boundaries of what constitutes justiciable climate harm.

A salient trend is the interplay between supposedly "specialised" treaty frameworks – like the UNFCCC regime – and general international law. Instead of displacing broader customary rules or human rights norms, the climate treaties often supplement them. As the cases before the HRC and the CRC demonstrate, the human rights lens has become a powerful vehicle for clarifying States' positive obligations and expanding remedies for those most vulnerable to a warming planet. Similarly, recent advisory proceedings before the ICJ and ITLOS confirm that obligations in environmental treaties can be interpreted in the wider matrix of customary law, general principles, human rights law, and State responsibility.

The structural question remains whether these converging streams of climate jurisprudence can deliver meaningful redress – especially for communities suffering immediate harm. In contentious proceedings, States remain reluctant to expose themselves to binding rulings; yet, the spate of advisory opinions underscores a strong appetite, particularly among smaller and more climate-vulnerable States, for the highest courts to articulate and enforce authoritative standards. Likewise, the emergence of "climate-based" human rights complaints suggests an evolving role for treaty bodies as forums for accountability, albeit with constraints on enforceability.

As new petitions and proceedings arise, the UN system will likely become more integral to shaping climate law. The cross-cutting nature of climate harm, especially in relation to human rights, sovereignty, and territorial integrity, underscores that no single institution or treaty can provide a neat, comprehensive response. It is precisely the diversity of these venues – and the interplay between them – that makes the UN system a fertile space for forging more coherent legal standards on climate obligations. Over time, decisions emanating from these institutions may harmonise discrete areas of law and push States, as well as private actors, to adapt their policies to a rapidly unfolding climate reality. Ultimately, the role of international adjudication in the UN system is not merely to adjudicate the past but to assist States and the international community in charting more equitable and effective pathways forward.

References

Bodansky D, Brunnée J, Rajamani L. International climate change law. 1st ed. Oxford: Oxford University Press; 2017.

Boyle A. Law of the sea perspectives on climate change. Int J Mar Coast Law. 2012;27:831–838.

Collier J, Lowe V. The settlement of disputes in international law: institutions and procedures. Reprint. Oxford: Oxford University Press; 2010.

Crawford E, Rayfuse R. Climate change and statehood. In: Rayfuse R, Scott SV, editors. International law in the era of climate change. Cheltenham: Edward Elgar; 2012.

de Sadeleer N. Environmental principles: from political slogans to legal rules. 2nd ed. Oxford: Oxford University Press; 2020.
Frost R, Hibberd P, Nidung M, Artack E. Redrawing the map of the pacific. Mar Policy. 2018;95:302–310.
Fruttero A, Halim D, Broccolini C, Coelho B; Gninafon H; Muller N. Gendered impacts of climate change: evidence from weather shock. World Bank Policy Research Paper. 2023; No. 10442.
Humphreys S. Human rights and climate change. Cambridge: Cambridge University Press; 2010.
Kohen M. Self-determination. In: Viñuales JE, editor. The UN Friendly Relations Declaration at 50: an assessment of the fundamental principles of international law. Cambridge: Cambridge University Press; 2020.
Leal Filho W, Krishnapiallai M, Minhas A, Ali S, Nagle Alverio G, Ahmed MSH, Naidu R, Prasad RR, Bhullar N, Sharifi A, Nagy GJ, Kovaleva M. Climate change, extreme events and mental health in the Pacific region. Int J Clim Chang Strateg Manag. 2023;15(1):20–40.
Mayer B. The "highest possible ambition" on climate change mitigation as a legal standard. Int Comp Law Q. 2024;73:285–317.
Mayer B. The international law on climate change. Cambridge: Cambridge University Press; 2018.
Mendenhall E. Interpreting the law of the sea "regime of islands": an opportunity for productive US leadership. Mar Policy. 2019;99:213–215.
Pörtner H-O, et al., editors. IPCC special report on the ocean and cryosphere in a changing climate. Cambridge: Cambridge University Press; 2019.
Rajamani L. The 2015 Paris Agreement: interplay between hard, soft and non-obligations. J Environ Law. 2016;28:337–358.
Rayfuse R. Sea level rise and maritime zones: preserving the maritime entitlements of "disappearing" states. In: Gerrard MB, Wannier GE, editors. Threatened island nations: legal implications of rising seas and a changing climate. Cambridge: Cambridge University Press; 2013.
Rocha A. Suing states – the role of courts in promoting states' responsibility for climate change. In: Garcia MG, Cortês A, editors. Blue planet law. Cham: Springer; 2023.
Rocha A, Sampaio R. Climate change before the European and the Inter-American court of human rights: comparing possible avenues before human rights bodies. Rev Eur Comp Int Environ Law. 2023;32(2):279–289.
Sands P, Peel J, Fabra A, MacKenzie R. Principles of international environmental law. 4th ed. Cambridge: Cambridge University Press; 2018.
Shelton D. The participation of nongovernmental organizations in international judicial proceedings. Am J Int Law. 1994;88: 611–642.
Stephan P. Privatizing international law. Va Law Rev. 2011;97:1573–1664.
Strauss A. Climate change litigation: opening the door of the International Court of Justice. In: Burns WCG, Osofsky HM, editors. Adjudicating climate change: state, national, and international approaches. Cambridge: Cambridge University Press; 2009.
Wewerinke-Singh M. State responsibility, climate change and human rights under international law. Oxford: Hart Publishing; 2019.
Wewerinke-Singh M, Aguon J, Hunter J. Bringing climate change before the international court of justice: prospects for contentious cases and advisory opinions. In: Alogna I, Bakker C, Gauci J-P, editors. *Climate change litigation: global perspectives*. Leiden: Brill; 2021.
Wewerinke-Singh M, Antoniadis M. Vessel for drowning persons? The standard-setting potential of international human rights litigation in addressing climate displacement. Yearb Int Disaster Law. 2022;3:238:255–257.

Wewerinke-Singh M, Viñuales J, Aguon J. The role of advocates in the conception of advisory opinion requests. Am J Int Law Unbound. 2023;117:277–281.
Xanthaki A. Indigenous rights and United Nations standards: self-determination, culture and land. Cambridge: Cambridge University Press; 2007.

2 The Inter-American Human Rights System and Climate Litigation

Maria Antonia Tigre and Thalia Viveros-Uehara

2.1 Introduction

For over five decades, the Inter-American Commission on Human Rights (IACHR) and the Inter-American Court of Human Rights (IACtHR), as foundational components of the Inter-American Human Rights System (IAHRS), have played a pivotal role in what is often termed *transformative constitutionalism*.[1] These institutions have provided structural guidance during the democratic transitions of numerous nations in the Americas, particularly those emerging from the authoritarian regimes of the 1970s.[2] Initially, their focus centred on civil and political rights, addressing egregious violations such as enforced disappearances and extrajudicial killings that typified dictatorial governance.[3] Over time, their scope has broadened, incorporating

1 A substantial body of scholarship has examined the transformative role of the IACtHR in relation to Latin American constitutional frameworks, noting the reciprocal influence between the Court and national constitutions. A prominent line of research contends that the Court has contributed to the development of a *ius constitutionale commune* in Latin America (ICCAL), a concept advanced under the coordination of Armin von Bogdandy and Mariela Morales Antoniazzi at the Max Planck Institute for Comparative Public Law and International Law. For a comprehensive overview of the Court's significance in the Latin American region and its impacts, see von Bogdandy A et al., eds. Transformative Constitutionalism in Latin America: The Emergence of a New *Ius Commune*. Oxford University Press; 2017; and von Bogdandy A et al., The Impact of the Inter-American Human Rights System: Transformations on the Ground. Oxford University Press; 2024.

2 Piovesan F. *Ius Constitutionale Commune* en América Latina: Context, Challenges, and Perspectives. In: von Bogdandy A et al., eds. Transformative Constitutionalism in Latin America: The Emergence of a New *Ius Commune*. Oxford University Press; 2017. p. 52.

3 For a mapping of the jurisprudential evolution of the IACtHR, particularly its early focus on civil and political rights corresponding to the 1970s and 1980s, when the system played a significant role in denouncing and documenting systematic, large-scale human rights violations, especially in the context of military dictatorships and abuses of states of emergency, see Vera OP. Impact of the Inter-American Human Rights System in the Struggle against Impunity. In: von Bogdandy A et al., The Impact of the Inter-American Human Rights System: Transformations on the Ground. Oxford University Press; 2024. p. 424.

DOI: 10.4324/9781003540977-4

environmental protection and, more recently, the pressing challenges posed by climate change.[4]

Particularly in the last 20 years, the IAHRS has established a pioneering framework of standards on environmental protection, with a strong emphasis on Indigenous peoples and the impacts of extractive industries, while laying a foundation for addressing the climate emergency.[5] This doctrinal evolution is particularly remarkable given the absence of explicit provisions for a right to a healthy environment (RHE) or any reference to climate change in the American Convention on Human Rights (ACHR) – the System's foundational instrument. Despite early obstacles, including the rejection of cases on these issues, both the IACHR and the IACtHR have progressively bridged these gaps. Through systematic and evolutive interpretation, they have redefined the ACHR's scope to address the pressing environmental and climate-related challenges of the present era.[6] Notably, among other developments, Advisory Opinion 23/17 by the IACtHR is widely regarded as the first decision by an international human rights tribunal to comprehensively address States' extraterritorial human rights obligations in the context of environmental protection.[7]

A defining characteristic of this progression is its regional contextualisation, facilitated by the process of "Inter-Americanization".[8] This refers to a dynamic, two-way exchange: on the one hand, the System's standards influence domestic legal frameworks, and, on the other, domestic developments inform and shape Inter-American developments. The resulting legal *corpus* is thus deeply rooted in the socio-legal realities of the region.

4 For a comprehensive view of the evolution of the environmental protection within the IHRS, see Jimenez Guanipa H, Barraco M. Inter-American Human Rights System's Impact on the Protection of the Right to a Healthy Environment. In: von Bogdandy A et al., The Impact of the Inter-American Human Rights System: Transformations on the Ground. Oxford University Press; 2024. pp. 238–253; Cavallo GA. El derecho humano a un medio ambiente sano, acceso a la información ambiental y el *ius Commune*. In: Jimenez Guanipa H, Leal ML, eds. Crisis climática, transacción energética y derechos humanos. Tomo II. Fundación Heinrich Böll; 2020. pp. 69–96; Cerqueira D. El Derecho a un medio ambiente sano en el marco normativo y jurisprudencia del Sistema Interamericano de Derechos Humanos. In: Jimenez Guanipa H, Leal ML, eds. Crisis climática, transacción energética y derechos humanos. Tomo II. Fundación Heinrich Böll; 2020. pp. 127–158.

5 Jimenez Guanipa H, Barraco M, (n 4), p. 241.

6 *Ibid*, p. 244. See also Tigre MA. International Recognition of the Right to a Healthy Environment: What Is the Added Value for Latin America and the Caribbean?. American Journal of International Law. Unbound. 2023.

7 Banda ML. Inter-American Court of Human Rights' Advisory Opinion on the Environment and Human Rights,. Asil Insights; 10 May 2018. Available from: https://www.asil.org/insights/volume/22/issue/6/inter-american-court-human-rights-advisory-opinion-environment-and-human#_edn32 [https://perma.cc/NUW3-Q9RQ].

8 Antoniazzi MM, Alessandri PS. Inter-Americanization: Its Legal Bases and Political Impact. In: von Bogdandy A et al., eds. Transformative Constitutionalism in Latin America: The Emergence of a New *Ius Commune*. Oxford University Press; 2017. pp. 255–276.

Such interplay is particularly significant given the disproportionate impacts of climate change across the Americas. Massive forest fires in the Amazon, intensified hurricanes, and Central American floods exemplify the escalating crisis.[9] Meanwhile, the melting of Andean glaciers has reduced water resources, jeopardising food security for populations already burdened by social and economic inequalities.[10] In the Caribbean, rising sea levels erode coastlines, degrade marine ecosystems, and destroy critical habitats, compounding biodiversity loss and increasing the risk of zoonotic diseases that could spark future pandemics.[11]

Latin America's climate challenges are further compounded by extreme climate injustices. Despite contributing minimally to global greenhouse gas (GHG) emissions – apart from large emitters like Brazil, Mexico, and Argentina – countries in the region face disproportionate vulnerability to both climate impacts and mitigation efforts.[12] Worsening food and water insecurity, driven by floods and droughts, affects communities in Central and South America and the Caribbean, particularly those located in low-lying coastal areas, small island states, and agricultural zones.[13] These regions, often home to non-white populations and characterised by significant development constraints, are identified by the IPCC as hotspots of high vulnerability.[14] At the same time, reliance on fossil fuels and agriculture makes many Latin American economies especially susceptible to the socioeconomic pressures of global energy transitions aimed at reducing GHG emissions.[15]

9 Tigre MA. COVID-19 and Amazonia: Right-based Approaches for the Pandemic Response. Review of European, Comparative & International Environmental Law. 2021;30:162.

10 Press Release, Org. Am. Sts., Statement on Entry into Force of the Escazú Agreement (Apr. 22, 2021), https://perma.cc/2Y47-YF7Y.

11 Fearnside PM. Will the Next Coronavirus Come from Amazonia? Deforestation and the Risk of Infectious Diseases. Mongabay. 8 April 2020. Available from: https://perma.cc/N4JB-B8P2.

12 Ivanova A et al. Climate Change Challenges in Latin America and the Caribbean. IMF. 2021;3. Available from: https://www.imf.org/-/media/Files/Publications/REO/WHD/2021/English/CH3.ashx; Auz J. Two Reputed Allies: Reconciling Climate Justice and Litigation in the Global South. In: Litigating the Climate Emergency: How Human Rights, Courts, and Legal Mobilization Can Bolster Climate Action. 2022. pp. 145–156; 148. Available from: https://doi.org/10.1017/9781009106214.009.

13 IPCC. Summary for Policymakers. H-O Pörtner et al., eds. In: H-O Pörtner et al., eds. Climate Change 2022: Impacts, Adaptation and Vulnerability. Contribution of Working Group II to the Sixth Assessment Report of the Intergovernmental Panel on Climate Change. Cambridge and New York: Cambridge University Press; 2022. p. 9. See also, Feld B, Galiani S. Climate Change in Latin America and the Caribbean: Policy Options and Research Priorities. Latin American Economic Review. 2025;24:14. Available from: https://doi.org/10.1007/s40503-015-0028-4.

14 For a more in-depth analysis of the racial aspect of climate change, see generally Gonzalez C. Climate Change, Race, and Migration. Journal of Law and Political Economy. 2020;1(1). Available from: http://dx.doi.org/10.5070/LP61146501. Retrieved from: https://escholarship.org/uc/item/4bw094qc.

15 Ivanova A, (n 12).

Amid escalating climate challenges and limited governmental action in Latin America, domestic climate litigation has gained momentum since 2015, emerging as a critical mechanism to address regulatory and enforcement gaps.[16] Such efforts operate within the broader legal *corpus* established by the IAHRS, where evolving standards on environmental protection provide a foundation for addressing climate-related harms.[17] To be sure, the System's standards, which have become an integral part of the region's legal landscape while reflecting its social realities, offer courts and claimants an alternative source of authority to support climate-related claims as the warming planet increasingly threatens fundamental human rights, including the RHE.[18]

This chapter examines the significance of the IAHRS in confronting climate challenges, both as a forum for adjudication and as a standard-setter for domestic legal proceedings. The analysis adopts a dual perspective. First, it situates climate litigation within the IAHRS by tracing the System's progressive development of "green jurisprudence", culminating in its application to climate change – a development that aligns with a broader trend of leveraging regional human rights courts to adjudicate climate change.[19] Second, the chapter analyses the influence of Inter-American standards on domestic climate lawsuits, emphasizing their role in shaping legal arguments. By contextualising contemporary climate litigation within the historical evolution

16 For example, deforestation in Brazil and Colombia is rising, with a continued overreliance on fossil fuel extraction throughout the region. See Martínez M. Beyond Pledges: Solidifying Climate Action in Latin America. NRDC. 17 November 2022. Available from: https://www.nrdc.org/experts/marilyn-martinez/beyond-pledges-solidifying-climate-action-latin-america.

17 Tigre MA, Urzola N. The 2017 Inter-American Court's Advisory Opinion: Changing the Paradigm for International Environmental Law in the Anthropocene. Journal of Human Rights & Environment. 2021;12(1):24. Viveros-Uehara T. The Fundamental Rights to Life and Health in Climate Litigation. e-Publica. 2022;9(3);147.

18 See Special Rapporteur of the U.N. Human Rights Council, *Report of the Special Rapporteur on the Issue of Human Rights Obligations Relating to the Enjoyment of a Safe, Clean, Healthy and Sustainable Environment*, U.N. Doc. A/HRC/31/52 (Feb. 1, 2016); *Understanding Human Rights and Climate Change*, Submission of the Off. of the High Comm'r for Hum. Rts. to the 21st Conf. of the Parties to the U.N. Framework Convention on Climate Change (Nov. 26, 2015), https://perma.cc/83BJ-JN27. In October 2021, the Human Rights Council adopted Resolution A/HRC/48/L.27, establishing the mandate of the Special Rapporteur on the promotion and protection of human rights in the context of climate change.

19 See, e.g., Chapman MS. Feature. Climate Change and the Regional Human Rights Systems. Sustainable Development Law and Policy. 2010;10(2):37. In Europe, for example, there are currently 12 climate litigation cases pending before the European Court of Human Rights. See Sabin Center for Climate Law's case chart at https://climatecasechart.com/non-us-jurisdiction/european-court-of-human-rights/. See also Bönnemann M, Tigre MA. The Transformation of European Climate Litigation. Verfassungsbooks; 2024; Heri C. Climate Change before the European Court of Human Rights: Capturing Risk, Ill-Treatment and Vulnerability. European Journal of International Law. August 2022;33(3):925–951. Available from: https://doi.org/10.1093/ejil/chac047; Keller K, Heri C. The Future is Now: Climate Cases before the ECtHR. Nordic Journal of Human Rights. 2022;40(1):153–174. Available from: DOI: 10.1080/18918131.2022.2064074.

of the System's environmental standards and its interplay with domestic litigation, this contribution underscores the interconnected dynamics between Inter-American legal frameworks and national efforts to advance climate justice.

Beginning with the IACHR, section 2 explores the Commission's role in addressing climate issues by analysing landmark petitions, including those filed by the Inuit, Athabaskan, and Cité Soleil communities, as well as Resolution 3/21 on the Climate Emergency. Section 3 shifts focus to the Inter-American Court, tracing its interpretative evolution through both advisory and contentious functions and highlighting three key doctrinal advancements stemming therefrom: (1) the recognition of the RHE, (2) the duty of due diligence, and (3) extraterritorial human rights obligations. In its contentious jurisdiction, the recognition of the RHE as a stand-alone right and the elaboration of the normative content of the due diligence duty are exemplified by *Lhaka Honhat v Argentina* and *La Oroya v Peru*. These cases mark a significant departure from earlier jurisprudence, which indirectly addressed environmental protection through rights such as life and communal property of Indigenous peoples and did not substantively engage with the obligations of non-State actors. In its advisory capacity, the chapter explores Advisory Opinion 23/17, as well as the recent advisory opinion request on the Climate Emergency and Human Rights submitted by Chile and Colombia.

Section 4 examines how domestic climate litigation incorporates and builds upon the standards set by the IAHRS, using landmark cases from Brazil and Panama to illustrate the interaction between regional norms and national legal frameworks. Section 5 concludes the chapter by synthesising insights into the IAHRS's evolving role in promoting climate justice. The conclusion underscores the importance of the System's evolutive interpretations of the ACHR, particularly through the integration of complementary instruments – including those related to climate change law – in developing context-specific standards tailored to the unique realities of Latin America.

2.2 Climate Change before the IACHR

As of December 2024, the IACHR has four relevant climate cases – one dismissed and three pending. This section briefly analyses these cases individually and how their climate claims relate to the IAHRS's developing green jurisprudence. Furthermore, it briefly introduces Resolution 3/21 on the Climate Emergency, adopted by the IAHRS in 2021.

2.2.1 Inuit Circumpolar Conference's Petition

In 2005, the Inuit Circumpolar Conference submitted a petition to the Commission seeking relief from human rights violations resulting from the impacts of global warming and climate change caused by acts and omissions of the United States.[20] The Inuit petition is one of the earliest attempts to use international human rights law in climate litigation. It articulates a novel "climate rights" frame emphasising climate change's moral dimensions and bringing marginalised communities' voices through state accountability.[21] The claim was lodged because of the historical GHG emissions and climate policy failures of the United States, contributing to climate change–related Arctic damage.

The Inuit alleged that the impacts of global warming constituted a violation of their human rights, including their right to the benefits of culture, property, the preservation of health, life, physical integrity, security, and a means of subsistence, and residence, movement, and inviolability of the home.[22] However, the IACHR rejected the petition, arguing a lack of proof of actual rights violation and damages suffered by the Inuit peoples, and no precautionary measures were issued, given the difficulty in proving the causal link between climate change and alleged harms and rights violations.[23] Since the petition was lodged, the development of climate attribution science has advanced significantly, precisely reinforcing the causal links that were then weak.[24]

While the petition ultimately failed in assigning any responsibility for climate change to the United States, it did exert legal influence at the international level by jumpstarting the connection between human rights and climate change[25] and indirectly influencing regulatory development,[26] as well as the recognition of an autonomous human RHE. It also advanced the development of environmental justice claims of Indigenous groups by opening the dialogue about the link between climate change and human rights and its

20 Petition to the Inter-American Commission on Human Rights Seeking Relief from Violations Resulting from Global Warming Caused by Acts and Omissions of the United States (Dec. 8, 2005). See also Osofsky HM. Inuit Petition as a Bridge? Beyond Dialectics of Climate Change and Indigenous Peoples' Rights. American Indian Law Review. 2007;31:675.

21 Allan JA, Hadden J. Exploring the Framing Power of NGOs in Global Climate Politics. Environmental Policy. 2017;26; Jodoin S, Corobow A, Snow S. Realizing the Right to Be Cold? Framing Processes and Outcomes Associated with the Inuit Petition on Human Rights and Global Warming. Law & Society. 2020;54(1):168–169.

22 Tsosie R. Indigenous People and Environmental Justice: The Impact of Climate Change. 78 University of Colorado Law Review. 2007;78:1625, 1663.

23 Letter from Dulitzky AE, Assistant Executive Secretary. Inter-American Court of Human Rights, to Paul Crowley, Barrister and Solicitor. 16 November 2006. Available from: https://perma.cc/M7EF-3Y9T. See also Gloppen S, Vallejo C. The Climate Crisis: Litigation and Economic, Social and Cultural Rights, Research Handbook on Economic, Social and Cultural Rights as Human Rights. 2020.

24 Burger M, Wentz J, Horton R. (2020). The Law and Science of Climate Change Attribution. *Columbia Journal of Environmental Law*, *45*(1). https://doi.org/10.7916/cjel.v45i1.4730.

25 Jodoin S et. al., (n 21) pp. 184–186.

26 Peel J, Osofsky HM. Climate Change Litigation's Regulatory Pathways: A Comparative Analysis of the United States and Australia. Law & Policy. 2013;35(3):160.

effects on Indigenous communities.[27] In sum, this early attempt to use human rights law to assign responsibility for global warming, albeit unsuccessful, opened the door for future cases, mainly regarding recognition of the intersection of climate change, Indigenous peoples, and human rights violations before the IACHR.

2.2.2 *Arctic Athabaskan Council's Petition*

The second petition presented to the IACHR alleging violation of human rights caused by the adverse effects of climate change concerns the rights of Arctic Athabaskan peoples resulting from rapid Arctic warming caused by Canada's carbon emissions.[28] In 2013, the Arctic Athabaskan Council asked the IACHR to declare that Canada's failure to implement adequate measures to reduce its black carbon emissions substantially violates their rights to the benefits of culture, property, health, and the means of subsistence, affirmed in the ADHR[29]; and recommend that Canada take steps to protect the rights of Athabaskan peoples by adopting measures to limit black carbon emissions.[30] They argue that Canada has a duty under the American Declaration not to degrade the Arctic environment, and continued degradation infringes upon their right to enjoy the benefits of their culture.[31] The petitioners comprehensively analysed and evidenced the human rights violations they suffered.[32] Given their close ties to their lands and environment, Arctic warming and melting adversely affect their traditional knowledge and ability to educate future generations, which is vital to their survival.[33] The petition is still pending.

The Athabaskan petition bears several similarities with the Inuit petition. Like the Inuit, the Athabaskan peoples are Indigenous groups in the Arctic that depend on natural resources for their livelihood and acutely feel the effects of climate change. The outcome and impact of this petition are yet to be seen. However, unlike the Inuit petition, which was met with stark resistance, the IACtHR's recent green jurisprudence shows an openness towards

27 Jaimes VR. The Arctic Athabaskan Petition: Where Accelerated Arctic Warming Meets Human Rights. California Western International Law Journal. 2014;45:213; Tigre MA. Climate Change and Indigenous Groups: The Rise of Indigenous Voices in Climate Litigation. E-Publica. 2022;9(3):214.

28 Petition to the Inter-American Commission on Human Rights Seeking Relief from Violations of the Rights of Arctic Athabaskan Peoples Resulting from Rapid Arctic Warming and Melting Caused by Emissions of Black Carbon by Canada [hereinafter Black Carbon Petition].

29 *Idem*, at 3–5; 78.

30 *Idem*, at 86.

31 *Idem*, at 61.

32 Szpak A. Arctic Athabaskan Council's Petition to the Inter-American Commission on Human Rights and Climate Change – Business as Usual or a Breakthrough?. Climatic Change. 2020;162:1575–1577.

33 *Idem*.

novel rights-based claims, which could prove helpful as this case progresses. As stated by Auz, "[t]he IACHR went from dismissing a petition on the impact of climate change on the rights of the Inuit filed in 2005, to specifying obligations for states in respect of climate change and human rights in reports and recommendations that date from 2017".[34] This paradigm shift, partly due to specific resolutions from the Organization of American States and grassroots movements, can potentially impact current and future climate-related cases.[35] Moreover, the fact that the IAHRS recognises an autonomous RHE could prove instrumental in solving this case, as it relates to the violation of human rights inherently connected to the RHE.

2.2.3 *Petition of Children in Cité Soleil, Haiti*

Third, in 2021, a group of Haitian children petitioned the IACHR to redress human rights violations stemming from waste disposal in their residential district of Cité Soleil.[36] The petition lays out a factual background of toxic trash disposal from Port-au-Prince, which causes short and long-term health harm that most acutely affects children. The petition further discusses climate change's aggravation of the harm to children through environmental displacement, food and water insecurity, and exacerbation of waterborne diseases. Petitioners allege violations of the American Convention's rights of the child, the right to dignity, the right to live in a healthy environment, and the right to judicial protection. The Commission is expected first to decide whether to assert jurisdiction.

Despite being in the early stages, the case could prove significant to advancing climate litigation, mainly because of the solid factual account of harms and their aggravation due to climate change. Moreover, it represents the first climate-related case filed following landmark case law established in the Court's evolving green jurisprudence (as section 3 maps). It also draws on the vulnerability of children, which has proven to strengthen the rights-based arguments in climate litigation elsewhere.[37] The case could become an instance for the Commission to advance climate liability from a rights-based perspective, drawing on the IAHRS green jurisprudence and the vulnerability of certain groups in framing climate claims.

34 Auz J. Human Rights-Based Climate Litigation: A Latin American Cartography. Journal of Human Rights and the Environment. 2022:13:114, 124.

35 *Ibid*, 125.

36 *In Re* Six Child. of Cité Soleil, Inter-Am Comm'n H.R., (petition filed 4 February 2021).

37 Donger E. Children and Youth in Strategic Climate Litigation: Advancing Rights through Legal Argument and Legal Mobilization. Transnational Environmental Law. 2022;11:263.

2.2.4 Public Hearing on Human Rights and Global Warming

It is worth mentioning that while the Inuit petition was dismissed, the IACHR agreed to hold a public hearing on Human Rights and Global Warming.[38] In 2019, a group of NGOs requested a hearing focused on the impacts of climate change on the human rights of groups in situations of vulnerability, including Indigenous peoples, women, children, and rural communities.[39] Thematic hearings represent a strategic mechanism available to human rights defenders to deliver updated information on developing different issues and push the IAHRS into the dynamic interpretation of the law concomitant to new social issues.[40]

Organisations have relied on the human rights impacts of GHG emissions, particularly due to extreme climate events and the response to climate change. They requested the Commission to, among others, recognise the climate crisis as a priority that threatens human rights and ecosystems and advance petitions and precautionary measures related to climate change and its response measures. They also requested the Commission to urge states to stop activities that aggravate climate change and threaten the effective enjoyment of human rights and take specific measures to guarantee access to information related to the impacts of climate change and its response measures.[41] The commissioners recognised the need to act urgently on the climate crisis, engage more deeply, and incorporate climate change considerations in their work.[42] In May 2020, the petitioners published a report regarding their requests.[43] These thematic hearings can give meaning to the diverse nature of

38 Press Release IACHR, IACHR Announces Webcast of Pub. Hearings of the 127th Regular Period of Sessions No. 8/07 (26 February 2007); See Audio Recording: Audio of Pub. Hearings of the 127th Regular Period of Sessions held by the Inter-Am. Comm'n H.R. (1 May 2007).

39 Inter-Am. Comm'n H.R.. Solicitud de Audiencia Temática Sobre Los Impactos del Cambio Climático en los Derechos en las Américas [Request for a Thematic Hearing on the Impacts of Climate Change on Rights in the Americas], (11 July 2019) [hereinafter Hearing on Climate Change]. Available from: https://perma.cc/6882-EP2M.

40 Juan Auz, Why Is the Inter-American Human Rights System lagging on Climate Change?, Open Global Rights (11 January 2018). Available from: https://perma.cc/H4XQ-PZTS.

41 Sabin Center for Climate Change Law. Climate Change Litigation Database. Hearing on Climate Change before the Inter-American Commission on Human Rights, Available from: http://climatecasechart.com/climate-change-litigation/non-us-case/hearing-on-climate-change-before-the-inter-american-commission-on-human-rights/.

42 Historic Hearing! Organizations Warn the IACHR of the Impacts of the #ClimateCrisis on Human Rights, DeJusticia. 22 May 2020. Available from: https://perma.cc/7PQY-D449.

43 Díaz MA et al., Cambio Climático y los Derechos de Mujeres, Pueblos Indígenas y Comunidades Rurales en las Américas [Climate Change and the Rights of Women, Indigenous Peoples and Rural Communities in the Americas]. Fundación Heinrich Böll. 2020. Available from: https://perma.cc/FZ3Y-WPGL.

climate claims, mainly as they stem from those experiencing its devastating effects.[44]

2.2.5 *Resolution 3/21*

Building on this jurisprudence, the IACHR and the Office of the Special Rapporteur on Economic, Social, Cultural and Environmental Rights (REDESCA) jointly published a resolution systematising the human rights obligations of States in the context of the climate crisis.[45] Resolution 3/21 specifically delineates the positive obligations of States concerning climate change, providing other legal grounds as to how a case can be brought to the IAHRS. Specifically, the Resolution highlights that "the right to a healthy, balanced and pollution-free environment is part of the set of rights that States must guarantee and protect by reason of their obligations at the national and regional levels".[46] The resolution explicitly states that the State obligations refer to the duty to implement mitigation targets consistent with the Paris Agreement.[47] In particular, the resolution specified the obligation of states to mitigate GHG emissions by adopting and implementing targets that "reflect a level of ambition consistent with the obligations of the Paris Agreement and other applicable instruments, particularly with the obligation not to exceed global temperature to such an extent as to jeopardize the enjoyment of human rights".[48] These include: a duty to (i) assess cumulative damages[49] and GHG emissions within its territory and transboundary in EIAs, (ii) reduce emissions in the public and private sectors, (iii) implement adaptation measures, and (iv) remedy any resulting damages,[50] in addition to (v) a series of procedural rights. The Resolution further notes that "[s]uch actions must be framed under the application of the principle of due diligence, from which the principles of precaution and prevention of environmental damage are derived, they must be seriously considered to avoid damage, both within the territory and transboundary".[51]

44 Auz J. "So, This Is Permanence": The Inter-American Human Rights System as a Liminal Space for Climate Justice. Melbourne Journal of International Law. 2022;22:20.
45 IACHR and REDESCA, Resolution No. 3/21, Climate Emergency: Scope of Inter-American Human Rights Obligations.
46 Resolution 3/21, para. 8.
47 Resolution 3/21, para. 41.
48 Resolution 3/21, para. 41.
49 Resolution 3/21, para. 10.
50 Resolution 3/21, para. 15.
51 Resolution 3/21, para. 10.

2.3 Climate Relevant Jurisprudential Trajectory of the IACtHR

In addition to the Commission's contributions, the IACtHR has established green jurisprudence with implications for climate litigation. This section explores the Court's case law evolution, focusing on three key developments: (1) recognition of the RHE, (2) the duty of due diligence, and (3) extraterritorial human rights obligations. Their application and refinement are illustrated through five landmark cases: *Mayagna (Sumo) Awas Tingni v Nicaragua*, *Yakye Axa Indigenous Community v Paraguay*, Advisory Opinion 23/17, *Lhaka Honhat v Argentina*, and *La Oroya v Peru*. Building on this foundation, the section concludes by reflecting on their potential implications for the forthcoming Advisory Opinion on the Climate Emergency – requested by the Republics of Chile and Colombia in January 2023 – and its likely influence on climate litigation.

2.3.1 Recognition of the RHE

The RHE, while explicitly recognised in the San Salvador Protocol, is absent from the ACHR, from which the IACtHR derives its jurisdiction.[52] Consequently, the Court lacks explicit *ratione materiae* authority over the RHE, meaning violations of this right could not initially be addressed through individual petitions, leaving a gap in the system for addressing environmental harm under this framework.[53] Over time, however, the Court employed an evolutive and systemic interpretation of the ACHR to overcome this limitation. Initially, it grounded environmental protection within the scope of established rights under the Convention and later explicitly recognised the RHE under Article 26 of the ACHR. The earlier approach focused on fundamental rights, such as the right to life (Article 4) and the right to property (Article 21), particularly in cases where environmental degradation impacted Indigenous and vulnerable communities.[54]

The case of *Mayagna (Sumo) Awas Tingni v Nicaragua* (2001) represents a landmark moment in this jurisprudential progression.[55] It marked the first instance in which the IACtHR, through separate opinions by individual judges, recognised the environment as integral to the cultural and physical integrity of the Awas Tingni Indigenous community – who had been adversely affected by the Nicaraguan state's granting of logging concessions on their

52 Article 11 on the right to a healthy environment provides that: "1. Everyone shall have the right to live in a healthy environment and to have access to basic public services. 2. The States Parties shall promote the protection, preservation, and improvement of the environment".

53 Additional Protocol to the American Convention on Human Rights in the Area of Economic, Social and Cultural Rights, Article 11. 11 November 1988, 28 ILM 156 [hereinafter Protocol of San Salvador].

54 Jimenez Guanipa H, Barraco M, (n 4) p. 243.

55 Inter-American Court of Human Rights, *Case of the Mayagna (Sumo) Awas Tingni Community v Nicaragua*, Judgment of 31 August 2001 (Merits, Reparations and Costs), para. 148.

traditional lands. This recognition was grounded in the community's newly established right to communal property under Article 21 of the ACHR. In their Joint Separate Opinion, Judges A.A. Cançado Trindade (Brazil), M. Pacheco Gómez (Chile), and A. Abreu Burelli (Venezuela) articulated that

> The communal concept of the land – including as a spiritual place – and its natural resources form part of [the community's] customary law; their link with the territory, even if not written, integrates their day-to-day life, and the right to communal property itself has a cultural dimension. In sum, the *habitat* forms an integral part of their culture, transmitted from generation to generation.[56]

The case of *Yakye Axa Indigenous Community v Paraguay* (2005) marked another significant step in the indirect recognition of environmental protection linked to the right to life under Article 4 of the ACHR. The Court determined that the Yakye Axa Indigenous community had been deprived of a dignified life due to their lack of access to ancestral lands, which hindered their ability to use natural resources essential for subsistence, cultural expression, and spiritual practices.[57] This deprivation subjected the community to precarious living conditions, severely affecting their health, nutrition, and overall well-being.[58] The Court underscored the particular vulnerability of children and elderly members within the community, emphasising the severe impact of these conditions on their lives.[59] Based on these findings, the Court held that Paraguay violated Article 4(1) of the American Convention, in conjunction with Article 1(1), by failing to adopt measures to address the living conditions that compromised the Yakye Axa community's right to a dignified life.[60]

The indirect protection of the right to a healthy environment through the rights to property and life gradually evolved into its direct recognition. In Advisory Opinion 23/17, the IACtHR established as a starting point that, under the IAHRS, the right to a healthy environment is expressly established in Article 11 of the Protocol of San Salvador.[61] The Court further interpreted that:

> [T]his right is included among the economic, social, and cultural rights protected by Article 26 of the American Convention, because this norm

56 *Ibid*, Joint Separate Opinion of Judges A.A. Cançado Trindade, M. Pacheco Gómez, and A. Abreu Burelli, para. 6.

57 *Mayagna (Sumo) Awas Tingni Community* (n 55) para. 164.

58 *Ibid.*

59 *Ibid*, para. 172.

60 *Ibid*, para. 176.

61 Inter-American Court of Human Rights, The Environment and Human Rights (Advisory Opinion OC-23/17, 2017), para. 56.

> protects the rights derived from the economic, social, educational, scientific and cultural provisions of the OAS Charter, the American Declaration of the Rights and Duties of Man [...] and those resulting from an interpretation of the Convention that accords with the criteria established in its Article 29. The Court reiterates the interdependence and indivisibility of civil and political rights, and economic, social, and cultural rights, as they should be understood integrally and comprehensively as human rights, with no order of precedence, enforceable in all cases before the competent authorities.[62]

The IACtHR also underscored the unquestionable link between environmental protection and the realisation of human rights affected by environmental degradation, reaffirming the interdependence and indivisibility of human rights.[63] It cited precedents from regional and international courts, international instruments, and UN resolutions, making clear that a wide range of rights could be adversely affected by the lack of a healthy environment. Hence, in addition to recognising the RHE, the Court expressly acknowledged the right to life–related to the environment, noting that an adequate environment, with access to water and food, is essential to human life. This interpretation relies on how the full enjoyment of all human rights depends on a favourable environment.[64] The Court further emphasised the mechanisms necessary to ensure that such rights are enforced, including the obligation of States to abstain from any practice that denies or restricts access to water or food and that illicitly contaminates the environment, affecting the conditions required for a dignified life.[65] This requirement implies a "positive environmental justice" dimension, where the benefits provided by human impact on the environment should be equitably accessed.[66]

More relevant to climate change, the Court underscored that the RHE encompasses both individual and collective dimensions, particularly concerning present and future generations.[67] It also acknowledged the disproportionate impact of climate change on vulnerable populations, including Indigenous peoples, children, and those living in extreme poverty.[68] By rendering the RHE directly *justiciable* under Article 26 of the ACHR[69] – and

62 *Ibid*, para. 57.

63 *Idem* at paras. 47, 54, 55, 57, 192. See Tigre MA, Urzola N, (n 17) p. 43.

64 *See* Christopher Campbell-Duruflé and Sumudu Anopama Atapattu, The Inter-American Court's Environment and Human Rights Advisory Opinion: Implications for International Climate Law, Climate Law 8.3–4 (2018), 321–337.

65 Tigre MA, Urzola N, (n 17), para. 117.

66 Ezio Costa Cordella and Gabriela Burdiles, El Derecho Humano Al Medio Ambiente: Nuevos Avances en su Comprensión en América Latina y El Caribe, 15(2) Anuario de Derechos Humanos 189–212 (2019).

67 Tigre MA, Urzola N, (n 17) para. 47; para. 59.

68 *Idem* at para. 47; para. 48.

69 This aspect has caused friction between the judges. See Tigre MA, Urzola N, (n 17) p. 44.

thereby opening the possibility of holding States accountable for failing to regulate and prevent environmental harm[70] – Advisory Opinion 23/17 provides a robust foundation for challenging activities that exacerbate GHG emissions, such as extractive operations in biodiversity-critical habitats that disproportionately impact vulnerable populations. This legal basis is essential for future climate litigation cases before the IACtHR, as it opens the door for claims grounded in violations of the RHE.

Despite this recognition in its advisory jurisdiction, the IACtHR did not extend the direct acknowledgment of the RHE to its contentious jurisdiction until 2019 in *Lhaka Honhat v Argentina*. In this landmark case, the IACtHR, drawing on Advisory Opinion 23/17, recognised the right to a healthy environment as an autonomous right for the first time, directly enforceable under Article 26 of the ACHR.[71] The Court further defined the scope of state obligations related to this right, particularly when addressing environmentally degrading activities by private companies.

> Regarding the right to a healthy environment, for the purposes of this case it should be pointed out States not only have the obligation to respect this, but also the obligation established in Article 1(1) of the Convention to ensure it, and one of the ways of complying with this is by preventing violations. This obligation extends to the "private sphere" in order to avoid "third parties violating the protected rights", and "encompasses all those legal, political, administrative and cultural measures that promote the safeguard of human rights and that ensure that eventual violations of those rights are examined and dealt with as wrongful acts". In this regard, the Court has indicated that, at times, the States have the obligation to establish adequate mechanisms to monitor and supervise certain activities in order to ensure human rights, protecting them from actions of public entities and also private individuals.[72]

As an autonomous right, the Court recognized that the RHE protects several components of the environment, including forests, seas, and rivers.[73] The IACtHR specified that the RHE requires not only an obligation to respect but also a duty to guarantee compliance as a way to prevent violations.[74] The interpretation of the RHE as an "autonomous" right indicates its dissociation, mainly from property rights, which may lead to more suitable forms of

70 Peel J, Osofsky HM, (n 26) p. 166.

71 Inter-American Court of Human Rights, *Case of the Indigenous Communities of the Lhaka Honhat (Our Land) Association v Argentina*, Judgment of 6 February 2020 (Merits, Reparations and Costs), para. 202.

72 *Ibid*, para. 207.

73 *Idem.*

74 American Convention, Article 1.1 (based on the general obligation to respect human rights).

reparation for environmental damages.[75] Clarifying the autonomous RHE can imply greater security for environmental standards through the progressive development of international environmental law when States must prevent environmental damage from a human rights perspective.[76]

This interpretation was further solidified in *La Oroya v Peru*, where the Court established state responsibility for violating the RHE to the detriment of La Oroya residents, who had suffered from air, water, and toxic pollution caused by mining activities.[77] Relying on Article 26, this case is particularly notable because, unlike *Lhaka Honhat*, it marks the first instance in which the Court upheld the right to a healthy environment in a case involving a non-Indigenous population. Here, the Court expanded on Advisory Opinion 23/17, shifting towards a more ecocentric understanding of the environment. It recognised that the right to a healthy environment entails the intrinsic value of nature itself, valued not solely for its utility to humans but for its own inherent significance. In this regard, the Court stated that

> the right to a healthy environment "protects components of the [...] environment, such as forests, rivers, seas, and others, as legal interests in themselves, even in the absence of certainty or evidence of risk to individuals". Thus, States are obligated to protect nature not solely for its utility or effects on human beings, but for its significance to other living organisms with whom we share the planet.[78]

75 Garcia B, Lixinski L. Beyond Culture: Reimagining the Adjudication of Indigenous Peoples' Rights in International Law. Intercultural Human Rights Law Review. 2020;15:127.

76 Boyle A. Human Rights and the Environment: Where Next? European Journal of International Law. 2012;23:613. See Boyd D, et al. The Case for Universal Recognition of the Right to a Safe, Clean, Healthy, and Sustainable Environment. Universal Rights Group. 2021 (on the need to recognise the right to a healthy environment at the international level).

77 See, generally, Boyd D. Landmark Court Decision on Right to a Healthy Environment: *La Oroya v Peru*. Global Network for Human Rights and the Environment. March 2024 [Accessed 20 November 2024]. Available from: https://gnhre.org/?p=17944; Puentes A. *La Oroya*: An Environmental Justice Lesson to Peru and the World. Medium. March 2024. [Accessed 20 November 20 2024]. Available from: https://medium.com/@astridpuentes/la-oroya-an-environmental-justice-lesson-to-peru-and-the-world-d44c62f47ce1; Kahl V, Rodríguez-Orúe JD. Upgrading Environmental Rights: La Oroya and its Significance for a Safer Climate. Verfassungsblog. 16 May 2024. [Accessed 20 November 20 2024]. Available from: https://verfassungsblog.de/upgrading-environmental-rights/; Viveros-Uehara T. La Oroya and Inter-American Innovations on the Right to a Healthy Environment. VerfBlog. 16 May 2024. [Accessed 20 November 20 2024]. Available from: https://verfassungsblog.de/la-oroya-and-inter-american-innovations-on-the-right-to-a-healthy-environment/ DOI: 10.59704/bc45e4a6c6e822d6.

78 Inter-American Court of Human Rights, *Case of the Residents of La Oroya v Peru*, Judgment of 27 November 2023 (Preliminary Objections, Merits, Reparations and Costs), para. 118.

Consequently, in line with its "integral reparations approach",[79] the Court mandated that the State implement restitution measures, including conducting a baseline assessment of air, soil, and water contamination in La Oroya and creating an action plan for prioritised remediation within 18 months, ensuring public participation throughout.[80] Decontamination efforts must focus on high-risk areas and affected homes, guided by scientific data.[81] For non-repetition, the State is required to align air quality standards with international benchmarks, establish a monitoring system with accessible, real-time data for residents and implement an effective alert system for contamination risks.[82] The State must also ensure specialised health care for pollution-related illnesses, enforce the "polluter pays" principle, and develop a compensation plan aimed at restoring and rehabilitating the local ecosystem in La Oroya.[83] The recognition of environmental compartments as legal interests themselves further expands the scope of climate and biodiversity cases before the IACtHR, as it potentially allows for cases to be brought on behalf of nature (and, therefore, in violation of the rights of nature in addition to the RHE of individuals and communities).

2.3.2 *Due Diligence Duty*

Recognition of the RHE within the IAHRS enables the IACtHR to assess whether measures undertaken by States to address climate change meet the duty of due diligence by being "reasonable and adequate" to prevent harm.[84] Voigt articulates a guiding framework for this analysis, posing the question of whether these measures reflect the "highest possible ambition" and effectively achieve significant reductions in GHG emissions, in conformity with the Paris Agreement's obligations and best available science.[85]

In *Lhaka Honhat*, the Court delineated the scope of States' positive obligations to protect the RHE, requiring mechanisms to monitor, regulate, and supervise activities capable of causing environmental harm, consistent with the principle of prevention.[86] The Court's interpretation of due diligence as an objective standard imposes a duty on States to implement *ex ante* meas-

79 Soley X. The Transformative Dimension of Inter-American Jurisprudence. In von Bogdandy A et al., eds. Transformative Constitutionalism in Latin America: The Emergence of a New *Ius Commune*. Oxford University Press; 2017. p. 346.

80 *Case of the Residents of La Oroya*, para. 333.

81 *Ibid*, para. 334.

82 *Ibid*, paras. 346–353.

83 *Ibid.*

84 Voigt C. The Climate Change Dimension of Human Rights Obligations. SSRN. 3 May 2021. 1; 13 (based on talk given at High Level Conference "Human Rights for the Planet" at the European Court on Human Rights and the Council of Europe, 5 October 2020). Available from: https://ssrn.com/abstract=3839012.

85 *Ibid.*

86 *Case of the Indigenous Communities of the Lhaka Honhat*, (n 71) para. 208.

ures aimed at avoiding foreseeable harm.[87] In the context of climate change, this translates into an obligation to adopt comprehensive strategies to mitigate GHG emissions commensurate with the severity and scale of the climate crisis.[88]

Building on this jurisprudential foundation, the IACtHR in *La Oroya* advanced the scope of due diligence by addressing State obligations involving third-party actors. The case involved a century-old polluting complex operated by both State entities and private foreign investors, where severe environmental degradation and health impacts had been documented for decades. Interpreting the due diligence standard in light of the UN Guiding Principles on Business and Human Rights, the Court emphasised that the obligations under Article 1(1) of the American Convention – to respect and ensure rights – apply equally to public and private entities.[89] To meet these obligations, Peru was required to regulate, supervise, and monitor the complex's activities effectively.[90] The Court identified critical failures in Peru's regulatory framework, particularly the absence of specific environmental legislation for mining and metallurgical activities before 1993.[91] While measures to supervise and monitor the polluting complex were eventually introduced, the Court criticised their delayed implementation, noting that meaningful enforcement only occurred after 2010.[92] The disconnect between the legislative measures implemented and the allowances the state permitted in practice facilitated the success of the case. This reasoning is also relevant to climate litigation. Several domestic climate cases, especially in Latin America, concern the lack of implementation of domestic climate legislation or commitments before the UNFCCC.[93]

Procedural dimensions of the RHE were also central to the Court's analysis. Recognising the interconnectedness of access to information and political participation with environmental governance, the Court scrutinised the

87 *Ibid.*
88 Voigt C, (n 84) p. 10.
89 *Case of the Residents of La Oroya*, para. 111. For an analysis of the significance of this judgment in distinguishing between public and private enterprises, see Pamplona DA. Relações entre empresas e direitos humanos e o caso La Oroya na Corte IDH. Jota. 7 May 2024. [Accessed 14 October 2024]. Available from: https://www.jota.info/opiniao-e-analise/colunas/direitos-humanos-sem-fronteiras/relacoes-entre-empresas-e-direitos-humanos-e-o-caso-la-oroya-na-corte-idh.
90 *Case of the Residents of La Oroya*, para. 157.
91 *Ibid*, para. 162.
92 *Ibid*, para. 163.
93 See, i.e., Burger B, Tigre MA. Global Climate Litigation Report: 2023 Status Review. Sabin Center for Climate Change Law, Columbia Law School and United Nations Environment Programme, 2023; Tigre MA, Urzola N, Goodman A. Climate Litigation in Latin America: Is the Region Quietly Leading a Regional Revolution?. Journal of Human Rights and Environment. 2023;14(1):67–93; Tigre MA. Climate Litigation in the Global South: Mapping Report. 2024. Available from: https://scholarship.law.columbia.edu/sabin_climate_change/230.

State's failures in this regard. Despite the Escazú Agreement offering a robust framework for procedural environmental rights, Peru's non-ratification led the Court to ground its findings in Articles 13 and 23 of the ACHR. It found that the State had withheld critical information on health risks from La Oroya's residents before 2003 and had failed to implement measures that allowed meaningful community participation in environmental decision-making.[94]

By defining due diligence as a dual obligation to regulate, supervise, and monitor activities and ensure accountability through robust procedural rights, *La Oroya* provides a framework with significant implications for addressing climate change. This interpretation obliges States to adopt measures not only to achieve substantial reductions in GHG emissions but also to guarantee transparency regarding emissions, the impacts of climate-related actions, and the broader effects of climate change. The duty extends to ensuring that private entities disclose equivalent information, fostering an environment of informed decision-making. States are further required to make this data accessible to the public, enabling affected communities to participate meaningfully in shaping climate policies and contributing to mitigation and adaptation strategies.

When read through the lens of Advisory Opinion 23/17, which extended jurisdiction to transboundary claims of environmental harm affecting human rights, the content of the due diligence duty acquires greater depth. The opinion introduced the concept of "diagonal" human rights claims, enabling individuals to hold States accountable for the harm caused by activities under their control, regardless of borders.[95] Combined with the standards articulated in *Lhaka Honhat* and later expanded in *La Oroya*, this jurisprudence underscores that States must employ all necessary measures to prevent significant environmental harm arising from activities within their jurisdiction, including those with transboundary impacts.

Building on this understanding, the principle of due diligence serves as an objective criterion in international law for assessing whether a State has met its obligations.[96] Assessments under this principle involve examining whether a breach of international law has occurred and evaluating the State's actions in light of the harm that could reasonably have been prevented.[97] They also include preventing transboundary environmental damage, cooperating with other States, providing information on environmental risks, applying the precautionary principle to avert irreversible harm, and guaranteeing procedural

94 *Case of the Residents of La Oroya*, para. 253.

95 Feria-Tinta M, Milnes SC. The Rise of Environmental Law in International Dispute Resolution: The Inter-American Court of Human Rights Issues a Landmark Advisory Opinion on the Environment and Human Rights. Blog of the European Journal of International Law EJIL:Talk! 2018;27:64, 75.

96 Kulesza J. Due Diligence in International Law. Brill; 2016. p. 2.

97 *Idem*, p. 2.

rights such as public participation and access to justice.[98] These requirements, alongside obligations to regulate, supervise, monitor, and address environmental harm, underscore the actionable dimensions of the due diligence duty.

In the context of climate change, the due diligence duty is shaped by factors such as the goals of the climate regime and the nature of harm resulting from a lack of diligence.[99] The concept of a State's "fair share" has gained traction as a tool for assessing compliance with these obligations by incorporating considerations of equity and fairness.[100] Maxwell et al. argue that fair share is central to evaluating whether a State has met its duty of care in addressing climate change.[101] Rajamani et al. have further elaborated on this principle, asserting that the harm prevention principle necessitates more ambitious targets within the scope of fair shares.[102]

This framework is particularly significant for countries in the Global South, which constitute the majority of States under the jurisdiction of the IAHRS and, as noted, are not among the major contributors to global GHG emissions. Despite their minimal historical contribution, the IACtHR's green jurisprudence confirms that these States hold positive obligations to prevent environmental harm. These obligations extend to implementing climate mitigation and adaptation measures, along with procedural safeguards such as ensuring access to information and public participation. By grounding the duty of due diligence in principles of equity and fairness, the concept of fair share underscores the importance of ambitious and inclusive climate action to protect both human rights and the environment. Rooted in the principle of common but differentiated responsibilities and respective capabilities (CBDR-RC), this due diligence obligation guarantees accountability. Rather than avoiding an obligation due to a more limited capacity, States must adhere to due diligence standards and ensure mitigation in alignment with equity standards.

98 Advisory Opinion OC-23/17, (n 55) para. 126; *Case of the Indigenous Communities of the Lhaka Honhat*, para. 208.

99 Rajamani L. Due Diligence in International Climate Change Law. In: Krieger H, Peters A, Kreuzer L, eds. Due Diligence in the International Legal Order. Oxford University Press; 2020. pp. 163–180.

100 See CLIMATE ACTION TRACKER. Available from: https://climateactiontracker.org/.

101 Maxwell L, et. al.. Standards for Adjudicating the Next Generation of Urgenda-Style Climate Cases. Journal of Human Rights and Environment. 2022;13(1):35; 50. See also Tigre MA. The "Fair Share" of Climate Mitigation: Can Litigation Increase National Ambition for Brazil? Journal of Human Rights Practice. 2024;16(1):25.

102 Rajamani L, et al.. National "Fair Shares" in Reducing Greenhouse Gas Emissions within the Principled Framework of International Environmental Law. Climate Policy. 2021;21(8):993.

2.3.3 *Extraterritorial Obligations concerning Environmental Harm*

Transboundary environmental and climate change harm fundamentally challenge the territorial foundation of State obligations in international law.[103] The IACtHR became the first human rights court to recognise an extraterritorial jurisdictional link grounded in control over domestic activities with extraterritorial effects.[104] By accepting a new jurisdictional nexus based on the factual connection between conduct within a State's territory and human rights violations abroad, the Court affirmed that States exercising effective control over damaging activities bear responsibility for preventing consequent harm.[105] As previously discussed, this reasoning broadens the scope of the duty to conduct due diligence within a State's territory to protect human rights beyond its borders.[106] Furthermore, when considered alongside Resolution 3/21, which clarified the specific obligations of States in the context of climate change, this interpretation gains further precision. Resolution 3/21 emphasises that States must adopt and implement GHG mitigation targets aligned with the ambitions of the Paris Agreement. Together, these developments underscore the inherently global nature of climate change and provide critical guidance for addressing its far-reaching impacts.

These evolving standards hold particular promise for cases like the Athabaskan petition (see section 2), which could enable the IACHR to hold Canada accountable for human rights violations resulting from climate change across all Athabaskan territories, including those beyond Canada's borders. Beyond the IAHRS, the Court's interpretation has influenced significant advancements in other contexts, as seen in *Sacchi v Argentina*.[107] In that case, the IACtHR's reasoning was instrumental in delineating extraterritorial obligations under climate change law, particularly regarding the rights of the child.[108] The European Court of Human Rights (ECtHR), in turn, had

103 See Shelton D. Legitimate and Necessary: Adjudicating Human Rights Violations Related to Activities Causing Environmental Harm or Risk. Journal of Human Rights and Environment. 2015;6:139, 142.

104 Banda ML. Inter-American Court of Human Rights' Advisory Opinion on the Environment and Human Rights. Asil Insights. 10 May 2018. Available from: https://www.asil.org/insights/volume/22/issue/6/inter-american-court-human-rights-advisory-opinion-environment-and-human#_edn32 [https://perma.cc/NUW3-Q9RQ].

105 Advisory Opinion OC-23/17 (n 55) para. 95, paras. 101–102.

106 Berkes A. A New Extraterritorial Jurisdictional Link Recognized by the IACtHR, EJIL: Talk! 28 March 2018. Available from: https://www.ejiltalk.org/a-new-extraterritorial-jurisdictional-link-recognised-by-the-iacthr/ [https://perma.cc/JC34-N7YW].

107 UNCRC, Decision adopted by the CRC under the Optional Protocol to the Convention on the Rights of the Child on a Communications Procedure in Respect of Communication No. 104/2019, CRC/C/88/D/104/2019 (8 October 2021).

108 *Sacchi et al., v Argentina et al.*, n. 147, para. 10.5. See Tigre MA, Lichet V. The CRC Decision in *Sacchi v. Argentina*. American Society of International Law Insights. 13 December 2021;25(26).

a stricter view of justiciability as it concerns extraterritorial obligations in *Duarte Agostinho*.[109]

2.3.4 *A Landmark Advisory Opinion on the Climate Emergency and Human Rights*

The IACtHR has just delivered a significant advisory opinion on the climate emergency and human rights, following a January 2023 request by Chile and Colombia.[110] This request sought to elucidate States' obligations under the ACHR in addressing climate change, presenting 21 questions across six thematic areas: due diligence, the right to life, children's rights, procedural rights, environmental defenders, and the principle of CBDR.[111] By leveraging its established green jurisprudence, particularly its recognition of the RHE and evolving approaches to transboundary and systemic harms, the Court was given the opportunity to define robust legal standards with potential global resonance.[112]

Chile and Colombia's request invited the Court to apply its innovative environment-related jurisprudence to critical questions that extend the scope of international human rights law. Among these is the issue of due diligence – whether states' obligations to prevent foreseeable harm require them to adopt mitigation measures consistent with the global temperature goal of limiting warming to 1.5°C. As previously discussed, building on *La Oroya v Peru*, where the IACtHR emphasised that states must implement *ex ante* measures to prevent environmental harm, the Court would extend this principle to require proactive regulation of GHG emissions. In *La Oroya*, the Court faulted Peru for failing to supervise and regulate the polluting activities

109 See, i.e., Rocha A. States' Extraterritorial Jurisdiction for Climate-Related Impacts. In: Bönnemann M, Tigre MA, eds.. The Transformation of European Climate Litigation. Verfassungsbooks; 2024. Available from: https://scholarship.law.columbia.edu/sabin_climate_change/235.

110 Opinión Consultiva OC-32/25, de 29 de Mayo de 2025, Solicitada por la República de Chile y La República de Colombia, Sobre Emergencia Climática y Derechos Humanos. Available at https://www.corteidh.or.cr/docs/opiniones/seriea_32_esp.pdf

111 *Ibid*, p. 8.

112 See, generally, Auz J, Viveros-Uehara T. Another Advisory Opinion on the Climate Emergency? The Added Value of the Inter-American Court of Human Rights. EJIL: Talk!. 2 March 2023. [Accessed 1 December 2024]. Available from: https://www.ejiltalk.org/another-advisory-opinion-on-the-climate-emergency-the-added-value-of-the-inter-american-court-of-human-rights/; Viveros-Uehara T, Auz J. The Climate Emergency at the Inter-American Court of Human Rights. OpenGlobalRights. 27 February 2023. [Accessed 1 December 2024]. Available from: https://www.openglobalrights.org/climate-emergency-interamerican-court-human-rights/?author_lang=2; Tigre MA, Urzola N, Castellanos JS. A Request for an Advisory Opinion at the Inter-American Court of Human Rights: Initial Reactions. (Climate Law Blog, 17 February 2023). [Accessed 1 December 2024]. Available from: https://blogs.law.columbia.edu/climatechange/2023/02/17/a-request-for-an-advisory-opinion-at-the-inter-american-court-of-human-rights-initial-reactions/.

of a mining complex, even though the harm was foreseeable and protracted. Applying this standard in the climate context would establish a direct link between failure to mitigate GHG emissions and State responsibility for human rights violations.

The Court's jurisprudence on the due diligence obligation also includes addressing the role of private actors. In *Lhaka Honhat v Argentina*, the Court highlighted States' duties to regulate and monitor private entities to ensure compliance with human rights standards.[113] This principle, reinforced by the Court's reliance on the UN Guiding Principles on Business and Human Rights in *La Oroya*, could be extended to climate governance.[114] For instance, states could be required to implement regulatory frameworks that hold corporations accountable for emissions and mandate transparency in their environmental practices. Such an interpretation would align with the IACtHR's emphasis on ensuring that the duty to prevent harm is applied comprehensively across both public and private spheres.

The request also probes the principle of CBDR, a concept that the Court had yet to engage directly but which has strong resonance with its existing jurisprudence. The Court's acknowledgement of differentiated obligations, as articulated in *Yakye Axa Indigenous Community v Paraguay* and the AO-23/17, establishes a foundation for considering how historical responsibility and capacity influence States' duties in the climate context. In *Yakye Axa*, the Court underscored States' obligations to provide heightened protections for populations whose vulnerability, rooted in historical marginalisation, made them more susceptible to environmental harm.[115] By analogy, the principle of CBDR would be integrated into the human rights framework to ensure that major emitters *within* the States provide financial and technical support to States and communities disproportionately affected by climate change. This would include obligations to fund adaptation efforts, compensate for loss and damage, and support the development of climate-resilient infrastructure in vulnerable regions.[116]

Procedural rights also emerge as a central theme in the request, reflecting their critical role in empowering communities to address climate harms. The Court has consistently underscored the importance of procedural guarantees in environmental governance, as evidenced in *La Oroya* and AO-23/17. In *La Oroya*, the Court held that States must ensure public access to information about environmental risks and facilitate meaningful participation in decision-making processes.[117] Chile and Colombia's questions suggest an extension of this principle to the climate context, where transparency regarding emissions,

113 See (n 86).
114 See (n 89).
115 See (n 59).
116 Viveros-Uehara T, Auz J. (n 112).
117 See (n 94).

adaptation measures, and mitigation strategies is essential for accountability. The Court was also given the opportunity to address the procedural rights of Indigenous and marginalised communities, emphasising their right to consultation and participation in the design and implementation of climate policies. This would be in line with its recognition in AO-23/17 of the need for an inclusive approach that accounts for the specific vulnerabilities of affected populations.

The transboundary nature of climate harm adds a complex dimension to the advisory opinion. The IACtHR has already addressed extraterritorial obligations in AO-23/17, where it recognised that states bear responsibility for activities within their jurisdiction that cause cross-border environmental harm. The Court's introduction of "diagonal" claims – where individuals affected by transboundary harm can hold States accountable – could be further developed to address climate-related impacts.[118] This would reinforce the principle that States must not only prevent harm within their borders but also cooperate internationally to address transboundary and systemic threats, aligning with the ACHR's obligations under Articles 1(1) and 2.

Chile and Colombia's request also signals the potential for the Court to address gaps in existing international climate governance frameworks. While treaties like the Paris Agreement provide a foundation for global action, they lack robust enforcement mechanisms and do not explicitly integrate human rights. The IACtHR's advisory opinion was expected tobridge these gaps by articulating the human rights dimensions of climate obligations, offering a complementary framework to enhance accountability and coherence in international climate law.[119]

The participatory nature of the advisory process enhanced the potential impact of the opinion. The Court's inclusion of over 200 amicus briefs and public hearings provides an opportunity for historically marginalised voices to shape the legal discourse.[120] This inclusivity aligns with the Court's jurisprudential commitment to interpreting rights in light of the lived experiences of affected populations. By grounding its analysis in these perspectives, the advisory opinion can provide a roadmap for addressing the systemic factors

118 Feria-Tinta M. Climate Change as a Human Rights Issue: Litigating Climate Change in the Inter-American System of Human Rights and the United Nations Human Rights Committee. In: Alogna I, Bakker C, Gauci J-P, eds. Climate Change Litigation: Global Perspectives. Brill Nijhoff; 2021. p. 320.

119 Auz J, Viveros-Uehara T, (n 112).

120 In Historic Hearing Process with the Participation of REDESCA, I/A Court Will Issue an Advisory Opinion on State Obligations on Climate Emergency. OAS. 5 June 2024. [Accessed 1 December 2024]. Available from: https://www.oas.org/fr/CIDH/jsForm/?File=/en/iachr/media_center/PReleases/2024/125.asp.

driving climate vulnerability, including structural inequalities and inadequate governance.[121]

The IACtHR did, in fact, seize this opportunity and delivered a landmark Advisory Opinion. A summary of the main novelties in presented in the conclusion of this chapter.

2.4 The IAHRS in Dialogue with National Courts: An Overview of Domestic Climate Litigation

The IAHRS's progressive engagement with environmental issues – and more recently with climate change – reflects a dynamic and reciprocal exchange of influence. Far from operating as isolated supraregional bodies headquartered in Washington, DC, and San José, the Commission and the Court are integral to a process often described as "Inter-Americanisation" – a continuous dialogue between regional organs, national courts, and legal communities across the Americas.[122] Domestic legal practices have shaped the IACHR's and the IACtHR's approach to environmental standards. In turn, the Commission's and the Court's evolving standards have influenced national courts, prompting the adaptation of domestic jurisprudence to reflect human rights–based environmental standards. This mutual influence is particularly evident in climate litigation, where litigants and domestic courts increasingly invoke IAHRS's green standards. The extent of this interplay is exemplified in the following landmark cases from Brazil and Panama.

2.4.1 PSB et al. v Brazil *(on Amazon Fund)*

A 2022 ruling of the Supreme Federal Court (STF) of Brazil in the Amazon Fund case addresses the federal government's constitutional omission in safeguarding the Amazon biome.[123] Brought by four political parties – *Partido Socialista Brasileiro*, *Partido Socialismo e Liberdade*, *Partido dos Trabalhadores*, and *Rede Sustentabilidade* – the action alleged that Brazil had failed to properly manage and operationalise the Amazon Fund.[124] This case exemplifies the increasing judicialisation of climate change in Brazil,

121 For an analysis of the consultative process before the Court, as well as its potential implications, see Lima LC. Balancing the Arguments before the Inter-American Court on the Climate Emergency and Human Rights Advisory Proceedings. Opinio Juris. 31 May 2024. [Accessed 1 December 2024]. Available from: https://opiniojuris.org/2024/05/31/balancing-the-arguments-before-the-inter-american-court-on-the-climate-emergency-and-human-rights-advisory-proceedings/; Jackson E. Potential Climate Remedies at the Inter-American Court of Human Rights. Opinio Juris. 1 August 2024. [Accessed 1 December 2024]. Available from: https://opiniojuris.org/2024/08/01/potential-climate-remedies-at-the-inter-american-court-of-human-rights/.

122 Antoniazzi MM, Alessandri PS, (n 8).

123 Supremo Tribunal Federal (Brazil), Ação Direta de Inconstitucionalidade por Omissão 59 Distrito Federal (Inteiro Teor do Acórdão, 3 November 2022).

124 *Ibid*, 84.

highlighting the intersection of domestic constitutional duties and international environmental and climate change standards.[125]

At the core of the dispute lay the federal government's alleged inaction in fulfilling its constitutional and administrative responsibilities towards the Amazon Fund, established in 2008 to combat deforestation and foster sustainable practices. The petitioners presented data underscoring the gravity of this omission. Between July 2018 and July 2019, deforestation alerts rose by 278%, and the area destroyed by forest fires surged by 67% from 2018 to 2019.[126] This failure to implement the Fund left more than 3 billion BRL in environmental project resources locked in suspension, halting essential anti-deforestation initiatives.[127] Compounding the issue, governance structures such as the Coordinating Committee of the Amazon Fund had been dismantled, further eroding administrative frameworks designed to safeguard the environment.[128]

The petitioners grounded their claims in Articles 225 and 23 of the Brazilian Constitution, which impose clear obligations to protect, maintain, and restore the environment for present and future generations.[129] In a majority opinion authored by Justice Rosa Weber, the STF partially upheld these claims. It found the government's omission unconstitutional and reaffirmed the doctrine of the non-retrogression of environmental protections.[130] The Court invalidated several decrees undermining the governance of the Amazon Fund and ordered the federal government to restore its operations within 60 days.[131] This outcome not only reinforced domestic environmental duties but also underscored that lapses in enforcement cannot be justified as policy choices devoid of legal consequences.

In reaching its determination, the STF explicitly relied on the jurisprudence of the IACtHR. Particularly, it drew guidance from the Inter-American Court's decision in *Lhaka Honhat*. Two principal themes emerged from this reliance. First, by citing the IACtHR, the STF embraced the principle of prevention as central to international environmental law. As it emphasised, "[t]he principle of prevention of environmental damage is part of customary international law and implies the obligation of States to adopt necessary

125 For a systematic analysis of climate litigation before the Brazilian Supreme Court and how these lawsuits have drawn a closer connection between climate change law and human rights standards, see Andrade Moreira D et al.. Rights-Based Climate Litigation in Brazil: An Assessment of Constitutional Cases before the Brazilian Supreme Court. Journal of Human Rights Practice. 2024;16:47. See also Tigre MA, Setzer J. Human Rights and Climate Change for Climate Litigation in Brazil and Beyond: An Analysis of the Climate Fund Decision. Georgetown Journal of International Law. 2023;54(4):593.

126 STF (n 123) 8.

127 *Ibid*, 2. As of December 2024, BRL 1.5 billion is approximately USD 600 million.

128 *Ibid*, 4.

129 *Ibid*, 10.

130 *Ibid*, 191.

131 *Ibid*.

measures *ex ante* to prevent environmental harm".[132] Second, the STF highlighted the IACtHR's understanding that environmental degradation can infringe upon fundamental rights, including the rights to life, dignity, and health. Through this lens, the STF argued that the weakening of environmental protections, particularly in the Amazon, not only breaches Brazil's constitutional and international human rights obligations but also provides a compelling basis for judicial intervention. By integrating these principles, the STF justified the judicialisation of climate change as a necessary response to ensure the protection of human rights. In this sense, it stated,

> To tolerate the repeated violation of what may be the most fundamental right of humanity – since it underpins the realization of all other rights by ensuring the very conditions for human existence – without empowering this Court, as the guardian of the Constitution with a counter-majoritarian role vis-à-vis the other branches of government, to act promptly to prevent climate chaos and the degradation of Amazonian biodiversity, is inconsistent with international agreements and the democratic commitments enshrined in the Constitutional Charter.[133]

This invocation of Inter-American green jurisprudence entails critical connotations. By linking Brazil's constitutional obligations to broader international standards, the STF strengthened its interpretation of Article 225 of the Brazilian Constitution, framing the State's environmental duties as judicially enforceable. The IACtHR's emphasis on prevention and human rights infuses this interpretation with additional legitimacy and scope. Moreover, by rejecting the notion that environmental policy is an exclusively political matter, the Court aligns with the IACtHR's reasoning in *Lhaka Honhat* to insist that state inaction constitutes a breach of legal obligations. The government's decision to dismantle the Amazon Fund's governance structures, the STF determined, was not merely a policy choice; it was an unconstitutional omission that demanded judicial intervention. Through this approach, the decision underscores that environmental stewardship, anchored in both domestic and Inter-American standards, is neither optional nor discretionary.

2.4.2 Sevillano Callejas and Others v Law No. 406 *(Panama)*

On 27 November 2023, Panama's Supreme Court invalidated Article 1 of Law No. 406, a landmark decision that effectively halted operations at Cerro Petaquilla, one of the world's largest copper mines.[134] Operated by Minera

132 *Ibid*, 133.
133 *Ibid*, 302.
134 Case concerning the unconstitutionality challenge by Juan Ramón Sevillano Callejas against Article 1 of Law No. 406 of 20 October 2023, Plenary, Supreme Court of Justice (Panama), 27 November 2023.

Panamá, the mine had been a major driver of Panama's economic growth, contributing significantly to GDP through copper exports.[135] However, its operations sparked intense debate, with critics raising concerns over environmental degradation, violations of constitutional principles, and Panama's obligations to address climate change.[136]

Cerro Petaquilla's operations were first authorised under a concession agreement ratified by Law No. 9 in 1997, granting Minera Panamá exclusive rights to explore, extract, and market minerals in a designated area.[137] In 2017, Panama's Supreme Court declared this original contract unconstitutional, citing procedural violations.[138] Subsequent renegotiations resulted in a revised agreement that extended Minera Panamá's rights for an additional 20 years, formalised through Law No. 406 on 20 October 2023.[139] The revised contract immediately became a flashpoint for legal challenges and widespread protests, reflecting broader concerns about transparency, accountability, environmental sustainability, and Panama's responsibility to meet international climate goals.

The case against Law No. 406 began with a lawsuit filed by Juan Ramón Sevillano Callejas, admitted by the Supreme Court on 26 October 2023. The plaintiffs argued that the concession violated Articles 257, 259, and 266 of Panama's Constitution, which establish requirements for public bidding, transparency in contracting, and prioritising collective interests in resource management.[140] According to the claims, the concession circumvented these constitutional mandates, undermining principles of fairness and accountability. The plaintiffs further contended that by enacting a law that disproportionately favoured the mining company, the country's National Assembly had failed in its duty to protect societal interests, particularly in addressing environmental and climate impacts tied to mining activities.[141]

Environmental and climate considerations were central to the Court's reasoning. The Environmental Impact Assessment (EIA) supporting the concession, conducted in 2011, was deemed obsolete for addressing the realities of 2023.[142] The Court highlighted that the ecological, social, and *climate* conditions of the mining area had changed significantly over the preceding decade. The outdated EIA failed to comply with updated regulatory standards

135 Intergovernmental Forum on Mining, Minerals, Metals and Sustainable Development, IGF Mining Policy Framework Assessment (Panama, December 2020), p. 8. [Accessed 1 December 2024]. Available from: https://www.iisd.org/system/files/2021-02/panama-mining-policy-framework-assessment-en.pdf.

136 *Ibid.*

137 *Juan Ramón Sevillano Callejas* (n 134) 2.

138 *Ibid.*

139 *Ibid*, 7.

140 *Ibid*, 72.

141 *Ibid.*

142 *Ibid*, 175.

established by Panama's General Environmental Law and Executive Decree No. 1 of March 2023, which set new requirements for EIAs.[143] The Court further criticised the approval process for failing to ensure public participation, denying affected communities access to updated information and the opportunity to voice concerns about decisions with profound environmental and climate consequences.[144] These procedural deficiencies violated Panama's obligations under the Escazú Agreement, which mandates transparency and public engagement in environmental decision-making.[145]

Underpinning such reasonings was the Court's reliance on key standards from the IAHRS, specifically Advisory Opinion OC-23/17 and Resolution 3/21 of the IACHR. These instruments provided a normative framework that shaped the Court's interpretation, enabling it to connect constitutional principles, environmental governance, and human rights obligations. The Court drew extensively on Advisory Opinion OC-23/17, which states that states have a duty to guarantee access to information, public participation in environmental decision-making, and access to justice for environmental harm.[146] These obligations, rooted in Articles 1.1, 2, 4, and 5 of the ACHR, are designed to ensure that the protection of the environment aligns with the protection of fundamental human rights, including the rights to life and dignity.[147] The Court invoked this standard to claim that the lack of transparency in approving the Cerro Petaquilla concession and the exclusion of communities from the decision-making process constituted violations of both constitutional guarantees and international obligations.[148] The outdated EIA, including its failure to assess changing climatic conditions, and the absence of meaningful public participation were found to be incompatible with these principles, highlighting procedural failures in the concession's approval.

Building on this foundation, the Court turned to Resolution 3/21, which emphasises that climate and environmental governance must adopt a rights-based approach.[149] This resolution clarifies that states must ensure transparency and participation in crafting policies and decisions affecting natural resources and climate action.[150] Moreover, it requires mechanisms allowing affected individuals to challenge decisions through judicial or administrative channels.[151] By referencing this standard, the Court highlighted the absence of participatory mechanisms and accountability measures in the concession agreement, underscoring the incompatibility of Law No. 406 with both

143 *Ibid.*
144 *Ibid*, 183.
145 *Ibid.*
146 *Ibid*, 178.
147 *Ibid.*
148 *Ibid*, 180.
149 *Ibid*, 207.
150 *Ibid*, 208.
151 *Ibid.*

domestic and international legal standards.[152] This deficiency, the Court concluded, further supported the law's invalidation.

The IAHRS green standards were instrumental in bolstering the Court's decision. They enabled the Court to consider sustainable development comprehensively, encompassing the protection of the environment and the adaptation to a changing climate as imperatives necessitating a delicate balance with economic activity. The ruling emphasised that this equilibrium cannot be achieved when transparency, public participation, and environmental management through EIA processes are deficient – practices that undermine both domestic constitutional principles and international human rights obligations.

2.5 Concluding Remarks

The IAHRS has significantly advanced its green jurisprudence, building on decades of systemic and evolutive interpretation of human rights and sustained dialogue with domestic courts, attuned to the region's distinct socio-environmental realities. This trajectory reflects the System's capacity to address emerging challenges – evident once more as this chapter went to press, marked by the Court's issuance, in July 2025, of Advisory Opinion 32/15 on the climate emergency and human rights, whose background was outlined in subsection 3.4.[153] The Court reformulated the questions submitted by the requesting states into three overarching thematic axes: (i) substantive rights, (ii) procedural rights, and (iii) vulnerable populations.

Under the first axis, the Court introduced several doctrinal innovations. It became the first supranational tribunal to articulate a *jus cogens* norm prohibiting irreversible environmental harm, recognize the legal personhood of nature, and affirm the right to a healthy climate as a standalone human right, derived from the RHE under Article 26 of the ACHR. This right was characterized as both individually justiciable and collectively held, capturing the intergenerational and interspecies dimensions of climate justice. The Court held that it imposes concrete state obligations, including the duty to mitigate GHG emissions through ambitious, binding, and progressively scaled targets.

On procedural rights, the Court elaborated on the three pillars of the Escazú Agreement: access to information, public participation, and access to justice. It emphasized the need for robust procedural guarantees to ensure

152 *Ibid*, 209.

153 As Advisory Opinion OC-32/23 was issued while this chapter was in press, a comprehensive analysis falls beyond its scope. For detailed commentary, see Maria Antonia Tigre, Maxim Bönnemann and Korey Silverman-Roati, 'A Blueprint for Rights-Based Climate Action: The Inter-American Court of Human Rights' Advisory Opinion on the Climate Emergency' (Climate Law Blog, 8 July 2025). Available from: https://blogs.law.columbia.edu/climatechange/2025/07/08/a-blueprint-for-rights-based-climate-action-the-inter-american-court-of-human-rights-advisory-opinion-on-the-climate-emergency/

effective environmental governance and accountability. Regarding vulnerable populations, the Court recognized that climate change disproportionately affects those already subject to structural and intersectional forms of discrimination, including children, Indigenous peoples, and Afro-descendant, ethnic, campesino, and fishing communities. It underscored the need for differentiated protection and highlighted the critical role of environmental defenders, outlining a range of state obligations to ensure their safety and participation.

This milestone within the IAHRS marks a potential turning point for the Commission. As it addresses climate change through the prism of human rights, it may issue decisions in the three currently pending cases that depart from its earlier approach in the Inuit petition. Such evolution would reinforce the IACtHR's role as a pioneering court capable of innovating in response to unprecedented global challenges – setting precedents that resonate not only within the realm of domestic climate litigation, as illustrated in this chapter, but also beyond the Americas. In a world increasingly bound together by the shared consequences of the climate emergency, the Court's jurisprudence – particularly its newly issued Advisory Opinion 32/15 – holds the potential to influence legal frameworks in Africa, Europe, and beyond, fostering a transnational dialogue essential for confronting this defining challenge of our time.

References

Allan JA, Hadden J. Exploring the framing power of NGOs in global climate politics. Environmental Policy. 2017;600–620.

Andrade Moreira D, Nina AL, Garrido CF, Barbosa Neves ME. Rights-based climate litigation in Brazil: an assessment of constitutional cases before the Brazilian supreme court. 16(1) J Hum Rights Pract. 2024;47–70.

Antoniazzi MM, Alessandri PS. Inter-Americanization: its legal bases and political impact. In: von Bogdandy A, Mac-Gregor EF, Antoniazzi MM, Piovesan F, Soley X, editors. Transformative constitutionalism in Latin America: the emergence of a new Ius commune. Oxford: Oxford University Press; 2017.

Auz J. Human rights-based climate litigation: a Latin American cartography. J Hum Rights Environ. 2022;114–136.

Auz J. "So, this is permanence": the Inter-American human rights system as a liminal space for climate justice. Melb J Int Law. 2022;22.

Auz J. Two reputed allies: reconciling climate justice and litigation in the Global South. In: Litigating the climate emergency: how human rights, courts, and legal mobilization can bolster climate action. 2022. p. 145–56. https://doi.org/10.1017/9781009106214.009.

Auz J, Viveros-Uehara T. Another advisory opinion on the climate emergency? The added value of the Inter-American court of human rights. EJIL: Talk! [Internet]. 2023 Mar 2 [Accessed 2024 Dec 1]. Available from: https://www.ejiltalk.org/another-advisory-opinion-on-the-climate-emergency-the-added-value-of-the-inter-american-court-of-human-rights/.

Banda ML. Inter-American court of human rights' advisory opinion on the environment and human rights. ASIL Insights [Internet]. 2018 May 10 [Accessed 2024 Dec 1]. Available from: https://www.asil.org/insights/volume/22/issue/6/

inter-american-court-human-rights-advisory-opinion-environment-and-human#_edn32 [https://perma.cc/NUW3-Q9RQ].
Berkes A. A new extraterritorial jurisdictional link recognized by the IACtHR. EJIL: Talk! [Internet]. 2018 Mar 28 [Accessed 2024 Dec 1]. Available from: https://www.ejiltalk.org/a-new-extraterritorial-jurisdictional-link-recognised-by-the-iacthr/ [https://perma.cc/JC34-N7YW].
Bönnemann M, Tigre MA. The transformation of European climate litigation. Verfassungsbooks; 2024.
Boyd D. Landmark court decision on right to a healthy environment: La Oroya v Peru. Global Network for Human Rights and the Environment [Internet]. 2024 Mar [Accessed 2024 Nov 20]. Available from: https://gnhre.org/?p=17944.
Boyd D, Knox J, Limon M. The case for universal recognition of the right to a safe, clean, healthy, and sustainable environment. Universal Rights Group; 2021.
Boyle A. Human rights and the environment: where next? Eur J Int Law. 2012;23:613–642.
Burger B, Tigre MA. Global climate litigation report: 2023 status review. New York: Sabin Center for Climate Change Law, Columbia Law School & United Nations Environment Programme; 2023.
Burger M, Wentz J, Horton R. The law and science of climate change attribution. Colum J Environ Law [Internet]. 2020;45(1). https://doi.org/10.7916/cjel.v45i1.4730.
Cavallo GA. El derecho humano a un medio ambiente sano, acceso a la información ambiental y el ius commune. In: Jimenez Guanipa H, Leal ML, editors. Crisis climática, transacción energética y derechos humanos. Tomo II. Fundación Heinrich Böll; 2020.
Cerqueira D. El Derecho a un medio ambiente sano en el marco normativo y jurisprudencia del Sistema Interamericano de Derechos Humanos. In: Jimenez Guanipa H, Leal ML, editors. Crisis climática, transacción energética y derechos humanos. Tomo II. Fundación Heinrich Böll; 2020.
Chapman MS. Feature. Climate change and the regional human rights systems. Sustain Dev Law Policy. 2010;10(2):37–38.
Díaz MA, Auz J, López JB, Bustos C, Carballo JM, Castillo Barnetche V, Medici-Colombo G, Lavayen AM, Martínez A, Pineda C, Tan J. Cambio climático y los derechos de mujeres, pueblos indígenas y comunidades rurales en las Américas [Internet]. Fundación Heinrich Böll; 2020 [Accessed 2024 Dec 1]. Available from: https://perma.cc/FZ3Y-WPGL.
Donger E. Children and youth in strategic climate litigation: advancing rights through legal argument and legal mobilization. Transnatl Environ Law. 2022;11:263–289.
Fearnside PM. Will the next coronavirus come from Amazonia? Deforestation and the risk of infectious diseases. Mongabay [Internet]. 2020 Apr 8 [Accessed 2024 Dec 1]. Available from: https://perma.cc/N4JB-B8P2.
Feld B, Galiani S. Climate change in Latin America and the Caribbean: policy options and research priorities. Lat Am Econ Rev [Internet]. 2025;24. Available from: https://doi.org/10.1007/s40503-015-0028-4.
Feria-Tinta M. Climate change as a human rights issue: litigating climate change in the Inter-American system of human rights and the United Nations human rights committee. In: Alogna I, Bakker C, Gauci J-P, editors. Climate change litigation: global perspectives. Brill Nijhoff; 2021.
Feria-Tinta M, Milnes SC. The rise of environmental law in international dispute resolution: the Inter-American court of human rights issues a landmark advisory opinion on the environment and human rights. EJIL: Talk! 2018;27.

Garcia B, Lixinski L. Beyond culture: reimagining the adjudication of Indigenous peoples' rights in international law. Intercult Hum Rights Law Rev. 2020;15:127–169.

Gloppen S, Vallejo C. The climate crisis: litigation and economic, social and cultural rights. In: Research handbook on economic, social and cultural rights as human rights. 2020;386–409.

Gonzalez C. Climate change, race, and migration. J Law Political Econ [Internet]. 2020;1(1). Available from: http://dx.doi.org/10.5070/LP61146501. Available from: https://escholarship.org/uc/item/4bw094qc.

Heri C. Climate change before the European court of human rights: capturing risk, ill-treatment and vulnerability. Eur J Int Law [Internet]. 2022 Aug;33(3):925–951. https://doi.org/10.1093/ejil/chac047.

IPCC. Summary for policymakers. In: Pörtner H-O, Roberts DC, Tignor MMB, et al., editors. Climate change 2022: impacts, adaptation and vulnerability. Cambridge and New York: Cambridge University Press; 2022.

Ivanova A, Kozack J, Roldós J, Muñoz S. Climate change challenges in Latin America and the Caribbean. IMF [Internet]. 2021;3. Available from: https://www.imf.org/-/media/Files/Publications/REO/WHD/2021/English/CH3.ashx.

Jackson E. Potential climate remedies at the Inter-American court of human rights. Opinio Juris [Internet]. 2024 Aug 1 [Accessed 2024 Dec 1]. Available from: https://opiniojuris.org/2024/08/01/potential-climate-remedies-at-the-inter-american-court-of-human-rights/.

Jaimes VR. The arctic athabaskan petition: where accelerated Arctic warming meets human rights. Cal West Int Law J. 2014;45:213–260.

Jimenez Guanipa H, Barraco M. Inter-American human rights system's impact on the protection of the right to a healthy environment. In: von Bogdandy A, Piovesan F, Mac-Gregor EF, Antoniazzi MM, editors. The impact of the Inter-American human rights system: transformations on the ground. Oxford University Press; 2024.

Kahl V, Rodríguez-Orúe JD. Upgrading environmental rights: La Oroya and its significance for a safer climate. Verfassungsblog [Internet]. 2024 May 16 [Accessed 2024 Nov 20]. Available from: https://verfassungsblog.de/upgrading-environmental-rights/.

Keller K, Heri C. The future is now: climate cases before the ECtHR. Nordic J Hum Rights. 2022;40(1):153–74. https://doi.org/10.1080/18918131.2022.2064074.

Kulesza J. Due diligence in international law. Brill; 2016.

Dulitzky AE. Letter from Dulitzky AE, Assistant executive secretary, Inter-American court of human rights, to paul crowley, barrister and solicitor. 2006 Nov 16. Available from: https://perma.cc/M7EF-3Y9T.

Lima LC. Balancing the arguments before the Inter-American court on the climate emergency and human rights advisory proceedings. Opinio Juris [Internet]. 2024 May 31 [Accessed 2024 Dec 1]. Available from: https://opiniojuris.org/2024/05/31/balancing-the-arguments-before-the-inter-american-court-on-the-climate-emergency-and-human-rights-advisory-proceedings/.

Martínez M. Beyond pledges: solidifying climate action in Latin America. NRDC [Internet]. 2022 Nov 17 [Accessed 2024 Dec 1]. Available from: https://www.nrdc.org/experts/marilyn-martinez/beyond-pledges-solidifying-climate-action-latin-america.

Maxwell L, et. al. Standards for adjudicating the next generation of Urgenda-style climate cases. J Hum Rights Environ. 2022;13(1):35–63.

Osofsky HM. Inuit petition as a bridge? Beyond dialectics of climate change and Indigenous peoples' rights. Am Indian Law Rev. 2007;31:675–697.

Pamplona DA. Relações entre empresas e direitos humanos e o caso La Oroya na Corte IDH. Jota [Internet]. 2024 May 7 [Accessed 2024 Oct 14]. Available from: https://www.jota.info/opiniao-e-analise/colunas/direitos-humanos-sem-fronteiras/relacoes-entre-empresas-e-direitos-humanos-e-o-caso-la-oroya-na-corte-idh.
Peel J, Osofsky HM. Climate change litigation's regulatory pathways: a comparative analysis of the United States and Australia. Law Policy. 2013;35(3):150–183.
Piovesan F. Ius constitutionale commune en América Latina: context, challenges, and perspectives. In: von Bogdandy A, Mac-Gregor EF, Antoniazzi MM, Piovesan F, Soley X, editors. Transformative constitutionalism in Latin America: the emergence of a new ius commune. Oxford University Press; 2017.
Puentes A. La Oroya: an environmental justice lesson to Peru and the world. Medium [Internet]. 2024 Mar [Accessed 2024 Nov 20]. Available from: https://medium.com/@astridpuentes/la-oroya-an-environmental-justice-lesson-to-peru-and-the-world-d44c62f47ce1.
Rajamani L. Due diligence in international climate change law. In: Krieger H, Peters A, Kreuzer L, editors. Due diligence in the international legal order. Oxford University Press; 2020.
Rajamani L, Jeffery L, Höhne N, Hans F, Glass A, Ganti G. National "fair shares" in reducing greenhouse gas emissions within the principled framework of international environmental law. Clim Policy. 2021;21(8):983–1004.
Rocha A. States' extraterritorial jurisdiction for climate-related impacts. In: Bönnemann M, Tigre MA, editors. The transformation of European climate litigation. Verfassungsbooks; 2024. Available from: https://scholarship.law.columbia.edu/sabin_climate_change/235.
Shelton D. Legitimate and necessary: adjudicating human rights violations related to activities causing environmental harm or risk. J Hum Rights Environ. 2015;6(2):139–155.
Soley X. The transformative dimension of Inter-American jurisprudence. In: von Bogdandy A, Mac-Gregor EF, Antoniazzi MM, Piovesan F, Soley X, editors. Transformative constitutionalism in Latin America: the emergence of a new ius commune. Oxford University Press; 2017.
Szpak A. Arctic Athabaskan Council's petition to the Inter-American commission on human rights and climate change – business as usual or a breakthrough?. Climatic Change. 2020;162:1575–1593.
Tigre MA. Climate change and Indigenous groups: the rise of Indigenous voices in climate litigation. e-Publica. 2022;9(3):214–260.
Tigre MA. Climate litigation in the Global South: mapping report. 2024. Available from: https://scholarship.law.columbia.edu/sabin_climate_change/230.
Tigre MA. COVID-19 and Amazonia: right-based approaches for the pandemic response. Rev Eur Comp Int Environ Law. 2021;30(2):162–172.
Tigre MA. International recognition of the right to a healthy environment: what is the added value for Latin America and the Caribbean?. Am J Int Law Unbound. 2023; 117:184–188.
Tigre MA. The "fair share" of climate mitigation: can litigation increase national ambition for Brazil?. J Hum Rights Pract. 2024;16(1):25–46.
Tigre MA, Lichet V. The CRC decision in Sacchi v. Argentina. Am Soc Int Law Insights. 2021 Dec 13;25(26).
Tigre MA, Setzer J. Human rights and climate change for climate litigation in Brazil and beyond: an analysis of the Climate Fund decision. Georgetown J Int Law. 2023;54(4):593–637.
Tigre MA, Urzola N. The 2017 Inter-American Court's advisory opinion: changing the paradigm for international environmental law in the Anthropocene. J Hum Rights Environ. 2021;12(1):24–50.

Tigre MA, Urzola N, Castellanos JS. A request for an advisory opinion at the Inter-American Court of Human Rights: initial reactions. Climate Law Blog [Internet]. 2023 Feb 17 [Accessed 2024 Dec 1]. Available from: https://blogs.law.columbia.edu/climatechange/2023/02/17/a-request-for-an-advisory-opinion-at-the-inter-american-court-of-human-rights-initial-reactions/.

Tigre MA, Urzola N, Goodman A. Climate litigation in Latin America: is the region quietly leading a regional revolution?. J Hum Rights Environ. 2023;14(1):67–93.

Tsosie R. Indigenous people and environmental justice: the impact of climate change. Univ Colo Law Rev. 2007;78:1625–1677.

Vera OP. Impact of the Inter-American human rights system in the struggle against impunity. In: von Bogdandy A, Piovesan F, Mac-Gregor EF, Antoniazzi MM, editors. The impact of the Inter-American human rights system: transformations on the ground. Oxford University Press; 2024.

Viveros-Uehara T. La Oroya and Inter-American innovations on the right to a healthy environment. VerfBlog [Internet]. 2024 May 16 [Accessed 2024 Nov 20]. Available from: https://verfassungsblog.de/la-oroya-and-inter-american-innovations-on-the-right-to-a-healthy-environment/ DOI: 10.59704/bc45e4a6c6e822d6.

Viveros-Uehara T. The fundamental rights to life and health in climate litigation. e-Publica. 2022;9(3):147–179.

Viveros-Uehara T, Auz J. The climate emergency at the Inter-American court of human rights. OpenGlobalRights [Internet]. 2023 Feb 27 [Accessed 2024 Dec 1]. Available from: https://www.openglobalrights.org/climate-emergency-interamerican-court-human-rights/?author_lang=2.

Voigt C. The climate change dimension of human rights obligations. SSRN [Internet]. 2021 May 3;1:13. Available from: https://ssrn.com/abstract=3839012.

von Bogdandy A, Mac-Gregor EF, Antoniazzi MM, Piovesan F, Soley X, editors. Transformative constitutionalism in Latin America: the emergence of a new ius commune. Oxford University Press; 2017.

von Bogdandy A, Piovesan F, Mac-Gregor EF, Antoniazzi MM, editors. The impact of the Inter-American human rights system: transformations on the ground. Oxford University Press; 2024.

3 In Search for the Content of States' Positive Obligations under the European Convention on Human Rights

KlimaSeniorinnen and Climate Change

Vladislava Stoyanova

3.1 Introduction

The European Court of Human Rights' (ECtHR) initial steps into the field of climate change led to mixed results. *Duarte Agostinho and Others v Portugal and 32 Other States* and *Carême v France* were declared inadmissible.[1] In *Verein KlimaSeniorinnen Schweiz and Others v Switzerland* all individual applications were dismissed.[2] Yet, it was the Swiss NGO Verein KlimaSeniorinnen's success that ultimately shaped the trajectory of this trio of cases and is likely to shape the future cases.

The reasoning in the three judgments is detailed. They synthesize a vast array of information on climate change and thoroughly address the arguments presented by the parties and interveners, which is commendable. The analysis of the victim status in *Verein KlimaSeniorinnen Schweiz* and the issue of extraterritoriality in *Duarte Agostinho and Others v Portugal* is particularly thorough. Notably, the Court showed a willingness to adapt its stance on the standing of associations in climate litigation under the European Convention on Human Rights (ECHR or the Convention). By modifying the standards under Article 34 of the Convention, the ECtHR could examine the substantive positive obligations under Article 8 of the Convention. By doing this modification, the Court acknowledged "the special feature of climate change as a common concern of humankind and the necessity of promoting intergenerational burden-sharing in this context".[3] No doubt, this new approach under Article 34 of the Convention will have serious implications for future litigation on the issue of climate change. In fact, it can have implications for many other areas characterised by *systemic* and *structural* harms with compound causes and complex causal connections. These would be generally areas where the causal links between causes and effects (understood as harms upon fundamental interests protected by human rights law) might be

1 *Duarte Agostinho and Others v Portugal and 32 Others* [GC] 39371/20 (ECtHR, dec, 9 April 2024); *Carême v France* [GC] 7189/21 (ECtHR, dec, 9 April 2024).

2 *Verein KlimaSeniorinnen Schweiz and Others v Switzerland* [GC] 53600/20 (ECtHR, 9 April 2024).

3 *KlimaSeniorinnen*, para. 488.

DOI: 10.4324/9781003540977-5

difficult to disentangle.[4] This question can be an object of a separate investigation, which at its core concerns the relevance and the distinctiveness of human rights law as a body of law and as a tool for "solving" complex social problems.

The question in this chapter is rather the following: What was the outcome of all these efforts by the Court in *Verein KlimaSeniorinnen Schweiz*? In other words, what substantive positive obligations did the Court formulate under Article 8 ECHR that can actually guide the future conduct of States?[5] To frame it even more specifically, what is the content of these positive obligations? More precisely, this content is clarified through the lens of the standard of causation. Causation is crucial because positive obligations in human rights law are grounded in the idea that, had the State acted (i.e., not failed/omitted to act), the fundamental interests protected by human rights law would have been better protected.[6] In this sense, the causal inquiry is actually an inquiry about the interpretation of the content of the positive obligations.[7] In other words, causation is a tool for specifying the content of these obligations.

To answer these questions, the reasoning in the judgment is subjected to a detailed scrutiny so that the logical and analytical movies performed by the Court can be exposed and explained. This effort of exposing and explaining leads to a critical engagement with the Court's reasoning. The critique should not be accepted as a denial of any factual or normative propositions related to climate change. It should be rather accepted as an attempt to urge in favour of better analytical and logical clarity. After all, the importance of the problem and its urgency should not lead to analytically flimsy legal reasoning.

To engage with the above-mentioned questions, the following path will be followed. Section 2 will explain how the Court chose to structure its review

4 V Stoyanova, 'Causation: Why and How for Establishing Breach of Positive Obligations under the European Convention on Human Rights?' in V. Stoyanova, & D. McGrogan (Eds.), The Limits of Positive Obligations in Human Rights Law: From Protection to Coercion (Hart Publishing, forthcoming).

5 This chapter does not cover Article 6 ECHR (the right to fair trial).

6 Stoyanova V. Positive Obligations under the European Convention on Human Rights: Within and beyond Boundaries. Oxford University Press; 2023; Stoyanova V. Causation: Why and How for Establishing Breach of Positive Obligations under the European Convention on Human Rights?. In: Stoyanova V, McGrogan D, eds. From Protection to Coercion: The Limits of Positive Obligations in Human Rights Law (forthcoming).

7 Stoyanova V, (n 6, forthcoming). See, more generally, Hoffmann L. Causation. In: Goldberg R, ed. Perspective on Causation. Hart Publishing; 2011. pp. 3, 5: "anyone is entitled to say that in treating X in some particular context as having caused Y, the courts are stretching the ordinary meaning of 'cause'. But this is *engaging in a legitimate argument over interpretation* and not introducing the concept of 'real' causation as a preliminary test which has to be satisfied before the question of interpretation arises". See also Green L. Are There Dependable Rules on Causation? University of Pennsylvania Law Review. 1929;77(5):601.

in *Verein KlimaSeniorinnen Schweiz* with reference to the question of causation. The four causal links identified in the reasoning are explained. Section 3 enquires how these four causal links were of any relevance in the determination of the content of the positive obligations held by the respondent State and in the finding of breach. The main argument is that, ultimately, these links did not matter much.

To advance this argument, section 3.1 first revisits the victim status requirement to explain that given the absence of harm to individual interests (and thus the absence of individual victims and the absence of specified harm), the analysis of breach on the merits cannot but be based on diffuse and very abstract causal assumptions. In this sense, as section 3.2 shows, the identification at a very abstract level of some general measures (i.e. adoption of regulatory framework, actual application of the framework, having procedures for allowing access to information and national decision-making process of sufficient quality) as forming the content of the positive obligations under Article 8 was not that controversial and difficult. Since the Court's review was allowed to proceed to the merits, the existence of positive obligations, *articulated in very abstract terms*, could be easily accepted as a starting point.

Section 3.3 continues to show that the tailoring of the content of these obligations to the context of climate change could not lead to further specification of the obligations, since causation was also sidestepped. This sidestepping was achieved in the following two ways: first, formulation of the obligation with reference to an abstract aim, and, second, the inclusion of procedural omissions in combination with substantive omissions as relevant. Finally, section 3.4 highlights that when the Court actually was meant to assess compliance, it never returned to the key standards (i.e., the "real prospect" causation standard and the "disproportionate burden" standard) that it itself had identified initially in the very same judgment.

In sum, the reasoning in *Verein KlimaSeniorinnen Schweiz* features a *disconnect* between the detailed discussions on causation and the content of any positive obligations. As a result, the obligations remained abstractly formulated and insufficiently specified. The categorical conclusion of breach might be celebrated; however, the search for the content of positive obligations, and, as I will also suggest, the search for the role and the essence of human rights law, has just began.

3.2 Structure of the Assessment and the Vexed Question(s) of Causation

Verein KlimaSeniorinnen Schweiz was not the usual case where the Court first decided on issues of admissibility, such as victim status, and then proceeded to the merits. Part C of the judgment titled "The Court's assessment" has four sections: 1. "Preliminary points", 2. "General considerations relating to climate-change cases", 3. "Admissibility", and 4. "Merits". Since the question at the centre of this chapter is about the substantive positive obligations under the ECHR, the focus will be on "Merits" (paragraphs 538–573). However, the formulation of any substantive positive obligations is related to the preliminary points, the general considerations, and the arguments on admissibility. In addition, it is useful to more generally gain a better understanding of the logical structure of the whole judgment and the overall consistency of the arguments and points made in the different sections and subsections. As importantly, the sections "Preliminary points", "General considerations relating to climate-change cases", and "Admissibility" expose the Court's approach to the standard of causation, which is key for the formulation of any substantive positive obligations. For these reasons, the implications from these three sections of the judgment will be also explained here.

In the "Preliminary points", the ECtHR offered numerous broad observations on the nature of climate change and the responsibilities of various actors in addressing it. For instance, the Court stated that "climate change is one of the most pressing issues of our times",[8] signalling to the public that it regards the issue with utmost seriousness. The Court also made general remarks on the separation of powers and the judiciary's role: "Judicial intervention, including by this Court, cannot replace or provide any substitute for the action which must be taken by the legislative and executive branches of government".[9] These statements aim at alleviating concerns among States regarding potential judicial overreach.

The main objective of the "Preliminary points", however, seems to be *explaining the distinctiveness* of the climate chance case in comparison with previous judgments delivered by the Court. All this distinctiveness pertain to the question of causation as evidenced here:

> The Court's existing case-law in environmental matters concerns situations involving specific sources from which environmental harm emanates. Accordingly, those exposed to that particular harm can be localised and identified with a reasonable degree of certainty, and the *existence of a causal link* between an identifiable source of harm and the actual harmful effects on groups of individuals is generally determinable. Furthermore, the measures taken, or omitted, with a view to reducing the impugned harm emanating from a given source, whether at the regulatory level or in terms of implementation, can also be specifically identified. In short, *there is a nexus* between a source of harm and those affected by the harm, and the requisite mitigation measures may be identifiable and available to be applied at the source of the harm.[10]

8 *KlimaSeniorinnen*, para. 410.
9 *KlimaSeniorinnen*, para. 412.
10 *KlimaSeniorinnen*, para. 415.

The Court continues to identify six distinctive features of the climate change case.[11] Only a brief overview is offered here. The first one concerns the multiple sources of GHG emissions. The second one concerns the fact that these emissions lead to harm only as "a result of a complex chain of events".[12] The third distinctive feature is related to the unpredictability of the effects in terms of time and place. Fourth, the emissions are produced by all activities within our societies and, therefore, "mitigation measures cannot generally be localized or limited to specific installations from which harmful effects emanate".[13] Fifth, since the mitigation measures cannot be localised and limited to single sectors, individuals have to "assume a share of responsibilities and burdens".[14] Lastly, mitigation and adaptation measures "may vary to some extent from one State to another".[15]

On the basis of these six distinctive features of the climate change case, the Court stated that it had to *tailor* its approach. While this tailoring seems to be quite clear on the victim status requirement, a point that I will revert to below in section 3.1, it is not very clear how the content and the scope of the positive obligations, and the specification of these obligations in Section 4 of the judgment titled "Merits", were tailored by these considerations. For example, it is not clear how the State's mitigation measures as to the content of any positive obligations were contingent upon and were to be balanced against individual "responsibilities and burdens". Similarly, it is not clear how the measures that form the content of any positive obligations varied and were to be balanced against any competing considerations, specifically for the respondent State. I shall return to these points below in section 3.4 in this chapter.

Neither is it clear how these six distinctive features identified in the "Preliminary points" in *Verein KlimaSeniorinnen Schweiz* are different from the points raised in Section 2, titled "General considerations relating to climate-change cases", in the same Part C. Rather, in Section 2 the Court tried to be slightly more specific by linking these six distinctive features with certain standards established in its case law.

In particular, the "general considerations relating to climate-change cases" are seven: (a) "questions of causation"; (b) "issues of proof"; (c) "effects

11 *KlimaSeniorinnen*, paras. 416–422.

12 *KlimaSeniorinnen*, para. 416. Here it should be also noted that the Court mixes different aspects, which makes the reasoning analytically confusing. For example, after noting that emissions lead to harm only as "a result of a complex chain of events", it added that the emissions have no regard to national borders. However, this addition pertains to a separate question.

13 *KlimaSeniorinnen*, para. 418. This paragraph also manifests a mixture of two aspects: the cause and the harmful effects on the one hand, and the measures to mitigate the harmful effects, on the other.

14 *KlimaSeniorinnen*, paras. 419–420. At this point, the Court also inserted some statements about "intergenerational burden-sharing".

15 *KlimaSeniorinnen*, para. 421.

of climate change on the enjoyment of Convention right's; (d) "the question of causation and positive obligations in the climate-change context"; (e) "the issue of proportion of State responsibility"; (f) "scope of the Court's assessment"; and (g) "relevant principles regarding the interpretation of the Convention". A mere overview of the names given to these "general considerations" reveals that the logical links between the "considerations" might be difficult to see. In what follows I will try to reconstruct these seven "general considerations" to make them more understandable and to explain how they might relate to each other.

In subsection (a), "questions of causation", the Court identified four dimensions of the causation question. Prior to explaining them, it should be noted that *KlimaSeniorinnen* is the first case in which the ECtHR dedicated entire sections to the issue of causation. As highlighted previously, causation has not traditionally been a focal point in the Court's case law, nor has it been systematically developed in relation to positive obligations under the ECHR.[16] In *KlimaSeniorinnen*, however, the Grand Chamber tackles causation directly, recognizing that the applicants' claims were unprecedented and called for a potential adjustment (or, more neutrally, evolution or development) of existing legal standards.[17]

To understand the four dimensions of the causation question, it is necessary to quote paragraph 425 from *KlimaSeniorinnen* in its entirety:

> The *first* dimension of the question of causation relates to the link between GHG emissions – and the resulting accumulation of GHG in the global atmosphere – and the various phenomena of climate change. *This is a matter of scientific knowledge and assessment.* The *second* relates to the link between the various adverse effects of the consequences of climate change, and the risks of such effects on the enjoyment of human rights at present and in the future. In general terms, this issue pertains to the *legal question* of how the scope of human rights protection is to be understood as regards the impacts arising for human beings from an existing degradation, or risk of degradation, in their living conditions. The *third* concerns the link, at the individual level, between a harm, or risk of harm, allegedly affecting specific persons or groups of persons, and the acts or omissions of State authorities against which a human rights–based complaint is directed. The *fourth* relates to the attributability of responsibility regarding the adverse effects arising from climate change claimed by individuals or groups against a particular State, given that multiple actors contribute to the aggregate amounts and effects of GHG emissions (emphasis added).

16 V Stoyanova, (n 6) p. 45.
17 Available from: KlimaSeniorinnen and the Question(s) of Causation – Verfassungsblog.

This paragraph reflects a conceptual quagmire, since different concepts/expressions are used. It might be difficult to understanding what the different concepts mean and how they analytically relate to each other. These include "enjoyment of human rights" and "scope of human rights protection". The first term appears to refer to the harms to fundamental interests that are protected by human rights.[18] However, as the text of paragraph 425 shows, it is not the harms themselves that matter, but the *risk* of such harms.[19] As to the "scope of human rights protection", it might also refer to harms and adverse impacts on fundamental interests; it seems, however, that the Court rather had in mind the scope of human rights *obligations* that might correspond to human rights. In then follows that the analytical distinctions between interests, rights, and obligations were all blurred.[20]

The term "adverse effects" is also used. It is not clear whether this is used to mean the same as "effects on the enjoyment of human rights", which would imply that the "adverse effects" are covered by the definitional scope of the human rights and, in this sense, the "effects" are actually harms to fundamental interests protected by human rights.

The expression "attributability of responsibility" is similarly confusing. For any responsibility to arise, it must first be established that the State has violated an obligation. A prior analytical step is the establishment that the State was actually under an obligation.[21] If the conceptual framework of the ILC Articles is adopted, it is not responsibility that is "attributed"; what is attributed is a conduct that might consist of an action or omission.

Let's set aside this conceptual quagmire for now and focus on reconstructing paragraph 425 and the following paragraphs in "General Considerations Relating to Climate-Change Cases". The aim of such a reconstruction is to make them more accessible and easier to understand. To achieve this better

18 Human rights are based on fundamental interests. See, e.g., Gerards J. Fundamental Rights and Other Interests. Should It Really Make a Difference?. In: Brems E, ed. Conflicts between Fundamental Rights. Intersentia; 2008. pp. 655–690; see also V Stoyanova, Positive Obligations as Coercive 'Rights' and Compulsory Vaccination under the European Convention on Human Rights, International Journal of Constitutional Law (forthcoming).

19 On the reframing of the harm, as risk of harm in human rights law, see V Stoyanova, 'Causation and Breach of Positive Obligations under the European Convention on Human Rights: Correcting the Past, Preventing the Future' in V Stoyanova and M Andenas (Eds), The Role of the Causal Inquiry under the European Convention on Human Rights (forthcoming).

20 Rights are intermediaries between interests and obligations. Raz J. On the Nature of Rights. Mind. 1984;XCIII(370):194, 208: "the interests are part of the justification of the rights which are part of the justification of the duties. Rights are intermediate conclusions in arguments from ultimate values to duties". Thomas J. Public Rights, Private Relations. Oxford University Press; 2015. p. 149: "The nature of rights [...] is coherently distinct from that of both interests and duties, and contains some analytical content that allows us to move from the former to the latter"; Besson S. The Morality of Conflict: Reasonable Disagreement and the Law. Hart Publishing; 2005. p. 423.

21 Crawford J. State Responsibility. The General Part. Cambridge University Press; 2013. p. 218.

understanding, it is very useful that these four dimensions of the causation question, as enumerated in paragraph 425 of the judgment, were renamed and reframed in the actual text of the judgment as (b) "issues of proof"; (c) "effects of climate change on the enjoyment of Convention rights"; (d) "the question of causation and positive obligations in the climate-change context"; and (e) "the issue of proportion of State responsibility". Prior to explaining this renaming and clarifications in the Court's reasoning, it is useful to clear our minds better as to what kind of causal links the Court actually invoked in paragraph 425. For the sake of achieving this clarity, a table will be offered below with the things being linked referred to as "A" and "B". "A" is the cause and "B" is the effect. The last row of the table indicates in which subsection the Court further clarified the link and how it chose to name it. The third row in the table indicates how the Court characterised the link in paragraph 425 of the judgment.

A (Cause)	*B (Effect)*	*Characterisation of the causal link by the Court in para. 425*	*Title of the subsection in the judgment where the causal link is further explained*
(1) Emissions	Climate change	"matter of scientific knowledge and assessment"	b) "issues of proof" paras. 427–430
(2) "adverse effects of the consequences of climate change"	"the risks of such effects on the enjoyment of human rights at present and in the future"	legal question about the interpretation of the scope of human rights protection	(c) "effects of climate change on the enjoyment of Convention rights" paras. 431–436
(3) "acts or omissions of State authorities"	Individual harm or "risk of harm"		(d) "the question of causation and positive obligations in the climate-change context" paras. 437–440
(4) Conduct of a particular State	"adverse effects arising from climate change claimed by individuals or groups" in this particular State	"attributability of responsibility"	(e) "the issue of proportion of State responsibility" paras. 441–444

3.2.1 *First Causal Link: Emissions Cause Climate Change, Presented as a Matter of Factual Causation*

The first causal link between emissions and climate change is characterised as a link reflecting factual causation since it pertains to issues about proof, which necessitates engagement with "complex scientific evidence".[22] Generally the Strasbourg case law features evidentiarily confusion: the questions how the Court approaches evidence and how well it does this have been understudied.[23] As a starting point, the Court refers to the criminal law standard of "beyond reasonable doubt". However, flexibility is applied to both the standard of proof and the burden of proof.[24]

This flexibility also implies that the Court uses proxies for "scientific evidence". These proxies include breaches of domestic regulations.[25] This means that if domestic legal standards have been adopted under the understanding/assumption that certain causes (A) factually lead to certain effects (B) and these effects are harmful, the Court will likely endorse this factual understanding/assumption. Similar endorsement can follow from assumptions underpinning international standards. In this sense, the evidence underpinning domestic and international regulatory standards is not likely to be questioned by the Court. It then follows that the Court does not really apply factual causation. It rather defers to preexisting standards where certain factual causal links are accepted. This deference is a *normative* acceptance of the casual links.

The same normative deference characterises the attachment of importance by the Court to "the findings of the domestic courts and other competent authorities in establishing the factual circumstances of the case".[26] The endorsement of the factual evidence discovered by the national institutions is *normatively* justified. The reason is that this endorsement has nothing to do with the scientific methods for collecting this evidence, the quality of the methods, or the possible limitations of the methods and factual findings. The endorsement is rather based on the normative justification related to the subsidiary role of the Court and that it is not a first-instance tribunal of fact.[27]

This deference, as justified by normative considerations that have little to do with facts and factual proofs, is also revealed by the following statements in *KlimaSeniorinnen*:

22 *KlimaSeniorinnen*, para. 427.

23 See, generally, Dembour M-B. The Evidentiary System of the European Court of Human Rights in Critical Perspective. European Convention on Human Rights Law Review. 2023;4:363.

24 Thienel T. The Burden and Standard of Proof in the European Court of Human Rights. German Yearbook of International Law. 2007;50:543; Kokott J. The Burden and Standard of Proof in Comparative and International Human Rights Law. 1998.

25 *KlimaSeniorinnen*, para. 428.

26 *KlimaSeniorinnen*, para. 430.

27 *KlimaSeniorinnen*, para. 430.

> As a general rule, where domestic proceedings have taken place, it is not the Court's task to substitute its own assessment of the facts for that of the domestic courts and it is for the latter to establish the facts on the basis of the evidence before them. However, it reiterates in this connection that, while sensitive to the subsidiary nature of its role and cautious about taking on the role of a first-instance tribunal of fact, the Court is nevertheless not bound by the findings of domestic courts and may depart from them where this is rendered unavoidable by the circumstances of a particular case. It is the Court's function *to review the reasoning* adduced by domestic judicial authorities from the point of view of the Convention and to determine whether the national authorities *have struck a fair balance* between the competing interests at stake.[28]

The last sentence refers to reviewing the domestic courts' reasoning as to how these domestic courts have struck a fair balance between competing interests. In line with what was mentioned above, this review is of a normative nature: it does not pertain to review of factual evidence and factual assumptions. This more generally relates to the role of the proportionality assessment in human rights law, where scientific/factual uncertainty does play a role.[29] Yet, it is only one element of the overall normative review that needs to be performed for reaching the conclusion whether competing interests have been fairly balanced. It then follows that by adding this last sentence from the above quotation in subsection (b), "Issues of proof", the Court introduces analytical confusion by conflating factual questions, such as issues of proof, with normative considerations.[30]

In subsection (b), "Issues of proof", there is, however, a whole paragraph that entirely pertains to factual evidence intended to scientifically prove the factual causal link between emissions and climate change:

> The Court also relies on studies and reports by relevant international bodies as regards the environmental impacts on individuals. As regards climate change, the Court points to the particular importance of the reports prepared by the IPCC, as the intergovernmental body of independent experts set up to review and assess the science related to climate change, which are based on comprehensive and rigorous methodology, including in relation to the choice of literature, the process of review

28 *KlimaSeniorinnen*, para. 430 (emphasis added).

29 Stoyanova V. The Disjunctive Structure of Positive Rights under the ECHR. Nordic Journal of International Law. 2018;87:344.

30 On the distinction between factual and legal causation, see Plakokefalos I. Causation in the Law of State Responsibility and the Problem of Overdetermination: In Search of Clarity. European Journal of International Law. 2015;26(2):471; Lanovoy V. Causation in the Law of State Responsibility. The British Yearbook of International Law. 2022;1.

and approval of its reports as well as the mechanisms for the investigation and, if necessary, correction of possible errors in the published reports. These reports provide scientific guidance on climate change regionally and globally, its impact and future risks, and options for adaptation and mitigation.[31]

It follows from this paragraph that the Court accepted the factual causal link between emissions and climate change as proven by the IPCC reports. Yet, this factual causation was still mixed with normative evaluations given the references to domestic standards, international standards, and balancing of interests in subsection (b) "Issues of proof".

3.2.2 *Second Causal Link: Climate Change Causes Risks to Human Rights, Presented as a Matter of Legal Causation*

The second causal link is that between climate change and risks for human rights, which is characterised as a link reflecting a legal causation. To refresh the issue, the Court observed in paragraph 425 that this link pertains to the "legal question of how the scope of human rights protection is to be understood". In subsection (c), "effects of climate change on the enjoyment of Convention rights" (paragraphs 431–436), the Court elaborated on this "legal question". Let's try to unpack subsection (c).

Subsection (c) is a conceptual quagmire on its own. In the first paragraph, the Court shifts *from* climate change *to* "protecting the environment, including in the context climate change" and to "environmental degradation".[32] This shift destabilises the reasoning – is the effects of climate change that matter or is the effects of the environmental degradation that matter? Then the Court immediately continues to make the unrelated assertion (or at least the relationship remained unaddressed) that the IPCC reports "have not been challenged or called into doubt",[33] and that the respondent State and other parties "have not contested that there is a climate emergency".[34] These considerations can be accepted as pertaining to legal causation in the sense that they reflect normative choices in terms of policy.[35] The interpretative tool of the "living instrument" doctrine, as traditionally used by the Court and added to the "stew" in subsection (c), also reflects a normative choice.[36]

31 *KlimaSeniorinnen*, para. 429 (referensers omitted).
32 *KlimaSeniorinnen*, para. 431.
33 *KlimaSeniorinnen*, para. 432.
34 *KlimaSeniorinnen*, para. 433.
35 *KlimaSeniorinnen*, para. 433: "the general policy aims in the respondent State in terms of the urgency of addressing climate change and its adverse effects on the lives, health and well-being of individuals".
36 *KlimaSeniorinnen*, para. 434.

The harmful effects of climate change are thus translated into harmful effects on "the enjoyment of Convention rights". To support this translation, the Court included risks as a relevant consideration. In other words, the effects on "the enjoyment of Convention rights" were reframed in the reasoning as effects on the risks upon the enjoyment:

> As the Court has already recognised, Article 8 is capable of being engaged because of adverse effects not only on individuals' health but on their well-being and quality of life and not only because of actual adverse effects but also *sufficiently severe risks of such effects* on individuals. [...] It has also held that the duty to regulate not only relates to actual harm arising from specific activities but extends to the *inherent risks involved*.[37]

The recharacterisation of the important interests (life, private life, family life, etc.) that the Convention protects, as risks to such interests (i.e., risks to life, risks to private life), has been performed before in the case law.[38] It then follows that, more generally, risk has become an object of regulation even under the ECHR.[39] Notably, in its reasoning in *KlimaSeniorinnen*, the Court introduced a severity threshold: the risks have to be "sufficiently severe". It is not entirely clear whether this severity threshold refers to the high likelihood of the harm ("adverse effects") to occur or to the seriousness of the harm ("the effects") itself. In an alternative, it might be an unclear combination of the two.[40] It is also relevant to note that in the concluding paragraph in subsection (c), instead of "risks", the Court changed the language by referring to "future threats to the enjoyment of human rights", in this way possibly conflating the concepts of "risk" and "threat".[41]

37 *KlimaSeniorinnen*, para. 435 (references omitted) (emphasis added).

38 Stoyanova V. Fault, Knowledge and Risk within the Framework of Positive Obligations under the European Convention on Human Rights. Leiden Journal of Internation Law. 2020;33:601; Ambrus M. The European Court of Human Rights as Governor or Risk. In: Ambrus M, Rayfuse R, Werner W, editors. Risk and Regulation of Uncertainty in International Law; 2017. p. 99.

39 See the chapter "The Rise of Risk in Regulatory Governance" in Yeung K, Ranchordas S, eds. An Introduction to Law and Regulation. Cambridge University Press; 2024. Researchers in regulatory law have observed a growing emphasis on risk regulation over the past few decades, both at the domestic and at the international levels. This trend has been accompanied by a widespread use of risk-related terminology in legal and policy documents. See Peel J. Science and Risk Regulation in International Law. Cambridge University Press; 2010.

40 Risk is generally defined by two components: first, a potential outcome that is harmful, undesirable, adverse, or hazardous, and second, an element of possibility, chance, probability, or likelihood that this outcome will occur in the future. See Steele J, Gardner JE. Introduction. In: Steele J, Gardner JE, eds. Risks and Legal Theory. Hart; 2004. p. 6; Dyson M, Steel S. Chapter 2 – Risk and English Tort Law. In: Dyson M, ed. Regulating Risk through Private Law. Intersentia; 2018.

41 *KlimaSeniorinnen*, para. 435.

The above quotation also refers to "inherent risks", which raises questions as to the meaning and the scope of risks meant to be covered by the definitional scope of Article 8 ECHR. The concept of "inherent risks" is problematic. "Inherent risks" to what? Are these risks from any economic activity that emits? Risks might then be completely diluted, since any human activity can be perceived as "inherently risky". Inherent risks might be also understood as risks that are possible to predict.

If the causal link at the heart of subsection (c) is the link between climate change and risks for human rights, the question of obligations should be irrelevant.[42] Putting it otherwise, the normative determination that certain forms of harms (or risks of harms) to important interests should be covered by the definitional scope of Article 8 is separate from the question of what conduct (in the form of obligations) States need to adopt to prevent and address these harms and risks. It then follows that the references to obligations in subsection (c) are confusing and analytically unnecessary.[43] In other words, the Court mixes considerations pertaining to the definitional scope of Article 8 with considerations pertaining to the existence of positive obligations and their content and scope. Subsection (c) should have been limited to the harmful effects on the important interests protected by the Convention rights. The question of obligation is a separate one, and it is, in fact, addressed in the subsection (d): "The question of causation and positive obligations in the climate-change context" of the judgment that will be scrutinized below.

3.2.3 *Third Causal Link: Omissions by States Cause Risk of Harm*

In the paragraphs included in subsection (d) of the *KlimaSeniorinnen*, the Court clarified what considerations were pertinent for determining the content of the positive obligations (i.e., "the measures to ensure effective protection") and what role causation played in this determination. The Court also acknowledged the need for adapting the considerations "in the context of climate change".

As to the pertinent considerations for determining the content of positive obligations, the context specific nature of these obligations was highlighted: the measures that form this content "may vary considerably from case to case".[44] The variation depended on the gravity of the harm, which was

42 The is based on the analytical distinction between, on the one hand, the definitional scope of Article 8, and the question of breach of any corresponding obligations. See, generally, Gerards J, Brems E. Introduction. In: Brems E, Gerards J. Shaping Rights in the ECHR. CUP; 2013. p. 1.

43 *KlimaSeniorinnen*, para. 435: "In other words, issues of causation must always be regarded in the light of the factual nature of the alleged violation and the nature and scope of the legal obligations at issue". See also para. 436.

44 *KlimaSeniorinnen*, para. 438.

also reframed as risk that meets "a certain threshold".[45] The variation also depended on "any burden" that the obligation might imply for the State.[46] The variation also depended on the causation between risks and omissions: "[t]here must be a relationship of causation between the risk and the alleged failure to fulfil positive obligations".[47] Crucially, the Court did not identify in subsection (d), "the question of causation and positive obligations in the climate-change context", any causation test that might address the question to what extend failures/omissions should have caused risks, so that these failures/omissions could be assessed as wrongful and, thus, as being in breach of positive obligations.

In the paragraph that immediately follows, the Court acknowledged the need to adapt the relationship of causation.[48] As mentioned above, this relationship was not clear to begin with – a clearer legal standard of causation had not been initially established. Adapting a standard that had never been clearly delineated to a different context might therefore appear strange.

What also comes as surprising is that the need for the adaptation of the causation standard had only one single justification in the reasoning of the Court. This justification pertains to the global nature of the emissions. Given this global nature, emissions from the single State "make up only part of the causes of the harm".[49] The Court continues to state that:

> Accordingly, the causal link between the acts or omissions on the part of State authorities in one country, and the harm, or risk of harm, arising there, is necessarily *more tenuous and indirect* compared to that in the context of local sources of harmful pollution.[50]

This is factually correct; however, it does not solve the problem as to the legal standard of causation: in human rights law, how much an omission by the State should have contributed to the harm (or the risk of harm) so that this omission becomes *legally* relevant and thus a basis for state responsibility? This is a normative question pertaining to the scope of the positive obligation.

In subsection (d) the Court did refer to a specific causation standard to make the point that this particular standard would *not* be applied as the legal standard in the case. In particular, it noted that the specific content of State obligations "cannot be determined on the basis of a strict *condition sine qua non* requirement".[51] This is a surprising statement, since the Court has *never*

45 *KlimaSeniorinnen*, para. 438.
46 *KlimaSeniorinnen*, para. 438.
47 *KlimaSeniorinnen*, para. 438.
48 *KlimaSeniorinnen*, para. 439.
49 *KlimaSeniorinnen*, para. 439.
50 *KlimaSeniorinnen*, para. 439.
51 *KlimaSeniorinnen*, para. 439.

applied this causation standard in its case law even in normal environmental cases or any other cases where breach of positive obligations have been adjudicated.[52] In fact, the Court has a long time ago explicitly rejected the *condition sine qua non* standard.[53] In sum, the rejection of this legal standard is not helpful for understanding the actual standard that needs to be applied.

3.2.4 *The Fourth Causal Link: Omissions by a Particular State Cause Risk to Specific Individuals in This State*

As noted above, one of the distinguishing features of the risk caused by climate change is that emissions are global, and any causal link between these risks and the conduct of a specific State is "necessaryly more tenuous".[54] This has been framed as the "drop in the ocean" argument, to which the Court responded that

> in the context of a State's positive obligations under the Convention, the Court has consistently held that it need not be determined with certainty that matters would have turned out differently if the authorities had acted otherwise. The relevant test does not require it to be shown that "but for" the failing or omission of the authorities the harm would not have occurred. Rather, what is important, and sufficient to engage the responsibility of the State, is that reasonable measures which the domestic authorities failed to take could have had a *real prospect of altering the outcome or mitigating the harm*. In the context of climate change, this principle should also be understood in the light of Article 3 § 3 of the UNFCCC according to which States should take measures to anticipate, prevent or minimise the causes of climate change and mitigate its adverse effects.[55]

The rejection of the "but for" test is a repetition of the above-mentioned rejection of the *condition sine qua non* standard. The "real prospect" test is instead proposed. This test has been applied previously in the case law in judgments where breaches of positive obligations are invoked and where, importantly, no complications arising from global (or multiactorial) contributions have arisen.[56] Just as importantly, the "real prospect" test has been

52 Stoyanova V. Causation between State Omission and Harm within the Framework of Positive Obligations under the European Convention on Human Rights. Human Rights Law Review. 2018;18:309.

53 *E. and Others v United Kingdom* App. no. 33218/96 (26 November 2002) para. 99.

54 *KlimaSeniorinnen*, para. 439.

55 *KlimaSeniorinnen*, para. 444 (emphasis added) (references omitted).

56 *O'Keeffe v. Ireland* [GC] App. no. 35810/09, para. 149; *Bljakaj and Others v. Croatia*, App. no. 74448/12, 18 September 2014, para. 124.

applied in the case law without consistency, since it has not been uniformly used.[57]

The pivotal point, based on the paragraph referenced above, is whether the relevance of the "real prospect" test is limited to rejecting the "drop in the ocean" argument or whether it might have wider significance. In case the latter, "real prospect" test would be actually the causation standard for delineating the content of positive obligations of the particular respondent State and finding breach. The next section in this chapter will revisit this issue to highlight that when the Court in *KlimaSeniorinnen* examined whether Switzerland breached its obligations, the "real prospect" test was not mentioned—in fact, no test was applied at all.

3.3 The Content of the Positive Obligation and the Irrelevance of Causation Test

3.3.1 No harm to individual interests

As mentioned above, the Court's assessment in *KlimaSeniorinnen* had four sections: "Preliminary points", "General considerations relating to climate-change cases", "Admissibility", and "Merits". Above, I already addressed the "Preliminary points" and "General considerations relating to climate-change cases" sections. Here I will briefly focus on the admissibility. Although the focus of this chapter is not on the preliminary procedural question of admissibility, it needs to be acknowledged that the admissibility requirement for victim status is not simply a procedural requirement. In fact, it has important substantive implications not only for the content of any positive obligations and therefore for the question of causation, but also for the distinctiveness of human rights law as a legal framework centred on the individual and on individual justice.[58]

To clarify the first implication regarding the content of positive obligations, it is essential to initially acknowledge that the determination of victim status also includes a causal inquiry. This is very obvious from the following paragraph: "in any event, whether the victim is direct, indirect or potential, there must *be a link between the applicant and the harm* which he or she claims to have sustained *as a result of the alleged violation*".[59] For direct victims, it needs to be demonstrated that the applicant "has been personally and actually affected" of "omissions of State authorities or private parties

57 Stoyanova V, (n 52) p. 309.

58 See, generally, Christoffersen J. Individual and Constitutional Justice: Can the Power Balance of Adjudication be Reversed? In Christoffersen J, Madsen M, eds. The European Court of Human Rights between Law and Politics. Oxford University Press; 2011. p. 181. See also Mayer B. Is Climate Change Mitigation within the Scope of Positive Human Rights Obligations? In Stoyanova V, McGrogan D, eds. The Limits of Positive Obligations in Human Rights Law: From Protection to Coercio. Hart Publishing (forthcoming).

59 *KlimaSeniorinnen*, para. 463.

allegedly infringing the applicant's Convention rights".[60] Very similarly, indirect victims have been also individually harmed or are individuals "who would have a valid and *personal interest* in seeing it [the violation] brought to an end".[61]

As to potential victims, two types could be identified in the case law. The first type refers to applicants who "contend that a law violates their rights, in the absence of an individual measure of implementation, if they belong to a class of people who risk being directly affected by the legislation, or if they are required either to modify their conduct or risk being prosecuted".[62] The second type of potential victims includes applicants who risk a future violation and who produce "reasonable and convincing evidence of the likelihood that a violation affecting him or her personally will occur".[63]

All these three conceptualisations of victim status (direct, indirect, and potential) point in one direction: human rights law is premised on individual interests that ground the ECHR rights and, accordingly, human rights law is premised on the idea of individual justice. If individual interests ground the ECHR rights, any obligations corresponding to these rights would also have to be grounded on individual interests. It then follows that any corresponding positive obligations are means to prevent *specified harms* suffered by individuals. If these fundamental premises of human rights law are followed, positive human rights obligations are not meant to prevent general harms to the population at large.[64]

The reasoning in *KlimaSeniorinnen* contains clear acknowledgements of these fundamental premises: "The Court's case-law on victim status is premised on the existence of a *direct impact* of the impugned action or omission *on the applicant* or a real risk thereof".[65] To claim victim status, "an applicant needs to show that he or she was *personally and directly affected* by the impugned failures".[66] Expectedly, when these requirements were applied in *KlimaSeniorinnen,* none of the individual applicants could fulfil the victim status criteria.[67] The wider point here is that since human rights law is

60 *KlimaSeniorinnen*, para. 465.
61 *KlimaSeniorinnen*, para. 468 (emphasis added).
62 *KlimaSeniorinnen*, para. 469.
63 *KlimaSeniorinnen*, para. 470.
64 For detailed theoretical discussion, see Stoyanova V. Positive Obligations as Coercive "Rights" and Compulsory Vaccination under the European Convention on Human Rights. International Journal of Constitutional Law Forthcoming.
65 *KlimaSeniorinnen*, para. 483.
66 *KlimaSeniorinnen*, para. 487. In the same para., the Court sets out the criteria for meeting this high threshold.
67 *KlimaSeniorinnen*, para. 527: "Two key criteria have been set out for recognising the victim status of natural persons in the climate-change context: (a) high intensity of exposure of the applicant to the adverse effects of climate change; and (b) a pressing need to ensure the applicant's individual protection (see paras. 487–488 above). The threshold for fulfilling these criteria is especially high (see paragraph 488 above)".

premised on individual justice it is meant to be relevant when the fundamental individual interests of a specific human being, have been harmed. Human rights law is not meant to protect general interests, which justifies the procedural limitation of not allowing public interest litigation before the Court.[68] In fact, if the distinction between individual interests and general interests is ignored, human rights law as a distinctive body of law collapses.[69]

Mitigation measures for combating climate change "appear to be a paradigm case of public interest",[70] in the sense that many can arguably benefit from the reduction of emissions and, if we fallow the accepted factual causal links by the Court, from the expected reduction of harms (or risks of harms). Certainly, public interests are relevant in human rights law since rights can be limited in service of public interests provided that such limitations meet certain conditions (i.e., legality and proportionality). In this sense, public interests can justify *limitations* of the rights. Public interests, however, do not justify the rights, since these are justified by individual interests. Yet, if public interests are allowed to justify the rights, we might face a case of some serious revision of human rights law itself. We appear to be also in a situation of a collapse of the distinction between individual interests and public interests.

This distinction apparently collapsed when the Court accepted that the applicant association in *KlimaSeniorinnen* had standing, which allowed the Court to make pronouncements about breach of positive obligations under Article 8.[71] The reason for the collapse is the following: no individual interests were affected (since no individual applicant was found to have victim status) and, relatedly, no specified harm could be identified, yet positive obligations corresponding to Article 8 were reviewed (and even found breached) since a collective body that serviced general interests had victim status. To

68 Letsas G. The European Court's Legitimacy after *KlimaSeniorinnen*. European Convention on Human Rights Law Review. 2024.

69 Alexy R. Individual Rights and Collective Goods. In: Nino C, ed. Rights. Dartmouth; 1992. p. 163. See Smet S. Resolving Conflicts between Human Rights: The Judge's Dilemma. Routledge; 2017, where the author tries to propose criteria for distinguishing general and individual interests.

70 Letsas G, (n 68). Letsas also adds climate change is a case of public interest "at least in the sense that everybody benefits from reducing greenhouse gas emissions". However, not everyone might benefit. See, generally, Mayer B. International Law Obligations on Climate Change Mitigation. Oxford University Press; 2022; Mayer B. Climate Change Mitigation as an Obligation under Human Rights Treaties?. American Journal of International Law. 2021;115:409; Mayer B. Is Climate Change Litigation within the Scope of Positive Human Rights Obligations. In Stoyanova V. and McGrogan D. Eds. The Limits of Positive Obligations in Human Rights Law: From Protection to Coercion. Hart Publishing (forthcoming).

71 For an interesting attempt to save the ECHR from this collapse, see Letsas G, (n 68): "*Klimaseniorinnen* can then be seen as having brought a claim not in the public interest, or on behalf of its members, but on behalf of victims who are currently unable to do so. To be sure, the Court did not say this in the judgment. But it cannot be true both that the applicant association did not bring the claim on behalf of victims and that the Convention prohibits *actio popularis*".

put it bluntly, the Court's reasoning worked backwards, and it can, therefore, be assessed as a revision of human rights law itself.

To explain this, note how the Court justified the standing of the association in the case:

> the special feature of climate change as a common concern of humankind and the necessity of promoting intergenerational burden-sharing in this context, speak in favour of recognising the standing of associations before the Court in climate-change cases. In view of the urgency of combating the adverse effects of climate change and the severity of its consequences, including the grave risk of their irreversibility, *States should take adequate action* notably through suitable general measures to secure not only the Convention rights of individuals who are currently affected by climate change, but also those individuals within their jurisdiction whose enjoyment of Convention rights may be severely and irreversibly affected in the future in the absence of timely action.[72]

The Court also developed a test for the standing of associations,[73] which we shall not explore presently. The applicant association was found to comply with the test and, therefore, was found to have standing, which allowed the Court to proceed to the question of obligations.[74]

Why is the reasoning in the above-quoted paragraph backwards? What mattered were not individual human rights that trigger corresponding obligations. The Court's reasoning started *from* the premise that there were general interests to do something about a general and urgent problem, and *then* it directly moved to the need that "States should take adequate action", which was transformed into a positive obligation upon the State, as demanded by a human rights treaty. Individual rights were basically lost. In this reasoning, individual interests and causality to individual interests were lost. In simple terms, the reasoning worked from obligations to "rights",[75] not from rights to obligations.

The bypassing of individual interests and causality to individual interests was analytically inevitable, if the Court's reasoning is followed. As Mayer has observed, the problem is not about some epistemological difficulty in identifying any individual victims.[76] The problem is rather more fundamental

72 *KlimaSeniorinnen*, para. 499.
73 *KlimaSeniorinnen*, para. 502.
74 *KlimaSeniorinnen*, para. 526.
75 I have placed the term "rights" in inverted commas to communicate the message that analytically it is not correct to accept that there were individual rights at stake.
76 This has been, for example, the case of surveillance regimes where data is collected about individuals without their knowledge. This clearly implicates the individual interest to private life, which means that they are victims, although they might not know, or, more generally, it might be difficult to know who the victims are.

and ontological: there *are* simply "no victims in any meaningful sense of the word".[77] Mayer has also added that "the causal relation between a state's failure to take appropriate measures to mitigate climate change and an individual's enjoyment of her human right is far too remote to characterize someone as a 'victim' of the state's action in any meaningful sense of the term".[78] All of this also comes down to the specification of the harm: if the harm remains unspecified and unindividualised, as it did in the Court's reasoning, the obligations (i.e., any measures for preventing the harm) have to necessarily also remain highly abstract. This was exactly what happened in *KlimaSeniorinnen* as the rest of this chapter will explain.

In sum, the procedural move by the Court in *KlimaSeniorinnen* is not simply a procedural technicality that we can easily brush aside. It affects the merits and the formulation of any corresponding positive obligations. There is a reason why, more generally, the substantive assessment of breach is preceded by the admissibility phase. The admissibility requirements, once fulfilled, allow and create the necessary conditions for performing the human rights law review on the merits. In this sense, this review is contingent upon and shaped by the admissibility filters.[79] If these filters are bypassed, problems emerge: How to apply the standards if there is no individual harm? How to apply human rights law if there is no individual harm? These questions concern, more generally, the role of human rights law as a distinctive body of law. The modification of the "victim status" as an admissibility requirement implies by necessity *modification* of the reasoning and the standards on the merits. What is this modification and what does it do to human rights law as a distinctive body of law? As the text below will show, the modification implied diffuse and abstract causal assumptions where general policy goals are framed.

3.3.2 Positive Obligations with Abstract and Unspecified Content

Having commented on the sections "Preliminary points", "General considerations relating to climate-change cases", and "Admissibility", I will now focus on the section in the judgment titled "Merits". The section "Merits" consisted of the following subsections: (a) "General principles", (b) "The States' positive obligations in the context of climate change", and (c) "Application of the above principles to the present case". The objective of subsection (a)

77 Mayer B. Is Climate Change Mitigation within the Scope of Positive Human Rights Obligations?. In: Stoyanova V, McGrogan D, eds. From Protection to Coercion: The Limits of Positive Obligations in Human Rights Law (forthcoming).

78 Mayer B, (n 70).

79 On the interplay between the admissibility phase and the other phases in the Court's review, see, generally, Gerards J, Buyse A, Andenas M. "Heads and Tails": Admissibility and Remedies at the European Court of Human Rights. European Convention on Human Rights Law Review. 2024;3:291.

was describing the general principles for identifying the content of State's positive obligations under Article 2 and 8 of the Convention. In the following subsection (b), these principles were specified given the particular context of climate change.

Prior to examining with some care what the Court named "general principles" for identifying the content of the State's positive obligations, it is relevant to clear our mind as to the meaning of the term "content". The content of the obligations are the measures that the State is required to perform.[80] The relevant question then is what measures the Court identified. These can be separated into substantive and procedural. As to the *substantive* measures, there were two. The first one was the adoption of effective "legislative and administrative framework"; in other words, adoption of "regulations geared to the specific features of the activity".[81] The second substantive measure that formed the content of the positive obligations was the application of the adopted regulatory framework in practice.[82]

These two positive obligations have been well-developed in the practice of the Court. As formulated at this abstract level in the reasoning in *KlimaSeniorinnen*, there was nothing controversial about them.[83] It is their specification, including the related causation link with the harm, that makes the positive obligations and the establishment of their breach more contentious; a point to which I will return below.

As to the *procedural* measures that form the content of the positive obligations, there were also two. The first was providing "access to essential information enabling individuals to assess risks to their health the lives", which has been also well-established in the case law.[84] The second procedural measure was having a national decision-making process of sufficient quality with sufficient procedural guarantees.[85] As to this second procedural measure, it is not entirely clear whether it formed the content of a separate independent procedural obligation or whether the national procedural guarantees were only a relevant consideration to be taken into account by the Court in determining the margin of appreciation. This ambiguous role of procedural guarantees is prevalent in the case law and, in this sense, the reasoning in *KlimaSeniorinnen* is not distinctive in comparison with other judgments.[86]

80 V Stoyanova, Positive Obligations under the European Convention on Human Rights: Within and Beyond Boundaries (Oxford University Press 2023).

81 *KlimaSeniorinnen*, para. 538(a).

82 *KlimaSeniorinnen*, para. 538(b).

83 Stoyanova V, (n 6).

84 *KlimaSeniorinnen*, para. 538(f).

85 *KlimaSeniorinnen*, para. 539.

86 See Gerards J. Procedural Review by the European Court of Human Rights – a Typology of Functions for the Court's Reasoning. In: Harvey D, Groussot X, eds. Process Federalism in EU Law. EULawLive Publishing. 2024.

In addition to identifying the content of the positive obligations in the form of substantive and procedural measures at abstract level, the Court also noted *two principles* relevant for the determination of breach. These are *discretion* and *proportionality*. As to first one, States are free to choose the measures that form the content of the positive obligations in terms of substantive and procedural measures.[87] This means that while the Court might formulate in general and abstract terms, for example, the positive obligation of adopting effective regulatory framework, States have multiple options at their disposal how to concretise the measures in their regulatory frameworks.[88] This discretion should be analytically distinguished from the structural margin of appreciation understood as subsidiarity.[89] This discretion (understood as multiple options of measures to comply) makes the finding of a breach of the positive obligation analytically difficult since there is no initial standard against which a breach can be assessed: there is no initial specification of the measures that should have been adopted, which can allow *a post factum* assessment as to whether these specific measures have been undertaken.[90] This analytical difficulty can be addressed by adopting a specific standard of causation to better define the required measures. In this context, causation plays a crucial role in specifying the content of positive obligations. The rationale is that the human rights review will include concrete examples of measures and an argument that if these measures were undertaken, this would have contributed to the prevention of the harm.[91] With this approach, the analytical operation of causally linking some concrete measures and the harm stabilises and strengthens the reasoning for establishing breach. As section 3.4 below will emphasise, in *KlimaSeniorinnen* such analytical operation was not performed in the establishment of breach, as the Court did not attempt to apply a "real prospect" causation test.

In addition to discretion (i.e., affording multiple compliance options), the proportionality standard further complicates the assessment of breach of positive obligations. As the Court reiterated in *KlimaSeniorinnen*, the measures forming the content of positive obligations cannot impose "an impossible or disproportionate burden" on the authorities. This means that authorities not only have the flexibility to choose between different measures, but must also

87 *KlimaSeniorinnen*, para. 538(d).

88 See, generally, Wibye J. Beyond Acts and Omissions – Distinguishing Positive and Negative Duties at the European Court of Human Rights. Human Rights Review. 2022; Klatt M. Positive Obligations under the European Convention on Human Rights. Heidelberg Journal of International Law. 2011:691.

89 Besson S. Subsidiarity in International Human Rights Law – What Is Subsidiary about Human Rights. The American Journal of Jurisprudence. 2016;61(1):69.

90 Stoyanova V. Framing Positive Obligations under the European Convention on Human Rights Law: Mediating between the Abstract and the Concrete. Human Rights Law Review. 2023;23:1.

91 Stoyanova V, (n 6).

weigh their priorities and resources when making those choices.[92] Similar to the issue of discretion, there is no predefined standard for determining what constitutes an impossible or disproportionate burden. In other words, no clear criteria exist for evaluating proportionality or suggesting which measures would impose a disproportionate burden. Once again, as noted earlier with regard to discretion, establishing a causal link between specific measures and the harm in question can aid in assessing proportionality. [93] Therefore, the process of analytically linking specific measures (that should have been implemented) to specific harms is crucial in this context as well.

In summary, in *KlimaSeniorinnen*, the Court broadly defined the content of positive obligations as including both substantive and procedural measures. These obligations were initially outlined in the "General Principles" section at a highly abstract level. The real challenge lies in specifying and tailoring these measures, especially given the lack of clear baseline standards to guide this process.

3.3.3 Tailoring the Content to the Context of Climate Change

The above-described abstract positive obligations whose content was expected not to impose a disproportionate burden and, at the same time, was characterised by discretion, were tailored to the context of climate change. How did the Court perform this tailoring in *KlimaSeniorinnen*?

3.3.3.1 The "Considerable Weight" Standard

On the standard of disproportionate burden, the Court noted the following: "the Court finds it justified to consider that climate protection should carry *considerable weight* in the weighing-up of any competing considerations".[94] Three arguments were advanced in support of this "considerable weight". The first one can be summarised as the scientific evidence that demonstrates the urgency and severity of climate change and that also demonstrates the "link between the adverse effects of climate change and the enjoyment of (various aspects of) human rights".[95] The second argument was the global nature of the effects of the emissions. The third argument was "the States' generally inadequate track record".[96]

Notably, any competing considerations were not even mentioned here. Even if climate protection is given "considerable weight", what considerations is it

92 *KlimaSeniorinnen*, para. 538(d).

93 For elaboration how the standard of "disproportionate burden" (also framed in the Court's case law as reasonableness) is related to the standard of causation in the content of adjudication of positive obligations, see Stoyanova V, (n 6).

94 *KlimaSeniorinnen*, para. 542 (emphasis added).

95 *KlimaSeniorinnen*, para. 542.

96 *KlimaSeniorinnen*, para. 542.

going to be weighed against? "Considerable weight" in comparison to what and in relationship to what? These questions were left out of the reasoning.

3.3.3.2 Differentiated Scope of the Margin

After determining that "climate protection should carry *considerable weight* in the weighing-up of any competing considerations", the Court proceeded to consider the margin of appreciation.[97] Put simply, the Court held that States must commit to the general aim of combating climate change, but retain discretion over the means of pursuing that aim. The fundamental distinction here was therefore between aims and means. However, this distinction is unstable, as the means—i.e. the specific measures constituting the content of positive obligations—can be framed at varying levels of abstraction.[98] The more abstract the framing is, the more they resemble aims, such as the general commitment to combat climate change. It then follows that the more abstract the positive obligations are articulated, which can make them resemble more general aim/commitments, the easier it is for the Court to find a violation. The reason is that the analysis remains at an abstract level, which allows overlooking causal links, difficult questions about degrees of causal contribution and about disproportionate burdens. This will be better explained in the text section.

3.3.3.3 Specification of the Obligation

As the Court held, Article 8 of the ECHR required that "each Contracting State undertake measures for the substantial and progressive reduction of their respective GHG emission levels, with a view to reaching *net neutrality* within, in principle, the next three decades".[99] The positive obligation was, therefore, articulated in terms of the aim that needs to be achieved and the timeframe.

In paragraph 550 of *KlimaSeniorinnen*, the Court outlined various mitigation measures. It is worth reproducing the entire paragraph here:

> When assessing whether a State has remained within its margin of appreciation, the Court *will examine* whether the competent domestic authorities, be it at the legislative, executive or judicial level, have had *due regard* to the need to:
>
> (a) adopt general measures specifying a target timeline for achieving carbon neutrality and the overall remaining carbon budget for the same time frame, or another equivalent method of quantification of future

97 *KlimaSeniorinnen*, para. 543.
98 Stoyanova V, (n 90).
99 *KlimaSeniorinnen*, para. 548.

GHG emissions, in line with the overarching goal for national and/or global climate-change mitigation commitments;

(b) set out intermediate GHG emissions reduction targets and pathways (by sector or other relevant methodologies) that are deemed capable, in principle, of meeting the overall national GHG reduction goals within the relevant time frames undertaken in national policies;

(c) provide evidence showing whether they have duly complied, or are in the process of complying, with the relevant GHG reduction targets (see sub-paragraphs (a)-(b) above);

(d) keep the relevant GHG reduction targets updated with due diligence, and based on the best available evidence; and

(e) act in good time and in an appropriate and consistent manner when devising and implementing the relevant legislation and measures.[100]

What is notable is the mixture of procedural and substantive review for determining breach. The Court observed that it would "examine whether the competent domestic authorities, [...] have had *due regard* to the need to [...]". This suggests a procedural review by the Court. In other words, the Court approached its task as one of examining what the national authorities had considered. Putting it differently, the task of the Court was not to examine whether the measures themselves were proportionate and contributed to achieving the aim: there was an additional procedural twist. The Court suggested that it would review the domestic review (double procedure review). In other words, the Court suggested that it would review *whether* the domestic authorities had a review.[101]

In sum, the Court's abstract framing of the obligation (e.g. 'achieving net neutrality'), combined with procedural reasoning, enabled it to sidestep the standard of causation. It avoided examining how the State's omission—or potential future omissions—to meet the carbon neutrality target actually caused harm. As discussed in Section 3.1, this was initially possible because no concrete harm to individual interests could be identified. Moreover, the procedural framing further obscured any specific causal link between procedural shortcomings and harm.[102]

100 Adaptation measures were also added. At para. 555, the Court clarified that the mitigation measures have autonomous standing: failure to comply with them suffices for finding a breach of Article 8.

101 *KlimaSeniorinnen*, para. 554.

102 This is an observation of a general nature, not pertaining specifically to *KlimaSeniorinnen*. The Court uses procedural failures as proxies for causation. See Stoyanova V, (n 52).

3.3.4 Assessing Compliance without Specification

Having explained the reasoning on the merits, regarding "General principles" and "The States' positive obligations in the context of climate change", here I will focus on the subsection in the judgment addressing the "Application of the above principles to the present case". The review of this application, which involved assessing whether the respondent State fulfilled its positive obligations, was covered in just four and a half pages. The reasoning is highly technical, with frequent references to scientific evidence. The main omissions underlying the finding of a breach of positive obligations under Article 8 ECHR were: the failure to adopt a regulatory framework (i.e. a "legislative lacuna"),[103] the failure to quantify national emission limits, and the failure to meet previously established emission reduction targets.

The omissions were framed in broad terms, without specifying the concrete measures that constituted the content of the obligations. This is not unique to *KlimaSeniorinnen*; more generally, the binary finding that a State has breached its positive obligations under the ECHR often lacks prescriptive clarity.[104] The conclusion of a violation, however, has to be read in light of "the spirit of the Court judgment",[105] understood as in light of the reasoning in the judgment. This is a suggestion that the reasoning might give some indications as to what could have been done differently, or what will need to be done in the future. Yet, indications do they remain, not prescriptions.

The lack of concrete measures specified in the operative part of the judgment – or the impossibility of specifying them – should not, in principle, prevent a judgment on the merits. However, this absence of specific prescriptions heightens the importance of the Court's reasoning and any indications of concrete measures. For the respondent State to understand how to remedy the omissions and effectively implement the judgment, the reasoning should offer clear guidance. Likewise, the Committee of Ministers requires this guidance to properly oversee the judgment's execution.

However, how useful and how analytically robust was the reasoning? To engage with this question, I will limit myself to two aspects: to wit, the related standards of causation and "disproportionate burden" that were already mentioned and explained in section 3.3 above.

103 *KlimaSeniorinnen*, para. 561.

104 Stoyanova V. Correlativity between Human Rights and Positive Obligations and Its Role for the Execution of Judgments Delivered by the European Court of Human Rights. European Convention on Human Rights Law Review. 2024.

105 *KlimaSeniorinnen*, para. 656: "The Court further points out that its judgments are essentially declaratory in nature and that, in general, it is primarily for the State concerned to choose, subject to supervision by the Committee of Ministers, the means to be used in its domestic legal order in order to discharge its obligation under Article 46 of the Convention, *provided that such means are compatible with the conclusions and spirit of the Court's judgment*" (emphasis added).

3.3.4.1 *The Causation Standard Was Not Relevant*

As noted earlier, the Court referenced the "real prospect" test for causation, yet this standard was absent from its actual assessment of the breach. This reveals a clear disconnect between the judgment's general principles and the brief four-page reasoning that followed. The concern is not the length of the reasoning but the fact that the finding of a breach of positive obligations was made without applying—or even engaging with—any causation analysis.

3.3.4.2 *The "Disproportionate Burden" Standard Was Not Relevant*

A similar omission concerns the "disproportionate burden" standard. Had the Court meaningfully applied this standard, it would have needed to account for the costs and adverse consequences of mitigation measures. The assumption that such measures are always beneficial—even for the individual interests protected by human rights—is untenable.[106] They may involve significant economic and social transformation, often at high cost. Yet, the judgment ignores these challenges entirely. This further underscores the disconnect between the Court's articulation of general principles, like "disproportionate burden," and their absence in the concrete reasoning leading to a finding of breach.

3.4 Conclusion

Causation is an essential element of any analysis of legal responsibility. It underpins every legal inquiry into responsibility, and the resulting consequences once responsibility is established. [107] At the same time, defining causation has proven challenging, particularly when the inquiry focuses on omissions as causal factors.[108]

This chapter offered a critical assessment as to how the Court framed the standard of causation and how it applied it *Verein KlimaSeniorinnen Schweiz*. Although the Court, in abstract terms, addressed causation upfront by devoting multiple paragraphs to this very question in the judgment, causal links had little role in the actual determination of breach. This determination featured casual assumptions in very abstract terms with little regard to the "real prospect" and the "disproportionate burden" standards. This feature

106 Mayer B, (n 70).

107 Honoré AM. Causation and Remoteness of Damage. In: Tunc A, ed. International Encyclopaedia of Comparative Law: Torts. Vol 11, ch 7. Mohr; 1983. pp. 1–156, 21–22.

108 Honoré T. Responsibility and Fault. Hart Publishing; 2002. pp. 41; Sartorio C. How to Be Responsible for Something without Causing It. Philosophical Perspectives. 2004;18(1):315; Moore MS. Causation and Responsibility: An Essay on Law, Morals, and Metaphysics. Oxford Academic. 2009. pp. 129–130; Schaffer J. Causes Need Not Be Physically Connected to Their Effects: The Case for Negative Causation. In: Hitchcock CR, ed. Contemporary Debates in Philosophy of Science. Blackwell Publishing; 2004. p. 197.

was in a way inevitable in the absence of specific harm and, therefore, harm to individual interests, which justified the denial of victim status to the individual applicants.

The breach analysis on the merits relied on diffuse and highly abstract causal assumptions, which easily underpinned the existence of broadly defined positive obligations. The tailoring of these obligations to the climate change context did not lead to greater specificity because the issue of causation was sidestepped. This was achieved by framing the obligation in terms of an abstract goal and by combining procedural omissions with substantive ones. When the Court assessed breach, it did not revisit the key standards of "real prospect" and "disproportionate burden". There was, therefore, a disconnect between the abstract discussion about causation and the determination of breach.

Although the definitive finding of a breach may be well-received, the work of defining the scope of positive obligations – and, more generally, understanding the role and core principles of human rights law – has only just started. The revision of human rights law as a body of law designed to also protect *general* interests, which was allowed by granting the applicant association victim status, must inevitably have implications that are yet to be better understood and articulated. This chapter clarified at least two things in this context. First, human rights law has been shifted away from more robust causal inquires. Second, human rights law has been shifted away from its historical origins that demand sensitivity and a certain level of reservation as to the idea that state interventions (framed as demanded by positive human rights law obligation) are necessary, positive, and beneficial.[109]

References

Alexy R. Individual rights and collective goods. In: Nino C, editor. Rights. Dartmouth; 1992.

Ambrus M. The European court of human rights as governor of risk. In: Ambrus M, Rayfuse R, Werner W, editors. Risk and regulation of uncertainty in international law. Oxford: Oxford University Press; 2017.

Besson S. The morality of conflict: reasonable disagreement and the law. Oxford: Hart Publishing; 2005.

Besson S. Subsidiarity in international human rights law—What is subsidiary about human rights. Am J Jurisprud. 2016;61(1):69–107.

Brems E, editor. Conflicts between fundamental rights. Cambridge: Intersentia; 2008.

Christoffersen J. Individual and constitutional justice: can the power balance of adjudication be reversed?. In: Christoffersen J, Madsen M, editors. The European court of human rights between law and politics. Oxford: Oxford University Press; 2011.

Crawford J. State responsibility: the general part. Cambridge: Cambridge University Press; 2013.

109 See, generally, McGrogan D. Critical Theory and Human Rights: From Compassion to Coercion. Manchester University Press; 2021.

Dembour M-B. The evidentiary system of the European court of human rights in critical perspective. Eur Conv Hum Rights Law Rev. 2023;4:363–374.
Dyson M, Steel S. Chapter 2 - Risk and English tort law. In: Dyson M, editor. Regulating risk through private law. Cambridge: Intersentia; 2018.
Gerards J. Procedural review by the European court of human rights – A typology of functions for the court's reasoning. In: Harvey D, Groussot X, editors. Process federalism in EU law. EULawLive Publishing; 2024.
Gerards J, Brems E. Introduction. In: Brems E, Gerards J, editors. Shaping rights in the ECHR. Cambridge: Cambridge University Press; 2013.
Gerards J, Buyse A, Andenas M. "Heads and tails": admissibility and remedies at the European court of human rights. Eur Conv Hum Rights Law Rev. 2024;3:291–301.
Green L. Are there dependable rules on causation?. Univ Pa Law Rev. 1929;77(5):601–628.
Hoffmann L. Causation. In: Goldberg R, editor. Perspective on causation. Oxford: Hart Publishing; 2011.
Honoré AM. Causation and remoteness of damage. In: Tunc A, editor. International encyclopaedia of comparative law: Torts. Vol. 11, ch. 7. Tübingen: Mohr; 1983.
Honoré T. Responsibility and fault. Oxford: Hart Publishing; 2002.
Klatt M. Positive obligations under the European convention on human rights. Heidelb J Int Law. 2011;71:691–718.
Kokott J. The burden *and standard of proof in comparative and international human rights law*. Springer; 1998.
Lanovoy V. Causation in the law of state responsibility. Br Yearb Int Law. 2022;1:1–84.
Letsas G. The European court's legitimacy after KlimaSeniorinnen. Eur Conv Hum Rights Law Rev. 2024;4(5):444–453.
Mayer B. Climate change mitigation as an obligation under human rights treaties?. Am J Int Law. 2021;115.
Mayer B. Is climate change mitigation within the scope of positive human rights obligations?. In: Stoyanova V, McGrogan D, editors. From protection to coercion: the limits of positive obligations in human rights law. Forthcoming.
Mayer B. International law obligations on climate change mitigation. Oxford: Oxford University Press; 2022.
McGrogan D. Critical theory and human rights: from compassion to coercion. Manchester: Manchester University Press; 2021.
Moore MS. Causation and responsibility: an essay on law, morals, and metaphysics. Oxford: Oxford Academic; 2009.
Peel J. Science and risk regulation in international law. Cambridge: Cambridge University Press; 2010.
Plakokefalos I. Causation in the law of state responsibility and the problem of overdetermination: in search of clarity. Eur J Int Law. 2015;26(2):471–492.
Raz J. On the nature of rights. Mind. 1984;XCIII(370):194–214.
Sartorio C. How to be responsible for something without causing it. Philosophical Perspectives. 2004;18(1):315–336.
Schaffer J. Causes need not be physically connected to their effects: the case for negative causation. In: Hitchcock CR, editor. Contemporary debates in philosophy of science. Oxford: Blackwell Publishing; 2004.
Smet S. Resolving conflicts between human rights: the judge's dilemma. London: Routledge; 2017.
Steele J, Gardner JE. Introduction. In: Steele J, Gardner JE, editors. Risks and legal theory. Oxford: Hart; 2004.

Stoyanova V. Causation between state omission and harm within the framework of positive obligations under the European Convention on Human Rights. Hum Rights Law Rev. 2018;18:309–346.
Stoyanova V. Causation: why and how for establishing breach of positive obligations under the European convention on human rights?. In: Stoyanova V, McGrogan D, editors. From protection to coercion: the limits of positive obligations in human rights law. Forthcoming.
Stoyanova V. Correlativity between human rights and positive obligations and its role for the execution of judgments delivered by the European Court of Human Rights. Eur Conv Hum Rights Law Rev. 2024.
Stoyanova V. Fault, knowledge and risk within the framework of positive obligations under the European convention on human rights. Leiden J Int Law. 2020;33:601–620.
Stoyanova V. Framing positive obligations under the European convention on human rights law: mediating between the abstract and the concrete. Hum Rights Law Rev. 2023;23:1–34.
Stoyanova V. *Positive obligations as coercive "rights" and compulsory vaccination under the European convention on human rights*. Forthcoming.
Stoyanova V. Positive obligations under the European convention on human rights: within and beyond boundaries. Oxford: Oxford University Press; 2023.
Stoyanova V. The disjunctive structure of positive rights under the ECHR. Nordic J Int Law. 2018;87:344–392.
Thienel T. The burden and standard of proof in the European court of human rights. Ger Yb Int Law. 2007;50:543–588.
Thomas J. Public rights, private relations. Oxford: Oxford University Press; 2015.
Wibye J. Beyond acts and omissions – Distinguishing positive and negative duties at the European Court of Human Rights. Hum Rights Rev. 2022:479–502.
Yeung K, Ranchordas S, editors. An introduction to law and regulation. Cambridge: Cambridge University Press; 2024.

4 The Protection of the Climate System in the African System of Human Rights – Possible Legal Grounds

Welena da Silva and Armando Rocha

4.1 Introduction

As climate change poses an immediate risk to the enjoyment of human rights, recent climate litigation has also been human rights–based.[1] Unsurprisingly, the UN Human Rights Committee[2] and the European Court of Human Rights[3] have recently affirmed that States bear a human rights obligation to adopt and effectively implement a regulatory framework aimed at reducing greenhouse gas emissions[4] and mitigating the impacts of climate change. As of 31 January 2025, it is also pending before the Inter-American Court of Human Rights[5] a request for an advisory opinion on States' obligations on climate change.[6]

However, no climate change–related case was yet brought before the African Court or Commission on Human and Peoples' Rights,[7] or the ECOWAS Court of Justice, or in which climate change was used as part of the legal argument.[8] Several reasons can explain the lack of climate litigation in the African human rights system, all of them related to domestic law

1 E.g., Setzer J, Higham C. Global Trends in Climate Change Litigation: 2024 Snapshot. Grantham Research Institute on Climate Change and the Environment & Centre for Climate Change Economics and Policy. 2024;2.

2 *Daniel Billy et al v Australia*, Communication No. CCPR/C/135/D/3624/2019, Views adopted on 21 July 2022. See, in this volume, Wewerinke-Singh M, Venkatachalam M, Rocha A. The United Nations System, Chapter 1.

3 *Verein KlimaSeniorinnen Schweiz et al v Switzerland*(App. No. 53600/20) ECtHR [GC] 9 April 2024. See, in this volume, Kwiędacz-Palosz M. The European Human Rights System, Chapter 8.

4 Hereinafter "GHG".

5 Hereinafter "IACtHR".

6 See, in this volume, Tigre MA, Viveros-Uehara T. The American Human Rights System, Chapter 2.

7 Hereinafter "African Court" and "African Commission", respectively.

8 Boshoff E. The Prospects and Challenges of Litigating Climate Change before African Regional Human Rights Bodies". In Bouwer K, et al., eds. Climate Litigation and Justice in Africa. Bristol University Press; 2024. pp. 125, 126.

DOI: 10.4324/9781003540977-6

factors[9]: the scarcity of advocacy groups' financial and human resources, the unclear domestic regulatory framework, the slow pace of courts' proceedings, the legal culture of a State, or the entrenched economic interests. These factors, linked with the need to exhaust domestic remedies[10] and the perception of other human rights priorities in Africa, explains the lack of climate litigation in the African human rights system.

Yet, although vulnerability is not uniform across the continent, Africa is particularly vulnerable to the detrimental consequences of climate change,[11] being African States also less equipped to cope with these consequences.[12] Furthemore, the African human rights system includes treaties that are germane to climate change, including the ACHPR, which enshrines a standalone right to a general satisfactory environment. This ultimately means that the African human rights system is a promising forum for human rights–based climate litigation.[13]

In this scenario, this chapter assesses how climate change can be incorporated into the legal arguments espoused in the context of the ACHPR. To that end, section 2 provides a brief overview of the African human rights system. Section 3 briefly looks at the sources of African States' climate mitigation obligations, at the international and regional levels (and how they interact). Section 4 considers how a right to a general satisfactory environment under Article 24 ACHPR can be used to espouse legal arguments related to the protection of the climate system, whereas section 5 makes the same analysis with regard to other human rights listed in the ACHPR.

9 *Ibid*, p. 126; Suedi Y, Fall M. Climate Change Litigation before the African Human Rights System: Prospects and Pitfalls Journal of Human Rights Practice. 2024;16:146, 147.

10 African Charter on Human and Peoples' Rights (adopted 27 June 1981, entered into force 21 October 1986) 1520 UNTS 363, Article 56(5) ("ACHPR"), applicable *ex vi* 1998 Protocol on the Establishment of an African Court on Human and Peoples' Rights (adopted 9 June 1998, entered into force 25 January 2004) OAU/LEG/MIN/AFCHPR/PROT.1/rev.2/1997, Article 6(2) ("1998 Protocol").

11 Trisos C, et al. Africa. In: Pörtner H-O, et al., eds. Climate Change 2022: Impacts, Adaptation and Vulnerability. Contribution of Working Group II to the Sixth Assessment Report of the Intergovernmental Panel on Climate Change. Cambridge University Press; 2022.

12 E.g., Addaney M, Boshoff E, Olutola B. The Climate Change and Human Rights Nexus in Africa. Amsterdam Law Forum. 2017;9(3):5, 6–7; Bouwer K, Field T-L. Editorial: The Emergence of Climate Litigation in Africa. Carbon and Climate Law Review. 2021;15(2):123, 124–125; Jegede A. Should a Human Right to a Safe Climate Be Recognized under the AU Human Rights System?. In: Addaney M, Jegede A, eds. Human Rights and the Environment under African Union Law. Springer; 2020. pp. 55–56, 58ff; Ruppel O. Climate Change Law and Policy Positions in the African Union and Related Developments in Selected African Countries. In: Ruppel O, Roschmann C, Ruppel-Schlichting K, eds. Climate Change: International Law and Global Governance. Vol. II. Policy, Diplomacy and Governance in a Changing Environment. Nomos; 2013. pp. 411–412; Scholtz W. The Promotion of Regional Environmental Security and Africa's Common Position on Climate Change. African Human Rights Law Journal. 2010;10:1–4.

13 Suedi Y, Fall M, (n 9) p. 147.

4.2 A Short Overview of the African System of Human Rights

4.2.1 General Overview

The African human rights system has several roots, all leading to the need to promote and fulfil civil, political, economic, social, and cultural rights across Africa. To some extent, this was the result of the colonial period, which left African States with a pressing need for development, i.e., institutional, technological, infrastructural, or economic, but also in the enjoyment of the most basic human rights, among which the healthy environment stands out. This explains why Article 24 ACHPR enshrines a human right to a "general satisfactory environment", therefore placing the ACHPR in that cluster of human rights treaties that autonomises a standalone and substantive human right to the environment.[14] Furthermore, the experience of the political processes of the newly created States, marked by a pattern of human rights abuses, highlighted the need for a certain assistance at the regional level, in order to secure the respect, protection, and fulfilment of human rights in Africa.[15]

Yet, the origins of the African human rights system date back to a period when most African States were still under colonial domination,[16] when a group of judges, scholars, and practitioners (assembled in Nigeria, in 1961) proclaimed the so-called Law of Lagos, in which they asked for the constitution of a regional human rights court in Africa.[17] However, the Charter of the Organisation of African Unity – although being the first major regional treaty in Africa – only refers to human rights in the context of the promotion of international cooperation,[18] suggesting that human rights protection and promotion was not conceived of as a priority for the organisation.[19]

Still, the ACHPR was adopted in 1981, not only as a reaction to an experience of human rights abuses in post-colonial Africa, but also to the need of

14 Rocha A, Oliveira H. Fundamental Rights and Human Rights. In: Amado Gomes C, Oliveira H, Perestrelo de Oliveira M, eds. A Treatise on Environmental Law. Vol. III. Environmental Law and Other Legal Fields. Lisbon Public Law Editions; 2024. pp. 22, 32.

15 E.g., Amechi EP. Enhancing Environmental Protection and Socio-economic Development in Africa: A Fresh Look at the Right to a General Satisfactory Environment under the African Charter on Human and Peoples' Rights. Law, Environment and Development Journal. 2009;5(1):58, 61.

16 Mutua M. Human Rights – A Political and Cultural Critique. University of Pennsylvania Press; 2002. pp. 71–74.

17 "Law of Lagos", para. 4. [Accessed 7 February 2025]. Available from: Africa-African-Conference-Rule-of-Law-conference-report-1961-eng.pdf. The "Law of Lagos" was revived in 1967 during the proceedings of the First Congress of French-Speaking African Jurists. See Africa-function-of-the-law-congress-report-conclusions-1967-fra.pdf [Accessed 7 February 2025].

18 Charter of the Organization of African Unity (adopted 25 May 1963, entered into force 13 September 1963) 479 UNTS 39, Article II(e).

19 Donnelly J, Whelan DJ. International Human Rights. 6th ed. Routledge; 2020. pp. 126 ff; Mutua M. African Human Rights System: A Critical Evaluation. Prepared for United Nations Development Programme, Human Development Report. 2000.

enhancing human rights standards as a condition for States having access to international funding and other forms of assistance. The ACHPR stands out as the major regional human rights treaty in Africa and covers a vast list of human rights and freedoms, in line with other major universal or regional human rights treaties, but it stands out for two reasons: first, it lists human and *peoples*' rights (Articles 19–24);[20] second, it sets out fundamental *duties* of individuals and peoples (Articles 27–29).[21] The African human rights system is also composed of other treaties, which are mentioned below in more detail in section 3.2.

From a more operative angle, the enforcement of the ACHPR is guaranteed by both the African Court (created by the 1998 Protocol) and the African Commission (ACHPR, Articles 30–61). In Chapter 9, Silva explains rules on the access of States, individuals, and civil society organisations to the African Court or Commission. With regard to the African Court, it holds contentious and advisory jurisdiction, and it is responsible for enforcing the ACHRP, the 1998 Protocol, and other human rights instruments ratified by the concerned States.[22] The African Court is a truly judicial body holding the power to render binding decisions, whilst the African Commission is a para-judicial body. Despite the limitedness of the system,[23] both the African Court and the Commission have effectively contributed to the enhancement of human rights protection in Africa. In 2008, a new regional court was created by treaty,[24] which aims to merge the African Court with the Court of Justice of the African Union, but this protocol is not yet in force.

The complexity of the African system also results from the fact that other regional courts hold jurisdiction on human rights matters. In this light, the protection and promotion of human rights is also a fundamental principle of the Economic Community of West African States (ECOWAS),[25] being the ECOWAS Court of Justice responsible for settling human rights disputes in Member States,[26] thus including the enforcement of the ACHPR. Human rights protection is also a fundamental principle of the East African Community,[27] being the East African Court of Justice also responsible for

20 See Smith R. International Human Rights Law. 10th ed. Oxford University Press; 2022. p. 132.

21 See, e.g., Boshoff E, (n 8) pp. 132–133; Mutua M, (n 16) pp. 82–84.

22 1998 Protocol, Article 3(1).

23 Mutua M, (n 19) pp. 22–34.

24 2008 Protocol on the African Court of Justice and Human Rights (adopted 1 July 2008).

25 Revised Treaty of the Economic Community of West African States (adopted 24 July 1993, entered into force 23 August 1995) 2373 UNTS 233, Article 4(g).

26 Supplementary Protocol A/SP.1/01/05 amending the Preamble and Articles 1, 2, 9, and 30 of Protocol A/P.1/7/91 relating to the Community Court of Justice and Article 4 Paragraph 1 of the English Version of the Said Protocol (adopted 19 January 2005, entered into force 14 June 2006) Article 3(4).

27 Treaty on the Establishment of the East African Community (adopted 30 November 1999, entered into force 7 July 2000) 2144 UNTS 255, Article 6(d) 27(2).

settling human rights disputes.[28] Accordingly, the case law of these regional courts can also provide valuable information regarding how a right to a general satisfactory environment can be used in climate litigation in the African system.

4.2.2 *An Advisory Opinion on Climate Change?*

In Chapter 9, Silva explains the access to the African Court in contentious cases, having in mind the difficulties faced by concerned and affected individuals and civil society groups in getting to domestic and regional courts. Yet, one must also note that according to Article 4(1) of the 1998 Protocol, "At the request of a Member State of the OAU, the OAU, any of its organs, or any African organisation recognised by the OAU, the Court may provide an opinion on any legal matter relating to the Charter or any other relevant human rights instruments, provided that the subject matter of the opinion is not related to a matter being examined by the Commission".[29] In this light, there was an initiative to bring climate change into the African Court's docket by means of a request for an advisory opinion,[30] seeking to get a judicial clarification on States' obligations under the ACHPR to mitigate and adapt to climate change. On May 2, 2025, an opinion from the African Court was requested by the Pan African Lawyers Union (PALU).

According to Article 4(1) of the 1998 Protocol, States have the right to request an advisory opinion from the African Court. Even though advisory opinions are less sensitive than a contentious case against another State, it is unclear why States would be interested in a judicial clarification of their obligations pursuant to the ACHPR since the lack of clarification is protective to States, as it provides a bigger margin in the domestic observance of those obligations. Another alternative is a request submitted by the African Union or one of its organs (which seems largely redundant), although international organisations and their organs work based on States Parties' votes. If States themselves are not comfortable with requesting an opinion on this topic, they are equally uncomfortable with doing it through an international organisation.

28 *Ibid*, Article 27(2).

29 On this matter, see Chenwi L. The Advisory Proceedings of the African Court on Human and Peoples' Rights. Nordic Journal of Human Rights. 2020;38:61; Van der Mei AP. The Advisory Jurisdiction of the African Court on Human and Peoples' Rights. African Human Rights Law Journal. 2005;5:27; Odinkalu CA. Advice without Consent? Assessing the Advisory Jurisdiction of the African Court on Human and Peoples' Rights. Human Rights Quarterly. 2023;45:365; Suedi Y, Fall M, (n 9).

30 Lupin D, Nekura R. An Advisory Opinion on Human Rights and Climate Change in the African Regional Human Rights System. In: Tigre MA, Rocha A, eds. The Role of Advisory Opinions in International Law in the Context of the Climate Crisis (forthcoming); Suedi Y, Fall M, (n 9) p. 152.

A final option is a request submitted by an African organisation recognised by the African Union, referring to non-governmental organisations. Although these organisations face the same constraints in terms of human and financial resources, they are less reluctant to ask for a clarification of States' obligations in respect of climate change and less likely to be captured by entrenched economic interests. The problem is that these organisations need to comply with certain requirements to be recognised by the African Union – which implies having observer status before the African Union in accordance with the criteria laid down in the Executive Council Decision EX.CL/Dec.230(VII): *Criteria for Granting African Union Observer Status to Non-Governmental Organizations (NGOs)*.[31] Unsurprisingly, the record of the organisations accepted to submit a request for an advisory opinion before the African Court is particularly narrow.[32]

Furthermore, according to Article 45(3) ACHPR, the African Commission can render advisory opinions requested by the same entities. However, the record on the exercise of advisory competence by the African Commission is much narrower than that of the African Court, with only one opinion rendered to date.[33] The opportunity here, in terms of climate litigation, is that a non-governmental organisation needs to be recognised as an observer only by the African Commission, and not by the African Union.[34]

4.3 The Obligation to Protect the Climate System and Global, (Sub) Regional, and Domestic Instruments

4.3.1 Obligations under UNFCCC Legal Complex

As almost all African States are Parties to the UN Framework Convention on Climate Change[35] and the Paris Agreement,[36] they bear the obligation to prepare, communicate, and maintain successive nationally determined contributions[37] that they intend to achieve, and to pursue domestic mitigation measures aimed at achieving the goals of such contributions.[38] A State's NDC shall be renewed every five years[39] and it must reflect a State's "highest

31 Decision on Advisory Opinion no. 001/2013 *On the Meaning of an African Organization Recognized by the African Union and whether extreme, systemic and widespread poverty is a violation of certain provisions of the African Charter on Human and Peoples' Rights, In particular, Article 2 thereof which prohibits discrimination based on "any other status", Requested by Socio-economic Rights and Accountability Project (SERAP)* (26 May 2017) paras. 59–64.

32 Suedi Y, Fall M, (n 9) p. 153.

33 *Ibid*, p. 154.

34 *Ibid*.

35 Adopted 9 May 1992, entered into force 21 March 1994 (1771 UNTS 107) ("UNFCCC").

36 Adopted 12 December 2015, entered into force 4 November 2016 (3156 UNTS 79).

37 Hereinafter "NDC".

38 Paris Agreement, Article 4(2).

39 Paris Agreement, Article 4(9).

possible ambition, reflecting its common but differentiated responsibilities and respective capabilities", and represent a progression beyond a Party's then current [NDC]".[40]

In the design of their NDCs, States must assess several variables, including the need to take into account the impact of climate change on the enjoyment of human rights, as well as the impact of the adoption of mitigation and adaptation policies on the enjoyment of the same human rights. In the case of African States, where the fulfilment of human rights lags behind the standards already achieved in other geographies, the human rights factor plays an important role in the design of States' NDCs. Thus, the same factors that led the drafters of the ACHPR to condition the right to a general satisfactory environment to the development of a people explain the difficulties of African States in submitting ambitious NDCs that might damage their capacity to enhance social and economic growth and fulfil other human rights.

4.3.2 Regional Sources of Climate-Related Obligations in Africa

If climate change affects the enjoyment of human rights, it means that human rights treaties can also entail a legal obligation to mitigate and adapt to climate change. Therefore, the ACHPR can also be used to design a legal argument regarding States' obligations: on the one hand, by using Article 24 on the right to a general satisfactory environment (section 4); on the other hand, by greening other human rights in the ACHPR (section 5). But before delving into these provisions, one must also emphasise that the African human rights system includes other instruments that can assist in identifying climate-related obligations.

To begin with, the Maputo Protocol to the ACHPR on the Rights of Women in Africa enshrines a right to a healthy and sustainable environment and lists detailed obligations on this matter.[41] In addition, under the umbrella of the right to adequate housing, it reads that "Women shall have the right [...] to acceptable living conditions in a healthy environment",[42] having in mind that climate-related events can affect the living conditions of individuals in an uneven manner, being more harmful to more vulnerable or historically discriminated groups as women. Moreover, the African Charter on the Rights and Welfare of the Child refers that "Every child shall have the right to education", which "shall be directed to [...] the development of

40 Paris Agreement, Article 4(3).

41 2003 Protocol to the African Charter on Human and People's Rights on the Rights of Women in Africa (adopted 1 July 2003, entered into force 25 November 2005) 3268 UNTS 1, Article XVIII. Regarding the use of this convention in the context of human rights and climate change, see Ruppel O, (n 12) pp. 423–424.

42 *Ibid*, Article XVI.

respect for the environment and natural resources".[43] Regarding the right to health, the convention also aspires to "ensure that all sectors of the society [...] are informed and supported in the use of basic knowledge of [...] environmental sanitation".[44] Children also rank among the groups most vulnerable to the detrimental effects of climate change. In addition, the Kampala Convention for the Protection and Assistance of Internally Displaced Persons aims to prevent, mitigate, protect, and assist internally displaced persons in Africa.[45] Aware of the fact that climate-related events (including heat waves and changes in weather patterns) increase the likelihood of human displacement, it sets out States' obligation to protect and assist persons who are internally displaced due to natural or human-made disasters, including an explicit reference to climate change.[46] Finally, the Revised African Convention on the Conservation of Nature and Natural Resources establishes as a core principle of its regime is "the right of all peoples to a satisfactory environment favourable to their development",[47] using a semantic element close to Article 24 ACHPR and suggesting that any reading of the ACHPR needs to be aligned with this latter Revised Convention.

As said, these instruments can be used for the purpose of enhancing climate-related States' obligations within the African human rights system, but notwithstanding the centrality of the ACHPR. Perhaps their main value here lies in assisting the interpretation of the ACHPR and clarifying States' obligation thereunder in relation to climate change. Moreover, although these are sectorial conventions, climate litigation seeks to pressure States to adopt not only mitigation policies, but also adaptation measures. African States may not be the major GHG emitters, but they are the major affected or vulnerable States. Treaties that seek to protect the most vulnerable layers of society against the adverse effects of climate change are of utmost relevance to clarify human rights–related adaptation obligations.

43 1990 African Charter on the Rights and Welfare of the Child (adopted 11 July 1990, entered into force 25 November 1999) CAB/LEG/24.9/49, Article 11(1) and (2)(g). Regarding the use of this convention in the context of human rights and climate change, see Boshoff E, (n 8) pp. 134–135; Fokala E, Muhumuza N. Eroding Children's Rights: An Analysis of the Utility of the African Charter on the Rights and Welfare of the Child to Climate Action in Africa. In: Fokala N, Assim U, Murungi N, eds. The Social, Economic and Cultural Rights of Children in Africa – Challenges and Reflections from the Perspective of the African Charter on the Rights and Welfare of the Child. Brill; 2025. p. 222; Ruppel O, (n 12) pp. 423–424.

44 *Ibid*, Article 14(2)(h).

45 African Union Convention for the Protection and Assistance of Internally Displaced Persons (adopted 23 October 2009, entered into force 6 December 2012) 3014 UNTS 3, Article II(b). Regarding the use of this convention in the context of human rights and climate change, see Addaney M, Jegede A, Matinda M. The Protection of Climate Refugees under the African Human Rights System: Proposing a Value-Driven Approach. African Human Rights Yearbook. 2019;3:242; Ruppel O, (n 12) pp. 420–423; Boshoff E, (n 8) pp. 133–134.

46 *Ibid*, Article V(4).

47 2003 Revised African Convention on the Conservation of Nature and Natural Resources (adopted 11 July 2003, entered into force 23 July 2016) 7782 AU Treaties 0029, Article 3(1).

4.4 The Protection of the Climate System under the Right to a Healthy Environment

The ACHPR was pioneer in framing a standalone right to a healthy environment as a *human* right, and as a human right of *peoples*. According to Article 24 ACHPR, "All peoples shall have the right to a general satisfactory environment favorable to their development". This is in line with African understanding of human rights, which is based, on the one hand, on a perception of the environment's importance for the observance of peoples' religion and cultural practices and values[48] and, on the other hand, on the idea that human rights are not just crafted for the protection of the individual against the State, but also for securing the belongingness of the individual to a group.[49]

Before assessing how this provision can be used in the context of climate litigation, a few preliminary words are needed.

First, a "general satisfactory environment" is to be read as a synonym of a "healthy", "clean", or "safe" environment.[50] Nonetheless, there is no definition of "general satisfactory" or "environment" under Article 24 ACHPR. It is rather an open-textured notion, from which one can easily derive procedural obligations, while allowing the institutions of the African human rights system to clarify substantive obligations.[51] However, being climate change and the related events the result of GHG emissions (i.e., the result of a form of atmospheric pollution), they can easily be included in the concept of environment under this provision. In this line, the ECOWAS Court of Justice referred to the environment "as an indivisible whole", comprising the "biotic and abiotic natural resources, notably air, land, fauna and flora and the interaction between these same factors".[52] Additionally, the practice of the African Commission has highlighted climate change as an environmental problem,[53] therefore linking GHG emissions to Article 24 ACHPR. This first reference is key when bringing climate-related cases before the African Court or Commission: as Vilchez and Savaresi observed, autonomising a

48 Amechi EP, (n 15) p. 62; Baldé A. O Sistema Africano de Direitos Humanos e a Experiência dos Países Africanos de Língua Oficial Portuguesa. UCE Editora; 2017. p. 129; Murray R. The African Charter on Human and Peoples' Rights – A Commentary. Oxford University Press; 2019. p. 548.

49 M'baye K. Les droits de l'homme en Afrique. In: Vasak K, ed. Les dimensions internationales des droits de l'homme. UNESCO; 1978. pp. 645, 651.

50 *Social and Economic Rights Action Center (SERAC) and Center for Economic and Social Rights (CESR) v Nigeria*, Communication No. 155/96, Decision 27 October 2001, para. 52 ("*SERAC*"). See also Murray R, (n 48) p. 548.

51 Amechi EP, (n 15) pp. 64–65.

52 ECOWAS Court of Justice, *SERAP v Federal Republic of Nigeria*, Judgment No. ECW/CCJ/JUD/18/12 (14 December 2012), para. 100 ("*SERAP*").

53 E.g., African Commission, "Resolution on Climate Change in Africa" ACHPR/Res.271(LV)2014, adopted at the 55th Ordinary Session of the African Commission on Human and Peoples' Rights held in Luanda, Angola, from 28 April to 12 May 2014.

standalone right to a healthy environment increases the likelihood of obtaining a favorable ruling in the context of climate litigation.[54] As said, although African States are not major GHG emitters, they still hold mitigation obligations and, more importantly, they bear an obligation to adapt to a warmer climate system in order to protect their populations.[55]

Second, Article 24 ACHPR establishes a right of "peoples" instead of individuals. This explains why the leading case *SERAC*[56] was brought to the African Commission by the Ogoni people from Nigeria. Framing the right to a general satisfactory environment as a peoples' right is rooted in the African cosmovision and understanding of a just world order, where life is understood as being established in connection with Nature and in a shared and communal manner.[57] The ACHPR's drafters intentionally left the concept of people undefined,[58] allowing it to be defined on a case-by-case basis. Yet, the African Commission has advanced a definition of a people as being a

> a group of individuals having a common identity on account of objective markers of shared language, racial or ethnic makeup, historical experience, religious, cultural or ideological affinity, connection to a particular territory and the subjective manifestations of self-identification and awareness as a distinct group possessing of shared identity. Peoples are therefore not to be equated solely with "Nation" or "State", but include subnational groups including communities of a particular region exhibiting the above characteristics, or people whose resources are exploited under foreign occupation.[59]

54 Vilchez P, Savaresi A. The Right to a Healthy Environment and Climate Litigation: A Game Changer?. Yearbook of International Environmental Law. 2021;32:3.

55 Boshoff E, (n 8) p. 137.

56 *SERAC*, (n 50).

57 E.g., Baldé A, (n 48) p. 129; Boshoff E, (n 8) p. 131; Buys E, Lewis B. Environmental Protection through European and African Human Rights Frameworks. International Journal of Human Rights. 2022;26(6):949, 960; Amado Gomes C. Artigo 24.°. In: Jerónimo P, Garrido R & Pereira MA, eds. Comentário Lusófono à Carta Africana dos Direitos Humanos e dos Povos. Observatório Lusófono dos Direitos Humanos da Universidade do Minho; 2018. pp. 247, 251. Amado Gomes C. Direito ao Meio Ambiente na Carta Africana dos Direitos do Homem e dos Povos: Direito do Homem, Direito dos Povos ou *Tertium Genus*? In: Amado Gomes C, ed. Direito Internacional do Ambiente: Uma Abordagem Temática. AAFDL; 2018. pp. 97, 102; Moco M. Direitos Humanos e seus Mecanismos de Protecção – As Particularidades do Sistema Africano. Almedina; 2010. p. 171; Moeckli D, Shah S, Sivakumaran S. International Human Rights Law. 4th ed. Oxford University Press; 2022. p. 487; Mutua M, (n 16) pp. 82 ff.

58 See the Report of the Rapporteur of the OAU ministerial meeting on the draft African Charter on Human and Peoples' Rights held in Banjul, The Gambia, from 9 to 15 June 1980 [CAB/LEG/67/3/Draft Rapt. Rpt (II)] at 4.

59 African Commission, "State Reporting on Guidelines and Principles on Articles 21 and 24 of the African Charter relating to Extractive Industries and the Environment", at 11. See also

Plus, it has also stated that "the notion of "peoples" [in the ACHPR] is closely related to collective rights",[60] which squares well with a certain understanding of collective rights as being held by peoples or collectivities.[61] This factor can be seen as an opportunity in climate litigation. On the one hand, because climate change affects the way of living of indigenous communities, which is based on a greater connection with Nature and its cycles. This ultimately means that it might be easier to establish an infringement of an indigenous group right resulting from climate change, than with respect to an individual (where the causation link might be distant and more difficult to establish). It is not a coincidence that the environmental case-law of the IACtHR is largely based on the rights of indigenous peoples,[62] and one can hint that the same is valid in the African human rights system. On the other hand, this means also that the right to a general satisfactory environment is established not in an individuals-based perspective, but rather in the interest of, and protected by, the community (current and future). This helps in identifying a violation resulting from GHG emissions, and it allows a group qualifying as a people to file a communication against a State (in lieu of individuals).

Yet, communications filed by peoples face a variety of obstacles (e.g., who represents the people? What is the appropriate compensation to be awarded?). This helps to explain why the ECOWAS Court of Justice, in a case related to Article 24 ACHPR, asked the defendant State to establish "a collective benefit adequate to repair, as completely as possible, the collective harm that a violation of a collective right causes".[63] More concretely, it asked the defendant State to "Take all effective measures, within the shortest possible time, to ensure restoration of the environment of the Niger Delta; Take all measures that are necessary to prevent the occurrence of damage to the environment; [and] Take all measures to hold the perpetrators of the environmental damage accountable".[64] In the context of climate litigation, claims for compensation are becoming more frequent, but applicants mostly seek for the adoption and effective implementation of domestic policies aimed at reducing GHG emissions and adapting to the future impacts of climate change. As such, the record of the ECOWAS Court of Justice in relation to

---

Principles and Guidelines on the Implementation of Economic, Social and Cultural Rights in the African Charter on Human and Peoples' Rights, para. 1(c).

60 *Centre for Minority Rights Development (Kenya) and Minority Rights Group International on behalf of Endorois Welfare Council v Kenya*, Communication No. 276 / 2003, Decision 4 February 2010, para. 149.

61 Viljoen F. The African Charter on Human and Peoples' Rights: The *Travaux Préparatoires* in the Light of Subsequent Practice. Human Rights Law Journal. 2004;25(9–12):313, 317.

62 See, e.g., *Case of Indigenous Communities of the Lhaka Honhat (Our Land) Association v Argentina* (Merits, Reparations and Costs). IACtHR Series C No. 400 (6 February 2020). See, generally, Tigre MA. Climate Change and Indigenous Groups: The Rise of Indigenous Voices in Climate Litigation. e-Publica. 2022;9(3):214.

63 *SERAP*, (n 52) para. 116.

64 *Ibid*, para. 121.

compensation to peoples' rights is in line with the restorative goals of climate litigation.

Third, the wording of Article 24 ACHPR might refer to peoples instead of individuals, but the underlying grammar is also one of individuals' rights.[65] This idea is echoed in the *SERAP* ruling, where the ECOWAS Court of Justice stated that "The environment is essential to every human being," for "The quality of human life depends on the quality of the environment".[66] Thus, in the *Adou Kouame and Others v Côte d'Ivoire* case,[67] the ECOWAS Court of Justice applied Article 24 ACHPR in the context of individuals' complaints.

Fourth, Article 24 ACHPR conditions the right to a general satisfactory environment to the development of a people. The link between development and the environment is clear and can be perceived as both contributory (if environmental degradation is a necessary side effect for social and economic development) or remedial (if social and technological development advances awareness and the capacity to protect and preserve the environment).[68] The link, therefore, can be problematic, if priority is given to "development" in case of conflict with the "environment".[69] However, this reading was ruled out by the African Commission[70] and the ECOWAS Court of Justice,[71] to whom development and environmental protection require reciprocal reconciliation, but without an abstract a priori preference of one variable. This point is particularly relevant, since mitigation policies entail a high social and economic cost, and they can conflict with valued-based, political options aimed at promoting social and economic development within a State. If "development" (which is also presented as a human right under Article 22 ACHPR) would always prevail over the "environment", Article 24 ACHPR would be of no use, since there are infinite social and economic excuses not to adopt climate change policies. Thus, clarifying the need for reconciliation between both variables and the eventual preference of the environment in a specific case is key in climate litigation, where the major obstacles do not

65 Murray R, (n 48) 549.

66 *SERAP*, (n 52) para. 100.

67 ECOWAS Court of Justice, *Adou Kouame and Others v Cote d'Ivoire*, Judgment No. ECW/CCJ/JUD/46/23 (30 November 2023) ("*Kouame*").

68 Linde M, Louw L. Considering the Interpretation and Implementation of Article 24 of the African Charter on Human and Peoples' Rights in Light of the *SERAC* Communication. African Human Rights Law Journal. 2003;3:167, 176; Maluwa T. International Law in Post-colonial Africa. Brill Nijhoff; 1999. p. 307.

69 E.g., Atapattu S. The Right to a Healthy Life or the Right to Die Polluted?: The Emergence of a Human Right to a Healthy Environment Under International Law. Tulane Environmental Law Journal. 2002;16:65, 88; Churchill R. Environmental Rights in Existing Human Rights Treaties. In: Boyle AE, Anderson MR, eds. Human Rights Approaches to Environmental Protection. Oxford University Press; 1998. pp. 90, 106; Linde M, Louw L, (n 68) p. 176.

70 *SERAC*, (n 50) para. 54. See also Amechi EP, (n 15) 60–61; Linde M, Louw L, (n 68) p. 179.

71 ECOWAS Court of Justice, *African Network for Animal Welfare v The Attorney General of Tanzania*, Reference No. 9 of 2010 (20 June 2014) para. 82.

refer to qualifying GHG emissions as pollution, or stating an obligation to mitigate or adapt to climate change, but rather to balance the duty to adopt climate policies with the pursuit of other societal goals.

Having in mind these observations, one can now assess what obligations derive from Article 24 ACHPR, and what can be used in the context of climate litigation. On this matter, the African Commission was the first to contribute to the clarification of Article 24 ACHPR in *SERAC*. In this case – related to the exploitation of oil fields in Nigeria that caused severe health problems in individuals of the Ogoni ethnicity – the African Commission looked at the right to a general satisfactory environment as a justiciable right that can be used as a source of States' obligations.[72] To that end, the *SERAC* decision follows the methodology of classifying States' duties as being obligations to respect, protect, and fulfil.[73] The Commission further mentioned that the right to a general satisfactory environment "imposes clear obligations [...]. It requires the State to take reasonable and other measures to prevent pollution and ecological degradation, to promote conservation, and to secure an ecologically sustainable development and use of natural resources".[74] Implied, thus, is an obligation of due diligence subject to the African Court's and Commission's oversight. However, *SERAC* left unanswered the question related to the minimum threshold of pollution to trigger Article 24 ACHPR[75]; and was unable to flesh out in more detail States' obligations, except for listing procedural obligations and a generic substantive obligation to prevent environmental degradation,[76] probably because it was reluctant to step in in the making of value-based judgements more appropriate for other branches of the government. On this matter, the African Commission was more comfortable in saying that a general satisfactory environment is a necessary condition for the enjoyment of other human rights (as the right to health) and to rely thereafter on a basket of human rights to support its findings – which means that the African Commission would have reached the exact same conclusion

72 Linde M, Louw L, (n 68) p. 171; Nwobike C. The African Commission on Human and Peoples' Rights and the Demystification of Second and Third Generation Rights under the African Charter: Social and Economic Rights Action Center (SERAC) and the Center for Economic and Social Rights (CESR) v. Nigeria. African Journal of Legal Studies. 2005;1-2:129, 134–135; Oliveira H. Direitos Humanos e Proteção do Ambiente. In Duarte ML, Gil AR, Fidalgo de Freitas T, eds. Direitos Humanos e Estado de Direito – Proteção no Quadro Europeu e Internacional. AAFDL; 2022. pp. 769, 778; Rocha A, Oliveira H, (n 14) p. 33; Scholtz W. Human Rights and the Environment in the African Union Context. In: Grear A, Kotzé JL, eds. Research Handbook on Human Rights and the Environment. Elgar; 2015. pp. 401, 406.

73 Buys E, Lewis B, (n 57) p. 951. See also *Kouame*, (n 67) paras. 176–178.

74 *SERAC*, (n 50) para. 52.

75 Amechi EP, (n 15) p. 65. See also Scholtz W, (n 72) p. 405.

76 Addaney A, Moyo CG. Experiences from African Regional Human Rights Courts and Tribunals in the Protection of Environmental Rights. In: Addaney M, Jegede A, (n 12) pp. 187, 201; Linde M, Louw L, (n 68) p. 167.

regarding those facts irrespective of a standalone right to the environment in the ACHPR.[77] In addition, as the facts referred to a polluting factor tolerated or authorised by State authorities, but produced by non-State actors, the African Commission also confirmed the indirect horizontal effect of Article 24 ACHPR, therefore imposing an obligation upon the State to regulate, monitor, and control non-State actors' conduct. This point is also relevant in climate litigation, since most GHG emissions are private-sourced.[78]

Article 24 ACHPR was also clarified by the ECOWAS Court of Justice in *SERAP*, a case ruled in 2012 regarding the exact same facts. The ECOWAS Court of Justice said that Article 24 ACHPR includes not only obligations of means, but also obligations of results,[79] which is an audacious stance in the environmental law context. It stated that

> Article 24 of the Charter [...] requires every State to take every measure to maintain the quality of the environment understood as an integrated whole, such that the state of the environment may satisfy the human beings who live there, and enhance their sustainable development. It is by examining the state of the environment and entirely objective factors, that one judges, by the result, whether the State has fulfilled this obligation. If the State is taking all the appropriate legislative, administrative and other measures, it must ensure that vigilance and diligence are being applied and observed towards attaining concrete results.[80]

Because the road to hell is paved with good intentions, it also added that

> the adoption of the legislation, no matter how advanced it may be, or the creation of agencies inspired by the world's best models, as well as the allocation of financial resources in equitable amounts, may still fall short of compliance with international obligations in matters of environmental protection if these measures just remain on paper and are not accompanied by additional and concrete measures aimed at preventing the occurrence of damage or ensuring accountability, with the effective reparation of the environmental damage suffered.[81]

This, in other words, is the exact same idea mentioned by the ECtHR in *KlimaSeniorinnen* and ITLOS in the *COSIS Opinion*, where an emphasis was placed on the adoption and *effective* implementation of mitigation policies.

77 Gomes CA. Artigo 24.°, (n 57) p. 256; Direito, (n 57) p. 108; Linde M, Louw L, (n 68) p. 178; Lumina M. The Right to a Clean, Safe and Healthy Environment under the African Human Rights System. In: Addaney M, Jegede A, (n 12) pp. 25, 38; Rocha A, Oliveira H, (n 14) p. 34.
78 Boshoff E, (n 8) p. 138.
79 *SERAP*, (n 52) paras. 100–101.
80 *Ibid*, para. 101.
81 *Ibid*, para. 105.

This means that a legal argument before the African Court or Commission must be based on this idea also. These views were endorsed in *Kouame*, where the Court was more clear in referring to States' duty to regulate non-State actors' conduct.[82] Yet, it cannot pass unnoticed that the ECOWAS Court of Justice also looked to Article 24 ACHPR as synthetising entitlements related to other human rights, such as the rights to life or health[83]; and it failed to flesh out in detail the content of States' substantive obligations in relation to climate change.

In this scenario, Article 24 ACPHR is conceived of as very broad, although apparently it has been used linked only to other ACHPR's provisions.[84] It includes varied obligations to respect, protect, and fulfil the right to general satisfactory environment, which includes the obligation to conserve and ameliorate the state of the environment,[85] and to protect peoples and individuals against the conduct of non-State actors and against natural disasters (including those resulting from climate change). However, the exact content of these obligations and the threshold of relevance of environmental factors are yet to be clarified by the institutions of the African human rights system.[86] In any case, the wording of Article 24 ACHPR and the findings of the African Commission and the ECOWAS Court of Justice allow us to agree with Jegede in saying that a right to a safe climate can be derived from Article 24 ACHPR,[87] hand in hand with the corresponding obligations to protect the stability of the climate, namely to regulate and effectively implement a regulatory framework targeting non-State actors' conduct linked to GHG emissions.

In this context, some efforts can be particularly important. *First*, a set of initiatives at a regional level, although mostly agnostic to human rights, put climate change atop of public policies priorities – including the 2009 Decision on the African Common Position on Climate Change,[88] the African

82 *Kouame*, (n 67) para. 225.
83 Gomes CA. Artigo 24.°, (n 57) p. 257; Direito, (n 57) p. 109.
84 In this context of the East African Community, however, the protection of the environment seems to have gained traction outside the scope of a human right to a healthy environment. See *African Network for Animal Welfare (ANAW) v The Attorney General of the United Republic of Tanzania* (Reference No. 9 of 2010), Judgment of 20 June 2014.
85 *SERAC*, (n 50) para. 52. Although the African Commission did not elaborate more on this notion, it can be part of a key legal argument in relation to adaptation and resilience building to cope with the consequences of climate change. For instance, protecting, preserving, and ameliorating the state of coastal ecosystems can be an important policy in order to deal with sea level rise and coastal erosion, the same way that the protection of ecosystems that are an integral part of a specific water cycle can be an important element to protect riparian ecosystems and populations. Therefore, the lack of adoption and effective implementation of such policies, with a view of adapting to climate change, can be considered as an infringement of Article 24 ACHPR.
86 E.g., Linde M, Louw L, (n 68) p. 179.
87 Jegede A, (n 12) pp. 62 ff. See also Ruppel O, (n 12) p. 418.
88 See Doc Assembly/AU/8(XII) Add.6 (3 February 2009).

Union Nairobi Declaration on the African Process for Combating Climate Change,[89] the 2014 African Union Draft Continental Strategy on Climate Change, the 2015 African Adaptation Initiative, and the African Union Climate Change and Resilient Development Strategy and Action Plan (2022–2032)[90] – and set out a possible pattern of "regionalisation"[91] of climate change action, thus building an autonomous framework of African States in relation to the Global South as a whole.[92] *Second*, a set of resolutions adopted by the African Commission in 2009,[93] 2014,[94] and 2016[95] highlighted the need for cooperation to achieve a strong, committed, and comprehensive climate action that secures human rights to the greatest extent possible, for current and future generations; requested States to adopt and implement special measures for the protection of vulnerable groups and victims of natural disasters, while emphasising that the implementation of the UNFCCC and the Paris Agreement should reflect the African perspective on human and peoples' rights and that African standards for the protection of the environment, management of natural resources, and human and peoples' rights are consistent with the UNFCCC; but also expressing concern with the detrimental consequences of climate change in Africa.[96] And *third*, as a result of these resolutions, a study group was constituted and eventually produced the Zero Draft Report (Study on the Impact of Climate Change on Human and Peoples' Rights in Africa), which has not been adopted formally yet, but which identified key issues and gaps in the protection of human rights in Africa in the context of climate change.

Although these instruments are non-binding, they also assist in the reading of Article 24 ACHPR and in linking climate change to the protection of human rights in Africa.

4.5 The Protection of the Climate System under Other Human Rights

As seen in the environmental cases brought before the African Commission and the ECOWAS Court of Justice, these bodies relied as much on Article 24 ACHPR as on other human rights. In fact, as human rights are indivisible,

89 Nairobi Declaration on the African Process for Combating Climate Change, ALLAFRICA (29 May 2009).

90 African Union Climate Change and Resilient Development Strategy and Action Plan (2022-2032). [Accessed 27 January 2025]. Available from: https://au.int/sites/default/files/documents/41959-doc-CC_Strategy_and_Action_Plan_2022-2032_08_02_23_Single_Print_Ready.pdf.

91 Murray R, (n 48) p. 555; Scholtz W, (n 12) p. 8.

92 Scholtz W, (n 12) pp. 7 ff.

93 See Doc ACHPR/Res.153(XLVI)09 (25 November 2009).

94 See Doc ACHPR/Res.271(LV)2014 (11 May 2014).

95 See Doc ACHPR/Res153 (XLVI) 09 (20 April 2016).

96 *Ibid*, Preamble, paras. 6, 7, 9.

interrelated, and interdependent,[97] and as a healthy environment is a pre-condition for the enjoyment of human rights, environmental values can be protected under non-environmental human rights. This is the very meaning of the "greening" of human rights[98] and this explains why the "environment" has been more frequent in the case law of the institutions of the African human rights system than the use of Article 24 ACHPR itself.[99]

A prime example is the *Endorois* case, also referring to Indigenous groups' rights to the enjoyment of their lands in certain environmental conditions appropriate for upholding their culture, traditions, and way of living, where applicants brought environmental concerns under the umbrella of other human rights.[100] Another example is the *Ogiek* case, where Article 24 ACHPR was not invoked, but the African Court

> note[d] that, in the context of traditional societies [...] the practice and profession of religion are usually *inextricably linked with land and the environment*. In indigenous societies in particular, the freedom to worship and to engage in religious ceremonies depends on access to land and the natural environment. Any impediment to, or interference with accessing the natural environment, including land, severely constrains their ability to conduct or engage in religious rituals with considerable repercussion on the enjoyment of their freedom of worship.[101]

The link between the environment, on the one hand, and the effective enjoyment of economic, social, and cultural rights, on the other hand, was highlighted in the Principles and Guidelines produced by the African Commission to assist States in the observance of their obligations under the ACHPR. To that end, the Commission specifically referred to the link with the right to *health* (protected under Article 16 ACHPR), as States have to "Ensure that national development plans and programmes are designed towards the realisation of a healthy environment that is conducive to the right to health, for example

97 In the *Kouame* case, the ECOWAS Court of Justice referred that the right to health is closely linked to the environment, whilst also referring that a healthy environment is an important condition for individuals' quality of life and safety, (n 67, paras. 186, 191). This also explains why Article 12(2)(b) ICESCR includes health and environment in one single provision (Nwobike C, [n 72] p. 137).

98 Dupuy P-M, Viñuales J. International Environmental Law. 2nd ed. Cambridge University Press; 2018. p. 374; Rocha A, Oliveira H, (n 14) p. 34.

99 Murray R, (n 48) pp. 549, 550.

100 Communication 276/03, *Centre for Minority Rights Development (Kenya) and Minority Rights Group (on behalf of Endorois Welfare Council) v Kenya*, Communication No. 276/03, Decision 25 May 2009.

101 *African Commission on Human and Peoples' Rights v Republic of Kenya* (App. No. 006/2012) African Court of Human and Peoples' Rights (Judgment, 26 May 2017) para. 164 (emphasis added).

in matters relating to water resources management and sanitation"[102]; the right to *education* (protected under Article 17 ACHPR), which is perceived as "ha[ving] a vital role in ... protecting the environment",[103] and thus States bear the obligation "To ensure that education systems are directed towards ... the development of respect for the environment and natural resources"[104]; the right to *housing* (protected under Articles 14, 16, and 18(1) ACHPR), which includes the obligation to "Take measures to ensure that women (...), internally displaced persons, refugees, indigenous communities/populations and other members of vulnerable and disadvantaged groups are guaranteed equal access to land, adequate housing or shelter and to acceptable living conditions in a healthy environment"[105]; the right to *food* (protected under Articles 4, 16, and 22 ACHPR), which forces States to "Ensure that all persons are able to feed themselves directly through environmentally, economically and socially sustainable methods from productive land or other natural resources"[106]; and the right to *water and sanitation* (protected under Articles 4, 5, 15, 16, 22, and 24 AfrCHPR), according to which "Everyone has the right to have access to adequate and safe sanitation that is conducive to the protection of public health and the environment".[107]

The effective enjoyment of all these human rights is (likely to be) affected by climate change–related events, meaning that the lack of adoption of measures aimed at protecting or securing these human rights against climate change–related events amounts to a breach of a State's obligations under the ACHPR. This was specifically mentioned by the Commission in relation to the right to health, namely by referring to States' obligation to "Protect individuals and peoples against environmental [...] hazards [...] and alleviating the adverse effects of [...] global warming on ecosystems, livelihood and food security".[108]

Yet, the detrimental effects of climate change threatens the effective enjoyment of the full gamut of human rights,[109] including the rights to life, physical integrity, private and family life, non-discrimination, self-determination, or to cultural identity. In other words, States bear an obligation to protect the stability of the climate system and, thereby, to mitigate and adapt to climate change, under the so-called civil and political rights *and* the economic, social,

102 "Principles and Guidelines on the Implementation of Economic, Social and Cultural Rights in the African Charter on Human and Peoples' Rights", 24 October 2011, para. 67(q).
103 *Ibid*, para. 69.
104 *Ibid*, para. 71(f)(6).
105 *Ibid*, para. 79(p).
106 *Ibid*, para. 86(g).
107 *Ibid*, para. 91.
108 *Ibid*, para. 67(s). See also *SERAC,* (n 50) paras. 52-53.
109 E.g., Addaney M, Boshoff E, Olutola B, (n 12) pp. 9 ff.

and cultural rights. This, in fact, was an approach *also* followed in *SERAC* and *SERAP*.[110]

The best case to exemplify this point is the right to life. In fact, the reports produced by the Intergovernmental Panel on Climate Change are clear, linking between extreme weather events (which are increasing in terms of frequency, duration, and intensity) and the loss of life, especially for vulnerable individuals, groups, and communities.[111] Life on a warmer planet is just more challenging for human beings and ever-more challenging for those who do not have the means to adapt and mitigate the risk. Thereby, the scale and harms related to climate change suggest that it is best understood under the lenses of the right to life. On this matter, the right to life is not just about a negative obligation not to take one's life: it also includes positive obligations to protect human life (e.g., against non-State actors' conduct or in case of natural disasters) and policies aimed at securing a life with dignity. In this sense, it envisages broad protection against any factor (such as GHG emissions or climate change) that may entail an unnatural or premature death of an individual. The right to life, therefore, entails a State's due diligence obligation to take the appropriate measures at its disposal in order to fulfil the right to life.

This picture was captured by the African Commission in the *General Comment* No. *3* (on the right to life), where it took the view that "the Charter envisages the protection not only of life in a narrow sense, but of dignified life. This requires a broad interpretation of States' responsibilities to protect life. Such actions extend to preventive steps to preserve and protect the natural environment. [...] Such an approach reflects the Charter's ambition to ensure a better life for all the people and peoples of Africa through its recognition of a wide range of rights, including the right to dignity".[112] In addition, the Commission also added that "The right to life should be interpreted broadly. The State has a positive duty to protect individuals and groups from real and immediate risks to their lives caused either by actions or inactions of third parties. [...] Such actions include, inter alia, preventive steps to preserve and protect the natural environment".[113] The link with the environment was made explicit by the African Commission and can easily incorporate the climate change–related risks to life.

110 Addaney M, Moyo CG, (n 76) p. 201; Linde M, Louw L, (n 68) p. 178; Lumina M, (n 77) p. 38; Nwobike C, (n 72) pp. 139–140; Scholtz W, (n 72) p. 406.

111 IPCC. Climate Change 2022: Impacts, Adaptation and Vulnerability. Contribution of Working Group II to the Sixth Assessment Report of the Intergovernmental Panel on Climate Change. IPCC; 2022. pp. 18, 50.

112 African Commission, *General Comment* No. *3 on the African Charter of Human and Peoples' Rights: The Right to Life (Article 4)*, 12 December 2015, para. 3.

113 *Ibid*, para. 41.

4.6 Conclusion

Pursuant to the ACHPR, States bear an *ex ante facto* responsibility for protecting and fulfilling the human rights of peoples and individuals against any form of environmental risk, which therefore includes the detrimental consequences of climate change.[114] This obligation derives from Article 24 ACHPR, but also from other provisions of the ACHPR that establish mainstream human rights. In fact, the different human rights protected in the African system (including those from sources other than the ACHPR) are not to be seen as alternative or exclusionary, but rather as concurrent and mutually reinforcing in the protection of peoples and individuals against the detrimental effects of climate change. Therefore, climate litigation before regional bodies in Africa (i.e., the African Court or Commission, the ECOWAS Court of Justice, or the EAC Court of Justice) is likely to rely on multiple human rights under the ACHPR and other regional treaties, including but not exclusive of the right to the environment. However, the lack of human and financial resources, the unclear domestic regulatory framework, the slow pace of courts' proceedings, the legal culture of States, or entrenched economic interests – in addition to the need to exhaust domestic remedies and a different cultural perception of human rights priorities in Africa – explain the difficult path lying ahead for climate litigation in Africa. In this scenario, resorting to an advisory opinion might be a way out to get some form of clarification on what are States' obligations under the ACHPR to mitigate and adapt to climate change.

References

Addaney A, Moyo CG. Experiences from African regional human rights courts and tribunals in the protection of environmental rights. In: Addaney M, Jegede A, editors. Human rights and the environment under African Union law. Springer; 2020:5–28.

Addaney M, Boshoff E, Olutola B. The climate change and human rights nexus in Africa. Amst Law Forum. 2017;9(3).

Addaney M, Jegede A, Matinda M. The protection of climate refugees under the African human rights system: proposing a value-driven approach. Afr Hum Rights Yearb. 2019;3:242–259.

Amado Gomes C. Artigo 24.°. In: Jerónimo P, Garrido R, Pereira MA, editors. Comentário lusófono à Carta Africana dos Direitos Humanos e dos Povos. Braga: Observatório Lusófono dos Direitos Humanos da Universidade do Minho; 2018.

Amado Gomes C. Direito ao meio ambiente na Carta Africana dos Direitos do Homem e dos Povos: Direito do homem, direito dos povos ou tertium genus? In: Amado Gomes C, editor. Direito internacional do ambiente: Uma abordagem temática. Lisboa: AAFDL; 2018.

Amechi EP. Enhancing environmental protection and socio-economic development in Africa: a fresh look at the right to a general satisfactory environment under the African charter on human and peoples' rights. Law Environ Dev J. 2009;5(1):58–72.

114 Addaney M, Boshoff E, Olutola B, (n 12) p. 12.

Atapattu S. The right to a healthy life or the right to die polluted?: the emergence of a human right to a healthy environment under international law. Tulane Environ Law J. 2002;16:65–126.

Baldé A. O sistema africano de direitos humanos e a experiência dos países africanos de língua oficial portuguesa. Lisbon: UCE Editora; 2017.

Boshoff E. The prospects and challenges of litigating climate change before African regional human rights bodies. In: Bouwer K, Etemire U, Field T-L, Jegede AO, editors. Climate litigation and justice in Africa. Bristol: Bristol University Press; 2024.

Bouwer K, Field T-L. Editorial: the emergence of climate litigation in Africa. Carbon Clim Law Rev. 2021;15(2):123–128.

Buys E, Lewis B. Environmental protection through European and African human rights frameworks. Int J Hum Rights. 2022;26(6):949–977.

Chenwi L. The advisory proceedings of the African court on human and peoples' rights. Nordic J Hum Rights. 2020;38:61–77.

Churchill R. Environmental rights in existing human rights treaties. In: Boyle AE, Anderson MR, editors. Human rights approaches to environmental protection. Oxford: Oxford University Press; 1998.

Donnelly J, Whelan DJ. International human rights. 6th ed. London: Routledge; 2020.

Dupuy P-M, Viñuales J. International environmental law. 2nd ed. Cambridge: Cambridge University Press; 2018.

Fokala E, Muhumuza N. Eroding children's rights: an analysis of the utility of the African Charter on the Rights and Welfare of the Child to climate action in Africa. In: Fokala N, Assim U, Murungi N, editors. The social, economic and cultural rights of children in Africa – Challenges and reflections from the perspective of the African Charter on the Rights and Welfare of the Child. Leiden: Brill; 2025.

IPCC. Climate change 2022: impacts, adaptation and vulnerability: contribution of working group II to the sixth assessment report of the intergovernmental panel on climate change. Geneva: IPCC; 2022.

Jegede A. Should a human right to a safe climate be recognized under the AU human rights system? In: Addaney M, Jegede A, editors. Human rights and the environment under African Union law. Springer; 2020.

Linde M, Louw L. Considering the interpretation and implementation of Article 24 of the African charter on human and peoples' rights in light of the SERAC communication. Afr Hum Rights Law J. 2003;3:167–187.

Lumina M. The right to a clean, safe and healthy environment under the African human rights system. In: Addaney M, Jegede A, editors. Human rights and the environment under African Union law. Springer; 2020.

Lupin D, Nekura R. An advisory opinion on human rights and climate change in the African regional human rights system. In: Tigre MA, Rocha A, editors. The role of advisory opinions in international law in the context of the climate crisis. Forthcoming.

M'baye K. Les droits de l'homme en Afrique. In: Vasak K, editor. Les dimensions internationales des droits de l'homme. Paris: UNESCO; 1978.

Maluwa T. International law in post-colonial Africa. Leiden: Brill Nijhoff; 1999.

Moco M. Direitos humanos e seus mecanismos de protecção – As particularidades do sistema africano. Coimbra: Almedina; 2010.

Moeckli D, Shah S, Sivakumaran S. International human rights law. 4th ed. Oxford: Oxford University Press; 2022.

Murray R. The African Charter on Human and Peoples' Rights – A commentary. Oxford: Oxford University Press; 2019.

Mutua M. African human rights system: a critical evaluation. Prepared for United Nations Development Programme, Human Development Report; 2000.
Mutua M. Human rights – A political and cultural critique. Philadelphia: University of Pennsylvania Press; 2002.
Nwobike C. The African commission on human and peoples' rights and the demystification of second and third generation rights under the African Charter: Social and Economic Rights Action Center (SERAC) and the Center for Economic and Social Rights (CESR) v. Nigeria. Afr J Leg Stud. 2005;1–2:129–146.
Odinkalu CA. Advice without consent? Assessing the advisory jurisdiction of the African Court on Human and Peoples' Rights. Hum Rights Q. 2023;45:365–405.
Oliveira H. Direitos humanos e proteção do ambiente. In: Duarte ML, Gil AR, Fidalgo de Freitas T, editors. Direitos humanos e estado de direito – Proteção no quadro europeu e internacional. Lisboa: AAFDL; 2022.
Rocha A, Oliveira H. Fundamental rights and human rights. In: Amado Gomes C, Oliveira H, Perestrelo de Oliveira M, editors. A treatise on environmental law. Vol. III. Environmental law and other legal fields. Lisbon: Lisbon Public Law Editions; 2024.
Ruppel O. Climate change law and policy positions in the African Union and related developments in selected African countries. In: Ruppel O, Roschmann C, Ruppel-Schlichting K, editors. Climate change: international law and global governance. Vol. II. Policy, diplomacy and governance in a changing environment. Baden-Baden: Nomos; 2013.
Scholtz W. Human rights and the environment in the African Union context. In: Grear A, Kotzé JL, editors. Research handbook on human rights and the environment. Cheltenham: Edward Elgar; 2015.
Scholtz W. The promotion of regional environmental security and Africa's common position on climate change. Afr Hum Rights Law J. 2010;10:1–25.
Setzer J, Higham C. Global trends in climate change litigation: 2024 snapshot. London: Grantham Research Institute on Climate Change and the Environment & Centre for Climate Change Economics and Policy; 2024. Vol. 2.
Smith R. International human rights law. 10th ed. Oxford: Oxford University Press; 2022.
Suedi Y, Fall M. Climate change litigation before the African human rights system: prospects and pitfalls. J Hum Rights Pract. 2024;16:146–159.
Tigre MA. Climate change and indigenous groups: the rise of indigenous voices in climate litigation. e-Publica. 2022;9(3):214–260.
Trisos C, Adelekan IO, Totin E, coords. Africa. In: Pörtner H-O, Roberts DC, Tignor MMB, Poloczanska E, Mintenbeck K, Alegría A, Craig M, Langsdorf S, Löschke S, Möller V, Okem A, Rama B, editors. Climate change 2022: impacts, adaptation and vulnerability: contribution of working group II to the sixth assessment report of the intergovernmental panel on climate change. Cambridge: Cambridge University Press; 2022.
Van der Mei AP. The advisory jurisdiction of the African court on human and peoples' rights. Afr Hum Rights Law J. 2005;5: 27–46.
Viljoen F. The African charter on human and peoples' rights: the travaux préparatoires in the light of subsequent practice. Hum Rights Law J. 2004;25(9–12):313–326.

5 Climate Litigation before the Court of Justice of the European Union

A Quantitative and Qualitative Review of Features and Legal Grounds

Heloísa Oliveira, Ana Ruiz, and Pedro Sampaio Minassa

5.1 Introduction

Although climate litigation is a global legal phenomenon, it was, until recently, almost exclusively confined to domestic courts. As detailed in other chapters of this book, only now are international courts[1] being called upon to decide cases or issue advisory opinions on climate change and international law – including human rights courts, despite having more permissive rules of access than most international courts.

As this chapter aims to demonstrate, the Court of Justice of the European Union ("CJEU")[2] is a notorious exception to this claim. The first climate cases were brought before the CJEU in 2001, and a total of 196 cases are registered to date.[3] In fact, even when considering non-judicial adjudicative bodies in the United Nations system, such as committees and other dispute settlement entities, climate litigation before the CJEU accounts for the vast majority of all international climate litigation.[4]

1 In this claim, we refer to courts *stricto sensu*, thus excluding non-judicial bodies and arbitration tribunals. For a more detailed view of climate cases before international courts and bodies, cf. Setzer J, Higham C. Global Trends in Climate Change Litigation; 2024 Snapshot. 16–17.

2 Article 19 (1) of the Treaty on European Union determines that the CJEU includes the Court of Justice, the General Court, and specialised courts. This chapter refers to cases brought before the Court of Justice and the General Court, since no climate cases have been brought before the only specialised court created to date (Civil Service Tribunal). When mentioning the CJEU, we are referring to both courts.

3 This number differs significantly from the number of cases (75) currently registered at the Sabin Center Climate Case Chart (climatecasechart.com/). The research methodology and criteria for filtering climate cases are explained in section 2.1.

4 Even when considering only the cases registered in the Sabin Center Climate Case Chart, CJEU climate cases accounted for half of all international cases, including those before non-judicial bodies – cf. Setzer J, Higham C. Global Trends in Climate Change Litigation: 2024 Snapshot. London: Grantham Research Institute on Climate Change and the Environment, London School of Economics and Political Science; 2024. p. 2.

DOI: 10.4324/9781003540977-7

An explanation for this scenario is so obvious that it can be provided in an introductory section. While it is true that the CJEU is an international court, created under international law and with strict access rules, it is also an uncontested assertion that European Union ("EU") law is an autonomous "*legal order of international law [...] and the subjects of which comprise not only the Member States but also their nationals*",[5] creating an "*independent source of law*" of a "special and original nature".[6] As EU law imposes strict and enforceable legal obligations on states and has a direct impact on citizens and companies, early judicial action was to be expected. Additionally, the expansion in quantity and depth of EU secondary law concerned with or related to climate change is unmatched by international law, creating a vast and diverse array of legal grounds and contexts for climate cases.[7] As a result, the early emergence of climate cases before the CJEU – either directly by States and private parties or through national courts via preliminary ruling proceedings – is unsurprising. Although judicial activism accusations have been made against the CJEU's case law on European integration, analyses made regarding a few climate cases[8] reveal a rather conservative, self-restrained standpoint by the Court, possibly undermining what could be its potential role in addressing modern complex issues. In fact, CJEU climate judgments have primarily focused on formal aspects, such as competence and standing, which, while relevant at a constitutional level, fail to address substantive climate challenges.[9] This conclusion is evident when examining the first 15 years of EU climate cases. However, a comprehensive and updated

5 As ruled in the landmark *NV Algemene Transport- en Expeditie Onderneming van Gend & Loos v Netherlands Inland Revenue Administration*, Judgement of the Court of Justice of the European Economic Community of 5 February 1963, Case 26/62.

6 As ruled in the landmark *Flaminio Costa v E.N.E.L*, Judgement of the Court of Justice of the European Economic Community of 15 April 1964, Case 6/64.

7 This growth of EU climate legislation is accelerating and brings new grounds for climate cases, as pointed out by Higham C et al. Climate Change Law in Europe. What Do New EU Climate Laws Mean for the Courts? London: Grantham Research Institute on Climate Change and the Environment and Centre for Climate Change Economics and Policy, London School of Economics and Political Science, 2023. pp. 11–27.

8 Garben S. The CJEU and Climate (in)Activism? Edward Elgar Publishing; 2024. pp. 247–268. Stoczkiewicz M. The Role of the Courts in EU Climate Policy. Cheltenham, UK: Edward Elgar Publishing; 2023. pp. 131–134. Peeters M, Misonne D. The European Union and Its Rule-Creating Force on the European Continent for Moving to Climate Neutrality by 2050 at the Latest. In: In: Reins L, Verschuuren J, eds. Research Handbook on Climate Change Mitigation Law. Edward Elgar Publishing; 2022. pp. 90–94. Available from: https://www.elgaronline.com/edcollbook/book/9781839101595/9781839101595.xml.

9 Bogojević S. EU Climate Change Litigation: All Quiet on the Luxembourgian Front?. In: Van Calster G et al., eds. Research Handbook on Climate Change Mitigation Law. Edward Elgar Publishing; 2015. pp. 545–559. Available from: https://china.elgaronline.com/edcollbook/edcoll/9781849803809/9781849803809.xml. Campins Eritja M. The European Union and Climate Change Litigation: Promising Much but Delivering Little? In: Sindico F et al., eds. Research Handbook on Climate Change Litigation. Edward Elgar Publishing; 2024. p. 372.

analysis of these cases – considering their legal grounds, objects, goals, and actors – is still missing in legal literature.

This chapter presents a systematised review of all CJEU climate cases. We begin with an overview of climate litigation before the CJEU (section 2), including a quantitative and qualitative review considering core themes, types of proceedings, outcomes, and actors. We then proceed to an in-depth examination of the most relevant legal grounds in climate cases (section 3), starting with ETS cases, given their significance in EU climate law, followed by non-ETS cases, exploring the increasing diversification of legal acts and issues involved. Finally, we present some concluding remarks.

5.2 Climate Litigation before the CJEU: An Overview

5.2.1 Methodology

In order to provide an overview of climate litigation before the CJEU, we conducted a quantitative and qualitative review of all existing – closed or pending – cases. The adopted methodology was as follows:

i. A compilation was made of all cases referenced as climate-related according to EuroVoc Thesaurus descriptors in EUR-Lex[10] or referring to climate change as delivered by the search form of the CJEU.
ii. Cases that did not concern the validity, interpretation, or application of climate-relevant laws (e.g., cases concerning combustion installations where GHG emissions were entirely irrelevant to the pleas and decision) were excluded. The concept of "climate-relevant laws" encompasses all legal acts with a clear material link with climate change (e.g., renewable energy, emissions trading scheme) or with other laws applied in a climate-relevant case (e.g., participatory rights or public procurement rules in the implementation of climate-relevant laws).
iii. Cases that were closed without a decision on the merits or admissibility (e.g., cases that were withdrawn or declared as no longer requiring a decision) were excluded.
iv. Duplicates (e.g., separate registrations of first-instance decisions and appeal decisions, since they refer to the same case) were eliminated.
v. Cases that were individually filed were registered separately, even when a joint decision was delivered.
vi. The remaining cases (196) were categorised according to eight criteria: year, type of proceedings, ETS or non-ETS, predominant area, decision on merits or admissibility, applicable EU legal acts, climate-friendly

10 For more information on the EuroVoc Thesaurus descriptors, cf. the European Commission's Science Hub section on Language and Technology Resources. Available from: https://joint-research-centre.ec.europa.eu.

outcomes,[11] and the type of party who initiated the case.[12] Due to their quantitative relevance and specific features, ETS cases were separated and not treated together with the other GHG reduction cases.

The aggregated results will be presented in the following section. The case law database that underpins this analysis and provides full references to all cases is fully accessible for the purpose of verifiability and replicability.[13]

5.2.2 A Qualitative and Quantitative Review

A comprehensive analysis of EU climate cases indicates that climate litigation before the CJEU has been steadily rising, albeit with significant yearly variation (cf. Figure 1). Regarding legal grounds, the majority of climate cases before the CJEU (110 out of 196) have the EU Emissions Trading Scheme ("ETS") as their exclusive theme, while a large minority (81) do not address the ETS at all. A small subset of cases (5) deals equally with both ETS and non-ETS issues. However, the focus has gradually shifted, with a growing number of cases addressing other legal acts since 2009. Since 2016, the majority of cases (66 out of 108) have focused exclusively on non-ETS legal issues, dealing with a diverse set of legal acts. This trend appears similar to domestic climate-related litigation, where an initial sharp increase in cases has now been followed by a deceleration in new filings but a broadening of legal grounds.[14]

A notable feature of climate litigation before the CJEU is that it was initially – and remains primarily – driven by companies, which started 136 out of 196 cases. Civil society played no role in climate litigation until the filing of the 2018 *Carvalho* case,[15] also known as *The People's Climate Case*. This case served as a stepping stone for climate litigation brought by civil society;

11 Categorised as positive, negative, or undetermined climate-friendly outcomes. An undetermined climate-friendly outcome can refer to four possibilities: (i) lack of information on the context of the case for a definitive assessment; (ii) both positive and negative outcomes that could not be balanced definitively; (iii) neutral effect due to the specific legal issues raised in the case.

12 Considering the existing cases, current subjects are companies, Member States, civil society (encompassing citizens and non-governmental organisations), municipalities, and the European Commission. When referring to a preliminary ruling, we considered who brought the case to the domestic court.

13 The database is available at https://lisbonpubliclaw.pt/en/lisbon-environmental-law/databases. The Climate Litigation Observatory database is an open science research output of the Lisbon Environmental Law cluster at the Lisbon Public Law Research Center, funded by FCT – Fundação para a Ciência e a Tecnologia, I.P. through national funds under UIDB/04310/2020 and UIDP/04310/2020.

14 Cf. Setzer J, Higham C, (n 4) p. 2.

15 *Carvalho and Others v Parliament and Council*, Order of the General Court of 8 May 2019, Case T-330/10, and Judgement of the Court of Justice of the European Union of 25 March 2021, Case 565/19 P.

since then, 21 additional cases have been filed by citizens and non-governmental organisations, representing a quarter of all cases.

A qualitative analysis of all cases (cf. Table 5.1) allows for the discovery of three separate phases in EU climate litigation:

(i) The early years of litigation (2001–2008), focused almost exclusively on the ETS and were dominated by a triangle of actors: companies, Member States, and the EU Commission (28 cases in total, with an average of 3.5 new cases per year).
(ii) An intermediate phase (2009–2015), still largely centred on ETS-related claims, increasingly addresses typical environmental issues, such as conflicting sustainability goals (especially in the energy transition) and participatory rights, and now including cases brought by municipalities (63 cases in total, with an average of nine new cases per year).
(iii) A third phase (2016–present), marked by a broader range of legal claims, where ETS topics have a relevant but frequently secondary relevance, the emerging leadership of citizens and non-governmental organisations, and the introduction of fundamental rights claims (108 cases in total, with an average of 12 cases per year).

Table 5.1 Climate Cases Brought before the CJEU, according to Type of Proceedings, Core Theme, Originating Entity, and Type of Decision

Year	*Cases*	*Type of Proceedings*	*Core Theme*	*Brought by*	*Decision on*
2001	1	Preliminary Ruling (1)	Public Procurement (1)	Company (1)	Merits (1)
2004	4	Annulment (4)	ETS (4)	Company (3) Member State (1)	Admissibility (2) Merits (2)
2005	3	Failure to Fulfil Obligations (2) Annulment (1)	ETS (3)	EU Commission (2) Member State (1)	Merits (3)
2006	2	Annulment (1) Annulment + Damages (1)	ETS (1)	Company (2)	Admissibility (1) Merits (1)
2007	17	Annulment (16) Preliminary Ruling (1)	ETS (17)	Company (13) Member State (4)	Admissibility (12) Merits (5)
2008	1	Annulment (1)	ETS (1)	Company (1)	Merits (1)
2009	4	Preliminary Ruling (2) Annulment (1) Failure to Fulfil Obligations (1)	ETS + Participatory Rights (2) ETS (1) GHG Emissions (1)	Municipality (2) Company (1) EU Commission (1)	Merits (4)
2010	2	Preliminary Ruling (2)	Energy (1) ETS (1)	Company (2)	Merits (2)
2011	9	Preliminary Ruling (6) Annulment (3)	ETS (9)	Company (8) Member State (1)	Merits (7) Admissibility (2)
2012	6	Preliminary Ruling (4) Damages (1) Annulment (1)	Energy (3) ETS (2) Participatory rights (1)	Companies (6)	Merits (6)

(*Continued*)

Table 5.1 (Continued)

Year	*Cases*	*Type of Proceedings*	*Core Theme*	*Brought by*	*Decision on*
2013	9	Annulment (7) Preliminary Ruling (2)	ETS (7) ETS + Participatory rights (1) Energy (1)	Companies (8) EU Commission (1)	Merits (8) Admissibility (1)
2014	16	Preliminary Ruling (13) Annulment (2) Failure to Fulfil Obligations (1)	ETS (13) GHG Emissions (2) Energy (1)	Company (14) Member State (1) EU Commission (1)	Merits (15) Admissibility (1)
2015	15	Preliminary Ruling (14) Annulment (1)	ETS (13) Energy (2)	Company (13) Member State (2)	Merits (15)
2016	13	Preliminary Ruling (7) Annulment (5) Failure to Fulfil Obligations (1)	GHG Emissions (4) Energy (4) ETS (3) ETS + Energy (1) Mobility – Public Funding (1)	Companies (8) Municipalities (3) Member State (1) EU Commission (1)	Merits (9) Admissibility (4)
2017	6	Preliminary Ruling (5) Annulment (1)	ETS (4) GHG Emissions (1) Energy (1)	Company (5) Member State (1)	Merits (6)
2018	7	Preliminary Ruling (4) Annulment (3)	GHG Emission Reduction (7)	Member States (4) Company (2) Civil Society (1)	Merits (5) Admissibility (2)
2019	14	Annulment (8) Preliminary Ruling (6)	GHG Emissions (6) Energy (3) ETS (4) ETS + Fundamental Rights (1)	Company (11) Civil society (3)	Merits (12) Admissibility (2)
2020	15	Preliminary Ruling (9) Annulment (5) Failure to Fulfil Obligations (1)	ETS (10) GHG Emissions (4) Taxes (1)	Company (11) Civil society (2) EU Commission (2)	Merits (9) Admissibility (6)
2021	8	Preliminary Ruling (4) Annulment (4)	ETS (4) Energy (2) GHG Emissions (2) ETS + Tax (1)	Company (7) Civil society (1)	Merits (7) Pending (1)
2022	18	Annulment (8) Preliminary Ruling (6) Annulment + Failure to Act (4)	Taxonomy Regulation (6) ETS (6) Participatory rights (4) Energy (2)	Civil society (9) Company (7) Member State (2)	Admissibility (5) Merits (9) Pending (4)
2023	16	Annulment (12) Preliminary Ruling (2) Failure to Fulfil Obligations (1) Damages (1)	GHG Emissions (6) Taxonomy Regulation (2) Energy (2) ETS (4) Participatory rights (1) CBAM (1)	Civil society (6) Member State (6) Company (5) EU Commission (1)	Merits (2) Pending (14)
2024	10	Annulment (7) Preliminary Ruling (3)	Energy (3) Taxonomy Regulation (2) GHG Emissions (2) State Aids (1) Fundamental Rights (1) ETS – Fundamental Rights (1)	Company (8) Civil society (2)	Merits (2) Pending (8)

Nevertheless, there has been a marked diversification in the range of actors involved, the legal instruments challenged, and the overall complexity of the issues at stake. This transformation is partly attributable to the evolution of EU environmental legislation, but it also seems to be further driven by the growing participation of civil society in climate litigation.

5.2.3 Core Themes and Type of Proceedings

A more specific review of legal grounds in climate cases allows for the identification of the core topics under discussion. As mentioned, ETS cases hold a central role and can be categorised under crucial topics that will be explored in more detail in section 3. However, ETS cases also cross with topics from other areas of environmental law and EU law in general.

As would be expected, most ETS cases are brought by companies (98 of a total of 115 cases) as a direct reaction to the adoption of implementing measures of the ETS Directive.[16] These cases reflect the ETS several trading phases: (i) 2005–2007; (ii) 2008–2012; (iii) 2013–2020; and (iv) 2021–2030.

The first and second trading periods of the ETS (2005–2012) were underpinned by a decentralised allocation model based on National Allocation Plans (NAPs). As a result, ETS cases during this period primarily involved challenges to the Commission's decisions to approve NAPs or to raise objections against them (22 out of a total of 43 cases). ETS litigation spiked in 2007 (cf. Figure 5.1), primarily challenging the Commission's decisions dated 2006 and 2007 concerning the NAPs for 2008–2012 – i.e., as the EU ETS transitioned into its second phase.

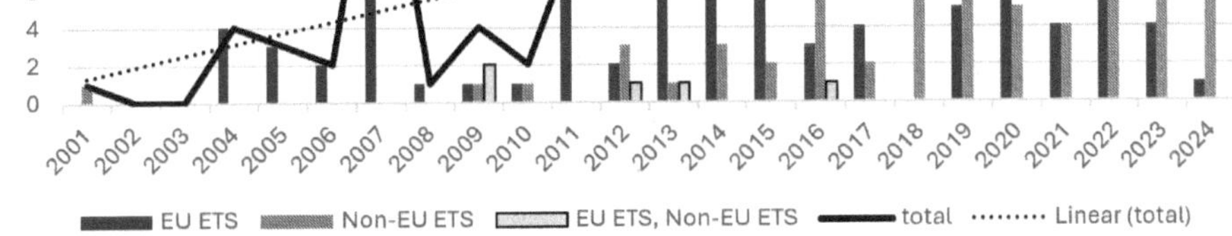

Figure 5.1 Number of Climate Cases before the CJEU: ETS-Non-ETS and Total.

16 Directive 2003/87/EC of the European Parliament and of the Council of 13 October 2003 establishing a scheme for greenhouse gas emission allowance trading within the Community and amending Council Directive 96/61/EC.

Table 5.2 ETS Cases Core Themes

ETS Cases Core Themes	*Cases*
Allowance allocation	61
National allocation plans	22
ETS Directive interpretation	20
Scope ETS	26
State aid	5
Participatory rights	4
Compensation for damages	3
Failure to transpose	2
Tax	2
Public procurement	2
Energy	2
ETS Directive validity	1

Some cases have two predominant areas, which is why the total number of cases in this table does not coincide with the total number of ETS cases.

The second most significant topic during this period (2005–2012) was allowance allocation, with a total of 10 cases, all initiated by companies. The remaining 8 cases during this period addressed various issues, including the scope and validity of the ETS Directive, participatory rights, and public procurement aspects related to ETS implementation.

The third phase (2013–2020) introduced a centralised ETS model, ending challenges related to NAPs and replacing them with harmonised allocation rules[17] as the primary focus of legal disputes. This shift led to a surge in ETS litigation in 2014–2015. During the third phase, allowance allocation was the core topic in the vast majority of cases (40 out of 57), namely issues related to the method of allocating free allowances.

The remaining 17 cases during this period covered a range of topics, including the scope and interpretation of the ETS Directive, participatory rights, fundamental rights, and a notable subset of four cases related to state aid.

Already in the fourth phase (2021–2030), with a peak in 2022–2023, a total of 15 cases are accounted for. Two of these were related to the guidelines on certain State aid measures within the greenhouse gas emission allowance trading system post-2021. The remaining cases addressed various issues, including transitional rules for the harmonised free allocation of emission allowances for the 2021–2030 period, the union registry, the market stability reserve for the EU emissions trading system, and the exclusion of units for the incineration of hazardous or municipal waste. As such, the fourth phase, unlike previous ones, lacks a predominant core theme.

17 Commission Decision of 27 April 2011 determining transitional EU-wide rules for harmonised free allocation, 2011/278/EU.

In what concerns non-ETS issues, an early case concerning public procurement was brought in 2001, but the second non-ETS climate case in the EU dates only from 2010. It concerned energy, following the adoption of the first Renewable Energy Directive[18] ("RED I") in 2009, and was soon followed by other energy-related cases. Such cases continue to play a central role in climate litigation before the CJEU, although issues surrounding GHG emissions are also among the most common core grounds for legal action (cf. Table 5.3).

The dominance of energy law and GHG emissions cases is, however, being challenged by a recent wave of cases raising other legal questions, driven mainly by non-governmental organisations, adding participatory rights and the Taxonomy Regulation[19] as persistent themes (cf. Figure 5.2). Taxonomy Regulation and participatory rights cases have been considered separately due to the distinct legal questions they raise; however, they address the broader topic of defining *sustainable energy*. Also, almost half of all energy cases (11 out of 25), including early climate cases, address the issue of conflicting sustainability goals in the energy sector. We can, therefore, conclude that the criteria for defining what constitutes sustainable energy have been – and remain – a pressing topic in EU climate litigation. In contrast, GHG emissions cases cover a very diverse range of topics, from monitoring emissions from engines to air conditioning gases, as well as reduction targets.

Table 5.3 Non-ETS Cases Core Themes

Non-ETS Cases Themes	*Cases*
GHG emissions	35
Energy	25
Taxonomy regulation	10
Participatory rights	7
State aid	2
Tax	1
Public procurement	1
Public funding – mobility	1
CBAM	1

Some cases have two predominant areas, which is why the total number of cases in this table does not coincide with the total number of non-ETS cases.

18 Directive 2009/28/EC of the European Parliament and of the Council of 23 April 2009 on the promotion of the use of energy from renewable sources and amending and subsequently repealing Directives 2001/77/EC and 2003/30/EC.

19 Regulation (EU) 2020/852 of the European Parliament and of the Council of 18 June 2020 on the establishment of a framework to facilitate sustainable investment, and amending Regulation (EU) 2019/2088.

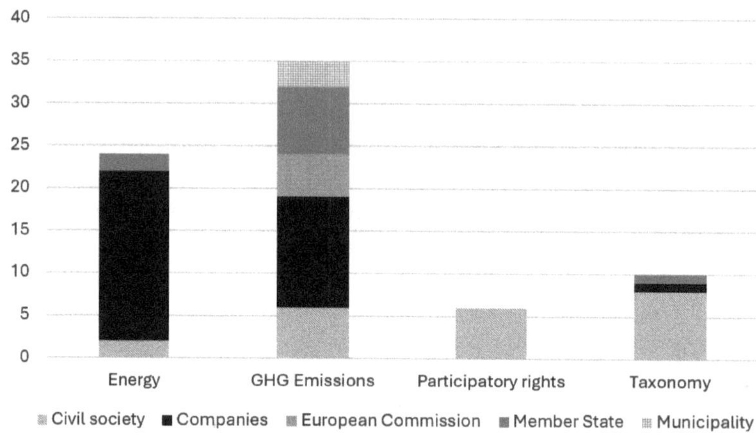

Figure 5.2 Non-ETS Cases by Issue and Type of Author.

One single case has been filed against CBAM in 2024. However, although the CBAM Regulation[20] is in force since May 2023, it is currently in a transitional phase imposing only reporting duties (2023–2025). Its restrictive effect is to be expected in the future, probably leading to more climate litigation.

So far, we have provided an overview of the legal acts in question in climate cases and can confidently conclude that a handful of legal acts have been the predominant subjects of legal action, with a strong and almost exclusive focus on laws regulating specific carbon-intensive economic activities. From the perspective of substantive EU law, this is a predictable outcome. However, a broader, intersectional view of the legal questions raised reveals another clear trend: the invocation of fundamental rights, specifically the Charter of Fundamental Rights of the European Union (CFREU), as a claim both for and against climate protection, in a total of 5 cases, 4 of which occurred in the third phase of EU climate litigation.[21] This shift is likely influenced by the growing adoption of rights-based approaches in climate litigation, both internationally and at the domestic level.[22]

Lastly, it should be noted that these grounds have reached the CJEU through four types of legal proceedings: preliminary rulings (91 cases),

20 Regulation (EU) 2023/956 of the European Parliament and of the Council of 10 May 2023 establishing a carbon border adjustment mechanism.

21 A summary of cases, including a table discriminating the invoked rights and number of cases, cf. Krommendijk J, Sanderink D. The Role of Fundamental Rights in the Environmental Case Law of the CJEU. European Law Open. 2023;2(3):618.

22 Many pieces have been published on the rights-turn in climate litigation. For an overview and mapping of these cases, cf. Savaresi A, Setzer J. Rights-Based Litigation in the Climate Emergency: Mapping the Landscape and New Knowledge Frontiers. Journal of Human Rights and the Environment. 2023;13(1):7–34.

Table 5.4 Climate Cases Brought before the CJEU, according to Phase and Type of Proceedings

	Preliminary Rulings	*Action for Annulment*	*Action for Failure to Fulfil Obligations*	*Action for Damages*
1st phase (2001–2008)	2	24	2	1
2nd phase (2009–2015)	43	15	2	1
3rd phase (2016–Present)	46	57	3	1

actions for annulment (96 cases, including 4 cases also grounded on failure to act), actions for failure to fulfil obligations (seven cases), actions for failure to act (four cases), and actions claiming compensation for damages (two cases, plus one other combined with an annulment request). The prevalence of annulment actions is growing rapidly.

5.2.4 Outcomes and Actors of Climate Cases

An overview of climate cases should include an assessment of how these cases have contributed to the enforcement of EU climate law and, overall, to enhancing climate protection. This assessment can be relatively straightforward in some cases and possibly in most cases before international courts. However, this is often not the case when analysing CJEU case law. Other than the structural reason that many cases are preliminary rulings and only provide the information required to reply to the specific validity or interpretation question(s) at hand, which does not provide enough context for assessment, there are three other reasons for this:

i. Many cases were decided based on admissibility requirements and therefore have an undetermined impact, except when initiated by civil society[23] and municipalities[24] in defence of high envi-

23 Along with the already cited *Carvalho and Others v Parliament and Council*, two other cases fall under this category: *Peter Sabo and Others v European Parliament and Council of the European Union*, Order of the General Court of 6 May 2020, Case T-141/19, and Order of the Court of 14 January 2021, Appeal Case C-297/20 P; and *ATPN v Commission*, Order of the General Court of 30 March 2023, Case T-567/22, and Judgment of the Court of 26 September 2024, Appeal Case C-340/23 P.

24 It should be noted that although initially decided on merits by the General Court, these cases were ultimately dismissed by the Court of Justice on the grounds that the municipalities lacked direct concern in the acts. Cf. Cases *Ville de Paris and Others v European Commission*, *Ville de Bruxelles v Commission*, and *Ayuntamiento de Madrid v Commission*, decided

ronmental standards, in which case the decision has a restrictive effect on access to justice for climate protection and was deemed unfavourable.

ii. EU law dealing with climate change is developed and complex, leading to cases regarding the interpretation of technical implementation aspects. This leads to a high number of cases whose impact is probably neutral in terms of climate protection, such as rules concerning free movement of good,[25] training and certifications of workers,[26] or procedural or institutional rules.[27]

iii. Due to the complex nature of climate problems and the fact that EU law is detailed, sustainability goals or other EU rules are often in tension, meaning that one decision will have positive and negative impacts, rendering difficult any definitive conclusion on its favourable and unfavourable consequences.[28]

This context results in a high number of decisions categorised as having an undetermined climate-friendly outcome, even when excluding cases decided exclusively on admissibility grounds (cf. Table 5.5). In an analysis limited to cases decided on merits, the majority have had a positive impact in terms

Table 5.5 Climate Protection Impacts of All Cases and Cases Decided on Merits

	Favourable Outcome	*Unfavourable Outcome*	*Undetermined*
All cases	63 (37.3%)	25 (14.8%)	81 (47.9%)
Cases decided on merits	63 (48.1%)	19 (14.5%)	49 (37.4%)

as Joined Cases T-339/16, T-352/16, and T-391/16, in Judgment of the General Court of 13 December 2018, and Judgment of the Court of 13 January 2022, Appeal Case C-177/19 P.

25 Cf. *Essent Belgium NV v [Flemish region of] Vlaams Gewest*, Judgment of the Court of 29 September 2016, Case C-492/14; or *BP France v Ministre de l'Économie, des Finances et de la Souveraineté industrielle et numérique*, Judgment of the Court of 29 July 2024, Case C-624/22; or *E.ON Biofor Sverige AB v Statens energimyndighet*, Judgment of the Court of 22 June 2017, Case C-549/15.

26 Cf. *Commission v Poland*, Judgment of the Court of 25 June 2015, Case C-303/14.

27 Cf. *European Commission v Council for the European Union*, Judgment of the Court of 16 July 2015, Case C-425/13; or *Republic of Latvia v European Commission*, Judgment of the General Court of 22 March 2011, Case T-369/07, and Judgment of the Court of 3 October 2013, Appeal Case C-267/11 P; or *Flachglas Torgau GmbH v Federal Republic of Germany*, Judgment of the Court of 14 February 2012, Case C-204/09; or *Green Network SpA v Autorità per l'energia elettrica e il gas*, Judgment of the Court of 26 November 2014, Case C-66/13.

28 Conflicting goals will probably also be a relevant in the several pending cases concerning the Taxonomy Regulation, namely those concerning nuclear energy. Cf. Section 3.2.1. on this topic.

of climate protection. Moreover, the number of favourable decisions significantly exceeds the number of unfavourable outcomes, in any circumstance.

This conclusion also evidences the relevance of standing rules in any analysis of cases before internacional courts. Aside from Member States and EU institutions, the rules for filing actions directly before the CJEU are strict, as outlined in Article 263 of the Treaty on the Functioning of the European Union (TFEU).[29] As a result, the number of cases dismissed is high, particularly when excluding preliminary rulings proceedings, as these are formally initiated by national courts rather than by the parties themselves (cf. Table 5.6). It should also be pointed out that civil society–led cases are significantly increasing. This was previously highlighted (section 2.2.) as a factor for the diversification of legal grounds in actions before the CJEU.

It should be noted at this point that admissibility rules have a substantive impact. To illustrate this, let us consider ETS cases. Early climate cases (2005–2012) were overwhelmingly industry-led (32 in 43). However, only five of these actions were decided on merits, excluding preliminary rulings. As a consequence, it is the minority of cases initiated by Member States (seven in 43), all decided on merits, that influence and determine EU climate law interpretation and implementation by courts.

As we will discuss in the following sections, access rules significantly impact the types of legal grounds currently being used in the third phase of climate litigation before the CJEU (2016–present) to circumvent previous failures in bringing strategic cases.

Table 5.6 Outcomes of Climate Cases and Pending Cases: All and by Subject

	Decided on Merits	*Decided on Merits (except Prelim. Rulings)*	*Decided on Admissibility*	*Pending*
All cases	131	49	38	27
Brought by civil society	10	6	3	9
Brought by companies	93	24	32	11
Brought by municipalities	2	1	3	0
Brought by Member States	18	10	0	6
Brought by the Commission	8	8	0	1

29 Standing rules for access to the CJEU will not be analysed here, as they are the specific focus of another chapter in this book.

5.2.5 The Strategic Nature of Climate Cases: An Elusive Question

Climate litigation can be further divided into strategic and non-strategic. Strategic litigation is not exclusive to environmental cases – on the contrary, it emerged as early as the 20th century in connection with human rights issues, in particular civil and labour rights – and it can be defined as litigation that has objectives beyond the interests of the parties to the lawsuit, in particular the resolution or evolution of relevant societal problems.[30] In the case of actions aimed at promoting legal, social, or political changes, this is a strategy usually associated with actions promoted, directly or indirectly, by civil society, namely non-governmental organisations. It is an established fact that there is a significant overlap between climate litigation brought by non-governmental organisations and strategic litigation.[31]

This is no different in climate litigation before the CJEU, which is therefore aligned with a global movement of increasing strategic litigation.[32] The *Carvalho* case embodies all the hallmarks of strategic climate litigation, advancing claims that challenge access to court and substantive rules while addressing complex legal and policy issues.[33] It aimed to promote the novel application of legal remedies in an area marked by legal uncertainty. Had it succeeded, it would have brought significant material advances in climate protection. Similarly, pending cases brought by non-governmental organisations concerning the Taxonomy Regulation and its implementation are built as a way of forcing the review of the EU's energy policy and indirectly opening the gates to the CJEU.[34]

This civil society–led strategic litigation is, though challenging, an acknowledged preexisting phenomenon in favour of societal evolution. However, it has recently been argued that the boundaries between strategic and non-strategic litigation, on the one hand, and the association of strategic litigation with public interest litigation, on the other, are being redefined in climate cases before the CJEU. Where the strategic ambition behind high-profile *pro-climate* lawsuits led by civil society in the public interest may be more easily perceptible, less can be said about the strategic nature of climate

30 Cf. Duffy H. Strategic Human Rights Litigation: Understanding and Maximising Impact. Oxford: Bloomsbury Publishing; 2018. p. 3. Van der Pas K. Conceptualising Strategic Litigation. Oñati Socio-Legal Series. 2021;11(6)(S):S116–145, 122.

31 Cf. Setzer J, Higham C, (n 4) p. 19.

32 Cebulak P, Morvillo M, Salomon S. Strategic Litigation in EU Law: Who Does It Empower? German Law Journal. 2024;25(6):800–821. Setzer J et al. Climate Litigation in Europe. A Summary Report for the European Union Forum of Judges for the Environment. Grantham Research Institute on Climate Change and the Environment and Centre for Climate Change Economics and Policy, London School of Economics and Political Science and the European Union Forum of Judges for the Environment; 2022. p. 11.

33 Cf. Section 3.2.2. for more details on the case.

34 Cf. Section 3.2.1. for more details on these cases.

cases characterised by an anti-climate or anti-regulatory agenda.[35] It has been argued that this overlooks the aggregated phenomena of hundreds of cases,[36] such as those concerning planning applications or the allocation of emission allowances under the ETS.[37] Mainly two assumptions are on the basis of this: (i) the nature of the litigants, primarily private economic actors pursuing self-interested objectives; and (ii) the substantive focus of these challenges, which primarily contest the scheme's implementation.

However, broader motives behind industry litigation can certainly be at play. As shown, despite the consistency of the Court's inadmissibility rulings, industry actions have persisted. Most notably, this trend in ETS litigation concerns the "futile" challenges by operators covered by the ETS contesting Commission decisions that approve or reject NAPs.[38] This strong opposition was particularly evident from energy-intensive industries, which represent a major business interest group within the "EU bubble" influencing the legislative process.[39] Among these, the steel sector has been identified as "the most active of all industries lobbying on emissions trading".[40] Leading this effort are Eurofer,[41] the trade association representing the European iron and steel industry, and ArcelorMittal, the largest steel producer in Europe and a dominant corporate player in the lobbying arena.[42]

Thus, if analysed in isolation, a case may *prima facie* appear to be non-strategic, when, together with other identical cases, it has a strategic ambition behind it. We can, therefore, conclude that although strategic litigation with its traditional features is not only present and increasing before the

35 Setzer J et al., (n 34) p. 7.

36 Fleerackers S. Hidden in Plain Sight? Corporate Strategic Litigation in the EU Emissions Trading System. German Law Journal. 2024;25(6):876.

37 Cf. Section 2.2.

38 Van Zeben J. The European Emissions Trading Scheme Case Law. Review of European Community & International Environmental Law. 2009;18(2):123–125.

39 Cf. Survival Guide to EU Carbon Market Lobby. Debunking Claims from Heavy Industry. Policy Briefing. For an account of lobbying of energy-intensive industries during the ETS development, see Braun M. The Evolution of Emissions Trading in the European Union – The Role of Policy Networks, Knowledge and Policy Entrepreneurs. Accounting, Organizations and Society. 2009;34(3):469–487.

40 Reyes O, Balanyá B. Carbon Warfare. How Big Polluters Plan to Profit from EU Emissions Trading Reform describe how energy intensive industries have undertaken "full spectrum lobbying" to spread their concerns, exert influence on ETS policy, and, ultimately, "extract more free subsidies from the ETS" through EU trade associations, echoed by national federations, and followed through by local companies. Corporate Europe Observatory; 2016.

41 Eurofer, or European Confederation of Iron and Steel Industries, is a trade association at sector level representing national steel federations and steel companies such as Arcelor Mittal, Corus/Tata Steel, and ThyssenKrupp on issues concerning the development of the European steel industry.

42 Industry Lobbying on Emissions Trading Scheme Hits the Jackpot: The Cases of Arcelor Mittal and Lafarge. See *Arcelor SA v Parliament and Council*, Judgment of the General Court of 2 March 2010, Case T-16/04; and *Société Arcelor Atlantique et Lorraine and Others v Premier Ministre and Others*, Judgment of the Court of 16 December 2008, Case C-127/07.

CJEU, but also that a more nuanced approach might be needed in assessing the strategic nature of strategic anti-climate litigation brought by corporate interests in EU law.

5.3 Legal Grounds of EU Climate Litigation

This section provides a more detailed analysis of the most relevant legal grounds for climate litigation before the CJEU divided into ETS and non-ETS cases. The selection is based on an assessment of frequency (a high number of cases citing specific legal grounds) and relevance in relation to potential novel avenues for climate cases. We will also conclude with a note on a specific strategy of anti-climate or possibly just transition litigation consistently used by Poland in climate cases.

5.3.1 ETS Cases

5.3.1.1 Cases during the Decentralised Model

One of the earliest challenges to the ETS before the CJEU offers an initial insight into the private interests of iron and steel corporations. The legal strategy employed in contesting the scope of the ETS Directive combined two distinct legal remedies. The first was an annulment filed in 2004,[43] by Arcelor, seeking partial annulment of the ETS Directive and claiming compensation for damages. The second was a preliminary ruling procedure initiated in 2007, also by Arcelor,[44] challenging the ETS Directive's validity, through national courts, based on the principle of equal treatment. Arcelor argued that the steel sector was included in the EU ETS, whereas the chemical and non-ferrous metal industries were excluded and, therefore, not subject to equivalent regulations. The Court acknowledged that these sectors were indeed comparable and that the steel sector faced a disadvantage due to its inclusion. However, it ruled that the difference in treatment was justified based on objective and reasonable criteria. The Court further held that excluding these sectors was proportionate, as including them would have imposed an excessive administrative burden.[45]

Member States have also filed ETS cases. In fact, although most cases were brought by companies, only states were able to obtain decisions on the merits, making these judgments particularly significant.[46] Government-

43 *Arcelor SA v Parliament and Council*, Case T-16/04.

44 *Société Arcelor Atlantique et Lorraine v Premier Minister*, Judgment of the Court of 16 December 2008, Case C-127/07.

45 *Arcelor v Parliament and Council*, Case T-16/04, paras. 65 ff. On this topic, cf. Weishaar SE. EU Emissions Trading – Its Regulatory Evolution and the Role of the Court. 452.

46 For a brief overview of early ETS cases in "privileged" and "non-privileged" annulment actions", cf. Bogojević S. Human Rights of Minors and Future Generations: Global Trends

led cases have occasionally succeeded in the CJEU, resulting in rulings considered unfavourable to climate action. For example, in a case brought by Estonia[47] and one brought by Poland,[48] these Member States challenged the Commission's mandate to reduce the total annual emission allowances in their National Allocation Plans (NAPs) by 47.8% and 26.7%, respectively. The General Court found that the Commission overstepped its authority, violating the principle of sound administration, as the discretion over NAPs largely rests with individual Member States to determine their total allocation for any given period. It clarified that the Commission's powers do not stretch to taking into account the effects of NAPs on the emissions market but rather are severely limited. The Commission appealed both cases to the CJEU on the basis that the General Court, *inter alia*, erred in law in its interpretation of the scope and the objective of its powers under the ETS Directive. The CJEU, nonetheless, dismissed the appeals in two almost identical judgments.

Conversely, in a 2006 case supporting climate action,[49] the Commission successfully argued that Italy had failed to adopt the necessary laws, regulations, and administrative measures required under Article 31(1) of the EU ETS Directive. Similarly, that same year, proceedings were furthermore successfully brought by the Commission in a comparable case against Finland[50] for providing an exemption to the Directive for the province of Åland.

Challenges against the Commission decisions also arose in the second trading period (2008–2012). These were often directed against decisions in which the Commission rejected the NAPs on the basis of suspected over-allocation of allowances.[51] For example, Latvia contested the Commission's decision, arguing that it was time-barred from requesting additional information on its NAP and that, as a result, the plan should be considered definitive.[52] The Court sided with Latvia, reaffirming its case law that the Commission's discretion in reviewing NAPs was limited to assessing their compliance with the criteria set out in Annex III and Article 10 of the Directive.

and EU Environmental Law Particularities. Review of European, Comparative & International Environmental Law. 2020;29(2):194–201.

47 *Republic of Estonia v Commission of the European Communities*, Judgment of the Court of First Instance of 23 September 2009, Case T-263/07, and Judgment of the Court of 29 March 2012, Appeal Case C-505/09 P.

48 *Republic of Poland v Commission of the European Communities*, Judgment of the Court of First Instance of 23 September 2009, Case T-183/07, and Judgment of the Court of 29 March 2012, C-504/09 P.

49 *Commission v Italy*, Judgment of the Court of 18 May 2006, Case C-122/05.

50 *Commission of the European Communities v Finland*, Judgment of the Court of 12 January 2006, Case C-107/05.

51 Cf. Weishaar SE. EU Emissions Trading – Its Regulatory Evolution and the Role of the Court. 454.

52 *Republic of Latvia v European Commission*, Judgment of the General Court of 22 March 2011, Case T-369/07, and Judgment of the Court of 3 October 2013, Appeal Case C-267/11 P.

5.3.1.2 Cases during the Centralised Model

With the introduction of a harmonised allocation format, legal challenges relating to NAPs came to an end. However, the harmonised allocation rules[53] themselves soon became the subject of legal disputes. In *Hüttenwerke Krupp Mannesmann and Others*,[54] several companies sought the annulment of the allocation rules, arguing, among other things, that the criteria for setting benchmarks had been disregarded and that incorrect data had been used in their calculation. The Court, however, declared the action inadmissible. Similarly, in *Borealis Polyolefine*,[55] the validity of Commission Decision 2011/278/EU was challenged through a preliminary ruling procedure but was ultimately upheld. However, the Court ruled that the Commission had incorrectly determined the uniform cross-sectoral correction factor set out in Article 4 of Decision 2013/448, leading to its invalidation.[56]

The extension of the ETS to aviation through Directive 2008/101 generated significant friction between the EU and third countries, including China and the United States. This tension led to a legal challenge by the Air Transport Association of America and two United States of America airlines, contesting the ETS Directive's implementation in the United Kingdom. The case resulted in a preliminary ruling request on the Directive's validity and its compatibility with the Chicago Convention,[57] the US-EU Air Transport Agreement, the Kyoto Protocol, and customary international law.[58] The Court ruled that the EU was not bound by the Chicago Convention, was entitled to include non-EU airlines in the ETS and had not infringed international law principles. Additionally, it found that the Directive did not violate the Open Skies Agreement.[59] The Court further clarified that the EU ETS did not impose a mandatory levy benefiting public authorities that could be classified as a tax, duty, fee, or charge on aircraft fuel. Instead, it was deemed a market-based mechanism rather than a fiscal measure.

53 2011/278/EU: Commission Decision of 27 April 2011 determining transitional EU-wide rules for harmonised free allocation.

54 *Hüttenwerke Krupp Mannesmann and Others v Commission*, Order of the General Court of 4 June 2012, Case T-379/11.

55 *Borealis Polyolefine GmbH v Minister for Land, Forestry, Environment, and Water Management*, Judgment of the Court of 28 April 2016, Case C-191/14.

56 *Ibid*, paras. 85, 95, 98–99.

57 Convention on International Civil Aviation, signed in Chicago, on 7 December 1994.

58 *Air Transport Association of America v Secretary of State for Energy and Climate Change*, Judgment of the Court of 21 December 2011, Case C-366/10.

59 This agreement between the United States and the EU opened up the market for more competition – cf. Decision of the Council and the Representatives of the Governments of the Member States of the European Union, meeting within the Council of 25 April 2007 on the signature and provisional application of the Air Transport Agreement between the European Community and its Member States, on the one hand, and the United States of America, on the other hand.

Despite this clear legal endorsement, political pressure persisted. Ultimately, the EU decided to suspend the application of the ETS for flights to and from airports in non-EU countries that are neither part of the European Free Trade Association (EFTA) nor the European Economic Area (EEA) and have not signed an EU accession treaty.[60] This demonstrates how, despite a definitive Court ruling, political considerations ultimately led to the limitation of the ETS's extraterritorial application in aviation.[61]

Another case worth mentioning is the Polish request for the annulment of Decision 2015/1814, which established the Market Stability Reserve (MSR), arguing that it should have been adopted under Article 192(2) TFEU – requiring unanimity – rather than Article 192(1) TFEU.[62] Poland claimed that the decision disproportionately affected its energy market, given its reliance on coal and lignite, by driving up the cost of emission allowances. The Court concluded that the MSR was designed to enhance the resilience of the EU ETS by ensuring orderly market functioning and addressing structural supply-demand imbalances.[63] It characterised the measure as a correction mechanism for the ETS rather than an instrument intended to influence national energy policies. Although the MSR's intended and actual effect – raising ETS prices – clearly impacts national energy policies, the Court deemed this effect too indirect to warrant a different legal basis.[64] Nonetheless, this line of reasoning has been brought repeatedly by Poland in subsequent cases, although concerning other EU laws.[65]

5.3.2 Non-ETS Cases

Non-ETS cases deal with a significant variety of legal acts, issues, and grounds (cf. Table 5.1). Among these, the most relevant concern energy and GHG emissions.[66] However, it should be noted that claims based on two cross-

60 Article 1, Decision No 377/2013/EU of the European Parliament and of the Council of 24 April 2013 derogating temporarily from Directive 2003/87/EC establishing a scheme for greenhouse gas emission allowance trading within the Community.

61 Cf. Scott J. Extraterritoriality and Territorial Extension in EU Law. The American Journal of Comparative Law. 2014;62:87–125. Peeters M, Misonne D, (n 8) p. 63. Bogojević S. Legalising Environmental Leadership: A Comment on the CJEU'S Ruling in C-366/10 on the Inclusion of Aviation in the EU Emissions Trading Scheme. Journal of Environmental Law. 2012;24(2):345–356.

62 *Republic of Poland v European Parliament and Council of the European Union*, Judgment of the Court of 21 June 2018, Case C-5/16.

63 *Ibid*, paras. 54 and 55.

64 Cf. Weishaar SE. EU Emissions Trading – Its Regulatory Evolution and the Role of the Court. In: Peeters M, Eliantonio M, eds. Research Handbook on EU Environmental Law. Edward Elgar Publishing; 2020. p. 456.

65 Cf. Section 3.3.

66 Other fields have been relevant in climate cases, such as state aids, taxes, but these cases will not be analysed in this section, but mentioned in section 2.3.

cutting legal grounds are increasing in frequency: participatory rights and fundamental rights. The following paragraphs summarise the most relevant cases and claims in each of these areas.

5.3.2.1 Energy

A significant number of energy cases deal with ordinary rules concerning the functioning of renewable energy markets, such as compatibility between rules on admissible green certificates and compatibility with free movement of goods,[67] stimulus measures for the production of non-fossil energy,[68] interpretation of rules on the incorporation of biofuels into motor fuels,[69] and the scope of rules on renewable energy's priority access to the electricity grid.[70] However, a core topic is common to many other cases in the field of energy production: the definition of criteria for sustainability. This has been brought before the CJEU through different angles.

The discussion around sustainable energy production is a core topic in EU law, because the production of renewable energy, a key aspect of the transition to a climate-neutral economy, has also negative environmental impacts. Balancing renewable energy production with the protection of habitats was

67 With a positive outcome for climate protection, we should highlight *Legatoria Editoriale Giovanni Olivotto (L.E.G.O.) SpA v Gestore dei servizi energetici (GSE) SpA and Others*, Judgment of the Court of 4 October 2018, Case C-242/17, where the Court found the imposition of additional requirements for certifying sustainability of bioliquids as compatible with the TFUE. As for other cases on the area of green certificates and/or free movement of goods, cf. *Industrie de bois de Vielsalm & Cie v Walloon Region*, Judgment of the Court of 26 September 2013, Case C-195/12; *Essent Belgium NV v Vlaamse Reguleringsinstantie voor de Elektriciteits- en Gasmarkt*, Judgment of the Court 11 September 2014, Case C-204/12; *Ålands Vindkraft AB v Swedish Energy Agency*, Judgment of the Court of 1 July 2014, Case C-573/12; *Green Network SpA v Autorità per l'energia elettrica e il gas*, Judgment of the Court of 26 November 2014, Case C-66/13; *Essent Belgium NV v Vlaams Gewest and Others*, Judgment of the Court of 29 September 2016, Case C-492/14; *E.ON Biofor Sverige AB v Statens energimyndighet*, Judgment of the Court of 22 June 2017, Case C-549/15; *Société BP France v Ministre de l'Économie, des Finances et de la Souveraineté industrielle et numérique*, Judgment of the Court of 29 July 2024, Case C-624/22; and *Autorità di Regolazione per Energia Reti e Ambiente v Fallimento Esperia and GSE*, Judgment of the Court of 7 March 2024, Case C-558/22.

68 For the production of renewable energy, cf. *Elecdey Carcelen SA and Others v Comunidad Autónoma de Castilla-La Mancha*, Judgment of the Court of 20 September 2017, Joined Cases C-215/16, C-216/16, C-220/16 and C-221/16; *Braila Winds SRL v Președintele Agenției Naționale de Administrare Fiscală and Others*, Case C-462/24 (pending). Concerning a state aid for the production of nuclear energy, cf. *Republic of Austria v European Commission*, Judgment of the General Court of 12 July 2018, Case T-356/15; Judgment of the Court of 22 September 2020 Appeal Case C-594/18 P).

69 *Vapo Atlantic SA v Entidade Nacional para o Setor Energético E.P.E.*, Judgment of the Court of 9 March 2023, Case C-604/21.

70 *EEW Energy from Waste v MNG Mitteldeutsche Netzgesellschaft Strom GmbH*, Judgment of the Court (Fifth Chamber) of 20 April 2023, Case C-580/21.

the core issue in *Azienda Agro-Zootecnica Franchini Sarl v Regione Puglia*,[71] with a decision deeming that RED I did not prevent national legislation from imposing a prior assessment of the environmental impact of renewable energy projects on sites forming part of the Natura 2000 network. This case highlights how, although a priority, transitioning to a low-carbon economy is not the only pressing sustainability goal. Significant concerns have been raised on RED III's[72] compatibility with biodiversity protection,[73] identifying a probable field for strategic biodiversity climate litigation in the future.[74]

With an opposite standpoint, but still on the topic of negative impacts of renewable energy production, is the action filed by *Lípidos Santiga*[75] against the Commission Delegated Regulation 2019/807[76] supplementing RED II, which defined rules relevant for limiting land-use change from farming to energy production. These rules seek to prevent the extension of agricultural land into areas with high carbon stock, such as forests, wetlands, and peatland – i.e., rules relevant both for GHG emissions and for biodiversity protection.

Claims against the sustainability of the production of renewable energy were also brought in *Sabo and Others v Parliament and Council*,[77] an action for annulment of certain provisions of RED II.[78] The focus of the case was on forest biomass, and the invoked legal grounds were breach of Article 191 TFEU for failing to provide a high level of environmental protection, not rectifying damage at source and not applying the precautionary principle or the polluter-pays principle. It was also argued the breach of several fun-

71 *Azienda Agro-Zootecnica Franchini Sarl v Regione Puglia*, Judgment of the Court of 21 July 2011, Case C-2/10.

72 Directive (EU) 2023/2413 of the European Parliament and of the Council of 18 October 2023 amending Directive (EU) 2018/2001, Regulation (EU) 2018/1999 and Directive 98/70/EC as regards the promotion of energy from renewable sources, and repealing Council Directive (EU) 2015/652.

73 Montini M. Addressing the conflicts between climate-related renewable energy goals and environmental protection interests under the RED Directive. European Law Open. 2024;3(1):209.

74 Schoukens H. Strategic Climate Change Litigation and the EU Habitats Directive: Squaring the Circle with the Help of the US Endangered Species Act? Journal for European Environmental & Planning Law. 2023;20(1):51–94.

75 The case was dismissed as inadmissible due to lack of standing. Cf. *Lípidos Santiga v Commission*, Order of the General Court of 11 June 2020, Case T-561/19, and Judgment of the Court of 21 October 2021, Appeal Case C-402/20 P.

76 Commission Delegated Regulation (EU) 2019/807 of 13 March 2019 supplementing Directive (EU) 2018/2001 of the European Parliament and of the Council as regards the determination of high indirect land-use change-risk feedstock for which a significant expansion of the production area into land with high carbon stock is observed and the certification of low indirect land-use change-risk biofuels, bioliquids, and biomass fuels.

77 *Sabo and Others v Parliament and Council*, Order of the General Court of 6 May 2020, Case T-141/19, and Order of the Court of 14 January 2021, Appeal Case C-297/20 P.

78 Directive (EU) 2018/2001 of the European Parliament and of the Council of 11 December 2018 on the promotion of the use of energy from renewable sources.

damental rights – namely the rights to respect for private and family life, education, property, and health care – protected under the CFREU. The concerns over sustainability of producing renewable energy with biomass were also the focus of ClientEarth's case against the European Investment Bank,[79] following a request for internal review under the Aarhus Regulation[80] of a resolution approving the financing of a biomass power generation plant, highlighting the instrumental role of this EU institution in climate action.[81]

In the end, ClientEarth's case, although successful and relevant, only addressed participatory rights. The *Sabo* case addressed substantive concerns but was ruled inadmissible due to lack of standing and was, therefore, not decided in substance. The recently filed *Föreningen Svenskt Landskapsskydd and Others v Council* Case,[82] against Council Regulation (EU) 2022/2577[83] also following an internal review request, is the repetition of this strategic action in the energy field – i.e., circumventing strict standing rules by challenging EU legislative acts, first, through an internal review procedure.[84]

Quite similarly, all recent cases against the Taxonomy Regulation's delegated acts address the problem of participatory rights in the definition of sustainability criteria by:

i. Questioning the labelling of bioplastics and the use of forest biomass for energy production, in one case,[85] and of fossil gas, in another case,[86] both brought by ClientEarth against the Commission, following requests for internal review.
ii. Deeming the consideration of gas and nuclear under the Taxonomy Regulation as unlawful, as claimed in an action filed by Greenpeace against the Commission, following a request for internal review.[87]

79 *ClientEarth v European Investment Bank*, Judgment of the General Court of 27 January 2021, Case T-9/19, and Judgment of the Court of 6 July 2023, Appeal Case C-212/21 P.
80 Regulation (EC) No 1367/2006 of the European Parliament and of the Council of 6 September 2006 on the application of the provisions of the Aarhus Convention on Access to Information, Public Participation in Decision-making and Access to Justice in Environmental Matters to Community institutions and bodies.
81 Cf. Mertens D, Thiemann M. The European Investment Bank: The EU's Climate Bank? Mertens D, Thiemann M. The European Investment Bank: The EU's Climate Bank? In: Handbook on European Union Climate Change Policy and Politics. In: Rayner T et al, eds. Cheltenham, UK: Edward Elgar Publishing; 2023. p. 73. Available from: https://www.elgaronline.com/edcollbook-oa/book/9781789906981/9781789906981.xml.
82 *Föreningen Svenskt Landskapsskydd and Others v Council*, Case T-534/23 (pending).
83 Council Regulation (EU) 2022/2577 of 22 December 2022 laying down a framework to accelerate the deployment of renewable energy.
84 Cf. Section 3.2.3.
85 *ClientEarth v Commission*, Case T-579/22 (pending).
86 *ClientEarth and Others v Commission*, Case T-215-23 (pending).
87 *Greenpeace and Others v Commission*, Case T-214/23 (pending).

iii. Maintaining that the Commission made a wrongful assessment of the "*substantial contribution to climate change mitigation*" and the "do no significant harm" criteria in what concerns forestry activities and forest bioenergy activities brought by the Robin Wood Association against the Commission, following a request for an internal review.[88]
iv. Claiming, among others, the breach of participatory rights and fundamental rights both with regard to the objective of climate mitigation and climate adaptation, following a request for an internal review.[89]
v. Invoking a wrongful interpretation of Taxonomy Regulation conditions in the adopted screening criteria and breach of the precautionary principle in what regards the aviation and maritime transport sectors, following a request for an internal review.[90]

With similar grounds substantively but not concerning participatory rights due to its qualified status, Austria also started an action for annulment of the Commission Delegated Regulation 2022/1214[91] by qualifying investments in fossil gas and nuclear energy rightly as *"environmentally sustainable"* under the Taxonomy Regulation.[92] An anti-climate litigation action requesting the annulment of part of the Commission Delegated Regulation 2021/2139[93] concerning the aviation sector and claiming breach of competence rules and procedural requirements, of the Taxonomy Regulation, legal certainty, and equality, as well as an error in assessment.[94]

All of these cases are pending. Conversely, a case addressing the same material problem – criteria used in the Taxonomy Regulation's delegated acts – was also filed by the Association Trinationale de Protection Nucléaire and already decided on. Because a preliminary request for an internal review was not filed, the case was ruled inadmissible on standing grounds.[95]

88 *Robin Wood and Others v Commission*, Case T-575/22 (pending).
89 *Fédération environnement durable and Others v Commission*, Case T-583/22 (pending).
90 *Dryade, Fossielvrij NL, and Protect our Winters Austria and Others v EU Commission*, Case T-449-24 (pending).
91 Commission Delegated Regulation (EU) 2022/1214 of 9 March 2022 amending Delegated Regulation (EU) 2021/2139 as regards economic activities in certain energy sectors and Delegated Regulation (EU) 2021/2178 as regards specific public disclosures for those economic activities.
92 *Austria v Commission*, Case T-625/22 (pending).
93 Commission Delegated Regulation (EU) 2021/2139 of 4 June 2021 supplementing Regulation (EU) 2020/852 of the European Parliament and of the Council by establishing the technical screening criteria for determining the conditions under which an economic activity qualifies as contributing substantially to climate change mitigation or climate change adaptation and for determining whether that economic activity causes no significant harm to any of the other environmental objectives.
94 *Dassault aviation v Commission*, Case T-77/24.
95 *ATPN v Commission*, Order of the General Court of 30 March 2023, Case T-567/22.

Other than the topic of compatibility within environmental goals, two relevant cases have also been brought concerning the ranking of sustainability of different sources of energy. Two cases started by ePURE and Pannonia Bio challenge two regulations. Specifically, these companies claim there was a wrongful assessment when comparing different sources of energy in the maritime transport[96] and the aviation sectors.[97] These companies invoke, among others, errors of assessment, breach of proportionality, and equality of treatment.

We can, therefore, conclude that energy cases have evolved from essentially market-condition cases to cases concerning the definition of sustainable energy, with a growing relevance of participatory rights, for strategic procedural reasons, but also claims of breach of fundamental rights.

5.3.2.2 GHG Emissions Reduction and Control

Most GHG emissions cases deal with two specific sectors: the automobile sector, with a focus on rules concerning GHG emissions from engines directly impacting climate change, and fluorinated GHG emissions. In these sectors, we can identify actions that question both legislative acts and implementing decisions, challenging:

i. Validity of rules setting more ambitious targets for reducing GHG emission values for new cars, alleging breach of the CFREU (freedom to conduct a business, property, equality, environmental protection, proportionality) and Article 191 TFEU.[98]
ii Validity of implementing decisions on performance values for manufacturers of new passenger cars and values for the calculation of emission targets, with a company invoking breach of EU law's objectives and effectiveness, non-discrimination, and proportionality.[99]
iii. Competence of the Commission for establishing not-to-exceed values for real-driving conditions, brought by municipalities[100] claiming interference with local powers.

96 *ePURE and Pannonia Bio v Parliament and Council*, Case T-1165/23 (pending).
97 ePURE and Pannonia Bio v Parliament and Council, Case T-45/24 (pending).
98 *Kiene and Others v European Parliament and Council of the European Union*, Order of the General Court of 2 May 2024, Case T-419/23; Appeal Case C-487/24 P (pending).
99 *London EV v Commission*, Case T-1024/23 (pending).
100 *Ville de Paris, Ville de Bruxelles and Ayuntamiento de Madrid v European Commission*, Judgment of the General Court of 13 December 2018, Joined Cases T-339/16, T-352/16 and T-391/16, and Judgment of the Court of 13 January 2022, Joined Cases C-177/19 P to C-179/19 P.

iv. Decisions concerning approval and certification of innovative technologies for reducing carbon dioxide emissions from passenger cars,[101] alleging procedural grounds and breach of law, filed by one company.
v. Admissibility of mechanisms that allow for higher values of emissions from engines in certain conditions and balancing of consumer protection with environmental protection goals,[102] in actions initiated by civil society and companies. The CJEU also decided on a case concerning non-governmental organizations' right to challenge decisions in this field before domestic courts,[103] considering the CFREU (right to an effective remedy) and the Aarhus Convention.
vi. Implementing decisions concerning quotas for fluorinated greenhouse gases[104] and hydrofluorocarbons,[105] brought by companies working on the sector.

Moreover, there is notably and, in relative terms, a significant number of actions for failure to fulfil obligations brought by the European Commission against Member States due to lack of adoption of national measures in the area of GHG emissions.[106]

However, two cases stand out for not being sector specific, but rather clear cases of strategic litigation pushing for more ambitions targets for GHG

101 *Daimler v Commission*, Order of the General Court of 22 January 2020, Case T-751/18; and Case *Daimler v Commission*, Judgment of the General Court of 15 September 2021, Case T-359/19.

102 *IR v Volkswagen AG*, Judgment of the Court of 14 July 2022, Case C-134/20; *DS v Porsche Inter Auto GmbH & Co. KG, Volkswagen AG*, Judgement of the Court of 14 July 2022, Case C-145/20; *QB v Mercedes-Benz Group AG*, Judgment of the Court of 21 March 2023, C-691/18; *CLCV and Others*, Judgment of the Court of 21 March 2023, Case C-100/21; *GSMB Invest GmbH & Co. KG v Auto Krainer GesmbH*, Judgement of the Court of 14 July 2022, C-128/20.

103 *Deutsche Umwelthilfe v Germany*, Judgment of the Court of 8 November 2022, Case C-873/19.

104 *GHC v Commission, Judgment of the General Court of 24 June 2015*, Case T-847/14; *Darment v Commission*, Judgment of the General Court of 28 May 2020, Case T-739/18; *Krajowa Izba Gospodarcza Chłodnictwa i Klimatyzacji v Commission*, Judgment of the General Court of 16 June 2021, T-126/19; *Darment v Commission*, Judgment of the General Court of 8 June 2022, T-92/21; *Stowarzyszenie chłodnictwa klimatyzacji i pomp ciepła v Commission*, Judgment of the General Court of 7 September 2022, Case T-123/21.

105 *Tazzetti v Commission*, Judgment of the General Court of 22 March 2023, Joined Cases T-825/19 and T-826/19; *Northtechnic v Commission*, Judgement of the General Court of 29 January 2025, Case T-6/24.

106 *European Commission v United Kingdom*, Judgment of the Court of 10 December 2009, Case C-187/09; *European Commission v Poland*, Judgment of the Court of 25 June 2015, Case C-303/14; *European Commission v Federal Republic of Germany*, Judgment of the Court of 4 October 2018, Case C-668/16; *European Commission v Bulgaria*, Case C-480/23 (pending).

emissions.[107] The already mentioned *Carvalho* case was the ignition factor for the current wave of civil society–led litigation for being the first of its kind, challenging the validity of several directives concerning GHG emissions, including the annual GHG emission reduction targets from 2021 to 2030. The legal grounds were varied, but with a strong resemblance to claims brought before national courts in leading climate cases: no harm principle; infringement of fundamental rights, including right to life and physical integrity, the right to pursue an occupation, the right to property, the rights of children and the right to equal treatment; breach of the Paris Agreement and UNFCCC.[108]

The *Carvalho* case was dismissed on standing rules, which might explain why a recent action brought a non-governmental organisation challenging a Commission's implementing decision revising Member States' annual emission allocations for the period from 2023 to 2030 has used a strategic preliminary request for internal review.[109] It should be noted that although the formal object of this action is a decision rejecting the review of the implementing decision, the arguments presented in the petition address the core of the reasons stated by the Commission, which, in turn, address the topics of EU's material duties to reduce GHG emissions.

This attempt for an incidental validity assessment of legal acts against which civil society holds no standing for annulment actions is a strategy also used in many cases against the Taxonomy Regulation's implementing acts mentioned in the previous section. All of these cases are pending. However, if the CJEU proceeds with the substantive analysis of the material arguments, a breach would be found that would allow access, although limited, to the CJEU in climate cases brought by citizens and non-governmental organisations. Moreover, the influence of the European Court of Human Right's recent case law over the CJEU reasoning is still to be assessed, namely in what concerns the standing of non-governmental organisations.[110]

It should also be noted that, at this point, in spite of growing relevance in terms of claims, fundamental rights have not played any relevant part in the

107 On the reasons why these cases are different from other EU climate cases, cf. Bogojević S, (n 48) pp. 197–199.

108 For a more detailed analysis on the legal reasoning behind the *Carvalho* case application, cf. Winter G. Armando Carvalho and Others v. EU. Invoking Human Rights and the Paris Agreement for Better Climate Protection Legislation. Transnational Environmental Law. 2020;9(1):137–164. Available from: https://www.cambridge.org/core/services/aop-cambridge-core/content/view/E88581624C67AEAD876CC2373F08FFAF/S2047102520000072a.pdf; cf. Garben S, (n 8) pp. 253–256.

109 *Global Legal Action Network and CAN-Europe v Commission*, Case T-120/24 (pending).

110 Eeckhout P. From Strasbourg to Luxembourg? The KlimaSeniorinnen Judgment and EU Remedies. In: Bönnemann M, Tigre MA, eds. The Transformation of European Climate Litigation. Verfassungsbooks; 2024. pp. 207–214.

existing EU climate case law,[111] raising questions as to a potential deficit of fundamental rights protection in the EU in the current climate crisis, particularly when taking into consideration the significant fundamental and human rights case law already delivered by domestic courts.[112] Notwithstanding, fundamental rights and EU environmental principles maintain the role of potentially solid legal grounds to be relevant in future decisions delivered by the European courts.[113]

5.3.3 The Polish Cases and Principles of EU Law

Only 16 climate cases have been filed directly by Member States with the CJEU, and Poland initiated 9 of them, making it by far the most frequent institutional litigant, aside from the Commission. Except for one early 2007 case concerning the Polish National Allocation Plan,[114] all the rest share common reasoning, although dealing with different issues: ETS allowance allocation,[115] ETS market stability reserve,[116] GHG emissions,[117] and CBAM.[118] They all challenge the legality of EU legislative acts: the ETS Directive, Directive

111 Reaching the same conclusion, cf. Campins Eritja M, (n 9) p. 381; Krommendijk J, Sanderink D (n 23) p. 618. The CFREU does, however, play a role in climate cases before national courts, although secondary to the European Convention on Human Rights. Cf. Van Zeben J. The Role of the EU Charter of Fundamental Rights in Climate Litigation. German Law Journal. 2021;22:1506.

112 Kalis M, Priebe A. The Right to Climate Protection and the Essentially Comparable Protection of Fundamental Rights: Applying *Solange* in European Climate Change Litigation? Review of European, Comparative & International Environmental Law. 2024;33(2):265–275.

113 On the possible conversion of EU environmental objectives enshrined in primary law to a right to a healthy environment in climate litigation, cf. Bouveresse A. Could the European Court of Justice Be a Decisive Player in Climate Justice? Athena: Critical Inquiries in Law, Philosophy and Globalization. 2023;3(2):176–182.

114 *Republic of Poland v Commission of the European Communities*, Judgement of the Court of First Instance of 23 September 2009, Case T-183/07, and Judgment of the Court of 29 March 2012, Appeal Case C-504/09 P.

115 *Republic of Poland v European Commission*, Judgment of the General Court of 7 March 2013, Case T-370/11.

116 *Republic of Poland v European Parliament and Council of the European Union*, Case C-5/16, analysed in section 3.1.2.; and *Poland v Parliament and Council*, Case C-445/23 (pending).

117 *Poland v Parliament and Council*, Judgment of the Court of 13 March 2019, Case C-128/17; *Poland v Parliament and Council*, Case C-442/23 (pending); *Poland v Parliament and Council*, Case C-444/23 (pending); *Poland v Parliament and Council*, Case C-451/23 (pending).

118 *Poland v Parliament and Council*, Case C-512/23 (pending).

2016/2284,[119] Decision 2015/1814,[120] Regulation 2023/839,[121] Regulation 2023/851,[122] Decision 2023/852,[123] Regulation 2023/857,[124] and the CBAM Regulation.

The common reasoning deals with validity claims grounded on EU primary law core principles, such as sincere cooperation, proportionality, legal certainty and protection of legitimate expectations, equality of Member States, fundamental rights, openness and transparency, and the duty to provide sufficient reasons. Poland has consistently argued, among other grounds, that not enough information was made available or assessed, that the challenged acts fail to consider the particular characteristics of individual Member States when adopting climate acts, or that they infringe upon the Member State's right to determine the conditions for exploiting its energy resources, and, therefore, constitute a breach of Article 194 TFEU. Moreover, Poland claims that these acts should have been adopted under a special legislative procedure requiring unanimity.

The 2023 cases (five in total) are pending, but, due to the similarity of legal claims, it is to be expected that the Court of Justice will, as in the three previous cases, reject these claims by considering that no breach of EU legal principles can be found, and that climate policy is well grounded in EU primary law and that the EU institutions are acting within their margin of discretion, complying with legislative procedural rules, and that there is no evidence of a

119 Directive (EU) 2016/2284 of the European Parliament and of the Council of 14 December 2016 on the reduction of national emissions of certain atmospheric pollutants, amending Directive 2003/35/EC and repealing Directive 2001/81/EC.

120 Decision (EU) 2015/1814 of the European Parliament and of the Council concerning the establishment and operation of a market stability reserve for the Union greenhouse gas emission trading scheme and amending Directive 2003/87/EC.

121 Regulation (EU) 2023/839 of the European Parliament and of the Council of 19 April 2023 amending Regulation (EU) 2018/841 as regards the scope, simplifying the reporting and compliance rules, and setting out the targets of the Member States for 2030, and Regulation (EU) 2018/1999 as regards improvement in monitoring, reporting, tracking of progress, and review.

122 Regulation (EU) 2023/851 of the European Parliament and of the Council of 19 April 2023 amending Regulation (EU) 2019/631 as regards strengthening the CO₂ emission performance standards for new passenger cars and new light commercial vehicles in line with the Union's increased climate ambition.

123 Decision (EU) 2023/852 of the European Parliament and of the Council of 19 April 2023 amending Decision (EU) 2015/1814 as regards the number of allowances to be placed in the market stability reserve for the Union greenhouse gas emission trading system until 2030.

124 Regulation (EU) 2023/857 of the European Parliament and of the Council of 19 April 2023 amending Regulation (EU) 2018/842 on binding annual greenhouse gas emission reductions by Member States from 2021 to 2030 contributing to climate action to meet commitments under the Paris Agreement, and Regulation (EU) 2018/1999.

lack of information or cooperation. This means that EU law principles have not played a significant role in climate litigation before the CJEU so far.[125]

The fact that previous dismissals did not prevent new cases using the same legal reasoning, despite small chances of success, is an indication of strategic anti-climate litigation, using actions before the CJEU to reinforce Poland's strong objections in this field. However, it should be noted that, although brought by a State, the legal grounds used by Poland echo those presented in just transition litigation.[126]

5.4 Concluding Remarks

As the highest judicial authority on the interpretation and application of EU law, the CJEU has delivered a significant number of rulings over the past 24 years. Unlike climate litigation in other legal systems, EU climate cases have primarily resulted from the adoption and implementation of laws designed to address climate change, mainly in three areas: the ETS, energy, and GHG emissions. These cases cover a wide range of topics, often interconnected with other areas of EU law, such as freedom of movement, state aid, public procurement, or tax law. This stands in contrast to most international climate cases, which deal with a context where climate norms are scarce and rely on general principles, human rights law, or the law of the sea as stepping stones to achieve climate protection in the absence of a robust climate legal framework.

However, the most recent cases demonstrate a shift. Although previous themes remain highly relevant, there has been a transformation in the reasoning behind the applications. This shift has moved litigation from the early cases concerning the technical aspects of EU climate laws to recent cases that address deeper questions about balancing social cohesion with environmental goals, as well as the broader challenge of intersectional sustainability. Moreover, two cross-cutting topics are consistently emerging: fundamental rights and participatory rights. The impact of these cases is still to be determined, as many are pending, and the first cases of this kind were dismissed due to strict standing rules. At this stage, despite their increasing prominence in legal claims, fundamental rights have not played a significant role in shaping EU climate case law.

125 Conversely, EU law principles have been invoked a significant role in climate cases before national courts, at least partially filling the gap left by strict access rules – cf. Colombo E. Principles of EU Law in Climate Litigation. China-EU Law Journal. 2024:1–23:sec. 4.

126 As conceptualised in a recent study, just transition litigation "is not brought with the stated purpose of undermining climate action. Instead, it contends that laws, policies and projects must better balance the pursuit of climate objectives with the rights and interests of adversely affected communities". Cf. Savaresi A et al. Conceptualizing Just Transition Litigation. Nature Sustainability. 2014;7(11):1379–1384.

In a prospective note, there are reasons to believe that EU climate litigation will continue to expand in quantity, scope, and complexity. The evolution of legal grounds will surely depend on how recently filed cases are decided by the CJEU. In any case, new EU climate laws have been adopted and are currently in a transition phase, while new climate-related legislative proposals are still progressing through the legislative process. It is therefore reasonable to conclude that new legal grounds for climate litigation will continue to emerge, fuelling new applications.

References

Bogojević S. EU climate change litigation: all quiet on the Luxembourgian front? In: Van Calster G, Vandenberghe W, Reins L, editors. Research handbook on climate change mitigation law. Cheltenham: Edward Elgar Publishing; 2015. p. 545–59. Available from: https://china.elgaronline.com/edcollbook/edcoll/9781849803809/9781849803809.xml.

Bogojević S. Human rights of minors and future generations: global trends and EU environmental law particularities. Rev Eur Comp Int Environ Law. 2020;29(2):191–200.

Bogojević S. Legalising environmental leadership: a comment on the CJEU's ruling in C-366/10 on the inclusion of aviation in the EU emissions trading scheme. J Environ Law. 2012;24(2):345–56.

Bouveresse A. Could the European court of justice be a decisive player in climate justice? Athena Crit Inq Law Philos Glob. 2023;3(2):157–86.

Braun M. The evolution of emissions trading in the European Union – The role of policy networks, knowledge and policy entrepreneurs. Account Organ Soc. 2009;34(3):69–87.

Campins Eritja M. The European Union and climate change litigation: promising much but delivering little? In: Sindico F, McKenzie K, Médici-Colombo G, editors. Research handbook on climate change litigation. Cheltenham: Edward Elgar Publishing; 2024. p. 364–83.

Carbon Market Watch. Survival guide to EU carbon market lobby: debunking claims from heavy industry. Policy Briefing. Brussels: Carbon Market Watch; 2021.

Cebulak P, Morvillo M, Salomon S. Strategic litigation in EU law: who does it empower? Ger Law J. 2024;25(6):800–21.

Colombo E. Principles of EU law in climate litigation. China-EU Law J. 2024:1–23.

Corporate Europe Observatory. *Industry lobbying on emissions trading scheme hits the jackpot: the cases of Arcelor Mittal and Lafarge.* Brussels: Corporate Europe Observatory; 2010.

Duffy H. Strategic human rights litigation: understanding and maximising impact. Oxford: Bloomsbury Publishing; 2018.

Eeckhout P. From Strasbourg to Luxembourg? The KlimaSeniorinnen judgment and EU remedies. In: Bönnemann M, Tigre MA, editors. The transformation of European climate litigation. Berlin: Verfassungsbooks; 2024. p. 207–14.

Fleerackers S. Hidden in plain sight? Corporate strategic litigation in the EU emissions trading system. Ger Law J. 2024;25(6):873–92.

Garben S. The CJEU and climate (in)activism?. Cheltenham: Edward Elgar Publishing; 2024. p. 247–268.

Higham C, Setzer J, Narulla H, Bradeen E. Climate change law in Europe: what do new EU climate laws mean for the courts? London: Grantham Research

Institute on Climate Change and the Environment and Centre for Climate Change Economics and Policy, London School of Economics and Political Science, 2023.
Kalis M, Priebe A. The right to climate protection and the essentially comparable protection of fundamental rights: applying Solange in European climate change litigation? Rev Eur Comp Int Environ Law. 2024;33(2):265–75.
Krommendijk J, Sanderink D. The role of fundamental rights in the environmental case law of the CJEU. Eur Law Open. 2023;2(3):616–35.
Mertens D, Thiemann M. The European Investment Bank: The EU's climate bank? In: Rayner T, Szulecki K, Jordan AJ, Oberthür S, editors. Handbook on European Union climate change policy and politics. Cheltenham: Edward Elgar Publishing; 2023. p. 68–82. Available from: https://www.elgaronline.com/edcollbook-oa/book/9781789906981/9781789906981.xml.
Montini M. Addressing the conflicts between climate-related renewable energy goals and environmental protection interests under the RED Directive. Eur Law Open. 2024;3(1):209–19.
Peeters M, Misonne D. The European Union and its rule-creating force on the European continent for moving to climate neutrality by 2050 at the latest. In: Reins L, Verschuuren J, editors. Research handbook on climate change mitigation law. Cheltenham: Edward Elgar Publishing; 2022. p. 59–102. Available from: https://www.elgaronline.com/edcollbook/book/9781839101595/9781839101595.xml.
Reyes O, Balanyá B. Carbon warfare: how big polluters plan to profit from EU emissions trading reform. Brussels: Corporate Europe Observatory; 2016.
Savaresi A, Setzer J. Rights-based litigation in the climate emergency: mapping the landscape and new knowledge frontiers. J Hum Rights Environ. 2023;13(1):7–34.
Savaresi A, Setzer J, Bookman S, Bouwer K, Chan T, Keuschnigg I, Armeni C, Harrington A, Heri C, Higham I, Hilson C, Luporini R, Macchi C, Nordlander L, Obani P, Peterson L, Schapper A, Ghaleigh NS, Tigre MA, Wewerinke-Singh M. Conceptualizing just transition litigation. Nat Sustain. 2014;7(11):1379–84.
Schoukens H. Strategic climate change litigation and the EU habitats directive: squaring the circle with the help of the US Endangered Species Act? J Eur Environ Plan Law. 2023;20(1):51–94.
Scott J. Extraterritoriality and territorial extension in EU law. Am J Comp Law. 2014;62:87–125.
Setzer J, Higham C. Global trends in climate change litigation: 2024 snapshot. London: Grantham Research Institute on Climate Change and the Environment, London School of Economics and Political Science; 2024.
Setzer J, Narulla H, Higham C, Bradeen E. Climate litigation in Europe: a summary report for the European Union Forum of Judges for the Environment. London: Grantham Research Institute on Climate Change and the Environment and Centre for Climate Change Economics and Policy, London School of Economics and Political Science and the European Union Forum of Judges for the Environment; 2022. Available from: https://www.lse.ac.uk/granthaminstitute/wp-content/uploads/2022/12/Climate-litigation-in-Europe_A-summary-report-for-the-EU-Forum-of-Judges-for-the-Environment.pdf.
Stoczkiewicz M. The role of the courts in EU climate policy. In: Rayner T, Szulecki K, Jordan AJ, Oberthür S, editors*Handbook on European Union climate change policy and politics*. Cheltenham: Edward Elgar Publishing; 2023. p. 129–42.
Van der Pas K. Conceptualising strategic litigation. Oñati Socio-Legal Ser. 2021;11(6)(S):S116–45.
Van Zeben J. The European emissions trading scheme case law. Rev Eur Community Int Environ Law. 2009;18(2):119–27.

Van Zeben J. The role of the EU Charter of Fundamental Rights in climate litigation. Ger Law J. 2021;22:1499–510.
Weishaar SE. EU emissions trading – Its regulatory evolution and the role of the court. In: Peeters M, Eliantonio M, editors. Research handbook on EU environmental law. Cheltenham: Edward Elgar Publishing; 2020. p. 443–57.
Winter G. Armando Carvalho and others v EU: invoking human rights and the Paris agreement for better climate protection legislation. Transnat Environ Law. 2020;9(1):137–64. Available from: https://www.cambridge.org/core/services/aop-cambridge-core/content/view/E88581624C67AEAD876CC2373F08FFAF/S2047102520000072a.pdf.

Part B

Procedural Issues in International Climate Litigation

6 Climate Litigation within the United Nations System – Unity, Pluralism, and a Common Goal

José Alberto Azeredo Lopes and Maria Isabel Tavares

6.1 Introduction

Discussing climate litigation within the United Nations (UN) system is increasingly important. Understandably, even the assessment of the conditions under which this system can be activated depends on the rules applicable to each litigation subsystem. However, it is based on concrete cases that the scope, relationships, and mutual legal leverage in the various judicial and para-judicial bodies of the UN can best be foreseen. Similarly, the influence of cases dealing with environmental protection (in general) before international tribunals, on the one hand, and those described under the heading of climate litigation, on the other, can already be assumed. For this reason, some attention will be paid, if only by way of reference, to the cases that have brought environmental issues to the fore.

Given the broad scope of the proposed concept of climate litigation, for the purposes of systematisation the option has been to depart from the judicial and quasi-judicial bodies to which the issue might be submitted. The focus will therefore be on the International Court of Justice (ICJ), the International Tribunal for the Law of the Sea (ITLOS), and the United Nations treaty-based mechanisms.

6.2 International Court of Justice

6.2.1 Jurisdiction

The ICJ is "the principal judicial organ of the United Nations"[1] and all members of the United Nations are "*ipso facto* parties to the Statute" of the ICJ.[2]

1 UN Charter, Article 92. As Dapo Akande stated in 2016, the ICJ "remains the pre-eminent standing tribunal for the adjudication of inter-State disputes, except with regard to trade disputes": Akande D. Selection of the International Court of Justice as a Forum for Contentious and Advisory Proceedings (Including Jurisdiction). Journal of International Dispute Settlement. 2016;7:320, 323. On the special characteristics that distinguish the ICJ from other institutional judicial institutions, D'Argent P. Article 92. In: Simma B, (ed). The Charter of the United Nations: A Commentary. 4th ed. Vol. II, Oxford University Press; 2024. pp. 2487, 2503–2506. The ICJ is indeed the principal judicial organ of the United Nations, which indicates that it was not designed to be the only one within the UN. On the other hand, it is the only judicial organ that is also "principal". See Tomka P. Article 92. In: Cot J-P, Pellet A, Forteau M, eds. La Charte des Nations Unies. Vol II. 3rd ed. Economica; 2005. pp. 1945, 1947.

2 UN Charter, Article 93(1).

DOI: 10.4324/9781003540977-9

Contentious cases and advisory proceedings may be brought before the ICJ. The difference on legal standing in both cases will be addressed as follows.

6.2.1.1 Contentious Cases

Contentious cases decided by the Court are of an inter-State nature.[3] In deciding, the Court shall apply international conventions, international customary law, and general principles of international law. If the Parties agree thereto by a special agreement, the Court may decide a case *ex aequo et bono*.[4] The decisions of the ICJ have an *inter partes* effect,[5] even if the material effect of the Court's decisions in this sphere always goes beyond the States involved in the dispute. As a rule, there is no right of appeal.[6]

Furthermore, the exercise of the ICJ's jurisdiction in contentious cases is subject to consent, normally referred to as the principle of voluntary jurisdiction. It may be accepted in three main ways: through a special agreement; a jurisdictional clause; or the acceptance of the compulsory jurisdiction of the ICJ.

Two or more States may reach an agreement through which they submit its dispute to the ICJ. In this *special agreement*, States normally delimit the scope of the ICJ's judgment, as they can determine, with precision, the object of the dispute and the applicable law. Thus, the answer of the Court will be restricted to the specific issues submitted by the Parties.

The ICJ will also be able to exercise its contentious jurisdiction when a treaty enshrines a *jurisdictional clause*[7] – i.e., when a treaty contains a provision whereby, in the event of a dispute of a given type or disagreement over the interpretation or application of the treaty, any State Party may refer the dispute to the Court involving another State Party. Attention must be given to the possible existence of reservations to the article of the treaty enshrining such jurisdictional clause.[8]

Finally, States Parties to the Statute of the ICJ may, through a unilateral declaration, accept the contentious jurisdiction as *compulsory*.[9] This declaration "may be made unconditionally or on condition of reciprocity on the part of several or certain states, or for a certain time".[10]

The ICJ has also interpreted[11] the possibility of "tacit or implicit consent: the so-called *forum prorogatum*". In the situation that "a State institutes

3 Statute of the International Court of Justice, Article 34(1) (ICJ Statute).
4 ICJ Statute, Article 39(2).
5 UN Charter, Article 94, and ICJ Statute, Article 59.
6 ICJ Statute, Article 60.
7 ICJ Statute, Article 36(1).
8 Under Article 19 of the 1969 Vienna Convention on the Law of Treaties, States might exclude the application of the jurisdictional clause. On reservations on jurisdiction and reciprocity, see D'Argent P, (n 1) pp. 2526–2527.
9 ICJ Statute, Article 36(2). In accordance with the information provided by the ICJ, 74 States have deposited such a declaration. See https://www.icj-cij.org/declarations.
10 ICJ Statute, Article 36(3).
11 ICJ, *Haya de la Torre Case* (Colombia/Peru), Judgment, 13 June 1951, 78.

proceedings before the Court against a State that has not previously accepted the Court's jurisdiction, the jurisdiction of the Court is established if the respondent State shows that it accepts the Court's jurisdiction by some act (such as appearing before the Court and arguing the case on its merits)".[12]

Third-State Parties may submit a request to the Court to intervene if they have an interest of a legal nature which may be affected by the concrete decision in that case.[13] It is for the Court to decide upon this request.[14] Furthermore, every State Party has the right to intervene "[w]henever the construction of a conventions to which States other than those concerned in the case are parties is in question."[15]

6.2.1.2 Advisory Opinions

The Security Council and the General Assembly may request advisory opinions on "any legal question".[16] Other UN organs and specialised agencies[17] might request advisory opinions from the Court on "legal questions arising from the scope of their activities".[18/19] In formal terms, advisory opinions are not legally binding.[20]

12 Gaeta P, Viñuales JE, Zappalà S. Cassese's International Law. 3rd ed. Oxford University Press; 2020. pp. 287, 288. See also Yee S. Forum Prorogatum in the International Court. German Yearbook of International Law. 1999;42:147; Yee S. Forum Prorogatum Returns to the International Court of Justice. Leiden Journal of International Law. 2003;16:701; Pouliot V. Forum Prorogatum before the International Court of Justice: The Djibouti v. France Case. Hague Justice Journal. 2008;3:28.

13 ICJ Statute, Article 62(1). "The existence of an interest of a legal nature is obviously the main element of an Article 62 intervention", Barrie GN. Third-Party State Intervention in Disputes Before the International Court of Justice: A Reassessment of Articles 62 and 63 of the ICJ Statute. Comparative and International Law Journal of Southern Africa. 2020;53:1, 8. Some guidance on what constitutes an interest of a legal nature based on the ICJ's case law, 8–9.

14 ICJ Statute, Article 62(2).

15 ICJ Statute, Article 63.

16 ICJ Statute, Article 96(1).

17 As of 31 December 2024, the UNGA has requested 18 advisory opinions, the UNSC has requested one, and the Economic and Social Council has made two requests for advisory opinion. Furthermore, 15 specialised agencies and one related organisation are acknowledged to have the competence to request for an advisory opinion.

18 ICJ Statute, Article 96(2). See, vg., ICJ, *Legality of the Use by a State of Nuclear Weapons in Armed Conflict* (Advisory Opinion) [1996], 8 July 1996, where the ICJ considered that the question raised in the request for an advisory opinion submitted to it by the World Health Organization did not arise "within the scope of its activities", paras. 18–26.

19 On the discussion of *erga omnes* violations and third-party intervention before the ICJ, see Alexander A, Guha SK. Critical Analysis of Third-Party Intervention before the International Court of Justice. The Indonesian Journal of International and Comparative Law. 2022;9:115, 133–136.

20 Pointing the different ways that the UNGA and UNSC have reacted to advisory opinions at their request, Oellers-Frahm K., Lagrange E. Article 96. In:: Simma B, (ed). The Charter of the United Nations: A Commentary. 4th ed. Vol. II, Oxford University Press; 2024, pp. 2585, 2601–2604.

The question put to the ICJ must be of a *legal nature* within the meaning of its Statute and the UN Charter, as opposed to a political question[21] (even though the distinction is sometimes blurred).[22] If the Court considers the question unclear or vague, not adequately formulated, or that it does not reflect the legal question really a stake, it has the power to reformulate and interpret the posed question.[23]

Regarding third Parties' intervention in advisory opinion proceedings, whether States or international organisations, the ICJ Statute enshrines great flexibility.[24]

6.2.2 *The UN General Assembly's Request to the ICJ for an Advisory Opinion on Climate Change*

Neither the United Nations Framework Convention on Climate Change nor the Kyoto Protocol or the Paris Agreement enshrine typical jurisdictional clauses, i.e., one in which the State is under a jurisdictional obligation *except* if it makes a reservation.[25]Prospectively, it is thus possible, even if not probable, that States accept a special agreement directly bringing climate litiga-

21 "The purpose of the advisory function aims at guiding the practice of the organ concerned and, as the case may be, also the States involved in the matter", *ibid*, pp. 2588–2589.

22 There is a relative proximity between this issue and the legal or political disputes brought before the Court under its contentious jurisdiction. The ICJ has consistently stated that the political elements of a given situation do not affect its competence to interpret and apply international law. The Court has been clear in stating that "legal disputes between sovereign States by their very nature are likely to occur in political contexts, and often form only one element in a wider and long-standing political dispute between the States concerned. Yet never has the view been put forward before that, because a legal dispute submitted to the Court is only one aspect of a political dispute, the Court should decline to resolve for the parties the legal questions at issue between them. Nor can any basis for such a view of the Court's functions or jurisdiction be found in the Charter or the Statute of the Court; if the Court were, contrary to its settled jurisprudence, to adopt such a view, it would impose a far-reaching and unwarranted restriction upon the role of the Court in the peaceful solution of international disputes". ICJ, *United States Diplomatic and Consular Staff in Tehran* (Merits) [1980] ICJ, Judgment of 24 May 1980, para. 37. See also ICJ, *Border and Transborder Armed Actions (Nicaragua v Honduras)* (Jurisdiction and Admissibility) [1988] ICJ, Judgment of 20 December 1988, para. 52 (a legal dispute being defined as a "a dispute capable of being settled by the application of principles and rules of international law").

23 See, for example, ICJ, *Application for Review of Judgment No. 271 of the United Nations Administrative Tribunal* (Advisory Opinion) [1982] ICJ, 20 July 1982, paras. 46–48 and *ICJ, Interpretation of the Agreement of 25 March 1951 between The WHO and Egypt* (Advisory Opinion) [1980] ICJ, 20 December 1980, para. 10.

24 ICJ Statute, Article 66.

25 Article 14 of the UNFCCC enshrines a dispute settlement provision, also incorporated in the Paris Agreement (Article 24). Article 14 (2) of the UNFCCC allows Parties to declare, at the time of ratification or thereafter, that they recognise as compulsory the submission of disputes regarding the interpretation or application of the Convention to the International Court of Justice or to arbitration procedures. Thus, an action of States is required for the ICJ's jurisdiction to be established.

tion before the ICJ. It is also possible that within the compulsory jurisdiction of the Court, or a jurisdictional clause on another treaty, States and or the ICJ raise environmental and climate issues, even if indirectly.[26]

In fact, the ICJ had a fundamental role in the development of environmental protection discussing and establishing important principles.[27] Seminal cases in this domain have had distinct origins in terms of legal standing. For example, the *Gabčikovo-Nagymaros* case[28] was brought before the ICJ through a Special Agreement.[29] On the other hand, the *Pulp Mills* case[30] was brought before the ICJ Court by Argentina[31] against Uruguay under a jurisdictional clause.[32] As for the *Whaling in the Antarctic* case,[33] the ICJ established its jurisdiction based on unilateral declarations of both States involved (Australia and Japan) pursuant to Article 36(2) ICJ Statute. In *Certain Activities carried out by Nicaragua in the Border Area*,[34] the jurisdiction of

---

Thus far, only one state, the Netherlands, as accepted the compulsory jurisdiction of the ICJ in this context. Two states – the Netherlands and the Solomon Islands – have recognised arbitration as a dispute resolution mechanism under Article 14(2) of the UNFCCC. The Netherlands is also the only state that has adopted a declaration under Article 24 of the Paris Agreement.

Furthermore, no such annex or formal arbitration procedures, established in Article 14 (2) UNFCCC, have been developed or finalised to date by the COP.

26 Daniel Bodansky, thanking Jay Butler for the suggestion, interestingly proposed that "to keep control of the issues presented to the ICJ, two similarly-inclined states might agree to have the ICJ hear a 'contentious' case between themselves": Bodansky D. The Role of the International Court of Justice in Addressing Climate Change: Some Preliminary Reflections. Arizona State Law Journal. 2017;49:689, 712.

27 See, for example, Viñuales JE. The Contribution of the International Court of Justice to the Development of International Environmental Law: A Contemporary Assessment. Fordham International Law Journal. 2008;32:232; Fitzmaurice M. The International Court of Justice and International Environmental Law. In: Tams CJ, Sloan J, eds. The Development of International Law by the International Court of Justice. Oxford University Press; 2013. pp. 353–374.

28 ICJ, *Case Concerning the Gabčíkovo-Nagymaros Project (Hungary/Slovakia)*, Judgment, 25 September 1997.

29 Special Agreement between the Republic of Hungary and the Slovak Republic for Submission to the International Court of Justice of the Differences between them concerning the Gabčíkovo-Nagymaros Project, signed at Brussels on 7 April 1993, https://www.icj-cij.org/sites/default/files/case-related/92/10835.pdf.

30 ICJ, *Case Concerning Pulp Mills on the River Uruguay (Argentina v Uruguay)*, Judgment, 20 April 2010.

31 For the text of the Argentinian Application of 4 May 2006 instituting proceedings, see https://www.icj-cij.org/sites/default/files/case-related/135/10779.pdf.

32 Article 60(1) of the Statute of the River Uruguay, signed by Argentina and Uruguay in 1975, https://treaties.un.org/doc/Publication/UNTS/Volume%201295/volume-1295-I-21425-English.pdf.

33 ICJ, *Whaling in the Antarctic (Australia v Japan: New Zealand intervening)*, Judgment, 31 March 2014.

34 ICJ, *Certain Activities Carried Out by Nicaragua in the Border Area (Costa Rica v Nicaragua) and Construction of a Road in Costa Rica along the San Juan River (Nicaragua v Costa Rica)*, Judgment, 16 December 2015.

the ICJ was based on a mixed legitimacy: on one hand, both parties invoked Article XXXI of the Pact of Bogotá and, on the other hand, both states made declarations in which they recognised the compulsory jurisdiction of the Court under Article 36(2) and (5) ICJ Statute. In the *Legality of Nuclear Weapons* opinion,[35] the ICJ addressed the environmental law applicable.[36]

On 29 March 2023, the UN General Assembly decided to request the ICJ for an advisory opinion on climate change. The forthcoming ICJ's Advisory Opinion will certainly clarify possible paths for future climate litigation not only before the ICJ itself but also within the UN system and beyond.[37]

The generic competence of the UN General Assembly invited, and enabled, an open question.[38] Furthermore, the persistent, strategic, and professional approach promoted by the Republic of Vanuatu as the main State sponsor shall be emphasised.[39] In fact, previous attempts to bring climate change before the ICJ in an advisory opinion had proven fruitless.[40]

The involvement of several States with different and worldwide representatives in the drafting and support of the request, as well as the involvement of civil society, was certainly an efficient approach that enabled not only the adoption of the request itself but also empowered the mandate of the ICJ.

Another aspect to be highlighted is the strategic drafting of the questions posed to the ICJ in a way that raises not only substantive questions but also enables the Court to give guidelines on possible future paths for litigation.[41]

35 ICJ, *Legality of the Threat or Use of Nuclear Weapons* (Advisory Opinion) [1996] ICJ, 8 July 1996.

36 Despite the generic terms of the question posed by the UN General Assembly ("Is the threat or use of nuclear weapons in any circumstance permitted under international law?"), some States argued in their written and oral statements the need for an assessment on applicable environmental law, which was done by the Court, paras. 27–33.

37 The impact will also reach non-legal spheres as recalled by Wewerinke-Singh M, Garg A, Hartmann J. The Advisory Proceedings on Climate Change before the International Court of Justice. Questions of International Law, Zoom-in. 2023;23, 42.

38 In 2017, Daniel Bodansky, considering that an advisory opinion request would be preferable to a contentious case on climate litigation, suggested that "the World Meteorological Organization might be a better choice than the U.N. General Assembly, since it is a more technical, less politicized forum, in which it might be easier to resist efforts to encumber the request with unhelpful baggage": Bodansky D, (n 26) p. 712.

39 Vanuatu successfully led a coalition of 132 nations. Vanuatu led a core group of nations which drafted a question to ask the Court: Vanuatu, Antigua and Barbuda, Costa Rica, Sierra Leone, Angola, Germany, Mozambique, Liechtenstein, Samoa, Federated States of Micronesia, Bangladesh, Morocco, Singapore, Uganda, New Zealand, Vietnam, Romania, and Portugal, see https://www.vanuatuicj.com/.

40 On previous attempts and the initiative of the Republic of Tuvalu that originated the UNGA request, see, for example, Wewerinke-Singh M, Garg A, Hartmann J, (n 37) pp. 25–28.

41 It can be framed as an advisory opinion request "generated as a result of a desire to clarify a legal question but where the opinion is not directed at a specific question"; the opinion is thus "intended to guide State behaviour in relation to the issues as such, whether those issues relate to a concrete factual situation or are pure questions of law that have not arisen in a particular factual setting", lending the classification by Akande, (n 1), pp. 340–341.

It is, first, interesting to note the wide range of treaties invoked to frame the posed questions by the UNGA.[42] On one hand, specific treaties on climate change and national obligations that lack jurisdictional clauses, namely the United Nations Framework Convention and the Paris Agreement. On the other hand, the establishment of a definite link between climate change and human rights, with the specific reference to the International Covenants on Civil and Political Rights (ICCPR) and on Economic, Social and Cultural Rights (ICESCR), as well as to the rights enshrined in the Universal Declaration on Human Rights. Last, but not least, the explicit reference to the United Nations Convention on the Law of the Sea (UNCLOS) is a necessary reminder not only of the substantive impact of climate change on the sea but also, on the advisory proceedings that were, at the time, already in motion, before ITLOS.[43]

Second, the request is designed on the basis of the structure of State responsibility. The first question addresses the existing legal obligations; the second question addresses the categories of "injured" or "specially affected", small island developing States and peoples and individuals of present and future generations. The underlining strategy seems clear: to identify the main holders of climate litigation standing in the future.[44]

These proceedings and the decision of the ICJ will certainly address, and hopefully give more clarity, to some of the difficult tasks involving climate litigation such as, for example, causality, making climate science and its concepts operational in legal context,[45] establishing a clearer standard of proof,[46] the role of the UN and its multiple bodies in providing evidence, or the role

42 Thus, encouraging "the adoption if a holistic approach in considering how international law applies to the relevant conduct of States", Wewerinke-Singh M, Garg A, Hartmann J, (n 37) p. 33.

43 The Commission of Small Island States on Climate Change and International Law requested an advisory opinion to the International Tribunal for the Law of the Sea on 12 December 2022. The advisory opinion was finally enacted by ITLOS on 21 May 2024.

44 Regarding small state islands, the reference to Article 42 of the Draft Articles on International State Responsibility for Internationally Wrongful Acts (ARSIWA) is evident. The identification of peoples and individuals in this context opens the path for individual complaints under human rights mechanisms (universal, regional, or domestic) and, also, to the possible invocation by third states based on communitarian values (ARSIWA, Article 48). However, despite this possible development, it is important to recall, with Akande, that the existence of *erga omnes* and/or *ius cogens* norms does not dispense the need of consent on jurisdiction: Akande D, (n 1) p. 326.

45 For example, addressing long-term implications of anthropogenic emissions in the existing legal system and concepts is certainly a challenging task, see Wewerinke-Singh M, Garg A, Hartmann J, (n 37) p. 34.

46 Sulyok K. Science, Legitimacy, and the Judicial Function: A Need for More Intrusive Standards of Review. In: Kajtár G, Çalı B, Milanovic M, eds. Secondary Rules of Primary Importance in International Law: Attribution, Causality, Evidence, and Standards of Review in the Practice of International Courts and Tribunals. Oxford University Press; 2022. pp. 83–101.

of third-party interventions in climate litigation.[47] Furthermore, this action of the ICJ will be – in fact, it already is, during the proceedings – subject to great scrutiny and, therefore, not free from criticism.[48]

The legal effects of an Advisory Opinion are limited and, thus, a necessary balance between wishful thinking and effectiveness is advisable. There is the risk that a certain judicial activism (to which the ICJ is being invited by many of the participants) might lead to a gap between the Court's *dictum* and the current and future foreseeable practice of States.[49] It would certainly be of no help if the Advisory Opinion of the Court was to be disregarded and contested by States. Some of the main challenges in this respect are certainly present in the need to identify, from some general obligations, concrete, palpable, and stringent legal obligations whose fulfilment may be easily addressed and monitored.

Without diminishing the importance of the Court's opinion, the proceedings themselves – along with the participation of more than one hundred States and organisations – present an excellent opportunity to better

47 By the end of 2024, the ICJ has authorised the International Union for Conservation of Nature, the European Union, the Commission of Small Islands States on Climate Change and International Law, the African Union, the Organization of the Petroleum Exporting Countries, the Organisation of African, Caribbean and Pacific States, the Melanesian Spearhead Group, the Forum Fisheries Agency, the Pacific Islands Forum, the Alliance of Small Island States, and the Parties to the Nauru Agreement Office to participate in the proceedings. As pointed by Wewerinke-Singh M, Garg A, Hartmann J, the authorization for the participation of the International Union for Conservation of Nature (IUCN) accepts an "unusual" broad concept of international organizations, (n 37) p. 30. In fact, the IUCN is not exclusively intergovernmental – its membership includes states, governmental agencies, NGOs, Indigenous people's organisations, academic institutions, and business associations. Paula Wojcikiewicz Almeida supports the enlargement of the procedural participation of third-Party States and the *Amicus Curiae* before the ICJ, particularly when communitarian interests are at stake, Almeida PW. International Procedure Regulation in the Common Interest: The Role of Third-Party Intervention and Amicus Curiae before the ICJ. The Law and Practice of International Courts and Tribunals. 2019;18:163, 188.

48 For example, the decision to invite a group of past and present authors of the reports of the Intergovernmental Panel on Climate Change (IPCC) to meet with Members of the Court in The Hague to enhance the Court's understanding of the key scientific findings which the IPCC has delivered through its periodic assessment reports covering the scientific basis, impacts, and future risks of climate change, and options for adaptation and mitigation on Climate Change (IPCC) (ICJ, Press Release, No. 2024/75, 26 November 2024) is not clear cut under the Statute. Pointing out this case as an opportunity to discuss more transparency in the proceedings, Deller RO. Experts Fantômes at the ICJ. EJIL Talk! 2 December 2024. Available from: https://www.ejiltalk.org/experts-fantomes-at-the-icj/.

49 For example, in the written statement presented before the Court by the Republic of India, it "contends that the Court should avoid creation of new or additional obligations beyond what is already agreed under the climate change regime, which takes due consideration of climate justice and the principles of equity and common but differentiated responsibilities and respective capabilities (CBDR-RC)", para. 8, 21 March 2024.

understand, through the transparency of both written and oral interventions, the practices and interpretations of States concerning climate change obligations.[50]

6.3 The International Tribunal for the Law of the Sea

6.3.1 Jurisdiction

UNCLOS establishes a general dispute settlement system, under which the jurisdiction of ITLOS is not exclusive.[51]

6.The importance of the law of the sea in the context of climate change is unquestionable, as confirmed by the recent ITLOS advisory opinion. Nevertheless, ITLOS is not the only judicial body which States may reach to when having questions on the interpretation or application of UNCLOS.

6.3.1.1 Contentious Jurisdiction

In accordance with Part XV and XI of UNCLOS and with its Annex VI,[52] ITLOS is one of the judicial bodies with comprehensive competence, amongst others. In general terms, ITLOS "shall have jurisdiction over any dispute concerning the interpretation or application of this Convention"[53] subject to consent by the Parties.[54] Furthermore, it "shall also have jurisdiction over any dispute concerning the interpretation or application of an international

50 The UN International Law Commission clarifies that "claims before national or international courts and tribunals" may be considered as a *forms of practice* (under conclusion 6, par. 2) and "assertions made in written and oral pleadings before courts and tribunals" as *forms of evidence of acceptance as law* (*opinio juris*) (under conclusion 10, par. 2), Draft Conclusions on identification of customary international law, with commentaries, A/73/10, Report of the International Law Commission, Seventieth session (30 April–1 June and 2 July–10 August 2018), https://legal.un.org/ilc/reports/2018/english/a_73_10_advance.pdf, 134 and 141, respectively.

51 In fact, ITLOS "is one of the four judicial bodies to which contracting parties to a dispute may turn, when the dispute cannot be solved through negotiations, conciliations, or other means (ITLOS has exclusive jurisdiction through its Seabed Disputes Chamber, over disputes relating to activities in the international seabed area; in addition, it has special jurisdiction in matters calling for provisional measures)". The ICJ, an arbitral tribunal set up in accordance with Annex VII to UNCLOS, and a special arbitral tribunal established under Annex VIII of the same convention are the other judicial bodies available to the parties. Gaeta P, Viñuales JE, Zappalà S, (n 12) p. 288.

52 Which contains the ITLOS Statute.

53 UNCLOS, Article 288(1), ITLOS Statute, Article 21.

54 In accordance with Article 297 UNCLOS, ITLOS might exercise its jurisdiction over all disputes and all applications submitted to it in accordance with UNCLOS, considering declarations by States under article 298. On the other hand, Article 297 and declarations made under Article 298 of the Convention do not prevent parties from agreeing to submit to the Tribunal a dispute otherwise excluded from the Tribunal's jurisdiction under these provisions, as stated in Article 299.

agreement related to the purposes of this Convention, which is submitted to it in accordance with the agreement".[55]

The decisions of the Tribunal are "final and shall be complied with by all the parties to the dispute". "In the event of dispute as to the meaning or scope of the decision, the Tribunal shall construe it upon the request of any party".[56]

Regarding third-State Party intervention, two situations might arise. A State Party that considers it has a legal interest potentially affected by the outcome of a specific dispute may request to intervene[57]. It is for the Tribunal "to decide upon the request".[58] If the request is given a positive answer, "the decision of the Tribunal in respect of the dispute shall be binding upon the intervening State Party in so far as it relates to matters in respect of which that State Party intervened".[59] On the other hand, every State Party has the right to intervene in a proceeding involving the interpretation or application of UNCLOS or the international agreement.[60] In that case, "the interpretation given by the judgment will be equally binding upon it".[61]

6.3.1.2 Advisory Jurisdiction

The competence of ITLOS to render advisory opinions is not expressly enshrined in UNCLOS. In fact, UNCLOS expressly gives advisory competence to the Seabed Disputes Chamber on legal questions arising within the scope of the activities of the Assembly or Council of the International Seabed Authority.[62]

However, it has been interpreted that the Tribunal may give an advisory opinion on a legal question if this is provided for by "an international agreement related to the purposes of the Convention".[63] The main legal reasoning developed by ITLOS is grounded on Articles 21 and 23 of its Statute, and on the idea that the meaning of the wording "disputes and applications"

55 UNCLOS, Article 288(2), ITLOS Statute, Article 21. For the list of multilateral and bilateral agreements that confer jurisdiction to ITLOS, see https://www.itlos.org/en/main/jurisdiction/international-agreements-conferring-jurisdiction-on-the-tribunal/. It should be added that "[i]f all the parties to a treaty or convention already in force [at the time of UNCLOS adoption] and concerning the subject-matter covered by this Convention so agree, any disputes concerning the interpretation or application of such treaty or convention may, in accordance with such agreement, be submitted to the Tribunal", ITLOS Statute, Article 22.

56 ITLOS Statute, Article 33(1) and (3). It should be added that in par. 2 of the article it is clearly stated that "[t]he decision shall have no binding force except between the parties in respect of that particular dispute".

57 ITLOS Statute, Article 31(1).

58 *Ibid*, Article 31(2).

59 *Ibid*, Article 31(3).

60 *Ibid*, Article 32.

61 *Ibid*, Article 32(3).

62 UNCLOS, Article 191.

63 ITLOS Statute, Article 21; Rules of the Tribunal, Article 138.

does not limit its authority to contentious cases. Thus, the "prerequisites [to establish the advisory jurisdiction of the Tribunal] are: an international agreement related to the purposes of the Convention specifically provides for the submission to the Tribunal of a request for an advisory opinion; the request must be transmitted to the Tribunal by a body authorized by or in accordance with the agreement mentioned above; and such an opinion may be given on 'a legal question'".[64]

All States Parties and intergovernmental organisations able to furnish information on the question may submit their statements to the Tribunal.[65]

6.3.2 *The ITLOS Advisory Opinion on Climate Change and International Law*

When discussing the possibility of climate litigation before ITLOS it is important to emphasise the Tribunal's non-exclusive competence.[66] The link between the sea and climate change is self-evident, and ITLOS will probably have future opportunities, in contentious cases, to address, directly or indirectly, substantive issues on climate change.[67] Nevertheless, transforming the Tribunal into "a" preferable climate ligation forum should be avoided, as it might contribute to an ocean-centred approach to climate change and, at the same time, lead to a certain distancing of States from the specialised jurisdiction that is crucial in the broader field of the law of the sea.[68]

On 12 December 2022, the Commission of Small Island States on Climate Change and International Law (COSIS) requested ITLOS to render an advisory opinion on specific obligations of States under UNCLOS with respect to climate change.

64 ITLOS, Case 21, *Request for an Advisory Opinion submitted by the Sub-Regional Fisheries Commission (SRFC Opinion)*, 2 April 2015, para. 60. For a full analysis on the reasoning of the Tribunal on its advisory jurisdiction, see paras. 37–69.

65 Rules of the Tribunal, Article 138(3) and Article 133(3). Defending the advantages of accepting *amicus curiae*, Rocha A. Amicus Curiae before the International Tribunal for the Law of the Sea: The Prospect of an Advisory Opinion on Climate Change and the Law of the Sea. Católica Law Review. 2022;VI:87–11.

66 Comparing ICJ and ITLOS, see, Yongming J. A Comparative Study on the International Tribunal for the Law of the Sea and the International Court of Justice – Focusing on the Tribunal's Characteristics in Respect of Constitution, Jurisdiction, Procedure and Judgment. China Oceans Law Review. 2005:289–313.

67 Doelle M, Sun Z, Schofield C. Potential Climate Change Litigation in the Law of the Sea. In: Sindico F, McKenzie K, Médici-Colombo G, Wegener L, eds. Research Handbook on Climate Change Litigation. Elgar; 2024. pp. 284–303.

68 The "underlying rationale for the creation of" the complex dispute settlement mechanism established in UNCLOS (to which ITLOS is an important of) "was the wish to safeguard the many delicate compromises enshrined in the Convention and to secure its uniform interpretation and application". Tuerk H. The Contribution of the International Tribunal for the Law of the Sea to International Law. Penn State International Law Review. 2007;26:289, 290.

In terms of the competence of the Tribunal and legal standing of COSIS, Article 138 of the Rules of the Tribunal and the international agreement creating the Commission must be revisited. The COSIS Agreement clearly enshrines the authority of the Commission to request an advisory opinion to the Tribunal "on any legal question within the scope of [UNCLOS], consistent with Article 21 of the ITLOS Statute and Article 138 of its Rules", considering "the fundamental importance of oceans as sinks and reservoirs of greenhouse gases and the direct relevance of the marine environment to the adverse effects of climate change on Small Island States".[69]

The unanimous advisory opinion was delivered by ITLOS on 21 May 2024.[70]

The *COSIS Opinion* reached important findings on the interpretation of UNCLOS and, consequently, the prospective role of ITLOS. First, the consideration that anthropogenic GHG emissions constitute "pollution of the marine environment" within the meaning of Article 1(1)(4) of UNCLOS[71] is of paramount importance, as it establishes the nexus between the law of the sea and climate change.

Second, although ITLOS states that "the UNFCCC and the Paris Agreement, as the primary legal instruments addressing the global problem of climate change, are relevant in interpreting and applying the Convention with respect to marine pollution from anthropogenic GHG emissions",[72] it adds that

> [t]he Convention and the Paris Agreement are separate agreements, with separate sets of obligations. While the Paris Agreement

69 Article 2, par. 2, Agreement for the Establishment of the Commission of Small Island States on Climate Change and International Law, signed by Antigua and Barbuda and Tuvalu on 31 October 2021. Available from: https://commonwealthfoundation.com/wp-content/uploads/2021/12/Commission-of-Small-Island-States-on-Climate-Change-and-International-Law.pdf. Following the signature, and some after the request for the advisory opinion was presented, several other States have acceded to it: Niue (13 September 2022), Palau (4 November 2021), Saint Lucia (7 December 2022), Republic of Vanuatu (2 December 2022), Saint Vincent and the Grenadines (9 June 2023), Saint Christopher (Saint Kitts) and Nevis (13 June 2023), and Commonwealth of the Bahamas (15 June 2023).

70 ITLOS, Request for an Advisory Opinion Submitted by the Commission of Small Island States on Climate Change and International Law, Advisory Opinion, 21 May 2024 (*COSIS Opinion*). As underlined by Christina Voigt, "the opinion was unanimously adopted by all 21 judges. There was no substantive dissent, and five separate declarations by judges seemed to advocate for interpreting the treaty even more broadly by way of including considerations of human rights into the advisory opinion deliberations. This represents a remarkable, unanimous willingness among the judiciary to interpret UNCLOS in a dynamic manner in the context of climate change". Voigt C. Overview and Noteworthy Elements of the Advisory Opinion. In: Reflections on the ITLOS Advisory Opinion. British Institute of International and Comparative Law. 30 May 2024. pp. 3–4, 3.

71 *Ibid*, paras. 159–179.

72 *Ibid*, para. 222.

complements the Convention in relation to the obligation to regulate marine pollution from anthropogenic GHG emissions, the former does not supersede the latter. Article 194, paragraph 1, imposes upon States a legal obligation to take all necessary measures to prevent, reduce and control marine pollution from anthropogenic GHG emissions, including measures to reduce such emissions. If a State fails to comply with this obligation, international responsibility would be engaged for that State.[73]

This reasoning leaves no room for doubt on the interpretation of the Tribunal on its competence to address in the future, including in contentious cases brought before it, the concrete fulfilment of State obligations under UNCLOS, and eventually, questions on state responsibility, on the obligation to adopt measures to prevent, reduce, and control pollution of the marine environment.[74]

Third, ITLOS identifies legal obligations under UNCLOS. On one hand, the obligation to undertake necessary measures (that meet a stringent, objective standard of case) to prevent, reduce, and control marine pollution, underlining the importance of due diligence when the activities in question are performed by private entities and the obligation of a precautionary approach. On the other hand, ITLOS adopts an overreaching approach on risk assessment and cumulative effects that will influence the possible interpretation of the previously identified obligations in a concrete situation.[75]

A final note on the expected address by the ICJ of the *COSIS Opinion*. It will be difficult and improbable for the ICJ to ignore the ITLOS advisory

73 *Ibid*, para. 223.

74 UNCLOS, Article 194.

75 For a more detailed analysis of the *COSIS Opinion*, see Khatri U, and Chowdhury J. How a Historic Opinion on Climate Change and Ocean Protection Sets the Bar for Climate Action. 27 June 2024. Available from: https://www.info-today.eu/2024/06/how-a-historic-opinion-on-climate-change-and-ocean-protection-sets-the-bar-for-climate-action/; Tigre MA, Carrillo Bañuelos JA. The ICJ's Advisory Opinion on Climate Change: What Happens Now? 29 March 2023. Available from: https://blogs.law.columbia.edu/climatechange/2023/03/29/the-icjs-advisory-opinion-on-climate-change-what-happens-now/; Yiallourides C, Deva S. A Commentary on ITLOS' Advisory Opinion on Climate Change. British Institute of International and Comparative Law. 24 May 2024. Available from: https://www.biicl.org/blog/77/a-commentary-on-itlos-advisory-opinion-on-climate-change; Anggadi F, et al. A First Reading of ITLOS' Advisory Opinion on Climate Change: Implications for Australia, New Zealand, and the Pacific. Australia and New Zealand Society of International Law Perspective. 2024;41. Available from: https://anzsilperspective.com/special-extended-perspective-a-first-reading-of-itlos-advisory-opinion-on-climate-change-implications-for-australia-new-zealand-and-the-pacific/.

opinion.[76] However, it is also unlikely that the ICJ will feel constrained, limited, or conditioned by the decision of ITLOS.[77]

6.4 United Nations Human Rights Treaty-Based Mechanisms

6.4.1 "Adversarial" Proceedings

The UN architecture on the protection of human rights is diverse and comprehensive. The implementation, monitoring, and evaluation mechanisms of those treaties and the Charter itself have a distinct nature. The focus of the following analysis will be treaty-based bodies and their competences,[78] assuming a possible specific link between the human rights enshrined and protected in those treaties and climate litigation.[79]

Furthermore, to identify possible mechanisms within the broad concept of "climate litigation", the need to meet a certain adversarial element is assumed. This being so, the possibility of individual complaints (usually known in this context as communications) and inter-State complaints, based in the different UN treaties on human rights, will be addressed.[80]

76 As would be expected, intervening States in the ICJ proceedings made explicit references to the *COSIS Opinion*, asking the Court to either confirm or restrain ITLOS's interpretation.

77 First, as seen previously, the ICJ is also an interpreter and applier of UNCLOS. Second, the question before the ICJ is broader and involves multiple legal regimes. Finally, in previous decisions, as in the *Genocide case* (when discussing the attribution standard presented by the International Criminal Tribunal for the former Yugoslavia), and, to say the least, the Court did not feel constrained by previous interpretations.

78 Thus, leaving aside the charter-based bodies that include the Human Rights Council, Special Procedures, the Universal Periodic Review, and Independent Investigations. Nevertheless, the existence of a Special rapporteur on the promotion and protection of human rights in the context of climate change should be underlined, see A/HRC/RES/48/14, Resolution adopted by the Human Rights Council on 8 October 2021.

79 A significant effort has been made to systematise and present these links in a comprehensive approach that may be explored in future climate litigation cases. Special attention should be given to the reports prepared by the distinct UN treaty-based bodies. For example: CRC/C/GC/26: General Comment No. 26 (2023) on children's rights and the environment with a special focus on climate change adopted 22 August 2023; A/HRC/52/33, Women, girls and the right to a clean, healthy and sustainable environment. Report of the Special Rapporteur on the issue of human rights obligations relating to the enjoyment of a safe, clean, healthy and sustainable environment, David R. Boyd, 5 January 2023 (Reissued for technical reasons on 3 March 2023); A/HRC/44/30, Analytical study on the promotion and protection of the rights of persons with disabilities in the context of climate change, Report of the Office of the United Nations High Commissioner for Human Rights, 22 April 2020; E/C.12/2018/1, CESCR, Climate change and the International Covenant on Economic, Social and Cultural Rights, Statement by the Committee on Economic, Social and Cultural Rights, 31 October 2018 (Reissued for technical reasons on 9 November 2018). Furthermore, the efforts to enshrine the Right to a clean, healthy, and sustainable environment led to two important resolutions within the UN: from the Human Rights Council in 2021 (A/HRC/RES/48/13) and from the General Assembly in 2022 (A/RES/76/300).

80 Thus, procedures based "on the examination of periodic reports submitted by States" will be left aside. "This is, of course, the *weakest* [supervisory procedure] and it is no coincidence

6.4.1.1 Individual Communications

The ICCPR and the ICESCR may be considered the main universal treaties on human rights. Both treaties have Optional Protocols that establish the possibility of communications. The United Nations Human Rights Committee receives communications on breaches of the ICCPR[81] and the Committee on Economic, Social and Cultural Rights receives communications on breaches of the ICESCR.[82]

The Committee on the Elimination of Racial Discrimination may "receive and consider communications from individuals or groups of individuals within its jurisdiction claiming to be victims of a violation by that State Party of any of the rights set forth in this Convention". The competence of the Committee may be declared by State Parties at any time. On the other hand, "[n]o communication shall be received by the Committee if it concerns a State Party which has not made such a declaration".[83]

The Optional Protocol to the Convention on the Elimination of All Forms of Discrimination against Women of 1999 has accepted the competence of the Committee on the Elimination of Discrimination against Women to consider requests of persons or groups of persons who claim to be victims of violations of their rights as laid down in the Convention.[84]

The Committee against Torture (CAT) may receive and consider individual complaints, from or on behalf of a person or group of persons claiming to be victims of a violation of the Convention against Torture and Other Cruel, Inhuman or Degrading Treatment or Punishment by a State party that has recognised the Committee's competence on individual complaints procedure.[85]

The Optional Protocol to the Convention on the Rights of the Child on a communications procedure, enshrined the Committee on the Rights of the Child with the competence to receive communications from an individual or group of individuals claiming to be victims of breaches of any the rights enshrined in the Convention on the Rights of the Child, the Optional Protocol to the Convention on the sale of children, child prostitution, and

that it is the scrutiny applicable to all contracting States". Gaeta P, Viñuales JE, Zappalà S, (n 12) p. 414.

81 Optional Protocol 1 to the ICCPR, Article 1.

82 Optional Protocol to the ICESCR, Article 1.

83 International Convention on the Elimination of all Forms of Racial Discrimination, Article 14(1) (CERD).

84 Optional Protocol to the Convention on the Elimination of All Forms of Discrimination against Women, Article 2.

85 Convention against Torture and Other Cruel, Inhuman or Degrading Treatment or Punishment, Article 22.

child pornography, and the Optional Protocol to the Convention on the involvement of children in armed conflict by a State Party to them.[86]

The Committee on the Rights of Persons with Disabilities is competent to receive and consider individual communications, also known as complaints, from or on behalf of a person or group of persons claiming to be victims of a violation of the Convention by a State Party.[87] Where a communication is submitted on behalf of individuals or groups of individuals, this shall be done with their consent unless the author can justify acting on their behalf without such consent.

Some general features may be identified in these different individual complaint's mechanisms. First, the voluntary nature on the acceptance of the competence of the different committees is a constant feature in line with general principles of international law. Second, the exhaustion of internal remedies as an admissibility requirement is omnipresent. Third, complaints may also be brought by third parties on behalf of individuals, provided they have given their written consent (without requirement as to its specific form).[88] Fourth, anonymous complaints are not admissible.[89]

A final note on the International Convention on the Protection of the Rights of All Migrant Workers and Members of Their Families (ICMW). In accordance with its Article 77, the Committee on Migrant Workers (CMW) shall have the competence to receive and consider individual communications alleging violations of the Convention by States Parties that made the necessary declaration under it. This individual complaint mechanism will become operative when ten State Parties have made the foresaid declaration and this requirement has not yet been met.[90]

6.4.1.2 State-to-State Comlaints

Several of the UN human rights treaties allow State Parties to complain to the relevant treaty body on alleged breaches of the treaty by another State Party.[91]

86 Optional Protocol to the Convention on the Rights of the Child on a communications procedure, Article 5.

87 Optional Protocol to the Convention on the Rights of Persons with Disabilities, Article 1.

88 In certain cases, a third Party may bring a case without such consent, for example, where a person is in prison without access to the outside world or is a victim of an enforced disappearance.

89 In certain situations, the consent of the complaints is necessary for the Committee to reveal their identity to the State in question; see, for example, CERD, Article 14(6).

90 Reservations and declarations on this treaty, including on Article 77, can be found in https://treaties.un.org/pages/viewdetails.aspx?src=treaty&mtdsg_no=iv-13&chapter=4&clang=_en.

91 Inter-State disputes concerning the interpretation or application of the specific conventions will be left outside of the analysis, as the trigger is not a question of breach of rights. Generally, disputes between State Parties concerning interpretation or application of the Convention are

The CAT,[92] the Committee on Enforced Disappearance,[93] the Committee on Economic, Social and Cultural Rights,[94] and the Committee on the Rights of the Child[95] may receive State-to-State complaint procedures, subject to reciprocity and a proven direct interest in the case.

On the other hand, the ICCPR[96] and the International Convention on the Elimination of all Forms of Racial Discrimination[97] enshrine a more complex procedure for the resolution of disputes between States Parties over a state's fulfilment of its obligations under the relevant treaty through the establishment of an *ad hoc* Conciliation Commission. This procedure normally applies to all States Party to CERD and applies only to States Party to the ICCPR that have made a declaration accepting the competence of the relevant Committee in this regard.

The ICMW establishes a similar complex procedure.[98] However, this mechanism has not yet entered into force.

6.4.2 *The Promising Results of Individual Communications*

In 2020, the Human Rights Committee adopted the first climate change decision of a UN human rights treaty-based body. The individual complaint had been brought before it in 2015 by Ioane Teitiota, a national of Kiribati, arguing that New Zealand violated his right to life as enshrined in the ICCPR by returning him to Kiribati despite the threats posed by climate change to his right to life.[99] The Committee accepted that climate change was affecting

to be solved by negotiation or, failing that, by arbitration. If the Parties fail to agree arbitration terms within six months, the dispute may be referred to the ICJ by any of the States involved. States Parties may exclude themselves from this procedure by making a declaration at the time of ratification or accession, in which case, in accordance with the principle of reciprocity, they are barred from bringing cases against other States Parties. See CERD, Article 22, Convention on the Elimination of All Forms of Discrimination against Women, Article 29, Convention against Torture and Other Cruel, Inhuman or Degrading Treatment or Punishment, Article 30, International Convention on the Protection of the Rights of All Migrant Workers and Members of Their Families, Article 92, and International Convention for the Protection of All Persons from Enforced Disappearance, Article 42.

92 Convention against Torture and Other Cruel, Inhuman or Degrading Treatment or Punishment, Article 21.

93 International Convention for the Protection of All Persons from Enforced Disappearance, Article 32.

94 Optional Protocol to the ICESCR, Article 10.

95 Optional Protocol to the Convention on the Rights of the Child on a communications procedure, Article 12.

96 ICCPR, Articles 41–43.

97 CERD, Articles 11–13.

98 International Convention on the Protection of the Rights of All Migrant Workers and Members of Their Families, Article 76.

99 CCPR/C/127/D/2728/2016, Views adopted by the Committee under Article 5 (4) of the Optional Protocol, concerning communication No. 2728/2016, 23 September 2020, in https://documents.un.org/doc/undoc/gen/g20/237/12/pdf/g2023712.pdf.

Ioane's and his family life in Kiribati, and that sea level rise was likely to render Kiribati uninhabitable in 10 to 15 years. Though confirming Teitiota faced a real, personal, and reasonably foreseeable risk of irreparable harm to his right to life, it did not consider the standard for non-refoulement to be met.[100]

Another communication on climate change was brought before the UN Human Rights Committee in May 2019.[101] Eight Australian nationals and inhabitants in the Torres Strait region,[102] acting on their own names and on behalf of six of their children, alleged that Australia, taking inadequate measures to reduce its greenhouse gas emissions and to help them to adapt to the anticipated effects of climate change, breached its obligations to protect their rights to life, private and family life, and to culture.

The Committee delivered its decision in 2022[103] and found that Australia's failure to adequately and timely protect Indigenous Torres Islanders against adverse impacts of climate change violated their rights to enjoy their culture and be free from arbitrary interferences with their private life, family, and home. In respect to the right to life, the Committee considered "that the information before it does not disclose a violation by the State party of the authors' rights under article 6 of the Covenant".[104] As remedies, the Committee asked Australia to compensate the Indigenous Islanders for the harm suffered, engage in meaningful consultations with their communities to assess their needs, and take measures to continue to secure the communities' safe existence on their respective islands.[105]

In 2019, fifteen children from around the world presented a communication to the Committee on the Rights of the Child against five States – Argentina,

100 Imminence was at the cornerstone of the discussion in the decision. Developing how imminence is interpreted differently in distinct contexts and in a very restrictive approach in this domain, Azeredo Lopes JA. Alterações climáticas, iminência e proteção de direitos humanos: algumas notas a propósito do caso Teitiota c. Nova Zelândia. Revista de Direito Econômico e Socioambiental. 2020;11(3):14–17.

101 Communication under the Optional Protocol to the ICCPR. 13 May 2019. Available from: https://climatecasechart.com/wp-content/uploads/non-us-case-documents/2019/20190513_CCPRC135D36242019_complaint.pdf.

102 The alleged victims petitioning before the Committee were all Indigenous inhabitants of Boigu, Poruma, Warraber, and Masig, four small, low-lying islands in Australia's Torres Strait region.

103 CCPR/C/135/D/3624/2019, Views adopted by the Committee under Article 5 (4) of the Optional Protocol, concerning communication No. 3624/2019. 18 September 2023. Available from: https://documents.un.org/doc/undoc/gen/g23/188/41/pdf/g2,318841.pdf.

104 Para. 8.8.

105 For a substantive and detailed analysis of the decision, see Luporini R. Climate Change Litigation before International Human Rights Bodies: Insights from Daniel Billy et al. v. Australia (Torres Strait Islanders Case). The Italian Review of International and Comparative Law. 2023;3:238–259.

Brazil, France, Germany, and Turkey.[106] The petitioners alleged the respondents were making insufficient cuts to greenhouse gas emissions and failing to use available tools to protect children from carbon pollution, thus asking the Committee to declare that they violated their rights by perpetuating climate change and to recommend actions for respondents to address climate change mitigation and adaptation. The invoked rights breached included the rights to life, health, and the prioritisation of the child's best interest, as well as the cultural rights of petitioners from Indigenous communities.

The Committee on the Rights of the Child analysed the complaint separately for each state and, in 2021,[107] found the communication inadmissible for failure to exhaust domestic remedies.[108] However, in its reasoning it accepted that States are legally responsible for the harmful effects of emissions originating in their territory on children outside their borders. It also considered that the fact that all States are causing climate change does not absolve States of individual responsibility to reduce their own share of

106 Communication to the Committee on the Rights of the Child, In the case of Chiara Sacchi (Argentina); Catarina Lorenzo (Brazil); Iris Duquesne (France); Raina Ivanova (Germany); Ridhima Pandey (India); David Ackley, III, Ranton A Njain, and Litokne Kabua (Marshall Islands); Deborah Adegbile (Nigeria); Carlos Manuel (Palau); Ayakha Melithafa (South Africa); Greta Thunberg (Sweden); Raslen J Beili (Tunisia); and Carl Smith and Alexandria Villaseñor (USA), as Petitioners V. Argentina, Brazil, France, Germany & Turkey, as Respondents, Submitted under Article 5 of the Third Optional Protocol to the United Nations Convention on the Rights of the Child. 23 September 2019. Available from: https://earthjustice.org/wp-content/uploads/2019.09.23-crc-communication-sacchi-et-al-v.-argentina-et-al-redacted.pdf.

107 CRC/C/88/D/104/2019, Committee on the Rights of the Child Decision adopted by the Committee under the Optional Protocol to the Convention on the Rights of the Child on a communications procedure, concerning communication No. 104/2019 (Argentina). Available from: https://documents.un.org/doc/undoc/gen/g21/322/87/pdf/g2132287.pdf; CRC/C/88/D/105/2019, Committee on the Rights of the Child, Decision adopted by the Committee under the Optional Protocol to the Convention on the Rights of the Child on a communications procedure, concerning communication No. 105/2019 (Brazil). Available from: https://documents.un.org/doc/undoc/gen/g21/320/72/pdf/g2132072.pdf; CRC/C/88/D/106/2019, Committee on the Rights of the Child, Decision adopted by the Committee under the Optional Protocol to the Convention on the Rights of the Child on a communications procedure, concerning communication No. 106/2019 (France). Available from: https://documents.un.org/doc/undoc/gen/g21/321/61/pdf/g2132161.pdf; CRC/C/88/D/107/2019, Committee on the Rights of the Child, Decision adopted by the Committee under the Optional Protocol to the Convention on the Rights of the Child on a communications procedure, concerning communication No. 107/2019 (Germany). Available from: https://documents.un.org/doc/undoc/gen/g21/322/67/pdf/g2132267.pdf; CRC/C/88/D/108/2019, Committee on the Rights of the Child, Decision adopted by the Committee under the Optional Protocol to the Convention on the Rights of the Child on a communications procedure, concerning communication No. 108/2019 (Turkey). Available from: https://documents.un.org/doc/undoc/gen/g21/320/59/pdf/g2132059.pdf.

108 Requirement established in Article 7(e) of the additional Protocol.

emissions. Furthermore, it found that the youth are victims of foreseeable threats to their rights to life, health, and culture.[109]

Though few, these cases confirm that the future path of climate litigation before the UN Human Rights treaty-based bodies is promising for several reasons. There is an evident link between the exercise and enjoyment of human rights and the effects of climate change.[110] This link, explored in the presented cases, will probably become clearer, as the framing of the question the ICJ is expected to answer points in the same direction. The concrete dimensions of the allegedly breached rights make the legal analysis more feasible and stringent.

The demanding requirement of exhaustion of domestic remedies will also, inevitably, promote domestic climate litigation before national jurisdictions. On the other hand, a human rights–based approach on climate litigation, of which the *Torres Strait* case is a paradigmatic demonstration, allows addressing the intersectionality of the impact of climate change in human rights in respect to vulnerable groups.[111]

Furthermore, these mechanisms empower individuals and groups of individuals, and the social movement on climate litigation will certainly have impact in more cases brought before the other committees.[112] Also, the para-jurisdictional nature of the system might be an advantage in the current context of crisis of formal processes on the development of international law.

Finally, focusing on addressing the impact of climate change on the enjoyment of human rights highlights a human-centred approach necessary to

109 For a substantive and detailed analysis of the decision, see Nolan A. Children's Rights and Climate Change at the UN Committee on the Rights of the Child: Pragmatism and Principle in *Sacchi v Argentina*. EJIL Talk! 20 October 2021. Available from: https://www.ejiltalk.org/childrens-rights-and-climate-change-at-the-un-committee-on-the-rights-of-the-child-pragmatism-and-principle-in-sacchi-v-argentina/.

110 Including for future generations. See Sulyok K. Transforming the Rule of Law in Environmental and Climate Litigation: Prohibiting the Arbitrary Treatment of Future Generations. Transnational Environmental Law. 2024;First View:1–27.

111 See, for example, Stein PJS, Stein MA. Disability, Human Rights, and Climate Justice. Human Rights Quarterly. 2022;44:81, 110; Stein PJS, et al. Advancing Disability-Inclusive Climate Research and Action, Climate Justice, and Climate-Resilient Development. Lancet Planetary Health. 2024;8:e242–e255; de Jong IJM. Beyond the Turn to Human Rights: A Call for an Intersectional Climate Justice Approach. The International Journal of Human Rights. 2024;28:738, 758; Urzola Gutiérrez N. Gender in Climate Litigation in Latin America: Epistemic Justice through Feminist Lens. Journal of Human Rights Practice. 2024;16:208, 226.

112 As is happening within the regional systems, namely the European Court of Human Rights and the Inter-American Court of Human Rights.

overcome the difficulties raised by causality[113] and a State-to-State bargain approach.[114]

6.5 Concluding Remarks

At this point, several conclusions might be drawn. The first is that the trend of climate change litigation at the UN level is an irreversible process, as few would question the centrality of climate change in contemporary political discourse and human rights debates, and the perception of the growing risks of inaction.

Within the framework of the United Nations, in a more traditional context, the International Court of Justice is undoubtedly the most sought-after and an indisputable point of reference. The thesis of an alleged fragmentation of international law is considerably weakened in state practice and in the academic debate. This has certainly led to an acceptance of the possibility that different jurisdictions may not have the same legal interpretation of the obligations to mitigate and prevent climate change. However, contrary to what has been admitted, this process of proliferation of judicial bodies does not diminish the authority of the ICJ. On the other hand, in view of the recent well-known cases, it would not be an exaggeration to say that the ICJ has strengthened the authority of its rulings, even if, as is certainly the case with this type of judicial impetus, its action is most likely to be in the sphere of its advisory powers. The question of the weight of the ICJ's pronouncements in the form of advisory opinions goes back a long way. However, the distinction between advisory and contentious jurisdiction is blurred in its legal and practical effect, if only because of the procedure that initiates one or the other.

Indeed, the UN General Assembly has always played a decisive role in submitting requests for advisory opinions to the ICJ. By way of illustration, of the 29 advisory opinions submitted to the Court, 21 were requested by the General Assembly (approximately 72.5% of the total). And without prejudice to the merit and importance of the issues raised by the other requesting bodies (from UNESCO to the WHO), it is quite clear that the General

113 Which are particularly challenging when due diligence obligations are at stake. See Ollino A. A "Missed" Secondary Rule? Causation and the Breach of Preventive and Due Diligence Obligations. In Kajtár G, Çalı B, Milanovic M, eds, (n 46) pp. 105–123.

114 For example, in its written statement before the ICJ on the Advisory Opinion, the People's Republic of China states: "International human rights law has limitations in addressing climate change. First, international human rights law is not specifically designed as a tailor-made legal regime for dealing with climate change issues. The obligations derived from international human rights law, such as mitigating and adapting to climate change, are applicable only to the extent that the provisions of international human rights law are compatible with those of the UNFCCC regime. They should not go beyond the scope of the obligations under the UNFCCC regime, which is specially designed to deal with climate change issues", 22 March 2024, para. 123.

Assembly is where the issues of greatest legal weight are concentrated, now including the problem of climate change and the obligations of States in this regard. The way in which the ICJ has interpreted its powers in advisory matters, or the way in which States attach importance to the positions that the Court may adopt, the very significant increase in the number of intervening States, are all aspects that contribute to the special weight that should be given, in this case, to the position that the ICJ may adopt with regard to the obligations of States in the field of climate change.

However, there are two other elements that should be added to the aforementioned. The fact that UNGA Resolution 77/276, which requested an advisory opinion on the matter, was adopted by consensus, does indeed confer a special responsibility on the ICJ. But it also gives the Court a special authority that should not be underestimated.

Attention should also be drawn to the very large number of States, groups of States, and international organisations that have decided to intervene in this process. On the one hand, it is legitimate to consider that this confirms the fundamental importance of the issue. Furthermore, it is better to draw from such interventions the possibility of a finer and more consistent interpretation of what scope the main international actors are willing to accept in the sphere of their obligations.

Finally, it is also interesting to note how States try to use Advisory Opinion requests as an instrument of benign pressure to induce international tribunals to harmonise, or at least approximate, positions in relation to previous decisions that they consider satisfactory. In the current case, the reference seems to be ITLOS. It remains to be seen whether the ICJ will accept this path or whether, on the contrary, it will want to mark its autonomy.[115] It is to be hoped, however, that it will not do so in the unfortunate way it reacted in the genocide case to the *Tadić* judgment of the ICTY.

In addition to the formal rules relating to questions of standing and jurisdiction, an integrated reading of the various jurisdictional approaches within

115 It will always be a relatively delicate exercise. The ICJ, for example, will certainly avoid giving an advisory opinion that appears to be too different from the position taken by ITLOS in the overlapping thematic areas. Moreover, this exercise is even more delicate because it has been difficult in recent years to achieve any significant consensus among states on climate change. It is, therefore, to be hoped that the ICJ will be able to find an inclusive formulation in which many states may agree. In other words, the creation of too obvious a gap between the ICJ's formulation of obligations and the practice of states is always to the detriment of this jurisdiction. Nevertheless, and to end in an optimistic note, the Court will certainly avoid the risk of fragmentation or of interfering with negotiations and ongoing processes. For an analysis on negotiating versus adjudicating climate and the discussion of the distinct normative legitimacy of them, see Bodansky D, (n 26) pp. 695–699 and 701–705. Adopting a negative approach on advisory opinions on climate litigation, Mayer B. International Advisory Proceedings on Climate Change. Michigan Journal of International Law 2023;44:41–116.

the UN system helps to understand how certain jurisdictions seek to mark out their territory in a logic of interesting and dynamic competition.

To take just one example, the fact that ITLOS has delivered its opinion before the ICJ has no bearing on the way in which the ICJ will exercise its jurisdiction in relation to the different subject matter of the application it has to consider. In a material sense, however, not only is the content of the *COSIS Opinion* itself a fact, but several States have referred to it in their interventions before the ICJ (either in criticism or in defence of the standard it sets). While other mechanisms within the UN system focus on human rights, this approach differs by emphasising protection and guarantees. It places less emphasis on state obligations detached from the immediate impact of a specific case and, instead, highlights the framework of prevention and due diligence responsibilities. Moreover, as recent cases show, there is no question of determining who, and under what circumstances, may be subject to certain obligations because of their past "contribution" to climate change. It is also a complaint mechanism that seeks to determine who will ultimately be held accountable, either because they have violated certain obligations in the sphere of private individuals (for example, by violating the principle of non-refoulement) or because they have refused, for example, to take the appropriate measures that would have made it possible to prevent harm from occurring, thereby violating a certain human right, including the right to life.

The UN Human Rights Committee was confronted with this type of "new" issue in the *Teitiota* case, which involved New Zealand and, to some extent, Kiribati.

However, we should note an indirect effect of the assessment of this individual case, in which, unfortunately, the HRC's overly restrictive interpretation of the concept of imminence played a decisive role in the outcome of the case (to the detriment of Teitiota's claim). This indirect, but potentially more frequent effect concerns the situation where a State suffers the effects of rising sea levels to such an extent that its territory or parts of its territory are submerged or no longer habitable. In this situation, which permeated the entire *Teitiota* case, the Human Rights Council had to deal with a hypothetical violation of the ICCPR, but at the same time, as a fact, with the possibility of the extinction of the State (which, according to the assessment made in the light of the concept of risk, prevailed in the HRC's analysis). From here, as analysed above, we can understand how the United Nations system, which seems to concentrate on somewhat fragmented assessments, can have a general coherence that amplifies the impact of any decision on climate change. The concept of climate refugee, which does not even seem viable, has already come into play. So has the right of self-determination of peoples. This reading, which is as coherent and integrated as possible, is what protects us from legal cacophony, which is interesting from the point of view of communication but less useful when it comes to proposing effective solutions. Therefore, the enunciation of clear obligations that would allow us to expect efficient processes prioritising this issue is likely to be achieved only when, rather than focusing on individual trees – each legally significant – it becomes more important to step back far enough to see the forest as a whole.

References

Akande D. Selection of the international court of justice as a forum for contentious and advisory proceedings (including jurisdiction). J Int Dispute Settl. 2016;7:320–344.

Alexander A, Guha SK. Critical analysis of third-party intervention before the international court of justice. Indones J Int Comp Law. 2022;9:115–137.

Almeida PW. International procedure regulation in the common interest: the role of third-party intervention and amicus curiae before the ICJ. Law Pract Int Courts Tribunals. 2019;18:163–188.

Anggadi F, Yiallourides C, Guilfoyle D, Scott KN, Stephens T. A first reading of ITLOS' advisory opinion on climate change: implications for Australia, New Zealand, and the Pacific. Aust N Z Soc Int Law Perspect. 2024;41. Available from: https://anzsilperspective.com/special-extended-perspective-a-first-reading-of-itlos-advisory-opinion-on-climate-change-implications-for-australia-new-zealand-and-the-pacific/.

Barrie GN. Third-party state intervention in disputes before the international court of justice: a reassessment of Articles 62 and 63 of the ICJ Statute. Comp Int Law J South Afr. 2020;53:1–20.

Bodansky D. The role of the international court of justice in addressing climate change: some preliminary reflections. Ariz State Law J. 2017;49:689–712.

D'Argent P. Article 92. In: Simma B, editor. The charter of the United Nations: a commentary. 4th ed. Oxford: Oxford University Press; 2024. Vol. II.

de Jong IJM. Beyond the turn to human rights: a call for an intersectional climate justice approach. Int J Hum Rights. 2024;28:738–758.

Deller RO. Experts fantômes at the ICJ. EJIL Talk! 2024 Dec 2. Available from: https://www.ejiltalk.org/experts-fantomes-at-the-icj/.

Doelle M, Sun Z, Schofield C. Potential climate change litigation in the law of the sea. In: Sindico F, McKenzie K, Médici-Colombo G, Wegener L, editors. Research handbook on climate change litigation. Cheltenham: Elgar; 2024.

Fitzmaurice M. The international court of justice and international environmental law. In: Tams CJ, Sloan J, editors. The development of international law by the international court of justice. Oxford: Oxford University Press; 2013.

Gaeta P, Viñuales JE, Zappalà S. Cassese's international law. 3rd ed. Oxford: Oxford University Press; 2020.

Khatri U, Chowdhury J. How a historic opinion on climate change and ocean protection sets the bar for climate action. 2024 Jun 27. Available from: https://www.info-today.eu/2024/06/how-a-historic-opinion-on-climate-change-and-ocean-protection-sets-the-bar-for-climate-action/.

Luporini R. Climate change litigation before international human rights bodies: insights from Daniel Billy et al. v. Australia (Torres Strait Islanders case). Ital Rev Int Comp Law. 2023;3:238–259.

Mayer B. International advisory proceedings on climate change. Mich J Int Law. 2023;44:41–116.

Nolan A. Children's rights and climate change at the UN committee on the rights of the child: pragmatism and principle in Sacchi v Argentina. EJIL Talk! 2021 Oct 20. Available from: https://www.ejiltalk.org/childrens-rights-and-climate-change

-at-the-un-committee-on-the-rights-of-the-child-pragmatism-and-principle-in-sacchi-v-argentina/.

Oellers-Frahm K., Lagrange E. Article 96. In: Simma B, editor. The charter of the United Nations: a commentary. 4th ed. Oxford: Oxford University Press; 2024. Vol. II.

Pouliot V. Forum prorogatum before the international court of justice: the Djibouti v. France case. Hague Justice J. 2008;3:28–40.

Rocha A. Amicus curiae before the international tribunal for the law of the sea: the prospect of an advisory opinion on climate change and the law of the sea. Católica Law Rev. 2022;VI:87–111.

Stein PJS, Ashley Stein M, Groce N, Kett M, Akyeampong EKA, Alford WP, Chakraborty J, Daniels-Mayes S, Eriksen SH, Fracht A, Gallegos L, Grech S, Gurung P, Hans A, Harpur P, Jodoin S, Lord JE, Macanawai SS, McClain-Nhlapo CV, Mezmur BD, Moore RJ, Muñoz Y, Patel V, Pham PN, Quinn G, Sadlier SA, Shachar C, Smith MS, Van Susteren L. Advancing disability-inclusive climate research and action, climate justice, and climate-resilient development. Lancet Planet Health. 2024;8:e242–e255.

Stein PJS, Stein MA. Disability, human rights, and climate justice. Hum Rights Q. 2022;44:81–110.

Sulyok K. Science, legitimacy, and the judicial function: A need for more intrusive standards of review. In: Kajtár G, Çalı B, Milanovic M, editors. Secondary rules of primary importance in international law: attribution, causality, evidence, and standards of review in the practice of international courts and tribunals. Oxford: Oxford University Press; 2022.

Sulyok K. Transforming the rule of law in environmental and climate litigation: prohibiting the arbitrary treatment of future generations. Transnat Environ Law. 2024;1:1–27.

Tigre MA, Carrillo Bañuelos JA. The ICJ's advisory opinion on climate change: what happens now? 2023 Mar 29. Available from: https://blogs.law.columbia.edu/climatechange/2023/03/29/the-icjs-advisory-opinion-on-climate-change-what-happens-now/.

Tomka P. Article 92. In: Cot J-P, Pellet A, Forteau M, editors. La Charte des Nations Unies. 3rd ed. Paris: Economica; 2005. Vol II.

Tuerk H. The contribution of the international tribunal for the law of the sea to international law. Penn State Int Law Rev. 2007;26:289–316.

Urzola Gutiérrez N. Gender in climate litigation in Latin America: Epistemic justice through feminist lens. J Hum Rights Pract. 2024;16:208–226.

Viñuales JE. The contribution of the international court of justice to the development of international environmental law: A contemporary assessment. Fordham Int Law J. 2008;32:232–258.

Voigt C. Overview and noteworthy elements of the advisory opinion. In: Reflections on the ITLOS advisory opinion. London: British Institute of International and Comparative Law; 2024 May 30.

Wewerinke-Singh M, Garg A, Hartmann J. The advisory proceedings on climate change before the International Court of Justice. Questions Int Law, Zoom-in. 2023;23:42:23–43.

Yee S. Forum prorogatum in the international court. Ger Yearb Int Law. 1999;42:147–191.

Yee S. Forum prorogatum returns to the international court of justice. Leiden J Int Law. 2003;16:710–713.

Yiallourides C, Deva S. A commentary on ITLOS' advisory opinion on climate change. British Institute of International and Comparative Law. 2024 May 24.

Available from: https://www.biicl.org/blog/77/a-commentary-on-itlos-advisory-opinion-on-climate-change.
Yongming J. A comparative study on the international tribunal for the law of the sea and the international court of justice – Focusing on the tribunal's characteristics in respect of constitution, jurisdiction, procedure and judgment. China Oceans Law Rev. 2005;289–313.

7 Climate Litigation in the Inter-American Human Rights System

Addressing Legal Standing

Délton Winter de Carvalho and Carolina Merida

7.1 Introduction

This chapter aims to demonstrate the evolution of the Inter-American Human Rights System (IARHS), especially with regard to the criteria and requirements for individuals' and moral persons' *locus standi* in cases of human rights implications related to climate change.

Indeed, as the impacts of climate change continue to escalate, there is a growing need for effective legal mechanisms to hold governments and corporations accountable for their contributions to environmental degradation and climate damage. However, navigating the nuances of *locus standi* in a human rights context presents unique challenges. This chapter explores the evolving jurisprudence within the Inter-American System, analysing key cases and decisions that have shaped the understanding of who can bring forth human rights claims related to climate change. By examining the intersection of environmental law and human rights, the chapter seeks to shed light on the opportunities and limitations facing individuals and groups pursuing redress for climate-related harm before the Inter-American Commission (IACmHR) and the Inter-American Court of Human Rights (IACtHR).

Additionally, the chapter analyses the growing participation of the *amicus curiae*, both in litigation and in requests for an advisory opinion addressed to the IACtHR. This examination is fundamental, since *amicus curiae* can help fill in gaps in legal representation and/or expertise that may exist in the parties directly involved, thus contributing to greater justice and equity in the judgment of climate cases.

Finally, considering the current state of climate emergency,[1,2] the chapters discuss who has *locus standi*; and what are the requirements for proposing

1 The climate emergency is "a situation in which immediate action is needed to reduce or stop climate change and prevent serious and permanent damage to the environment". Oxford Learner's Dictionaries. Climate emergency. [Accessed 20 August 2024]. Available from: https://www.oxfordlearnersdictionaries.com/definition/english/climate-emergency.

2 According to Carvalho, the term "climate emergency" is presented in three central dimensions: a scientific one, which demonstrates the climate crisis, its urgency, and its potential catastrophic effects; a political one, which is characterised as a movement arising from social

DOI: 10.4324/9781003540977-10

provisional measures before the Inter-American Court in cases of extreme gravity and urgency, aiming to protect the stability of the climate as derived from a human right set out in the ACHR, including the right to a healthy environment under Article 26 ACHR.

To this end, the chapter is structured into four main sections: an overview of the Inter-American Human Rights System, *locus standi* in the Inter-American Human Rights System, the potential role of provisional measures in cases of climate change, and final reflections on the topic.

7.2 Overview of the Inter-American Human Rights System

The IAHRS is intended to promote and protect human rights in the Americas, encompassing several general normative instruments, such as the American Declaration of the Rights and Duties of Man,[3] the Charter of the Organization of American States,[4] and the American Convention on Human Rights[5] (San José Pact) and its two additional protocols – Protocol Relating to Social and Economic Rights[6] (San Salvador Protocol) and Protocol Relating to the Abolition of the Death Penalty.[7]

From such normative instruments, two protection systems were developed.[8] The first system, which applies to all 35 Member States of the Organization of American States (OAS), is based on the Charter creating the OAS itself and the American Declaration of the Rights and Duties of Man. Within it, the IACmHR, created in 1959 and formally incorporated as the main and autonomous body of the OAS with the publication of the Buenos Aires Protocol (1967),[9] is responsible for monitoring, promoting, and protecting human rights expressed in the Charter and the American Declaration, thus holding States responsible in case of non-compliance.

---

pressure on the political system, with the engagement of various institutions and sectors of society in favor of urgent climate commitments and actions; and a legal one, which consists of a manifestation of the normative effects resulting from the institution of an emergency operational mode. Winter de Carvalho D. Desvendando a emergência climática. Revista Jurídica do Ministério Público Catarinense. 2022;17(36):39–64.

3 American Declaration of the Rights and Duties of Man, adopted on 2 May 1948, in Bogotá.

4 Charter of the Organization of American States, signed in Bogotá on 30 April 1948.

5 American Convention on Human Rights (adopted 22 November 1969, entered into force 18 July 1978) OAS Treaty Series No. 36.

6 Additional Protocol to the American Convention on Human Rights in the Area of Economic, Social and Cultural Rights ("Protocol of San Salvador"), adopted 17 November 1988, entered into force 16 November 1999.

7 Additional Protocol to the American Convention on Human Rights to Abolish the Death Penalty (adopted 8 June 1990, entered into force 28 August 1991).

8 Carvalho Ramos A. Processo Internacional de Direitos Humanos: Análise dos mecanismos de apuração de violações de direitos humanos e a implementação das decisões no Brasil. 7ª ed. SaraivaJur; 2022. p. 512.

9 Protocol of Amendment to the Charter of the Organization of American States ("Protocol of Buenos Aires"), signed on 27 February 1967.

In the words of André de Carvalho Ramos, with the authorisation to receive and examine individual petitions, inquire States, and make recommendations, the IACmHR "became a true international body for monitoring compliance by OAS States with their commitments (listed in the OAS Charter and the American Declaration) of respect for human rights".[10]

The second is the so-called American Convention on Human Rights (ACHR) system, signed in 1969 and in force since 1978, after the eleventh ratification. The procedure is two phase, consisting of a first stage before the IACmHR and a second stage before the Inter-American Court of Human Rights (IACtHR), the system's judicial body, which has both a contentious and an advisory role. The Convention has 23 States Parties[11] among the 35 Member States of the OAS.

Thus, after the entry into force of the ACHR, the IACmHR began to play a dual role, since in addition to the responsibilities it exercises in the OAS system, "the Commission also became an organ of the Convention Association of Human Rights, analysing individual petitions and filing an action of international responsibility against a State before the Inter-American Court".[12]

However, despite the advances promoted by the American Convention system, countries such as the USA, Canada, and most Caribbean countries are not under the contentious jurisdiction of the IACtHR, which is a problem from the perspective of climate litigation, since the USA and Canada are major emitters of GHG, and many Caribbean countries are significantly vulnerable to climate-induced disasters.[13]

With this background in mind, this chapter analyses the issue of legal standing in the Inter-American Human Rights System, both before the IACmHR and before the IACtHR, with an emphasis on its consequences in cases of violations of the obligations to protect the stability of the climate as derived from a human right set out in the ACHR, including the right to a healthy environment under Article 26 ACHR.

7.3 Legal Standing in the Inter-American Human Rights System

7.3.1 Definition of Legal Standing within the Inter-American Human Rights Framework

Legal standing refers to the ability of interested parties, such as non-governmental organisations (NGOs), affected communities, or individuals, to lodge

10 Carvalho Ramos A, (n 10) p. 275.

11 The withdrawals from Trinidad and Tobago (1998) and Venezuela (2012) have already been considered.

12 Carvalho Ramos A. Curso de Direitos Humanos SaraivaJur; 2022. p. 647.

13 Auz J. "So, This Is Permanence": The Inter-American Human Rights System as a Liminal Space for Climate Justice. Melbourne JIL. 2021;22:187.

petitions before the IACmHR,[14] which filters petitions before reaching the IACtHR.[15] As a group, these can be qualified as "private petitioners".

The issue of legal standing in the context of the IAHRS has acquired relevant contours, especially with regard to cases of environmental and climate litigation. Legal standing refers to the right of individuals or groups of individuals to lodge petitions and seek protection or redress for human rights violations.

In the specific case of climate litigation, it is important to recognise that the IACtHR acknowledged the existence of an autonomous right to a healthy environment in Advisory Opinion OC-23/17. This distinction sets the right to a healthy environment apart from other rights and emphasises the legal status of environmental components – such as forests, rivers, and oceans – as legal interests themselves. Consequently, even in the absence of definitive evidence about the risks posed to individuals, it is possible for private petitioners to be classified as victims without the need to demonstrate that their human rights have been directly and individually affected by climate change.

Furthermore, regarding legal standing in environmental cases, the framework allows for not only the protection of individual rights but also the safeguarding of collective interests. This is particularly relevant given that affected parties typically belong to identifiable groups connected by shared factual circumstances, legal considerations, or conditions of socio-environmental vulnerability.[16] In the environmental context, this legal standing is vital for the exercise of rights that are intrinsically linked to the quality of the environment, the protection of natural resources, and the stability of the climate system. Legal standing in climate litigation is also linked to the fundamental rights of access to justice and public participation in decision-making processes related to the environment. Rising concerns about climate change and environmental degradation have led civil society organisations, Indigenous communities, and vulnerable groups to seek recognition of their legal standing before the IACmHR.

Establishing legal standing in climate change cases requires a comprehensive understanding of the applicable legal standards and the mechanisms by which individuals, groups of individuals, and civil society organisations can assert their rights.

Individual petitions must be filed by individuals, groups of individuals, or NGOs before the IACmHR, pursuant to Article 44 of the ACHR and Article

14 ACHR, Article 44.

15 ACHR, Article 61(1).

16 Amado Gomes C, Schramm da Silva J, Moura do Carmo W. Opinião Consultiva 23/2017 da Corte Interamericana de Direitos Humanos e as Inovações à Tutela do Meio Ambiente no Direito Internacional. Veredas do Direito: Direito Ambiental e Desenvolvimento Sustentável. 2020;17(38):25. [Accessed 21 October 2024]. Available from: http://dx.doi.org/10.18623/rvd.v17i38.1841.

23 of the Rules of Procedure of the Inter-American Commission on Human Rights,[17] which state that:

> Any person or group of persons, or any nongovernmental entity legally recognized in one or more member states of the Organization, may lodge petitions with the Commission containing denunciations or complaints of violation of this Convention by a State Party. (ACHR, art 44)
>
> Any person or group of persons or nongovernmental entity legally recognized in one or more of the Member States of the OAS may submit petitions to the Commission, on their behalf or on behalf of third persons, concerning alleged violations of a human right recognized in, as the case may be, the American Declaration of the Rights and Duties of Man, the American Convention on Human Rights "Pact of San José, Costa Rica", the Additional Protocol to the American Convention on Human Rights in the Area of Economic, Social and Cultural Rights "Protocol of San Salvador", the Protocol to the American Convention on Human Rights to Abolish the Death Penalty, the Inter-American Convention to Prevent and Punish Torture, the Inter-American Convention on Forced Disappearance of Persons, and/or the Inter-American Convention on the Prevention, Punishment and Eradication of Violence Against Women "Convention of Belém do Pará", in accordance with their respective provisions, the Statute of the Commission, and these Rules of Procedure. The petitioner may designate an attorney or other person to represent him or her before the Commission, either in the petition itself or in a separate document. (Article 23 of the Rules of Procedure of the ACHR)

The IACmHR analyses and studies the petitions submitted to determine whether there has been a violation of one or more rights established in the ACHR and/or the American Declaration. Depending on its findings, the IACmHR may admit the petition and issue a report on admissibility or inadmissibility[18]; negotiate an amicable solution between the parties[19]; issue a report on the merits[20]; and finally, present the case to the IACtHR, requesting that the State be declared internationally responsible.[21]

The admissibility requirements for individual petitions are set forth in Article 46 of the ACHR and repeated in Article 28 of the Regulations of the

17 Rules of Procedure of the Inter-American Commission on Human Rights, approved by the Commission at its 137th regular period of sessions, held from 28 October to 13 November 2009, and modified on 2 September 2011 and during the 147th Regular Period of Sessions, held from 8 to 22 March 2013, for entry into force on 1 August 2013.

18 ACHR, Articles 46 and 47.

19 ACHR, Article 48(1)(f).

20 ACHR, Article 50.

21 ACHR, Article 61(1).

Inter-American Commission on Human Rights. The admissibility requirements include, among others: a) the need to identify the name of the person or persons making the complaint or, in the case of a non-governmental entity, its legal representative or representatives, and the Member State in which it is legally recognised; b) the e-mail address for receiving correspondence from the Commission and, where applicable, telephone number, fax number, and address; c) a report of the fact or situation reported, specifying the place and date of the alleged violations; d) if possible, the name of the victim and of any public authority that has become aware of the fact or situation reported; e) the indication of the State that the petitioner considers responsible, by action or omission, for the violation of any of the human rights enshrined in the ACHR and other applicable instruments, although without specific reference to the article(s) allegedly violated (the petition will not be admitted if it does not set forth facts that characterise a violation of the rights guaranteed by the applicable normative instruments and enforceable by the IAHRS); e) compliance with the six-month deadline from the date on which the alleged victim was notified of the decision exhausting domestic remedies; f) the measures taken to exhaust domestic remedies or the impossibility of doing so in accordance with Article 31 of the Regulations; and g) the lack of international *lis pendens*.

It should be noted that, unlike what occurs in the European Human Rights System, there is no provision that legitimises the direct submission of a case by individuals, groups of individuals, or non-governmental organisations before the IACtHR. At the contentious level, only the IACmHR and the States Parties to the ACHR can submit a case to the Inter-American Court of Human Rights.[22]

Likewise, only the Member States of the Organization of American States, the Commission, and other bodies listed in Chapter X of the Charter of the Organization of American States may invoke the advisory function of the IACtHR on the interpretation of the ACHR or other treaties concerning the protection of human rights in the American States, as well as on their domestic laws with these latter treaties.[23]

A critical analysis of the *locus standi* of private petitioners in the case of climate change–related disputes in the Inter-American Human Rights System requires a careful assessment of the legal and jurisprudential bases that support the participation of interested parties in these cases, which is done below.

22 ACHR, Article 61(1). On this subject, see Piovesan F. Direitos humanos e o direito constitucional internacional. 7th ed. Editora Saraiva; 2006. p. 35.

23 ACHR, Article 64.

7.3.2 *Criteria and Requirements for Individuals and Groups to Establish Legal Standing in Climate Change Cases*

In the IAHRS, climate change–related human rights discussions emerged and developed from a bottom-up strategy.[24] The petition presented by the Inuit People (Canada) before the IACmHR in 2005, arguing that the United States of America was violating their human rights, impacting the petitioners' traditional practices and way of living through its contribution to global warming (unrestricted emission of greenhouse gases), is considered the first climate-related petition before an international human rights body.[25]

Despite the significance and pioneering nature of the aforementioned case (with the Inuit petition being recognised as the inception of a movement that links climate change to human rights), the IACmHR declined to process the petition for procedural reasons, not questioning the *locus standi* of the private petitioners.[26] The IACmHR stated that the petitioners had provided insufficient information for it to determine, "for the moment", whether the alleged facts constituted a violation of rights protected by the American Declaration. It is also important to clarify that the petition was grounded in the provisions of the American Declaration because the United States is not a party to the ACHR.

In the second case regarded as climate litigation within the Inter-American Human Rights System (IAHRS), the Athabaskan community submitted a communication to the IACmHR in 2013, alleging that Canada's failure to implement measures for reducing black carbon emissions posed a threat to their human rights as Indigenous peoples.[27] On this occasion, even prior to the IACtHR's recognition of an independent right to a healthy environment, the petitioners invoked the American Declaration of the Rights and Duties of Man, along with the ACHR and the Protocol of San Salvador, as key interpretative standards.

To establish legal standing, individuals and communities typically need to demonstrate a link between their grievances and actions or inactions of States

24 Auz J, (n 15) p. 187.

25 Hohmann J. Igloo as Icon: A Human Rights Approach to Climate Change for the Inuit. Transnational Law & Contemporary Problems. 2009;18:295.

26 Auz J. Climate crisis and the testing of international human rights remedies: Forecasting the Inter American Court of Human Rights. Centre for Studies and Research in International Law and International Relations Serie. Climate change and the testing of international law/ Le droit international au défi des changements climatiques. Vol 26. Brill | Martinus Nijhoff Publishers; 2023. [Accessed 5 July 2024]. Available from: https://doi.org/10.1163/1875-8096_pplcdu_a9789004682399_13; Rocha A, Sampaio R. Climate change before the European and Inter-American Courts of Human Rights: Comparing possible avenues before human rights bodies. RECIEL. 2023. Available from: 10.1111/reel.12502.

27 Petition Seeking from Violations of the Rights of Artic Athabaskan Peoples Resulting from Rapid Artic Warming and Melting Caused by Emissions of Black Carbon by Vanada (IACmHR, submitted on 23 April 2013).

that contribute to climate change. This involves highlighting how climate change–related impacts – such as extreme weather events, rising sea levels, or deforestation – threaten rights as set out in the American Declaration of the Rights and Duties of Man, the Charter of the Organization of American States, the ACHR, or in another applicable and enforceable instrument within the scope of the IAHRS.

Furthermore, as seen, given the subsidiary nature of the IAHRS, applicants must exhaust their internal resources before submitting a complaint of violation to the IACmHR, which, added to the impossibility of directly petitioning the IACtHR, ends up delaying access to justice for those affected by climate-related issues.

In any case, the jurisprudence of the IACmHR and the IACtHR reflects an evolution in the interpretation of active legitimacy. In recent years, there has been an increase in the acceptance of cases that address the violation of human rights as a result of practices related to the environment.

The Inter-American Court, in decisions such as in the cases *Kichwa Indigenous People of Sarayaku v Ecuador*[28] and *Saramaka v Suriname*,[29] highlighted the importance of protecting the rights of Indigenous and tribal peoples, recognising their legitimacy to claim rights collectively against the State. This trend has allowed active legitimacy to be expanded to include not only directly affected individuals, but also groups whose rights are threatened by harmful or insufficient environmental (and why not climate?) policies.

The consolidation of the recognition that Indigenous and tribal communities are holders of rights protected in the ACHR and have the capacity to access the Inter-American System by the contentious jurisprudence of the IACtHR, as well and in its Advisory Opinion OC-22/16,[30] denotes a paradigmatic change in the perception of *locus standi*, which is now seen as an instrument of struggle for socio-environmental and climate justice.

In fact, over time, the development of the possibility of protecting environmental issues by both the IACmHR and the IACtHR is evident, despite the absence of express reference to the right to environment or/and climate change in the ACHR. The worsening degradation of natural resources and the absence of an international court with specific jurisdiction in environmental matters contributed to this movement called "*greening*" of international human rights law.[31]

28 *Kichwa Indigenous People of Sarayaku v Ecuador* (IACtHR, 27 June 2012).

29 *Saramaka v Suriname* (IACtHR, 28 November 2007).

30 Advisory Opinion 22/16 (IACtHR, 26 February 2016).

31 Greening is hereby referred as the technique through which the environment is protected in regional human rights protection systems, which, *a priori*, do not have specific protection on this topic. Merida C. Governança Global da Água nas Cidades: a Atuação dos Governos Locais na Concretização do Direito Humano à Água no Atual Contexto de Mudanças Climáticas. Tese de Doutorado. Universidade do Vale do Rio dos Sinos – UNISINOS; 2022. p. 119.

In this sense, it is noteworthy that the IACtHR gradually began to attribute an environmental dimension to the human rights under its jurisdiction. Initially, the protection of the environment in the IAHRS took place indirectly or reflexively, "recognizing the human right to the environment through jurisprudence when environmental factors prevented or, in some way, limited the enjoyment of human rights expressly provided for in the ACHR",[32] based on the civil and political rights protected by the ACHR, such as the right to life (article 4), personal integrity (article 5), property (article 21), information and participation public policy (article 13), and the right of access to Justice (articles 8 and 25), among others.[33] The understanding hitherto in force in the jurisprudence of the IACtHR was "the impossibility of justiciability (direct and objective protection) of the 'right to a healthy environment' [...] provided for in article 11 of the Additional Protocol of San Salvador of 1988, instrument in which economic, social and cultural rights are housed within the scope of the IAHRS",[34] namely, as a result of Article 19(6) of the San Salvador Protocol itself.

The major evolution of the IAHRS in environmental matters occurred with the issuance of Advisory Opinion OC-23/2017 – *Environment and Human Rights*, rendered on 15 November 2017,[35] through which the IACtHR, provoked to express its understanding on the obligations of States in relation to the environment within the scope of protecting and guaranteeing the rights to life and personal integrity, recognised the right to the environment as an autonomous right, of an individual and collective nature, contemplated in article 26 of the ACHR (Right to Progressive Development) and, therefore, capable of being invoked directly and exclusively before the IAHRS.[36]

For the purpose of delimiting *locus standi* in climate disputes, it is important to highlight that, in addition to an individual dimension (connection with rights such as health, personal integrity, life, among others), the human right to a healthy environment has a collective dimension, constituting a universal interest for both present and future generations. It is, therefore, a fundamental right to the existence of humanity.[37]

Particularly in cases on territorial rights of Indigenous and tribal peoples, the IACtHR highlighted that the right to collective property of these peoples is linked to the protection and access to resources found in the peoples' territories, as natural resources are necessary for their own survival, development,

32 Merida C, (n 33) p. 119.
33 Monteiro Danese P. Meio ambiente na contemporaneidade: De sua proteção à luz do Sistema Interamericano de Direitos Humanos. Editora Juruá; 2019.
34 Merida C, (n 33) p. 120.
35 Advisory Opinion 23/17 (IACtHR 15 November 2017).
36 Merida C, (n 33) p. 126.
37 Advisory Opinion 23/17 (IACtHR 15 November 2017), para. 59.

and continuity of the lifestyle of such people.[38] On these premises, the close link between the right to a dignified life and the protection of ancestral territory and natural resources was recognised.

In this context, in consideration of the special vulnerability of Indigenous and tribal peoples, the IACtHR determined that States "must adopt positive measures aimed at ensuring that members of these peoples have access to a dignified life – which includes the protection of the close relationship they maintain with the earth – and his life project, both in its individual and collective dimensions".[39]

Regarding the definition of jurisdiction, through OC 23/2017, the Inter-American Court presented "an understanding that goes beyond other international courts regarding the concept of extraterritorial jurisdiction in the case of damage to the environment",[40] establishing the existence of state obligations to prevent transboundary environmental damage that may affect the human rights of people outside its territory, in the following terms:

> When cross-border damage occurs, a person is under the jurisdiction of the State of origin if there is a causal relationship between the action occurring in its territory and the negative impact on the human rights of people outside its territory. The exercise of jurisdiction arises when the State of origin exercises effective control over the activities carried out that caused the damage and consequent violation of human rights.[41]

It appears, therefore, that the IACtHR, by adopting a standard of control over the source by the State of origin of the activity causing environmental damage that involves human rights visible to people residing outside its territory,[42] admitted the possibility of extraterritorial exercise of jurisdiction in the framework of compliance with obligations in environmental matters, which may result in the expansion of the concept of victim in future climate conflicts before IAHRS.

38 In this sense, see *Yakye Axa Indigenous Community v Paraguay* (IACtHR 17 June 2005), para. 137; *Sawhoyamaxa Indigenous Community v Paraguay* (IACtHR 29 March 2006), para. 118; *Saramaka People v Suriname* (IACtHR 28 November 2007) paras. 121 and 122, among others.

39 Advisory Opinion 23/17 (IACtHR 15 November 2017), para. 48.

40 Montovani de Lima R, Mucelli Rezende Veloso N. A conceituação ampliada da jurisdição extraterritorial no Sistema Interamericano pela OC-23/17: os avanços na internacionalização ambiental. Revista do Programa de Pós-Graduação em Direito da UFC. 2018;8(2):646. [Accessed 20 November 2024]. Available from: https://periodicos.ufc.br/nomos/article/view/39819/95987.

41 Advisory Opinion 23/17 (IACtHR 15 November 2017), para. 104.

42 Winter de Carvalho D. Constitucionalismo climático: Estado de direito e justiça climática. Livraria do Advogado; 2025. p. 85.

Based on this latter Advisory Opinion, the IACtHR, in the case *Lhaka Honhat (Nuestra Tierra) v Argentina*, delivered on 6 February 2020,[43] acknowledged the right to a healthy environment within the framework of its contentious jurisdiction for the first time. This development paves the way for the eventual recognition of the human right to climate stability, or at least an obligation to protect climate stability as derived from the right to a healthy environment. The collective dimension and inherently diffuse nature of the right to a healthy environment "lightens the requirement of victimhood and opens the door to measures aimed at compensating for damages beyond the harm suffered by the applicant".[44]

Finally, it is worth highlighting the recent ruling published by the IACtHR in relation to the Case *Habitantes de La Oroya v Peru,* judged in November 2023.[45] In this decision, the IACtHR held the Peruvian State responsible for violations of the human rights of 80 inhabitants of the Peruvian community of La Oroya as a result of the contamination of air, water, and soil produced by mining and metallurgical activities carried out by a private company on-site. This is the first case judged by the IAHRS in which the obligation of governments to respect, protect, and guarantee the right to a healthy environment in relation to industrial pollution is recognised.

The ruling in this second contentious case on the human right to the environment after the Advisory Opinion OC-23/17 advances on several points in relation to the decision given in the Case of *Indigenous Communities Members of the Lhaka Honhat Association (nuestra tierra) v Argentina.* In this sense, the convergent vote delivered by judges Ricardo C. Pérez Manrique (Uruguay), Eduardo Ferrer Mac-Gregor Poisot (Mexico), and Rodrigo Mudrovitsch (Brazil) in the Case *La Oroya v. Peru* recognised the importance of international obligations to protect the environment in the current scenario of climate crisis, which progressively come to be recognised as peremptory norms of international law (*jus cogens*).[46]

In addition, within the scope of the IACmHR, the *La Oroya* Case[47] addresses state climate duties that radiate from the human right to a healthy environment. In the aforementioned case, the IACmHR established, under the provisions of art. 26 of the ACHR, the obligations of States to continuously and progressively reduce GHG emissions (duty of prevention)[48] in accordance with the commitments assumed in the international climate regime,

43 *Lhaka Honhat (nuestra tierra) v Argentina* (IACtHR, 6 February 2020).
44 Rocha A, Sampaio R, (n 28).
45 *La Oroya v Peru* (IACtHR, 27 November 2023).
46 Concurrent vote of judges Ricardo C. Pérez Manrique, Eduardo Ferrer Mac-Gregor Poisot and Rodrigo Mudrovitsch in the case Comunidad de *La Oroya v Peru* (IACtHR, 27 November 2023), paras. 71, 78, 82.
47 *Comunidad de La Oroya v Peru* (IACmHR, 19 November 2020), para. 142.
48 Legale S et al. Direito Climático Interamericano. NIDH. 2024:114–120.

notably in the Paris Agreement and Nationally Determined Contributions (NDCs), as well as to implement adaptation policies.[49]

More recently, the IACmHR published Resolution 3/2021, with the goal of systematising the obligations that States have in matters of human rights in the current context of the climate crisis, so that they can take decisions on public policies structured on an approach based on human rights.

In this sense, the IACmHR states that for the effective protection of human rights:

> States must take appropriate measures to mitigate greenhouse gases, implement adaptation measures and remedy consequential damages. Such obligations should not be neglected due to the multi-causal nature of the climate crisis, as all States have common but differentiated obligations in the context of climate action. As with economic issues, social, cultural rights and environmental rights, in the context of climate change, maximum resources must be available to the State to progressively achieve its full effectiveness by all appropriate means.[50]

The Resolution concludes that in the current context of climate emergency, the obligation of States to prevent transborder environmental damage requires them "to develop and implement GHG mitigation targets that reflect a level of ambition in accordance with the obligations of the Paris Agreement", among other applicable standards and instruments, with emphasis on the "obligation not to exceed the global temperature to such a point that it compromises the enjoyment of human rights".[51]

Thus, the IACHR indicates that the absence or insufficiency of mitigation and adaptation policies in comparison with the obligations internationally assumed allow the jurisdiction of the Inter-American Human Rights System to be activated.

This resolution issued by the IACmHR, interpreted together with the aforementioned rulings and opinions handed down by the IACtHR, in light of the scientifically declared and politically recognised state of climate emergency, brings important perspectives for a new interpretation of the ACHR that admits the protection of the right to climate stability as a human right,

49 Merida C. Emergência Climática e Direitos Humanos: Contribuições para o reconhecimento e a delimitação do direito humano à estabilidade climática a partir do Sistema Interamericano de Direitos Humanos. Direito Internacional e Decolonialismo. Editora Arraes; 2024. Winter de Carvalho D, (n 44) p. 86.

50 IACmRH. *Resolution 03/2021*. Climate Emergency. Scope and Inter-American Human Rights Obligations, p. 15. [Accessed 10 April 2024]. Available from: https://www.oas.org/es/cidh/decisiones/pdf/2021/Resolucion_3-21_SPA.pdf.

51 IACmRH. *Resolution 03/2021* Climate Emergency. Scope and Inter-American Human Rights Obligations, p. 22. [Accessed 10 April 2024]. Available from: https://www.oas.org/es/cidh/decisiones/pdf/2021/Resolucion_3-21_SPA.pdf.

since climate security is a condition of possibility for the existence of a fundamental human right to an ecologically balanced environment.

It should also be noted that in January 2023, the Republics of Colombia and Chile presented, in accordance with Article 64 of the ACHR, a request for an Advisory Opinion to the Inter-American Court containing 16 detailed questions, with the aim of clarifying the scope of State obligations, in their individual and collective dimensions, to respond to the climate emergency within the scope of International Human Rights Law.

This is a unique opportunity for the IAHRS to take, in a pioneering way, a more concrete step towards not only recognising the existence of a human right to climate stability subject to unionisation before the IACtHR, but, above all, delimiting State obligations regarding the adoption of legal, political, and administrative measures to protect the human right to a stable climate, as well as the duties to respect and guarantee the enjoyment of human rights in the context of climate emergency, particularly regarding their differentiated effects on vulnerable people and groups.[52]

While the framework of the IAHRS established mechanisms for legal redress, numerous obstacles impede access to justice for those confronting climate change. Many individuals, especially Indigenous communities and marginalised groups, encounter systemic challenges that hinder their ability to effectively assert their legal rights. This underscores the critical need to examine the role of *amicus curiae* in environmental and climate litigation.

7.3.3 The Role Played by the amicus curiae

At the international level, the *amicus curiae* (in the literal translation, "friend of the Court or Tribunal") consists of "an entity that is not a party to the dispute and that offers the particular International Court its own perspective, arguments or certain specialised knowledge, which may be useful in decision making".[53]

Even though the *amicus curiae* institute had already intervened in the processes of the IACtHR since the beginning of its jurisdictional activity, this mechanism only began to be regulated in 2009.

In this sense, Article 2(3) of the current Rules of Procedure of the Inter-American Court of Human Rights regulates the role of the *amicus curiae*, providing that it is an instrument through which a third Party intervenes with the purpose of promoting clarifications regarding the case, thus aiming to protect human rights; while Article 44 establishes the respective procedure

52 Merida C, (n 51) *passim*.
53 Carvalho Ramos A, (n 10) p. 275.

for manifestation before the IACtHR, regulating the means and deadlines for voluntary presentation of the petition.[54]

In accordance with Article 73(3) of the aforementioned Rules of Procedure of the Inter-American Court of Human Rights,[55] it is possible that the IACtHR may invite interested persons to present their opinion in writing, so that their statements may collaborate with the case at hand. Thus, intervention in the form of *amicus curiae* either can occur voluntarily or requested by the Inter-American Court *ex officio*. Specifically in matters of the environment and climate change, the wide use of the *amicus curiae* mechanism by State actors, non-governmental organisations, universities, and human rights experts stands out both in the case of Advisory Opinion 23/17 and in relation to the request for an *Advisory Opinion on the scope of States' obligations in terms of Human Rights in the context of the Climate Emergency* (OC-32), still to be rendered by the IACtHR, which included unprecedented participation in the jurisprudence of the IACtHR and other international courts. There were almost 300 written statements between States,[56] state organisations, OAS bodies, international organisations, NGOs, academic institutions, civil society organisations, and companies.[57]

The important role played by the *amici curiae* in the case *Comunidades Indígenas Miembros de la Asociación Lhaka Honhat (Nuestra Tierra) v Argentina* also stands out, in which the written contributions presented by civil society regarding the autonomous protection of economic and social rights, cultural and environmental rights (including, among others, human rights to food, cultural identity, a healthy environment, and water), as well as the importance of studies on environmental impacts carried out by independent technical entities as a fundamental component in public policies that aim to tackle climate change, were widely cited throughout the decision.[58]

In this sense, as can be seen from the vote of judge Eduardo Ferrer Mac-Gregor Poisot in *Lhaka Honhat*, the IACtHR's fundamental pillar of its jurisdictional activity is in permanent communication with organisations, institutions, and society in general.[59]

Indeed, by providing expert opinions, additional evidence, and legal insights, *amici curiae* can not only enhance the understanding of the rights

54 Rules of Procedure of the Inter-American Court of Human Rights. San José da Costa Rica, 2009.

55 Article 73. "Procedure [...] 3. The Presidency may invite or authorize any interested person to present their opinion in writing on the items submitted for consultation. If the request refers to the provisions of article 64.2 of the Convention, it may be done through prior consultation with the Agent". Rules of Procedure of the Inter-American Court of Human Rights. San José da Costa Rica, 2009.

56 Including State of Tuvalu, which is not a member of the OAS.

57 Lima CL, et al. Os argumentos jurídicos perante a Corte Interamericana na Opinião Consultiva sobre Direitos Humanos e Emergência Climática. Stylus Curiarum; 2024. pp. 8–9.

58 *Lhaka Honhat (nuestra tierra) v Argentina* (IACtHR, 6 February 2020) 21–22.

59 *Lhaka Honhat (nuestra tierra) v Argentina* (IACtHR, 6 February 2020) 23.

at stake and the human rights implications of climate change but also contribute to defining victim status. Considering that within the Inter-American Human Rights System (IAHRS) the roster of entities qualified to engage in advisory functions is broader than that found in other human rights protection frameworks, alongside the volume and diversity of contributions from *amicus curiae* in Advisory Opinion OC 23/17 and Advisory Opinion OC 32 (pending a ruling by the IACtHR), their participation is deemed particularly significant. Such active engagement fosters the establishment of a fairer and more inclusive system wherein human rights are respected and safeguarded, irrespective of an individual's origin, gender, age, or sexual orientation.

It is believed, therefore, that the action of the *amicus curiae* increases the probability of a more qualified decision, either through additional information added to the case that provides substantial elements for the decision[60] or through the reinforcement of legitimacy that it provides to the IAHRS through the openness to dialogue with society, especially in cases of complexity and transcendence of the object of the process,[61] as occurs in climate disputes.

Furthermore, the figure of the *amicus curiae* also plays a fundamental role in monitoring government actions and ensuring compliance with international obligations related to the environment. This is because, by providing information and analysis on public policies and their consequences for the climate, they contribute to holding States accountable and protecting the human rights of communities affected by climate change.

Finally, it is important to emphasise that the participation of the *amicus curiae* does not replace the role of the parties involved in the litigation. On the contrary, its role is carried out in parallel with the work of the parties, offering a more comprehensive and enriching view of the case.

7.4 Provisional Measures in Climate Change Cases

Provisional measures within the scope of the IAHRS have gained prominence in recent decades. Just as occurs in domestic Procedural Law, international Procedural Law also has urgent measures so that irreparable harm to people can be avoided or, at least, stopped.

Inspired by the precautionary procedures of domestic legal systems, provisional measures are instruments that aim to protect human rights in urgent situations, providing a rapid response to violations or potential violations

60 Torres Manrique JI. Agenda pendiente de los amici curiai: Análisis a la luz de los derechos fundamentales. Revista Brasileira de Direito. 2021;29(11):218. [Accessed 10 July 2024]. Available from: https://doi.org/10.26668/IndexLawJournals/2358-1352/2021.v29i11.7538.

61 Leal MCH, Hoffmann GB. Amicus Curiae na Corte Interamericana de Direitos Humanos a partir do Caso *Honhat Vs. Argentina*. Journal of Institutional Studies. 2021;7(1):331. [Accessed 18 August 2024]. Available from: https://doi.org/10.21783/rei.v7i1.524.

of human rights, which is fundamental in the current climate emergency context.

As stated by Cançado Trindade, in International Human Rights Law (IHRL), provisional measures "began to go further in terms of protection, revealing an unprecedented reach, by starting to protect the very substantive rights of human beings, insofar as they seek to prevent irreparable damage to the human person as a subject of IHRL".[62]

The IACtHR, in particular, has the power to grant provisional measures in cases where an extremely serious and urgent situation arises that involves a risk of irreparable damage to human rights, as determined by the provisions of Article 63(2) of the ACHR:

> In cases of extreme gravity and urgency, and when necessary to avoid irreparable damage to persons, the Court shall adopt such provisional measures as it deems pertinent in matters it has under consideration. With respect to a case not yet submitted to the Court, it may act at the request of the Commission.

The legal standing for requesting provisional measures varies depending on whether or not the case is being processed before the IACtHR. Once the case is pending before the Court, provisional measures may be granted *ex officio*, at the request of the IACmHR or the victims and their representatives. However, if the case is not yet in progress before the IACtHR, only the IACmHR will have the legitimacy to request the measure.

At the IAHRS, provisional measures are applicable in three cases, namely: the first, of a general nature, refers to the prevention of irreparable harm to people in the context of cases pending before the IACtHR; ii) the second, with a view to protecting the object of a case pending before the IACtHR; and ultimately, to prevent irreparable harm regardless of the case system.

Considering that the IACtHR is not a permanent court[63] and that urgent situations may arise at any time, in addition to the provisional measures provided for in the ACHR (addressed to the Court), the Regulations of the Inter-American Court of Human Rights, in its Article 27(6), stipulate the possibility of urgent measures directed to the Presidency of the Inter-American Court when it is not in session.[64]

Also, the IACmHR, in accordance with Article 25 of its Regulations, may adopt precautionary measures to protect various human rights, both *ex officio* and at the request of the interested party.[65]

62 Excerpt taken from the vote given in the resolution of provisional measures in the Case of Haitians and Dominicans of Haitian origin in the Dominican Republic, 2000.

63 In other words, the IACtHR is not permanently installed, but it operates in session periods throughout the year.

64 Article 27 of the Rules of Procedure of the Inter-American Court of Human Rights 2009.

65 Article 25 of the Rules of Procedure of the Inter-American Court of Human Rights 2009.

Although the IACtHR has not yet granted a provisional measure on climate matters, direct victims of environmental violations, such as Indigenous communities and rural populations, have the legitimacy to request provisional measures. This is essential in scenarios where their lives, health, and well-being are threatened by harmful activities such as mining, deforestation, and pollution. As a recent example, we mention the resolution issued by the IACtHR, in 2023, in relation to members of the Yanomami, Ye'Kwana, and Munduruku Indigenous peoples against Brazil,[66] aiming at the immediate adoption of measures necessary to protect life and personal integrity, health, and access to food and drinking water for members of the aforementioned Indigenous peoples, from a culturally appropriate perspective.

In this scenario, faced with serious threats, attacks and contamination of rivers, among others, due to the presence of unauthorised people and the advancement of illegal mining exploration in their territories, the IACtHR recognised that the lack of adequate measures on the part of the State could result in irreparable damage, justifying the urgency of measures to protect territorial rights and the integrity of affected communities. Precedents like this[67] demonstrate the possibility of intervention by the inter-American system in situations of serious environmental and climate risk.

7.5 Conclusion

This chapter examines the connection between legal standing and climate change within the Inter-American Human Rights System. It highlights the criteria for establishing legal standing, the barriers faced by claimants, and the vital role of *amici curiae*. It also emphasises the importance of provisional measures as a means of providing urgent protection to individuals affected by climate change.

Legal standing and provisional measures are instrumental in advancing climate justice in the Inter-American region. By improving access to justice mechanisms and facilitating urgent responses to climate-induced human rights abuses, the IAHRS can foster greater accountability among states. Moving forward, it is crucial that the system continually adapts and emerges as a robust platform for addressing the intersections of human rights and climate change, promoting sustainable development and environmental and climate protection in the Americas.

66 *Miembros de los Pueblos Indígenas Yanomami, Ye'kwana y Munduruku v Brasil* (IACtHR, 12 December 2023).

67 In a similar sense, we recommend consulting the Case *Kichwa Indigenous People of Sarayaku regarding Ecuador. Provisional Measures.* Order of the Inter American Court of 6 July 2004. Available from: https://www.Cortetidh.or.cr/docs/medidas/sarayaku_se_01.pdf . In Orders of 17 July 2005, and 4 February 2010, the Court ratified the provisional measures in force with regard to Ecuador. Orders available at: https://www.Corteidh.or.cr/docs/medidas/sarayaku_se_02.pdf medidas/sarayaku_se_04.pdf.

It is essential to acknowledge that active legitimacy serves as a vital instrument for promoting human rights in a context marked by environmental degradation and climate change, which give rise to new forms of vulnerability. Enhancing this legitimacy within the framework of the IAHRS can ensure that more victims of human rights violations linked to climate issues have their cases formally addressed and considered. Facilitating dialogue among the State, civil society, and international organisations is crucial for aligning the protection of human rights with sustainable development.

In summary, the concept of active legitimacy within the Inter-American Human Rights System, particularly in the realm of environmental and climate litigation, presents a significant opportunity for advancing human rights in response to contemporary global challenges. Expanding active legitimacy not only amplifies the voices of historically marginalised groups but also reaffirms the commitment of States to environmental protection and climate stability as fundamental human rights.

Moreover, the limitations and challenges encountered, alongside potential academic contributions, underscore the necessity of significantly broadening the discourse on active legitimacy in climate litigation within the IAHRS. In this context, it is crucial to highlight the need for robust mechanisms for international cooperation to effectively address transboundary challenges and the limited capacity of individual nations to manage the impacts of climate change. The pursuit of innovative and adaptable solutions is essential to ensure the protection of human rights amid rapid environmental transformations. Only through a collaborative and coordinated approach can we make the necessary advancements to secure justice and equity in the face of the challenges presented by climate change.

In conclusion, to enhance the accountability mechanisms within the Inter-American Human Rights System, it is recommended to bolster the active legitimacy of individuals and groups by implementing a reform that enables direct individual petitioning to the IACtHR. This reform would facilitate access to justice and streamline procedures, ensuring the availability of adequate resources to address pressing climate challenges effectively.

References

Amado Gomes C, Schramm da Silva J, Moura do Carmo W. Opinião consultiva 23/2017 da Corte Interamericana de Direitos Humanos e as inovações à tutela do meio ambiente no direito internacional. Veredas do Direito: Direito Ambiental e Desenvolvimento Sustentável. 2020;17(38):25. [Accessed 2024 Oct 21]. http://dx.doi.org/10.18623/rvd.v17i38.1841.

Auz J. Climate crisis and the testing of international human rights remedies: forecasting the inter American court of human rights. In: Centre for studies and research in international law and international relations serie: climate change and the testing of international law/Le droit international au défi des changements climatiques. Vol 26. Brill | Martinus Nijhoff Publishers; 2023. [Accessed 2024 Jul 5]. https://doi.org/10.1163/1875-8096_pplcdu_a9789004682399_13.

Auz J. "So, this is permanence": the Inter-American human rights system as a liminal space for climate justice. Melbourne JIL. 2021;22:1–34.

Carvalho Ramos A. Curso de direitos humanos. SaraivaJur; 2022.

Carvalho Ramos A. Processo internacional de direitos humanos: análise dos mecanismos de apuração de violações de direitos humanos e a implementação das decisões no Brasil. 7th ed. SaraivaJur; 2022.

Hohmann J. Igloo as icon: a human rights approach to climate change for the Inuit. Transnatl Law Contemp Probl. 2009;18:295–316.

Leal MCH, Hoffmann GB. Amicus curiae na Corte Interamericana de Direitos Humanos a partir do caso Honhat vs. Argentina. J Inst Stud. 2021;7(1). [Accessed 2024 Aug 18]. https://doi.org/10.21783/rei.v7i1.524.

Legale S, Deschamps L, Causanilhas T. Direito climático interamericano. NIDH; 2024.

Lima CL, Franco RM, Melo RF, Ribeiro STC. Os argumentos jurídicos perante a Corte Interamericana na opinião consultiva sobre direitos humanos e emergência climática. Stylus Curiarum; 2024;1:1–93.

Merida C. Emergência climática e direitos humanos: contribuições para o reconhecimento e a delimitação do direito humano à estabilidade climática a partir do Sistema Interamericano de Direitos Humanos. In: Wagner Menezes, editor. Direito internacional e decolonialismo. Editora Arraes; 2024.

Merida C. Governança global da água nas cidades: a atuação dos governos locais na concretização do direito humano à água no atual contexto de mudanças climáticas. Doctoral thesis, Universidade do Vale do Rio dos Sinos – UNISINOS; 2022.

Monteiro Danese P. Meio ambiente na contemporaneidade: de sua proteção à luz do Sistema Interamericano de Direitos Humanos. Editora Juruá; 2019.

Montovani de Lima R, Mucelli Rezende Veloso N. A conceituação ampliada da jurisdição extraterritorial no Sistema Interamericano pela OC-23/17: os avanços na internacionalização ambiental. Revista do Programa de Pós-Graduação em Direito da UFC. 2018;8(2):646. [Accessed 2024 Nov 20]. Available from: http://periodicos.ufc.br/nomos/article/view/39819/95987.

Oxford Learner's Dictionaries. Climate emergency. [Accessed 2024 Aug 20]. Available from: https://www.oxfordlearnersdictionaries.com/definition/english/climate-emergency.

Piovesan F. Direitos humanos e o direito constitucional internacional. 7th ed. Editora Saraiva; 2006.

Rocha A, Sampaio R. Climate change before the European and Inter-American courts of human rights: comparing possible avenues before human rights bodies. RECIEL. 2023. https://doi.org/10.1111/reel.12502.

Torres Manrique JI. Agenda pendiente de los amici curiai: análisis a la luz de los derechos fundamentales. Revista Brasileira de Direito. 2021;29(11):218. [Accessed 2024 Jul 10]. https://doi.org/10.26668/IndexLawJournals/2358-1352/2021.v29i11.7538.

Winter de Carvalho D. Constitucionalismo climático: estado de direito e justiça climática. Livraria do Advogado; 2025.

Winter de Carvalho D. Desvendando a emergência climática. Revista Jurídica do Ministério Público Catarinense. 2022;17(36):39–64.

8 Climate Litigation before the European Court of Human Rights

A Catalyst for Reevaluating Prerequisites for Legal Standing

Małgorzata Kwiędacz-Palosz

8.1 Introduction

The heart of the European system of human rights protection is the Convention for the Protection of Human Rights and Fundamental Freedoms (also called the European Convention on Human Rights, the Convention, or the ECHR) adopted in 1950 under the auspices of the Council of Europe. The rising tide of European climate litigation relying on human rights, such as the right to life or the right to private and family life, reaches the European Court of Human Rights ("ECtHR") and is a challenge to its existing case law on the legal standing, which refers to the capacity to bring an application to the ECtHR as it does not envisage bringing of an *actio popularis*. The climate litigation serves as a catalyst for reevaluating prerequisites for legal standing, which requires a link between the applicant and the harm that he or she claims to have sustained as a result of the alleged violation of the Convention and provides a significant opportunity to explore the implications of these interpretations for individuals and the capacity of environmental non-governmental organisations ("NGOs") to bring cases before the ECtHR.

8.2 The Legal Standing before the European Court of Human Rights

In the Strasbourg system, Article 34 ECHR regulates legal standing: "The Court may receive applications from any person, non-governmental organisation or group of individuals claiming to be the victim of a violation by one of the High Contracting Parties of the rights set forth in the Convention or the Protocols thereto". This provision clearly does not provide for an *actio popularis*, meaning that applicants cannot complain of a violation of the Convention unless they claim that their rights or freedoms under the ECHR have been infringed.

The notion of legal standing refers to the capacity to bring an application to the ECtHR and englobes both terms, victim status and *locus standi*, which are separate and should be distinguished. The ECHR has introduced the notion of victim status of individuals, NGOs, and group of individuals. Interestingly, the initial text of Article 25 (currently Article 34) ECHR included the following list of applicants: "any natural or legal person or the

DOI: 10.4324/9781003540977-11

group of individuals", and only its final version incorporated the "non-governmental organisation" instead of "legal person".[1] Therefore, in the preparatory works of the ECHR, "non-governmental organisation" means a legal or moral person such as a private law association, foundation, or commercial company. The Founding Fathers did not cover an NGO bringing the case on behalf of the affected persons.

Therefore, the case law of the ECtHR has introduced the term *locus standi* of representatives who are acting on behalf of persons whose ECHR's rights are alleged to be violated.[2] Consequently, the application was successfully brought by an NGO. It is also described as "representation" and was introduced in the Grand Chamber judgment issued in *Centre for Legal Resources on behalf of Valentin Câmpeanu v Romania*, in which the ECtHR for the first time held that there might be "special considerations" where it could be accepted that applications could be lodged by others on behalf of the victims without a specific authority to act.[3] This term would be crucial in adapting the legal standing before the ECtHR to the context of climate litigation.

8.3 The Concepts of "Victim" and *locus standi*

The ECtHR interprets the concept of "victim" autonomously and irrespective of domestic concepts such as those concerning an interest or capacity to act.[4] The ECtHR's well-established case law ruled that this victim-status criterion should not be applied in a rigid, mechanical, and inflexible way.[5] Additionally, like the other provisions of the Convention, the term "victim" must also be interpreted in an evolutive manner in the light of conditions in contemporary society as any excessively formalistic interpretation of that concept would make protection of the rights guaranteed by the Convention ineffectual and illusory.[6]

There are three categories of victims: those directly affected by the alleged violation of the ECHR (the direct victims); those indirectly affected by the alleged violation of the ECHR (the indirect victims); and those potentially affected by the alleged violation of the ECHR (the potential victims). Regardless of whether the victim is direct, indirect, or potential, there must be a link between the applicant and the harm that he or she claims to have

1 Tymofeyeva A. Non-governmental organisations under the European Convention on Human Rights: Exceptional Legal Standing. RWW. 2015;43.

2 ECtHR. Key Theme - Article 34/35 The locus standi of representatives to bring/pursue a case before the Court when the direct victim has died. August 2024. [Accessed 10 September 2024]. Available from: The locus standi of representatives to bring/pursue a case (coe.int).

3 *Centre for Legal Resources on behalf of Valentin Câmpeanu v Romania* App. No. 47848/08 (ECtHR [GC] 17 July 2014) paras. 103 and 105.

4 *Aksu v Turkey* App. Nos. 4149/04 and 41029/04 (ECtHR [GC] 15 March 2012) para. 52.

5 *Albert and Others v Hungary* App. No. 5294/14 (ECtHR [GC] 7 July 2020) para. 121.

6 *Gorraiz Lizarraga and Others v Spain* App. No. 62543/00 (ECtHR 27 April 2004) para. 38.

sustained as a result of the alleged violation of the ECHR as it does not envisage bringing of an *actio popularis* for the interpretation of the rights set out therein or permit individuals to complain about a provision of national law simply because they consider that it may contravene the Convention.[7]

To qualify as a direct victim, a person must normally be "personally and directly affected" by the alleged violation.[8] They can be affected by past or ongoing harm. In environmental cases, for example, in the *Cordella* judgment,[9] the Court stated that individuals are "personally affected" by the measure complained of if they find themselves in a situation "of high environmental risk", in which the environmental threat "becomes potentially dangerous for the health and well-being of those who are exposed to it".[10]

If the alleged victim of a violation has passed away before the submission of the application, it may be possible for the person with the requisite legal interest as next of kin to submit an application raising concerns related to the death or disappearance of his or her relative. In this situation, the ECtHR examines whether relatives can be considered indirect victims of the alleged violation of the ECHR suffered by the deceased direct victim. In short, the indirect victims must demonstrate a "ricochet effect" created by the alleged violation affecting the direct victim on their Convention rights for them to prove harm or a valid personal interest in bringing the situation complained of to an end.

As the ECHR does not permit complaints *in abstracto* (i.e., without a human right or freedom being infringed), individuals are not entitled to complain simply because of the existence of incompatibilities with the Convention in the national legal order or in the practice of the State. Applicants must demonstrate that incompatibilities with the Convention are at least potentially detrimental to them. The ECtHR may accept the existence of victim status where applicants contend that a law violates their rights, in the absence of an individual measure of implementation, if they belong to a class of people who risk being directly affected by the legislation or if they are required either to modify their conduct or risk being prosecuted.[11] Also, the individuals who argue that they may be affected at some future point in time and only in highly exceptional circumstances may claim to be a victims of a violation

7 *Mansur Yalçın and Others v Turkey* App no 21163/11 (ECtHR 16 September 2014) para. 40, *in fine*.

8 *Tănase v Moldova* App no 7/08 (ECtHR [GC] 27 April 2010) para. 104; *Burden v the United Kingdom* App no 13378/05 (ECtHR [GC] 20 April 2008) para. 33; *Lambert and Others v France* App no 46043/14 (ECtHR [GC] 25 June 2015) para. 89.

9 *Cordella and Others v Italy* App. Nos. 54414/13 and 54264/15 (ECtHR 24 January 2019).

10 Schmid E. Victim status before the ECtHR in cases of alleged omissions: The Swiss Climate Case. Blog of the European Journal of International Law EJIL: Talk!; 30 April 2022. [accessed on 10 September 2024]. Available from: Victim Status before the ECtHR in Cases of Alleged Omissions: The Swiss Climate Case – EJIL: Talk! (ejiltalk.org).

11 *Tănase v Moldova* App. No. 7/08 (ECtHR [GC] 27 April 2010) para. 104.

of the ECHR owing to the risk of a future violation.[12] Such an applicant "must produce reasonable and convincing evidence of the likelihood that a violation affecting him or her will occur as mere suspicion or conjecture is insufficient".[13]

The ECtHR accepted the *locus standi* of associations to lodge or pursue applications on behalf of victims, including where the victim had been able, while alive, to lodge complaints himself or herself.[14] The main objective of this approach is that the *locus standi* "[served] not only to decide those cases brought before [it] but, more generally, to elucidate, safeguard and develop the rules instituted by the Convention, thereby contributing to the observance by the States of the engagements undertaken by them as Contracting Parties".[15]

Consequently, to have legal standing, the applicant must show that they meet the relevant criteria elaborated in the case law. As the ECHR is a living instrument which must respond to the realities of the present[16] and the climate cases, as their nature differs from environmental litigation, as explained below, the ECtHR needed to reevaluate the prerequisites for legal standing in the climate context.

8.4 Climate Change and Legal Standing

This chapter analyses the principles pertinent to climate change litigation, based on the landmark judgments in three cases examining States' obligations concerning climate change under the ECHR: *Verein KlimaSeniorinnen Schweiz and Others v Switzerland*[17] ("*KlimaSeniorinnen*"); *Carême v France*[18] ("*Carême*"); and *Duarte Agostinho and Others v Portugal and 32 Others*[19] ("*Duarte Agostinho*"). All rulings were issued on 9 April 2024. The *KlimaSeniorinnen* case was brought by individuals and an association complaining about the Swiss authorities' lack of action to mitigate climate change. The ECtHR found a violation of the right to respect for private and family life (Article 8 ECHR) and the right to a fair hearing (Article 6(1) ECHR) by Switzerland. In *Carême*, a complaint by a former inhabitant and mayor of Grande-Synthe concerning France's insufficient steps to prevent

12 *Berger-Krall and Others v Slovenia* App. No. 14717/4 (ECtHR 12 June 2014) para. 258, with further references.

13 *Centre for Legal Resources on behalf of Valentin Câmpeanu* (n 7) para. 101.

14 *Association for the Defence of Human Rights in Romania – Helsinki Committee on behalf of Ionel Garcea v Romania* App. No. 2959/11 (ECtHR 24 March 2015) paras. 42–46.

15 *Ibid*, para. 105.

16 *Tyrer v the United Kingdom* App. No. 5856/72 (ECtHR 25 April 1978) para. 31.

17 *Verein KlimaSeniorinnen Schweiz and Others v Switzerland* App. No. 53600/20 (ECtHR [GC] 9 April 2024).

18 *Carême v France* App no 7189/21 (ECtHR [GC] 9 April 2024).

19 *Duarte Agostinho and Others v Portugal and 32 Others* App. No. 39371/20 (ECtHR [GC] 9 April 2024).

global warming was declared inadmissible. Finally, in *Duarte Agostinho*, the applicants' complaints regarding the severe effects of climate change and the extraterritorial jurisdiction of respondent States were also declared inadmissible. In *Duarte Agostinho*, the Court did not examine the issue of victim status under Article 34 ECHR, noting that the applicants' failure to exhaust domestic remedies made it difficult to examine whether they satisfied the victim-status criteria.

Therefore, only the judgment issued in *KlimaSeniorinnen* offers a complete and thorough analysis of the issue of legal standing, as the ECtHR dealt with not only the standing to lodge the complaints related to the right to life and the right to private and family life, as well as the right to a fair trial, but it also assessed the legal standing of individual applicants and the applicant association, securing a comprehensive panorama of who can bring climate change cases before the ECtHR.

Undoubtedly, the climate change context, owing to its exceptional features described below, impacts the legal standing. At the outset, the main challenge in climate change litigation before the ECtHR lies in the reconciliation of the complaints about the alleged harm linked to State actions and/or omissions, affecting individuals' Convention rights, and the exclusion of *actio popularis* from the ECHR system. All of this keeping in mind that "the nature of the Court's judicial function, which is by definition reactive rather than proactive".[20]

In environmental cases, in order to assess the victim status of the applicants complaining about the violation of their rights guarantee under Article 8 ECHR, namely the right to private and family life, the ECtHR relied on "the minimum level of severity of the harm in question, its duration and the existence of a sufficient link with the applicant or applicants, including in some instances, the geographical proximity between the applicant and the impugned environmental harm".[21] This was possible as, in those cases, there is a nexus between specific sources from which environmental harm emanates and those affected by the harm – and "the requisite mitigation measures may be identifiable and available to be applied at the source of the harm".[22] Conversely, in the context of climate change, there is no single or specific source of harm and the emissions (regardless of national borders) produce harmful consequences worldwide as a result of a complex chain of effects.[23] Moreover, this chain of effects is both complex and unpredictable in terms of time and place.[24] Additionally, the sources of greenhouse gas emissions (GHG) are not restricted to specific activities that could be considered

20 *KlimaSeniorinnen*, (n 1) para. 481.
21 *Ibid*, para. 472.
22 *Ibid*, para. 415.
23 *Ibid*, para. 416.
24 *Ibid*, para. 417.

dangerous and, as a result, mitigation measures must be part of comprehensive regulatory policies across various sectors.

Therefore, the test applied in environmental matters could not be just copy-pasted to climate context and "the Court's environmental case-law to date [...] can offer guidance up to a point".[25]

As the victim status is premised on the existence of a direct impact of the impugned action or omission on the applicant, or a real risk thereof, "in the climate-change context, everyone may be, one way or another and to some degree, directly affected, or at a real risk of being directly affected, by the adverse effects of climate change".[26]

Setting aside the matter of jurisdiction, "given the fact that almost anyone could have a legitimate reason to feel some form of anxiety linked to the risks of the adverse effects of climate change in the future",[27] in *KlimaSenniorinen* the ECtHR was looking for a limiting criterion to lodge an application on account of the alleged failure of a State to take adequate measures to mitigate climate change that would ensure, on the one hand, the effective protection of the ECHR rights and, on the other hand, that the criteria for legal standing are not inadvertently treated as an admission of *actio popularis*.

8.5 Legal Standing in Climate Change Context under Articles 2 and 8 ECHR

In *KlimaSeniorinnen*, four women, aged between 78 and 89, and a Swiss association, Verein KlimaSeniorinnen Schweiz, whose members are all older women concerned about the consequences of global warming on their living conditions and health, complained under Articles 2 and 8 ECHR that the Swiss authorities are not taking sufficient action, despite their duties under the ECHR, to mitigate the effects of climate change.

As correctly described by some scholars, victim status in climate cases is inextricably intertwined with the substance of the disputes.[28] In the ECtHR's case law, three approaches prevail in examining the existence of legal standing: it has been examined as a separate preliminary issue in the case,[29] it may be examined in the context of an assessment of the applicability of the relevant Convention provision,[30] or it may be considered to be "closely bound up with" the issues to be considered on the merits and thus

25 *Ibid*, para. 414.
26 *Ibid*, para. 483.
27 *Carême v France*, para. 84.
28 Keller H, Heri C. The Future is Now: Climate Change Cases before the ECtHR. Nordic Journal of Human Rights, 40(1): 153–174. [Accessed 27 August 2024] Available from: Full article: The Future Is Now: Climate Cases before the ECtHR (tandfonline.com).
29 *S.A.S. v France* App. No. 43835/11 (ECtHR [GC] 1 July 2014) paras. 53–58.
30 *Greenpeace e.V. and Others v Germany* App. No. 18215/06 (ECtHR 12 May 2009).

joined to the examination of the complaint on the merits.[31] Accordingly, in *KlimaSeniorinnen*, the applicants' legal standing was examined together with the assessment of the applicability of the right to life and right to private and family life, as well as the right to a fair trial. As far as all the judges approved the adopted approach under Articles 2 and 8 ECHR, the choice of this approach to the right to a fair trial has been criticised by Judge Eicke in his partly concurring and partly dissenting opinion,[32] which is discussed in more detail below.

8.6 The Victim Status of the Individual Applicants

In *KlimaSeniorinnen*, one of the individual applicants passed away after the submission of the application in the course of the proceedings before the ECtHR. Thus, in line with the above-mentioned approach of ECtHR which allows the right of relatives of a deceased applicant to pursue an application, provided that they have a legitimate and sufficient interest in the continued examination of the application,[33] the ECtHR accepted that the son of the deceased applicant continued the proceedings on his mother's behalf.

The ECtHR has ruled that to be considered a victim in the context of complaints about harm or risk of harm resulting from alleged State failures to address climate change, an applicant must demonstrate personal and direct impact from the impugned failures. Therefore, the ECtHR "rel[ied] on distinguishing criteria for victim status such as a particular level and severity of the risk of adverse consequences of climate change affecting the individuals, taking into account the pressing nature of their need for individual protection".[34] Consequently, the ECtHR set up the two-criteria test that will check the applicant's victim status. First, "the applicant should be subject to a high intensity of exposure to the adverse effects of climate change, that is, the level and severity of (the risk of) adverse consequences of governmental action or inaction affecting the applicant must be significant".[35] Second, "there must be a pressing need to ensure the applicant's individual protection, owing to the absence or inadequacy of any reasonable measures to reduce harm".[36]

In assessing the victim status of individual applicants, the ECtHR examines the specific circumstances of the applicant's situation to determine their eligibility and to assess whether they meet the aforementioned criteria, both

31 *Hirsi Jamaa and Others v Italy* App. No. 27765/09 (ECtHR [GC] 23 February 2012) para. 111.

32 *KlimaSeniorinnen* (n 1). Partly Concurring Partly Dissenting Opinion of Judge Eicke, para. 22.

33 *Taşkın and Others v. Turkey* App. No. 46117/99 (ECtHR 10 November 2005) para. 102; *Jivan v Romania* App. No. 62250/19 (ECtHR 8 February 2022) paras. 25–26.

34 *Ibid*, para. 486.

35 *Ibid*, para. 487.

36 *Ibid*, para. 487.

of which must be fulfilled. The concrete circumstances of the case, such as the prevailing local conditions and individual specificities and vulnerabilities, would matter. To that end, "[t]he Court's assessment will also include, but will not necessarily be limited to, considerations relating to: the nature and scope of the applicant's Convention complaint, the actuality/remoteness and/or probability of the adverse effects of climate change in time, the specific impact on the applicant's life, health or well-being, the magnitude and duration of the harmful effects, the scope of the risk (localised or general), and the nature of the applicant's vulnerability".[37]

In *KlimaSeniorinnen*, although the ECtHR acknowledged the undeniable adverse impact of heatwaves on the quality of life of elderly women, it found that the applicants did not exhibit severe medical conditions that could not be mitigated by the adaptation measures available in Switzerland or by reasonable personal adjustments to address the extent of heatwaves in the country. Consequently, they were not exposed to the detrimental effects of climate change, nor were they at risk of encountering such effects in the future with an intensity that would necessitate immediate individual protection. Therefore, this test has not been met by the four Swiss women in *KlimaSeniorinnen.* Undoubtedly, the threshold for fulfilling the new victim status criteria is especially high.

In *Carême,* the Court did not even reach the step of checking whether the French Mayor had fulfilled the test. M. Carême's current residence outside of France and a lack of substantial connections to the town of Grande Synthe resulted in his application being dismissed as incompatible *ratione personae.*

Thus, it seems that "the Court's reasoning appears to leave the door open to granting victim status in cases where an individual applicant can be shown to be suffering from a serious, heat-affected, medical condition".[38] More clarity would be provided in the already communicated case *Müllner against Austria*, where the applicant suffers from multiple sclerosis and asserts that his symptoms worsen in higher temperatures, leading to temporary paralysis and restricted mobility, an effect known as Uhthoff's Syndrome.[39]

37 *Ibid*, para. 488.

38 Hösli A, Rehmann M. *Verein KlimaSeniorinnen Schweiz and Others v Switzerland:* the European Court of Human Rights' Answer to Climate Change. Climate Law; 2024 *1-22* [Accessed 27 August 2024]. Available from: 240805_Verein-KlimaSeniorinnen-Schweiz.pdf (walderwyss.com).

39 *Müllner v Austria* App. No. 18859/21 (ECtHR communicated on 18 June 2024).

8.7 The *locus standi* of Associations

This chapter takes the view that the most significant consequence of climate litigation at the ECtHR in terms of legal standing is the upgraded role of associations under the ECHR system.[40]

In fact, a review of the ECtHR's practice reveals differences in approach as regards the associations' legal standing depending on which ECHR provision they are complaining about. In its case law regarding Article 6 ECHR, which guarantees the right to a fair trial, NGOs have a victim status if they meet certain criteria. However, as far as the right to life under Article 2 ECHR or the right to private and family life guaranteed by Article 8 ECHR are concerned, the well-established case law of the Court does not allow NGOs' standing as direct victims under those provisions, since, in principle, the association is not in a position to rely on health considerations to allege a violation of Article 8 ECHR[41] – and, in general, it cannot complain of nuisances or problems which can only be encountered by natural persons.[42] Essentially, the rights and freedoms the NGOs can invoke (such as for example those under Article 6 ECHR) are their rights and freedoms as associations and not the rights or freedoms of the public, whose protection they may seek at the domestic level. This is because according to the above-mentioned preparatory works under Article 34 ECHR, the term "NGOs" refers to the legal or moral person, which englobes a large number of subjects who may act in the capacity of an applicant NGO, such as traditional non-profit NGOs, religious organisations, trade unions, political parties, and even business companies and corporations.[43] There are numerous examples in the case law of the Court where NGOs have claimed that they were subjected to a violation of Articles 9 (freedom of thought, conscience, and religion),[44] 10 (freedom of expression),[45] and 11 (freedom of assembly and association)[46] ECHR, as

40 Abel P. Mixed Signals for Domestic Climate Law: The Climate Rulings of the European Court of Human Rights. Verfassungsblog; 17 April 2024. [Accessed 27 August 2024]. Available from: https://verfassungsblog.de/mixed-signals-for-domestic-climate-law/.

41 *Greenpeace e.V. and Others v Germany* App. No. 18215/06 (ECtHR 12 May 2009).

42 *Yusufeli İlçesini Güzelleştirme Yaşatma Kültür Varlıklarını Koruma Derneği v Turkey* App. No. 37857/14 (ECtHR 7 December 2021).

43 Tymofeyeva A, (n 6); 42.

44 *Church of Scientology of St Petersburg and Others v Russia* App. No. 47191/06 (ECtHR 2 October 2014); *The Church of Jesus Christ of Latter-Day Saints v the United Kingdom* App. No. 7552/09 (ECtHR 4 March 2014); *Jehovas Zeugen in Österreich v Austria* App. No. 27540/05 (ECtHR 25 September 2012).

45 *Scharsach and News Verlagsgesellschaft v Austria* App. No. 39394/98 (ECtHR 13 February 2003); *RTBF v Belgium* App. No. 50084/06 (ECtHR 15 September 2011); *Radio Twist a.s. v. Slovakia* App. No. 62202/00 (ECtHR 19 December 2006).

46 *Christian Democratic People's Party v Moldova* App. No. 28793/02 (ECtHR 14 February 2006); *Grande Oriente d'Italia di Palazzo Giustiniani v Italy* App No. 35972/97 (ECtHR 12 December 2001); *Wilson, National Union of Journalists and Others v the United Kingdom* App. Nos. 30668/96, 30671/96 and 30678/96 (ECtHR 2 July 2002).

well as Article 1 of Protocol No. 1 (protection of property),[47] and they were recognised as a direct victim.

Consequently, according to the traditional case law of the ECtHR, an association could not be granted victim status in a climate change–related case – at least, based on substantive human rights, as it cannot rely on health considerations or nuisances and problems associated with climate change. To cope with this narrow understanding of NGOs' legal standing, in *KlimaSeniorinnen* the ECtHR relied on the following three main factors as a reason for granting legal standing to the associations complaining about the alleged violation of the substantive rights due to lack of the State's sufficient action to mitigate the effects of climate change.

First, it recalled the distinction between the victim status of individuals and the *locus standi* of representatives who are acting on behalf of persons whose Convention rights are allegedly violated.[48] Two other rationales behind the upgraded role of associations in climate litigation were the evolution in contemporary society as regards recognition of the importance of associations to litigate issues of climate change on behalf of affected persons, and, lastly, the special feature of climate change as a common concern of humankind and the necessity of promoting intergenerational burden-sharing in this context.

These three factors allowed the ECtHR to grant legal standing to the associations. However, similar to the individual applicants' victim status, the ECtHR needed to find the limiting criterion which would not allow abstract complaints about a general deterioration of the living conditions of people without considering its impact on a particular person or group of persons.

This is how the ECtHR developed the associations' *locus standi* test, named by Pedersen as the Aarhus Convention[49] test with an ECHR twist.[50] In environmental matters, the Court has already referred to the Aarhus Convention in its case law. The Aarhus Convention is premised on the idea of environmental protection as a public good and grants a prominent role to NGOs in that respect. It emphasises the need to ensure that NGOs have wide access to justice in environmental matters.[51] The Aarhus Convention contains, as its title suggests, three broad "pillars": access to information, public participation, and access to justice. There are 47 Parties to the Convention, and out of 46 Council of Europe Member States, only five have not ratified

47 *Oferta Plus S.R.L. v Moldova* App. No. 14385/04 (ECtHR 19 December 2006); *Microintelect OOD v Bulgaria* App. No. 34129/03 (ECtHR 4 March 2014).

48 *KlimaSeniorinnen*, (n 1) para. 496.

49 Aarhus Convention on Access to Information, Public Participation in Decision-Making and Access to Justice in Environmental Matters, adopted 25 June 1998, entered into force 30 October 2001, 2161 UNTS 447.

50 Pedersen OW. Climate Change and the ECHR: The Results Are In. Blog of the European Journal of International Law EJIL: Talk!; 11 April 2024. [Accessed 27 August 2024]. Available from: Climate Change and the ECHR: The Results Are In – EJIL: Talk! (ejiltalk.org).

51 In particular, its Preamble and Article 9 on access to justice.

it.[52] Furthermore, Article 2(5) Aarhus Convention explicitly incorporates within the category of "the interested public" NGOs whose statutory goals include the promotion of environmental protection, provided that they also meet "any requirements under national law".[53] According to the Aarhus Convention Implementation Guide, this reference should not be read as leaving absolute discretion to States in defining these requirements, but rather in the context of the important role the Aarhus Convention assigns to NGOs.[54]

During its assessment of the *locus standi* of associations in *KlimaSeniorinnen*, the ECtHR referenced the Aarhus Convention no less than 51 times, which is a record for an ECtHR decision.[55] Although the Court heavily relied on the Aarhus Convention, it has stated that its scope does not cover the standing of associations in the context of climate change litigation.[56] The scope of the Aarhus Convention has been unjustifiably limited as it applies to any national law relating to the environment, and the national laws regulating emissions and the climate crisis have not been excluded from this field.[57] Eckes and Trapp consider that "the Aarhus Convention seems to be most relevant to the ECtHR in relation to the definition of victimhood, and the consequential question of standing for non-governmental organisations like the Verein KlimaSeniorinnen".[58] In this judgment, for the first time, the ECtHR relied on the Aarhus Convention to establish a new concept of the *locus standi* for NGOs in climate matters.

52 Andorra, Lichtenstein, Monaco, San Marino, and Turkey.

53 "The public concerned" means the public affected or likely to be affected by, or having an interest in, the environmental decision-making; for the purposes of this definition, non-governmental organisations promoting environmental protection and meeting any requirements under national law shall be deemed to have an interest.

54 The Aarhus Convention: An Implementation Guide (second edition). [Accessed 27 August 2024. Available from: Aarhus_Implementation_Guide_interactive_eng.pdf (unece.org).

55 James Maurici KC. 30 – The Aarhus Convention and the European Convention on Human Rights–Part 2. Landmark Chambers – Aarhus blog series; 10 April 2024. [Accessed 10 September 2024]. Available from: 30 – The Aarhus Convention and the European... – Landmark Chambers.

56 *KlimaSeniorinnen,* (n 1) para. 494.

57 See, for example, the Aarhus Convention Compliance Committee findings: "*Article 9, paragraph 3, is not limited to "environmental laws", e.g., laws that explicitly include the term "environment" in their title or provisions. Rather, it covers any law that relates to the environment, i.e. a law under any policy, including and not limited to, chemicals control and waste management, planning, transport, mining and exploitation of natural resources, agriculture, energy, taxation or maritime affairs, which may relate in general to, or help to protect, or harm or otherwise impact on the environment*" (emphasis added). (Austria ACCC/C/2011/63; ECE/MP.PP/C.1/2014/3, 13 January 2014, para. 52).

58 Eckes C, Trapp T. The Aarhus Convention's Relevance for Climate Litigation Through the Lens of KlimaSeniorinnen. European Law Blog; 11 September 2024. [Accessed 30 September 2024]. Available from: The Aarhus Convention's Relevance for Climate Litigation through the Lens of KlimaSeniorinnen. European Law Blog.

It appears that it enabled the ECtHR to strike a balance between permitting effective challenges to be brought before it and preventing the incorporation of a genuine *actio popularis* in the ECHR system.

Consequently, to be recognised as having *locus standi* to lodge an application due to the alleged failure of a State to take adequate measures to reduce GHG emissions, an NGO must fulfil three criteria of the newly established test. First, it must be lawfully established in the jurisdiction concerned or have standing to act there. Second, it must be able to demonstrate that it pursues a dedicated purpose following its statutory objectives in the defence of the human rights of its members or other affected individuals within the jurisdiction concerned, whether limited to or including collective action for the protection of those rights against the threats arising from climate change. Third, it must be able to demonstrate that it can be regarded as genuinely qualified and representative to act on behalf of members or other affected individuals within the jurisdiction who are subject to specific threats or adverse effects of climate change on their lives, health, or well-being as protected under the ECHR.[59]

This test demands almost the same as the Aarhus Convention, but it is slightly more lenient. It requires that the association must be established in accordance with domestic law, whereas the Aarhus Convention requires that the association should fulfil "any requirements under national law".[60]

Additionally, when evaluating if an association meets the criteria, the ECtHR considers factors such as "the purpose for which the association was established, that it is of non-profit character, the nature and extent of its activities within the relevant jurisdiction, its membership and representativeness, its principles and transparency of governance, and whether on the whole, in the particular circumstances of a case, the grant of such standing is in the interest of the proper administration of justice".[61]

It is important to note that this *locus standi* of an association does not depend on showing that the individuals on whose behalf the case has been brought meet the victim-status requirements for such cases.

The ECtHR applied the new test to the Verein KlimaSeniorinnen Schweiz, which is a non-profit association established under Swiss law to promote and implement effective climate protection on behalf of its members. It has more than 2,000 female members who live in Switzerland and whose average age is 73. Close to 650 members are 75 or older. The NGOs' bylaws state its commitment to engaging in various activities aimed at reducing GHG emissions in Switzerland and addressing its effects on global warming. It acts not only in the interest of its members but also in the interest of the general public and future generations to ensure effective climate protection. It pursues its goals

59 *KlimaSeniorinnen*, (n 1) para. 502.
60 The definition of "the public concerned", (n 78).
61 *Ibid*, para. 502.

through various actions, including taking legal action to address the effects of climate change in the interests of its members.[62]

The ECtHR accepted that the Verein KlimaSeniorinnen Schweiz represents a vehicle of collective recourse aimed at defending the rights and interests of individuals against the threats of climate change in the respondent State.[63] Consequently, the ECtHR found that the applicant association is lawfully established, it has demonstrated that it pursues a dedicated purpose in accordance with its statutory objectives in defence of the human rights of its members and other affected individuals against the threats arising from climate change in the respondent State, and that it is genuinely qualified and representative to act on behalf of those individuals who may arguably claim to be subject to specific threats or adverse effects of climate change on their life, health, well-being, and quality of life as protected under the ECHR.[64] For those reasons, the ECtHR held that Verein KlimaSeniorinnen Schweiz has *locus standi* and its complaint was examined on merits.

In his partly concurring partly dissenting opinion, Judge Eicke assessed this newly established test and concluded that the Grand Chamber "created exactly what the judgment repeatedly asserts it wishes to avoid, namely a basis for *actio popularis* type complaints".[65] However, an important factor should be kept in mind when assessing those criteria: the conditions to establish an NGO are not the same in 46 Member States of the Council of Europe. Thus, those remarks could be "only true for jurisdictions in which it is relatively straightforward to establish human rights focused NGOs", as pointed out by Raible.[66]

One must agree with Sicilianos (a former president of the ECtHR), who mentioned that "when it comes to the admissibility stage, the judgment's main added value is the generous understanding of NGOs' standing that fits squarely with the adjudication of disputes decided in the public interest".[67] Additionally, the ECtHR expanded the *locus standi* of associations to lodge or pursue applications not only on behalf of victims but also affected individuals.

62 *Ibid*, para. 521.

63 *Ibid*, para. 523.

64 *Ibid*, para. 524.

65 *Ibid*, "Opinion of Judge Eicke", para. 45.

66 Raible L. Priorities for Climate Litigation at the European Court of Human Rights. Blog of the European Journal of International Law EJIL: Talk!; 2 May 2024. [Accessed 27 August 2024]. Available from: Priorities for Climate Litigation at the European Court of Human Rights – EJIL: Talk! (ejiltalk.org).

67 Sicilianos L-A, Deftou M-L. Breaking New Ground: Climate Change before the Strasbourg Court. Blog of the European Journal of International Law EJIL: Talk!; 12 April 2024. [accessed 27 August 2024]. Available from: Breaking New Ground: Climate Change before the Strasbourg Court – EJIL: Talk! (ejiltalk.org).

8.8 Legal Standing under Article 6(1) ECHR – Individual Applicants and Association

Out of the three ECtHR rulings on climate change–related issues, only in *KlimaSeniorinnen* did the applicants (both the individuals and the NGO) rely on Article 6(1) ECHR. They complained that they had not had access to a court concerning the State's failure to take the necessary action to reduce GHG emissions. In a similar manner to its approach under Articles 2 and 8 ECHR, the ECtHR decided to examine the issue of the legal standing of the applicants under Article 6(1) ECHR by joining it to the assessment of the applicability of that provision.

Article 6(1) ECHR guarantees the right to a fair trial but it does not guarantee a right of access to a court with the power to invalidate or override a law enacted by the legislature.[68] In general terms (and thus also in the environmental and climate sphere), for Article 6(1) ECHR to be applicable, there must be a dispute over "civil rights", which should be recognised under domestic law.[69] Such a dispute must be "genuine and serious".[70] Further, it may relate not only to the actual existence of a right but also to its scope and the manner of its exercise.[71] The outcome of the proceedings must be "directly decisive" for the right in question.[72] All of the specified conditions must be met concurrently.

A narrow reading of this provision might suggest that it is inapplicable to proceedings aimed at environmental protection as a public interest value. However, the ECtHR has adopted a flexible approach to the issue of who holds civil rights in a series of cases brought by environmental protection associations. Consequently, they qualify for protection under Article 6(1) ECHR if they seek recognition of specific rights and interests of their members,[73] of particular rights to which they have a claim as legal persons, such as the right to take part in decisions regarding the environment[74] or when there was a sufficient link between the dispute and the right claimed by the local environmental protection association, in particular given the status

68 *Project-Trade d.o.o. v Croatia* App. No. 1920/14 (ECtHR 19 November 2020) para. 68.

69 *König v Germany* App. No. 6232/73 28 June 1978, para. 89.

70 *Sporrong and Lönnroth v Sweden* App. No. 7151/75 and 7152/75 (ECtHR 23 September 1982) para. 81; *Cipolletta v Italy* App. No. 38259/09 (ECtHR 11 January 2018) para. 31.

71 ECtHR. Guide on Article 6 of the European Convention on Human Rights, right to a fair trial (civil limb). [Accessed on 27 August 2024]. Available from: Guide on Article 6 – Right to a fair trial (civil limb) (coe.int).

72 *Ulyanov v Ukraine* App. No. 16472/04 (ECtHR 5 October 2010); *Alminovich v Russia* App. No. 24192/05 (ECtHR 22 October 2019) paras. 31–32.

73 *Gorraiz Lizarraga and Others v Spain* App. No. 62543/00 (ECtHR 27 April 2004).

74 *Collectif national d'information et d'opposition à l'usine Melox – Collectif Stop Melox and Mox v France* App. No. 75218/01 (ECtHR 28 March 2006).

of the association and its founders, and the fact that the aim it pursued was limited in space and substance.[75]

These general principles also prevail in the climate change context. However, their application needs to take into account the specificities of climate change litigation, such as the fact that the object of the climate litigation proceedings may be broader than in the environmental cases. This is why the question of whether their object can be considered directly decisive for the rights relied on becomes more critical and distinct. Moreover, the harm of climate change–related risks "is not strictly imminent, which should not, on its own, lead to the conclusion that the outcome of the proceedings would not be decisive for its alleviation or reduction".[76] Lastly, as the ECtHR underlined, "the intergenerational burden-sharing impact of the climate crisis implies that the associations instituting climate-related legal actions must be seen as a means through which the Convention rights of those affected by climate change, including those at a distinct representational disadvantage, can be defended and through which they can seek to obtain an adequate corrective action for the alleged authorities' failures and omissions".[77]

In *Klimaseniorinnen*, the ECtHR analysed whether, within the context of climate matters, the individuals and the association satisfied the criteria outlined in Article 6(1) ECHR to qualify for victim status. The applicants' action instituted at the domestic level concerned both the requests for legislative and regulatory action as well as the implementation of measures within the competence of the respective authorities. Following its case law, the legislative and regulatory action falls outside the scope of Article 6(1) ECHR. Thus, only a part of their complaint related to the implementation measures falls into the remit of the protection guaranteed by this provision, and only if the three criteria listed above are met.

The first criterion of the "civil" nature of the right was fulfilled as the applicants relied, *inter alia*, on the right to life under the Swiss Constitution, and, following the ECtHR's case law, this is a right that is civil in nature.[78] The second criterion, the existence of a genuine and serious dispute over respect for the relevant right, was also met as the ECtHR held that the individual applicants' claim was not frivolous or vexatious. As regards the association, the ECtHR was satisfied that the interests defended by it are such that the "dispute" raised had a direct and sufficient link to its members' rights in question, bearing in mind the specific role of associations in the climate change context. As regards the third criterion, the ECtHR found that this requirement of a "directly decisive" outcome must be taken in the

75 *L'Érablière A.S.B.L. v Belgium* App. No. 49230/07 (ECtHR 24 February 2009).
76 *KlimaSeniorinnen*, (n 1) para. 614.
77 *Ibid.*
78 *Balmer-Schafroth and Others v Switzerland* App no 22110/93 (ECtHR 26 August 1997) paras. 33–34.

broader sense of seeking to obtain a form of correction of the authorities' actions and omissions affecting the civil rights of the association's members under national law. The association met this criterion as it acted "as a means through which the rights of those affected by climate change, including those at a distinct representational disadvantage could be defended and through which they could seek to obtain adequate corrective action"[79] for the State's failure to effectively implement mitigation measures under the existing law. However, the ECtHR considered that the dispute brought by individual applicants was not directly decisive for their specific rights. They have not demonstrated that "the requested action by the authorities alone would have created sufficiently imminent and certain effects on their rights in the context of climate change".[80]

As a result, the ECtHR found that Article 6(1) ECHR applied to the complaint of the association and it can be considered to have victim status under that provision. However, it was inapplicable to the complaints of individual applicants.

In his partly concurring and partly dissenting opinion, Judge Eicke pointed out there is no need to join the question of victim status to the merits and that this finding of inadmissibility breaks with a long tradition of Article 6(1) ECHR case law where the victim status is granted to any individual applicant demonstrating that they have been a party in proceedings brought by them before domestic courts.[81] He further suggested that the choice of the approach made by the majority negatively impacted the victim status of the individuals. This approach is followed by Brucher and De Spiegeleir, who noted that "by granting legal standing only to the association, *KlimaSeniorinnen* indirectly entitled member states to impair the essence of individuals" right to access to court, even though this essence was found to be threatened by domestic authorities' failures".[82]

8.9 Conclusion

In relation to the legal standing in climate change–related cases, the ECtHR adopted a new approach which both acknowledges and takes into account the particularities of climate change and is tailored to address its specific characteristics. Pagano said that the ECtHR established the "innovative

79 *KlimaSeniorinnen*, (n 1) para. 614.
80 *Ibid*, para. 624.
81 *Ibid*, Opinion of Judge Eicke, para. 23.
82 Brucher A, De Spiegeleir A. *Verein KlimaSeniorinnen Schweiz v. Switzerland* and Article 6(1) of the ECHR: Of Climate Change and Craftsmanship. EU Law Live; 8 May 2024. [Accessed 27 August 2024]. Available from: https://eulawlive.com/op-ed-verein-klimaseniorinnen-schweiz-v-switzerland-and-article-61-of-the-echr-of-climate-change-and-craftsmanship-by-anais-brucher-and-antoine-de-spiegeleir/.

criteria acting as 'filters' to be applied with rigour on a case-by-case basis".[83] The ruling in *KlimaSeniorinnen* has significant implications for legal actions in climate litigation, as Article 34 ECHR now allows associations to bring cases related to climate change without demonstrating that their members would individually meet victim-status requirements. While the Court has shown receptiveness to associations, it has set a high threshold for individual applicants. One must agree with Brucher and De Spiegeleir that "the ECtHR built a clear common thread for climate change cases: if one hopes to be successful in Strasbourg, one might wish to resort to associations".[84] This implies that NGOs may find it comparatively easier to access the ECtHR in climate change–related cases than individual litigants. The influence of the Aarhus Convention has been instrumental in facilitating this development.

The outcome of pending climate cases and those to be filed in the future by individuals and NGOs will inevitably hinge upon the application of the legal standing criteria elaborated in this chapter. New rulings eventually issued by the ECtHR will serve to elucidate the criteria delineating who may be deemed to have legal standing in climate litigation before the ECtHR.

References

Abel P. Mixed signals for domestic climate law: the climate rulings of the European court of human rights. Verfassungsblog [Internet]. 2024 Apr 17 [Accessed 2024 Aug 27]. Available from: https://verfassungsblog.de/mixed-signals-for-domestic-climate-law/.

Arntz S, Krommendijk J. Historic and unprecedented: climate justice in Strasbourg. Verfassungsblog [Internet]. 2024 Apr 9 [Accessed 2024 Aug 27]. Available from: https://verfassungsblog.de/historic-and-unprecedented/.

Brucher A, De Spiegeleir A. Verein KlimaSeniorinnen Schweiz v. Switzerland and Article 6(1) of the ECHR: of climate change and craftsmanship. EU Law Live [Internet]. 2024 May 8 [Accessed 2024 Aug 27]. Available from: https://eulawlive.com/op-ed-verein-klimaseniorinnen-schweiz-v-switzerland-and-article-61-of-the-echr-of-climate-change-and-craftsmanship-by-anais-brucher-and-antoine-de-spiegeleir/.

Eckes Ch, Trapp T. The Aarhus Convention's relevance for climate litigation through the lens of KlimaSeniorinnen. European Law Blog [Internet]. 2024 Sep 11 [Accessed 2024 Sep 30]. Available from: https://verfassungsblog.de/from-strasbourg-to-luxembourg/.

Hösli A, Rehmann M. Verein KlimaSeniorinnen Schweiz and others v Switzerland: the European court of human rights' answer to climate change. Climate Law. 2024;I–22. [Accessed 2024 Aug 27]. Available from: 240805_Verein-KlimaSeniorinnen-Schweiz.pdf (walderwyss.com).

83 Pagano M. Op-Ed: Legal Standing in Climate Litigation before the ECtHR and the CJEU. EU Law Live, 28 May 2024. [Accessed 27 August 2024]. https://eulawlive.com/op-ed-legal-standing-in-climate-litigation-before-the-ecthr-and-the-cjeu-by-mario-pagano/.

84 Brucher A, De Spiegeleir A, (n. 82).

Keller H, Heri C. The future is now: climate change cases before the ECtHR. Nordic J Hum Rights. 2023;40(1):153–74. [Accessed 2024 Aug 27]. Available from: https://www.tandfonline.com/doi/full/10.1080/18918131.2023.2173842.

Maurici KCJ. 30 - The Aarhus convention and the European convention on human rights - Part 2. Landmark Chambers - Aarhus blog series [Internet]. 2024 Apr 10 [Accessed 2024 Sep 30]. Available from: https://landmarkchambers.co.uk/30-the-aarhus-convention-and-the-european/.

Pagano M. Op-ed: legal standing in climate litigation before the ECtHR and the CJEU. EU Law Live [Internet]. 2024 May 28 [Accessed 2024 Aug 27]. Available from: https://eulawlive.com/op-ed-legal-standing-in-climate-litigation-before-the-ecthr-and-the-cjeu-by-mario-pagano/.

Pedersen OW. Climate change and the ECHR: the results are in. Blog of the European Journal of International Law EJIL: Talk! [Internet]. 2024 Apr 11 [Accessed 2024 Aug 27]. Available from: https://www.ejiltalk.org/climate-change-and-the-echr-the-results-are-in/.

Raible L. Priorities for climate litigation at the European court of human rights. Blog of the European Journal of International Law EJIL: Talk! [Internet]. 2024 May 2 [Accessed 2024 Aug 27]. Available from: https://www.ejiltalk.org/priorities-for-climate-litigation-at-the-european-court-of-human-rights/.

Schmid E. Victim status before the ECtHR in cases of alleged omissions: the Swiss climate case. Blog of the European Journal of International Law EJIL: Talk! [Internet]. 2022 Apr 30 [Accessed 2024 Sep 30]. Available from: https://www.ejiltalk.org/victim-status-before-the-ecthr-in-cases-of-alleged-omissions-the-swiss-climate-case/.

Sicilianos L, Deftou M. Breaking new ground: climate change before the Strasbourg court. Blog of the European Journal of International Law EJIL: Talk! [Internet]. 2024 Apr 12 [Accessed 2024 Aug 27]. Available from: https://www.ejiltalk.org/breaking-new-ground-climate-change-before-the-strasbourg-court/.

Tymofeyeva A. Non-governmental organisations under the European convention on human rights: exceptional legal standing. RWW. 2015;42–43.

9 Climate Litigation in the African Human Rights System

Possibilities, Limits, and Constraints

Welena da Silva

9.1 Introduction

Nowadays, the relationship between climate change and human rights is unquestionable, as the adverse effects of climate change on the effective enjoyment of human rights and on human life itself become more visible.[1] This explains why the international community increasingly recognises this connection between climate change and human rights.

The Intergovernmental Panel on Climate Change, hereinafter IPCC, has sought to elucidate climate science by pointing out the global scope of the adverse effects of climate change on environmental components and human populations in all regions of the world in the periodic reports it has published since 1990. In its latest report, the IPCC testifies that climate change will intensify in all regions of the globe in the coming decades and that, even with the aspiration to limit global warming to 1.5°C, there will be increasing heatwaves, longer hot seasons, and shorter cold seasons. In addition, sea levels will continue to rise throughout the 21st century, further increasing the risk of flooding in low-lying regions as wind, snow, sea ice, drought, or humidity change, leading to painful repercussions.[2]

Although the African continent's contribution to the climate crisis that humanity is witnessing is very low compared to other regions,[3] it is certain

1 Through Resolutions A/HRC/RES/47/24 of 2021; A/HRC/RES/32/34 of 2016; A/HRC26L/33 of 2014; A/HRC/RES/ 18/22 of 2011 and A/HRC/RES/10/4 of 2009, the United Nations Human Rights Council has acknowledged the relationship between climate change and human rights. In Africa, the African Commission's ACHPR Resolution 153(XLVI) 09 calls on the Conference of Heads of State and Government of the African Union to ensure that safeguards of human rights standards, such as the principle of free, prior, and informed consent, are included in any legal text adopted on climate change, such as preventive measures against forced resettlement, unjust dispossession, loss of livelihoods, and other similar human rights violations. On the subject, Jegede AO. State Duty to "Protect" Rights and Legal Obstacles to Climate Litigation. In: Climate Litigation and Justice in Africa. Bristol, UK: Bristol University Press; 2024. p. 43.

2 Climate Change 2023. Synthesis Report. [Accessed 25 August 2024]. Available from: IPCC _AR6_SYR_LongerReport.pdf.

3 The IPCC's Sixth Assessment Report (AR6) reports that in 2018, Africa contributed only 3% to the global fossil fuel industry. However, South Africa is in the top 20 countries that emit the

DOI: 10.4324/9781003540977-12

that Africa is one of the regions in the world most vulnerable to climate change. According to the draft *Study on the Impact of Climate Change on Human and Peoples' Rights in Africa*,[4] prepared by the African Commission, by virtue of Resolutions 153(XLVI) 09 and 271(LV)2014, sectors identified as vulnerable to the impact of actual or projected climate change in Africa include water resources, nutritional security, natural resource and biodiversity management, human health, human settlements, infrastructure, and desertification. Due to generally high temperatures in many regions, greater drought is expected in parts of the continent, such as northern and southern Africa; other areas, such as East Africa, could have higher humidity, with different consequences for food production and sanitary conditions.[5]

To address the challenge of combating climate change, a number of instruments have been adopted at regional, sub-regional, and national levels on the continent. Some examples are the Nairobi Declaration, adopted at the first African Climate Summit in 2009, which recognises that climate change is the greatest challenge facing humanity, that it is one of the main threats to life on earth, and that urgent and concerted action is therefore needed to reduce emissions and the concentration of greenhouse gases in the atmosphere; the African Union's Climate Change Strategy (2014); Aspiration 1 of the African Union's Agenda 2063 "A prosperous Africa based on inclusive growth and sustainable development", and the Africa Adaptation Initiative launched in 2015 by the African Ministerial Conference on the environment.

At the sub-regional level, sub-regional action plans and policy responses to adverse climate impacts have been developed. The Southern African Development Community (SADC/CCSAP) Climate Change Strategy and Action Plan highlights the need to establish a standardised monitoring, evaluation, and reporting framework for climate change programmes. Similarly, the East African Community (EAC) Climate Change Policy Framework emphasises research, monitoring, and projection. The Economic Community of West African States (ECOWAS) adopted the Lomé Declaration on Climate Change and the Protection of Civilians in West Africa in 2009, calling for a human rights approach to climate change. The organisation also has a Regional Strategy and a Regional Climate Action Plan (2022–2030) of a

---

most GHGs. For further developments, Jegede AO. Should a Human Right to a Safe Climate Be Recognized under the AU Human Rights System?. In: Addaney M, Jegede AO, eds. Human Rights and the Environment under African Union Law. Springer Nature; 2020. p. 55 ff; Mo Ibrahim Foundation. The road to COP27 making Africa's case in the global climate debate. Forum Report 12; 2022. [Accessed 28 October 2024]. Available from: 2022-Ibrahim-Forum _Facts-Figures.pdf.

4 Call for Comments to the Study on the Impact of Climate Change on Human and Peoples' Rights in Africa. African Commission on Human and Peoples' Rights. [Accessed on 25 August 2024]. Available from: au.int.

5 Kabaseke C, Odaghara CT, Ashukem JCN. The Interface between Loss and Damage, Vulnerability and Human Rights in Africa. African Journal of Climate Law and Justice. 2024(1):76–77.

Regulation on environmental and social assessment (C/Regulation 16/12/13, of 8 December 2023), which mandates that climate change must be foreseen and considered in the design of projects and in carrying out environmental and social assessment.[6]

At the domestic level, African states are not only adopting political and legislative measures in response to climate change,[7] but they have also made commitments at the multilateral level, ratifying instruments of international law, such as the United Nations Framework Convention on Climate Change (UNFCCC)[8] and the Paris Agreement.[9] On this point, it should be noted that the text of the African Charter on Human and Peoples' Rights[10] (the Charter), unlike other regional human rights treaties[11] in Europe[12] and America,[13]

6 Article 46 of the Regulation 12/16/13, of 8 December 2023.

7 Examples include Uganda's National Climate Change Act of 2021. [Accessed 5 September 2024]. Available from: https://disasterlaw.ifrc.org/sites/default/files/media/disaster_law/2022-05/National%20Climate%20Change%20Act%2C%202021.pdf; Nigeria's Climate Change Act 2021. [Accessed 5 September 2024]. Available from: NIG208055.pdf (fao.org); Kenya's Climate Change Act 2016 revised 2023. [Accessed 5 September 2024]. Available from: Climate ChangeAct11of2016.pdf (kenyalaw.org); South African Climate Change Act 2024. [Accessed 5 September 2024]. Available from: https://www.gov.za/sites/default/files/gcis_document/202407/50966climatechangeact222024.pdf (English/Tshivenda) (www.gov.za).

8 1992 United Nations Framework Convention on Climate Change (adopted 9 May 1992, entered into force 21 March 1994) 1771 UNTS 107.

9 2015 Paris Agreement (adopted 12 December 2015, entered into force 4 November 2016) 3156 UNTS 79. 52 African States are Parties to the Paris Agreement. [Accessed 25 August 2024]. List updated on: UNTC.

10 1981 African Charter on Human and Peoples' Rights (adopted 27 June 1981, entered into force 21 October 1986) 1520 UNTS 217.

11 The Declaration of the Human Rights of the States of South-East Asia adopted in 2012 within ASEAN, although not legally binding, embraces the right to the environment in Article 28(f).

12 1950 (European) Convention for the Protection of Human Rights and Fundamental Freedoms (adopted 4 November 1950, entered into force 3 September 1953) ETS No. 5. The European Convention on Human Rights and its protocols do not expressly enshrine the right to the environment. However, this gap has not prevented the European Court of Human Rights from indirectly protecting the environment through the rights enshrined in Articles 2 (right to life), 8 (right to respect for private and family life) and 10 (freedom of expression).

13 1969 American Convention on Human Rights (adopted 22 November 1969, entered into force 18 July 1978) OAS Treaty Series No. 36. Even though this latter convention and the 1948 American Declaration of Human Rights and Duties (adopted at the 9th International Conference of American States, in Bogotá, on 2 May 1948) do not expressly provide for the right to a healthy environment, the 1988 San Salvador Additional Protocol on Human Rights in the Area of Economic, Social, and Cultural Rights (adopted 17 November 1988, entered into force 16 November 1999, OAS Treaty Series No. 69) recognises such a right in Article 11, by providing that all rights to the environment are not expressly provided for people have the right to live in a healthy environment and to have access to basic public services, and it is the duty of States to promote, preserve, and improve the environment. However, pursuant to Article 19(6) of the same San Salvador Protocol, the Article 11 is non-justiciable. Accordingly, the Inter-American Court has been forced to deal with the environmental issue in a more indirect manner (e.g., through the rights of Indigenous peoples, to life or health).

enshrines a standalone right to a healthy environment. More particularly, Article 24 of the African Charter states that "All peoples have the right to a satisfactory general healthy environment, to their development". Moreover, Article III(1) of the African Conservation Convention on the Protection of Nature and Natural Resources in Africa[14] recognises the right to the environment under the terms of the Charter.[15]

Without getting involved in the analysis of the meaning and scope of the right to a healthy environment in the light of the Charter, a subject hotly debated among practitioners and scholars, this chapter is limited to two brief considerations:

The right to a healthy environment, despite being considered by the Charter as a "right of peoples", which, *prima facie*, insinuates its (exclusively) collective nature, with all the legal difficulties associated with this status, especially in terms of its enforceability,[16] has been seen by scholars and in the case-law of African courts as also a subjective right of individuals. In addition to the procedural dimension associated with it (i.e., the rights to environmental information, to participation in decision-making procedures related to environmental matters, and of access to justice for the protection of the environment), the right to a healthy environment

---

However, in 2017, at the request of Colombia, the Court rendered an advisory opinion in which it acknowledged the existence of a right to a healthy environment under the American Convention on Human Rights, by operation of Article 26, which is therefore as justiciable as any other human rights. *The Environment and Human Rights (State Obligations in Relation to the Environment in the Context of the Protection and Guarantee of the Rights to Life and to Personal Integrity – Interpretation and Scope of Articles 4(1) and 5(1) of the American Convention on Human Rights)* Advisory Opinion OC-23/17, Inter-American Court of Human Rights Series A No. 23 (15 November 2017).

14 1968/2013 African Convention on the Conservation of Nature and Natural Resources (adopted 15 September 1968, revised 24 January 2013, entry into force 16 June 1969). Out of the 53 Member States of the African Union, only 17 have ratified the Convention.

15 At the regional level, other relevant instruments in the environmental and climate context, namely the 1990 African Charter on the Rights and Welfare of the Child (adopted 11 July 1990, entered into force 25 November 1999) CAB/LEG/24.9/49 (Maputo Protocol), the 2003 Protocol to the African Charter on Human and People's Rights on the Rights of Women in Africa (adopted 1 July 2003, entered into force 25 November 2005) 3268 UNTS 1, and the 2009 African Union Convention for the Protection and Assistance of Internally Displaced Persons (adopted 23 October 2009, entered into force 6 December 2012) 3014 UNTS 3 (Kampala Convention).

16 Lumina M. The Right to a Clean, Safe and Healthy Environment under the African Human Rights System. In: Addaney M, Jagede AO, eds. Human Rights and the Environment under African Union Law. Springer Nature; 2020. p. 26; Rocha A, Oliveira H. Human Rights and Fundamental Rights. Lisbon Public Law Working Paper Series No 2024-1:12–13. [Accessed 5 September 2024]. Available from: https://papers.ssrn.com/sol3/papers.cfm?abstract_id=4714724.

has a substantive dimension from which one can derive an obligation to protect, preserve, and ameliorate the environment.[17]

The African Commission on Human and Peoples' Rights (AfrCmHPR) has argued that the rights guaranteed in the Charter are inseparable and interdependent – both civil and political rights, as well as economic, social, and cultural rights – living up to the preamble of the Charter in which it is stated that all rights are at the same level in terms of conception and universality. This thesis explains the position the AfrCmHPR has taken in several cases submitted to it,[18] and in the guidance documents it has prepared.[19] Seen in this way, the right to a healthy environment does not gain autonomy in relation to the other rights enshrined in the Charter, despite the fact that it is justiciable.

The legally binding nature of the right to a healthy environment under the Charter results, therefore, from the duties of promotion and protection of the environment by the Member States, but also from the fact that it is a subjective right, inseparable and interdependent from other enshrined rights. Thus, although the Charter does not provide for the right to a balanced climate system, it seems to us that it fits into the content of Article 24,[20] insofar as climate change not only impacts the effective enjoyment of human rights, but can also significantly affect natural environmental components and the ecosystem services they provide, jeopardising the quality of human life.[21] Therefore, in the climate context, States are

17 On the State's duty to protect climate rights and litigation, Jegede AO, (n 1) pp. 44 ff.

18 ComADHP, Social and Economic Action Center, *Center for Economic and Social Rights c. Nigeria*, Communication n. ° 155/96, para. 51, "the environment affects the quality of life and safety of the individual" *SERAP v. Federal Republic of Nigeria*, ECW/CCJ/JUD/18/12, December 14 2012, para. 100.

19 This thesis is also supported by the explanatory note on the reporting guidelines on articles 21 to 24 of the ACHPR regarding mining operations. [Accessed 25 August 2024]. Avaliable from: state-reporting-guidelines-and-principles-articles-21-and-24fre.pdf.

20 See the case *KlimaSeniorinnen v Switzerland* (ECtHR). [Accessed 5 September 2024]. Available from: coe.int. *Verein KlimaSeniorinnen Schweiz and others v. Switzerland* (communicated case), in which the European Court of Human Rights found a violation of the right to respect for private and family life (Article 8) and to access the courts (Article 6(1)) of the European Convention on Human Rights. It asserted that Article 8 of the Convention covers the right to effective protection by State authorities against the serious adverse effects of climate change on life, health, well-being, and quality of life. The Court further found that Switzerland had failed to meet its positive obligations under the Convention on Climate Change, with critical gaps in establishing a relevant domestic regulatory framework, including through a carbon budget or national GHG emission limitations.

21 Based on the analysis of criteria proposed by the doctrine for the classification of a new human right, Ademola argues that the right to a safe climate can emerge in AU law. Jegede AO, (n 1) pp. 62 ff. In the same vein, Suedi Y, Fall M. Climate Change Litigation before the African Human Rights System: Prospects and Pitfalls. Journal of Human Rights Practice. February 2024:16(1):147.

> obliged not only to limit and condition activities that cause global warming, but also to implement proportionate preventive and adaptive measures to address them.[22]

In recent years, as a result of a greater awareness by the civil society for the defence of the planet, there has been recourse to the courts, domestic and international, mainly by concerned individuals and non-governmental actors, who pursue more altruistic goals, such as an answer to global environmental problems.[23]

Scholars have pointed out two types of actions that have been brought before the courts, namely, actions based on the violation of the right to the environment through human rights (life, physical and mental integrity, property, etc.) and actions aimed at condemning States to the obligation to create, specify, adapt, or complement internal policies with the international commitments assumed, particularly in the climate field.[24]

In April 2024, the Sabin Center's[25] Global Climate Litigation[26] Database identified cases in five jurisdictions on the African continent, namely: Kenya, Namibia, Nigeria, South Africa, and Uganda. With 19 cases in total, climate litigation in Africa accounts for 9.0% of cases in the Global South.[27] In regional and sub-regional human rights courts, the United Nations

22 Arguing that the inclusion of environmental rights in the Charter is an ideal way to protect against adverse impacts related to climate change, cf. Mativo J. Climate Change Displacement Litigation in Africa: A Human Rights and Refugee Law–Based Approach. In: Climate Litigation and Justice in Africa. Bristol, UK: Bristol University Press; 2024. pp. 157–158.

23 Bouwer K. The Emergence of Climate Litigation in Africa. Carbon & Climate Law Review. 2021(15):123 ff.

24 Boshoff E. The Prospects and Challenges of Litigating Climate Change before African Regional Human Rights Bodies. In: Climate Litigation and Justice in Africa. Bristol, UK: Bristol University Press; 2024. pp. 125–128; Jegede AO, (n 1), p. 45 ff; Amado Gomes C, Minassa PS. As alterações climáticas, em breve num tribunal constitucional perto de si. Revista do Ministério Público. outubro-dezembro 2021;a.42(168):15; Burger M, Wentz J, Metzger DJ, Climate Science and Human Rights: Using Attribution Science to Frame Government Mitigation and Adaptation Obligations. In: Rodríguez-Garavito C, ed. Litigating the Climate Emergency: How Human Rights, Courts, and Legal Mobilization Can Bolster Climate Action. Globalization and Human Rights. Cambridge University Press; 2022. pp. 224–230.

25 Burger M, Tigre MA. Global Climate Litigation Report: 2023 Status Review Sabin Center for Climate Change Law. Columbia Law School and United Nations Environment Programme; 2023. [Accessed 5 September 2024]. Available from: columbia.edu.

26 About trends in climate litigation in the world, see: Setzer J, Higham C. Global Trends in Climate Change Litigation: 2024 Snapshot. London: Grantham Research Institute on Climate Change and the Environment, London School of Economics and Political Science; 2024. [Accessed 30 September 2024]. Available from: Global-trends-in-climate-change-litigation-2024-snapshot.pdf.

27 Tigre MA. Climate Litigation in the Global South: Mapping Report. June 2024. [Accessed 25 August 2024]. Available from: https://climate.law.columbia.edu/content/climate-litigation-global-south-mapping-report.

Environment Programme's Global Climate Litigation Report (2023 Review)[28] awards 2.3% of the world's total climate litigation cases in Africa.[29] The registered case was heard in the Court of Justice of the Community of East African States in 2020, which pitted a civil society organisation against the Tanzanian Government.[30]

In view of the statistics presented above, it is necessary to question what the reason for the "handful" number of cases of climate litigation in the African system of Human and Peoples' Rights is. Thus, in the following pages, we will seek to answer the question posed by analysing the possibilities, limits, and obstacles of access to the courts for climate protection in Africa.

9.2 The Right of Access to Courts in the African System of Human and Peoples' Rights

9.2.1 Preliminary Note

At the regional level, there are two bodies charged with the task of promoting and protecting human rights, namely the African Commission on Human and Peoples' Rights, whose organisation and functioning are regulated by Articles 30 to 61 of the Charter, and the African Court on Human and Peoples' Rights, established by an Additional Protocol to the Charter,[31] that disciplines its organisation and functioning. One of the obstacles to the (direct) protection of the environment in other regional systems for the promotion and protection of human rights is the fact that proof of victim status is required.

In the African system, the requirement of victimhood is a circumvention, as regional bodies consider victims not only to be people who, individually or collectively, suffer harm, including physical or psychological harm, through acts or omissions that constitute violations of the Charter, but also to those affected direct family members or dependents of the victim, as well as people who have suffered harm during the intervention to help victims or prevent victimhood.[32] However, in order for moral persons, for example, NGOs, to

28 United Nations Environment Programme. Global Climate Litigation Report: 2023 Status Review. Nairobi.

29 United Nations Environment Programme, (n 28) p. 32.

30 *Center for Food and Adequate Living Rights et al. v Tanzania and Uganda*, East African Court of Justice, 6 November 2020 (East African Court of Justice). [Accessed 5 September 2024]. Available from: Reference-No.-39-of-2019-CEFROHT-3-Others-v.-The-AG-of-the-Republic-of-Uganda-The-AG-of-United-Republic-of-Tanzania-and-The-Secretary-General-of-the-East-African-Community.pdf.

31 1998 Protocol on the Establishment of an African Court on Human and Peoples' Rights (adopted 9 June 1998, entered into force 25 January 2004).

32 ACmHPR 2017 (General Comment No. 4 on the African Charter on Human and Peoples' Rights: The Right to Redress for Victims of Torture and Other Cruel, Inhuman or Degrading Punishment or Treatment (Article 5). [Accessed 30 September 2024]. Available from: achpr_general_comment_no._4_english.pdf.

be able to act on behalf of a victim, the Commission requires the consent of the victim.[33]

As long as the conditions for access to regional bodies for environmental protection are met, which we will analyse below, the African system opens the door for the defence for concerned applicants, who act in order to pursue environmental and climate goals.[34] In some domestic jurisdictions, proving a causal link has been problematic in the context of climate litigation,[35] which, in the African regional context, as we will see, can be circumvented by the possibility of holding States accountable for the violation of human rights caused by the adverse effects of climate change.

In addition to regional bodies, the African system for the promotion and protection of human rights also has sub-regional bodies. Due to their relevance in the promotion and protection of human rights, the Economic Community of West African States and the Community of East African States stand out, both having an established court competent to hear and decide cases of human rights violations. At the internal level of States, in addition to the promotion of human rights by legislative and administrative bodies, courts have played an important role in protecting the environment through human rights.

9.2.2 *Access to the African Commission on Human and Peoples' Rights (AfrCmHPR)*

The AfrCmHPR, established by Article 30 of the Charter, is a quasi-judicial body that is responsible for promoting[36] and protecting the human rights and freedoms enshrined in the Charter.[37] The responsibility for protecting is manifested in its competence to receive and assess communications regarding alleged human rights violations, namely submitted by States,[38] and to bring them before the AfrCtHPR[39] – although individuals and civil society organisations with an observer status may also submit them directly to the AfCtHPR.[40]

With regard to intra-State communications, provided for and regulated in Articles 47 to 54 of the Charter, it is the Commission's responsibility to assess and make recommendations in relation to allegations of violations of human and peoples' rights set out in the Charter. This expedient can be used by States to, *inter alia*, denounce violations of Article 24 of the Charter,

33 ACmHPR 2020.
34 Suedi Y, Fall M, (n 21) pp. 150–151.
35 *Idem.*
36 Charter, art 45(1).
37 Charter, art 45(3).
38 Charter, arts 47 ff.
39 Protocol to the ACHPR, art 5(1)(a).
40 Protocol to the ACHPR, art 5(3).

especially in cases where domestic activities, by virtue of their location, nature, or size, are likely to cause cross-border impacts.

In addition to intra-State communications, Article 55 of the Charter admits "other communications", that is, all those that do not emanate from the States. Thus, pursuant to this provisions, the AfrCmHPR can receive communications submitted by natural and legal persons, provided that they meet the conditions of admissibility provided for in Article 56 of the Charter.[41] Looking at the communications regime, both State and non-State vis-à-vis the Commission's competences, it seems safe to say that there is a strong political dependence of the Commission on the Conference of Heads of State and Government,[42] to the extent that, in relation to inter-State communications, for example, a detailed study can be carried out only at the request of the Conference of Heads of State and Government.[43]

On the other hand, the Commission's recommendations and decisions are not binding, and there are no mechanisms for redressing the damage caused by States. This regime is explained by the fact that the African Union is an international organisation of the classic type in which States are the only protagonists,[44] but different from the European Union in which the Member States have created their own legal order, distinct from that of the Member States and superior to them.[45]

To date, the only Communication in which Article 24 of the Charter has been under discussion is 155/96 of 27 October 2001. In it, the Social and Economic Rights Action Center (SERAC) and the Center for Economic and Social Rights (CESR) denounced the inertia of the Nigerian State in the face of pollution in the Niger Delta caused by oil companies, having caused social and ecological damage to the resident community. In this case, the AfrCmHPR found that the Nigerian State had violated, among others, Article 24 of the Charter, which in its opinion obliged the State to take reasonable measures to prevent pollution and ecological degradation and to promote the conservation and ecologically sustainable use of natural resources. The AfrCmHPR also asserted that Article 24 of the Charter includes the duty of the State to

41 For a critical analysis of the admissibility requirements, Baldé A. O Sistema Africano de Direitos Humanos e a Experiência dos Países Africanos de Língua Oficial Portuguesa. UCE Editora; 2017. p. 167.

42 Martorana CS. The New African Union: Will It Promote Enforcement of the Decisions of the African Court of Human and Peoples Rights? George Washington International Review. 2008;40:597.

43 Article 59 (1).

44 In this sense, Sow AI. The Primacy of Member States in the Institutional Structure of the African Union. Hellenic Journal of International Law, 57th year, ANT Editions. N. Sakkoulas; 2004. p. 15.

45 In this sense, Loureiro Bastos F. A União Europeia e a União Africana: Pode um puzzle de que não se conhece a imagem final servir de modelo a integração do continente africano? In: Legal and Economic Studies in Honour of Professor António de Sousa Franco. Lisbon: Faculdade de Direito da Universidade de Lisboa; 2006. 1st v., pp. 1038 ff.

disclose environmental and social impact studies before any industrial activity, to carry out monitoring, to provide information to the affected communities, and to ensure their participation in the decision-making procedure that may affect their protected rights or interests.[46]

Despite the criticisms of this decision, especially regarding doubts about the autonomy of the right to a healthy environment in relation to other human rights,[47] it is notable for its clarity and sharpness in relation to the duties of the State in the promotion and protection of the environment under Article 24 of the Charter; either directly, through its organs and services, or indirectly, through the conduct of non-State actors, namely private companies. Thus, although it is not a case of "climate litigation", the communication in question, considering the growing trend of "acclimatization of the right to the environment" is a "*feu vert*" for the submission of future communications that denounce state actions and omissions that violate international commitments or that may jeopardise climate stability.[48]

9.2.3 *Access to the African Court on Human and Peoples' Rights (AfrCtHPR)*

9.2.3.1 *Introduction*

The AfrCtHPR, hereinafter the Court, was established by the 1998 Additional Protocol to the Charter adopted in Ouagadougou, Burkina Faso, which is in force since 2004. In 2008, the African Court on Justice and Human Rights was established, a merger of the African Court on Human and Peoples' Rights and the Court of Justice of the African Union.[49] Although the formal requirements for the entry into operation of the latter are met,[50] it has not been established in practice. The ongoing reform in the African Union and financial issues, considering that with the reform judges will start working full-time, are some reasons that may explain the imperative of the new

46 Social and Economic Rights Action Center (SERAC) and Center for Economic and Social Rights (CESR) / Nigeria – 155/96 | African Commission on Human and Peoples' Rights (au .int).

47 Gomes CA. Comentário ao artigo 24° da Carta Africana dos Direitos do Homem e dos Povos. In: Jerónimo P, et al., coords. Comentário Lusófono à Carta Africana dos Direitos do Homem e dos Povos. Lusophone Observatory of Human Rights of the University of Minho and Human Rights – Interdisciplinary Research Center; 2018. p. 255.

48 Boshoff B, (n 24) pp. 136–140; Suedi Y, Fall M, (n 21) p. 147.

49 African Court on Justice and Human Rights. Available from: https://www.african-court .org/wpafc/wp-content/uploads/2020/10/23-PROTOCOL-ON-AMENDMENTS-TO-THE -PROTOCOL-ON-THE-STATUTE-OF-THE-AFRICAN-COURT-OF-JUSTICE-AND -HUMAN-RIGHTS.pdf

50 African Court on Justice and Human Rights. 24-SIGNED-PROTOCOL-ON-AMENDMEN TS-TO-THE-PROTOCOL-ON-THE-STATUTE-OF-THE-AFRICAN-COURT.pdf

Court.[51] Hence, considering that the Court has operated on the basis of the Ouagadougou Protocol, we will, in this text, use it as a tool for our exercise.

The Court complements the protective functions conferred on the AfrCmHPR by the Charter,[52] and its jurisdiction extends to all cases and disputes submitted to it concerning the interpretation and application of the Charter, the Protocol, and any human rights instrument ratified by the States concerned.[53] With regard to the system of sources, it is stated that the Court may apply the provisions of the Charter, as well as any other relevant human rights instrument ratified by the States.[54]

The scope of AfrCtHPR's jurisdiction and the system of sources of law allow decisions to be based on the Paris Agreement or other legal instruments that impose obligations on the State in the environmental and climate fields. It is important to note that the jurisdiction of the Court is not mandatory, and that the ratification of the respective Protocol is necessary, under the terms of Article 34 thereof. Of the 54 States Parties to the Charter, 31 have ratified the Protocol to the AfrCtHPR. In addition to contentious jurisdiction, the AfrCtHPR has advisory competence and may, under this cover, and at the request of any AU Member State, any of its organs, or any African organisation recognised by the AU, issue opinions on any legal question relating to the Charter or any other instrument, provided that it is not related to a matter under consideration by the AfrCtHPR.[55]

9.2.3.2 *Access to the AfrCtHPR by Individuals and Organisations: Between Breakthroughs and Setbacks*

Individuals and non-governmental organisations with observer status with the Commission may submit cases directly to the Court,[56] provided that the State against which they complain has ratified the Protocol and, if in the act, declares that it recognises the jurisdiction of the Court to hear cases submitted directly by individuals or NGOs.[57] For the admissibility of cases, it is also necessary to comply with the conditions laid down in Article 50 of the Rules of Procedure of the Court *ex vi* Article 56 (5) of the Charter and Article 6(2)

51 Clarke KM, Jalloh CC, Nmehielle VO. Introduction: Origins and Issues of the African Court of Justice and Human and Peoples' Rights. In: Jalloh CC, Clarke KM, Nmehielle VO, eds. The African Court of Justice and Human and Peoples' Rights in Context: Development and Challenges. Cambridge University Press; 2019. pp. 1–54; Murray R. The Human Rights Jurisdiction of the African Court of Justice and Human and Peoples´ Rights. In: Jalloh CC, Clarke KM, Nmehielle VO, eds. The African Court of Justice and Human and Peoples' Rights in Context: Development and Challenges. Cambridge University Press; 2019. pp. 33 ff.

52 Article 2 of the Protocol.

53 Article 3 of the Protocol.

54 Article 7 of the Protocol.

55 Article 4 of the Protocol.

56 Article 5(3) of the Protocol.

57 Article 34(6) ex vi of Article 5(3) of the Protocol.

of the Protocol. As expected, scholarship has not spared criticism of this regime, in particular the condition of the exhaustion of domestic remedies, which it considers to be limiting and incongruous,[58] despite recognising that is an old rule of international human rights law and it is a strategy and a political commitment to induce States to ratify the Protocol.[59]

We support the criticisms made at the regime of access of individuals and NGOs to the Court for the Defence of Human Rights to the extent that it does not align with the rationale and historical-political principles of human rights, much less with the increasingly pressing need to protect human rights across borders. However, such a regime does not surprise us, given the nature of the African Union. Therefore, in order to avoid being poorly regarded and/or condemned in the international arena for violation of human rights, many States prefer that cases be heard only by national jurisdictions, which are controlled, in some contexts, by political power. The retreat of some States that had declared the admissibility of direct access to the Court by individuals and NGOs confirms this diagnosis.

In this regard, it should be noted that of the 31 States Parties to the Protocol, only 12 (Burkina Faso, Malawi, Mali, Tanzania, Ghana, Rwanda, Côte d'Ivoire, Benin, Tunisia, The Gambia, Niger, and Guinea-Bissau) have deposited the Declaration. Of these, Tanzania, Rwanda, Benin, and Côte d'Ivoire withdrew their Declarations. On the subject, the Court, in several cases, concluded that the withdrawal of the Declaration does not have any retroactive effect, and doing so has no influence on the issues pending before the filing of the Declaration.[60]

The arguments invoked by Tanzania,[61] Benin,[62] and Rwanda[63] to justify the withdrawal of the Declaration, and the possibility for States to make this decision on the basis of the principle of sovereignty, are symptomatic of the fragility of the African human rights system,[64] denoting, on the one hand, the conflict of jurisdiction (state and regional) and, on the other hand,

58 Vljoen F. A Human Rights Court for Africa and Africans. Brooklyn Journal of International Law. 2004:9; Suedi Y, Fall M, (n 21) pp. 148–150.

59 Mutua M. The African Human Rights Court: A Two-Legged Stool? Human Rights Quarterly: the Johns Hopkins University. 1999:6.

60 *Jebra Kambole v United Republic of Tanzania*, Case No. 018/2018, Judgment of 15 July 2020, pp. 6–7; *Ambrose Cheusi v United Republic of Tanzania*, TADHP, Case No. 004/2015, Judgment of 26 June 2020, pp. 37–39.

61 African Union Commission. Available from: https://www.african-court.org/wpafc/wp-content/uploads/2020/10/Withdrawal-Tanzania_E.pdf.

62 African Union Commission. Available from: https://www.african-court.org/wpafc/wp-content/uploads/2020/10/Withdrawal-Benin.pdf.

63 African Union Commission. Available from: https://www.african-court.org/wpafc/wp-content/uploads/2020/10/Withdrawal-Rwanda.pdf.

64 In this sense, Moumouni I. The slow evolution of the international status of the individual in Africa. Revue de Droit Public. Jan/Fév. 2020;136(1): 299–302.

reinforcing what has been said above about the legal nature of the African Union and the role of States in the legal architecture of the organisation.

There are no records[65] of cases of climate litigation in the Court, which, in addition to other factors, especially extra-legal ones, can be explained by the very restrictive and conditioned access regime described above, and the need to exhaust domestic remedies.[66] Regarding the insufficiency of financial means as an obstacle to access to the Court, it is worth noting the fact that in 2012 a legal assistance programme was created by the Court with the aim of providing free legal aid to individuals or groups of individuals. The latest report on the Court's activities shows that in 2023, the Court examined a total of twenty (20) requests for legal aid: eight (8) petitioners benefited from legal aid, ten (10) did not benefit from legal aid, and two (2) were still awaiting the Court's decision. Of the 10 applications that were rejected, the report testifies that four petitioners were already represented by a lawyer, while six petitioners had requested legal assistance for their cases brought in the national courts, where the African Court does not have jurisdiction.[67]

9.2.1 *Access to African Sub-regional Courts*

9.2.1.1 *The ECOWAS Experiences*

The Economic Community of West African States is a sub-regional integration organisation comprising 15 West African countries.[68] The treaty that created ECOWAS[69] was signed in May 1975 and revised in 1993 with the aim of promoting regional trade, cooperation, and development in the region, as well as the harmonisation and coordination of policies with a view to protecting the environment.[70,71]

The Court of Justice[72] is one of the institutions of the organisation, in addition to the Conference of Heads of State and Government, Council of Ministers, or Parliament, among others.[73] Its organisation and operation are based on Protocol 1/7/91 and Additional Protocol A/SP.1/01/05. All Member States are *ipso facto* parties to the Court, which is competent to, *inter alia*,

65 African Court Cases. Available from: african-court.org.

66 Boshoff E, (n 24) pp. 126–127; Suedi Y, Fall M, (n 21) p. 147.

67 Activity Report of the African Court on Human and Peoples' Rights 1 January – 31 December 2023. [Accessed 30 September 2024]. Available from: EX-CL-1492-XLIV-Report-AfCHPR-_-EN.pdf.

68 The ECOWAS member countries are: Benin, The Gambia, Mali, Ghana, Burkina Faso, Niger, Cape Verde, Guinea-Bissau, Senegal, Côte d'Ivoire, Liberia, Sierra Leone, and Togo.

69 See UNTS ecowas.int/wp-content/uploads/2022/08/Revised-treaty-1.pdf.

70 Article 2(2)(b).

71 On environmental protection within ECOWAS, Bilgho PTR. The Protection of the Right to a Healthy Environment Before e ECOWAS Court of Justice. Revue Africaine de Droit de l'environnement. 2020;5: 87–96.

72 Article 15 of the Revised Treaty.

73 Article 3 of the Revised Treaty.

deal with cases of human rights violations by Member States, as well as the examination of Member States' failure to comply with their obligations under the Treaty, Conventions and Protocols, Regulations, Decisions, and Directives.[74] Since, under the revised Treaty, it incorporates the African Charter, it can be directly invoked for the protection of the environment in the community.

This was the case in the case of *SERAP v Nigeria* (ECW/CCJ/JUD/18/12) in which the Court, in accordance with Article 1 of the Charter, reinforced the normative content of Article 24 of that instrument, concluding that it encompasses the rights to life, dignity, information, work, property, and the use of natural resources, among others, whose promotion and protection is a state task. In that vein, it condemned Nigeria for failing to take all effective measures to ensure the restoration of the environment in the Niger Delta, prevention of environmental damage, and accountability of the perpetrators of the damage.

It should be emphasised that, unlike what happens at regional level, citizens and NGOs can apply directly to the Community Court without the need to exhaust domestic mechanisms,[75] provided that the request is not anonymous and that it is not being examined by another international court.[76] The ECOWAS Treaty further provides that the Court's decisions have general binding force for Member States, community institutions, and natural and legal persons.[77] The negative aspect that deserves to be highlighted is that the Protocol has not created mechanisms for monitoring and holding States accountable for non-implementation of their decisions.

9.2.1.2 The EAC Experience

The East African Community (EAC) is a regional intergovernmental organisation of seven states, namely the Democratic Republic of the Congo, the Republic of Burundi, Kenya, Rwanda, South Sudan, Uganda, and the United Republic of Tanzania, based in Arusha, Tanzania.

Within the framework of this organisation, whose treaty provides in Articles 11 and 12 for the duty of the Community and each Member State to protect the environment, individuals and NGOs may appeal directly to the East African Court of Justice if there is an action or omission by a Member State or community bodies that violates the Treaty.[78] In the case of *Africa Network for Animal Welfare (ANAW) v The Attorney General of the United*

74 Article 9 of the Additional Protocol (A/SP.1/01/05)
75 Moumoni I, (n 63) pp. 284–287.
76 Article 10(d) of the Additional Protocol (A/SP.1/01/05).
77 Article 15(4) of the ECOWAS Treaty.
78 Article 30(1) of the Treaty.

Republic of Tanzania[79] the Court ordered the Republic of Tanzania not to proceed with its initial plan to build a road in the Serengeti National Park because it could have adverse effects on the environment and cause irreversible damage to the Serengeti Park ecosystem and surrounding parks, such as the Masai Mara in Kenya. The potential damages invoked are, among others, the destruction of species and their habitats, disruption of migrations and habits of fauna, destruction of flora, increase in poaching, and destruction of the soil.

9.3 Climate Litigation in Domestic Law

As previously stated, African states have not only ratified international instruments applicable to the fight against global warming, which is one of the main causes of climate change – *one of the main existential threats of our time* – but they have also adopted political and legislative measures to respond to the problems and challenges posed by this phenomenon. As a result, administrative and judicial bodies have been confronted with cases of climate litigation.

As it is impossible to list all the cases that fit the concept of "climate litigation" in the 54 countries of the African continent, we resorted to the records of the Sabin Center to, by way of example and without the ambition to analyse the merits of the allegations made and decisions taken, illustrate the way in which domestic jurisdictions in Africa have dealt with the issue. The following are the experiences of Kenya, South Africa, Namibia, Nigeria, and Uganda.

9.3.1 *South Africa*

South Africa is on the list of countries with one of the highest GHG emissions *per capita* in the world due to, among others, its heavy dependence on coal for energy production.[80] The Sabin Center has registered ten cases of climate litigation in that African country. The first case was decided in 2016, followed by four in 2017, four in 2021, and one in 2024. Of these, six cases are pending and four have been decided.[81] In case 61561/17[82] (*Trustees*

79 EACJ, *Africa Network for Animal Welfare (ANAW) v The Attorney General of the United Republic of Tanzania*, Reference 9 of 2010.

80 Obani P. Climate Litigation in South Africa and Nigeria: Legal Opportunities and Gender Perspectives. In: Climate Litigation and Justice in Africa. Bristol, UK: Bristol University Press; 2024. pp. 295 ff. For further details, UNEP Climate Action Note | Data you need to know [Accessed 5 September 2024]. Available from: https://www.unep.org/explore-topics/climate-action/what-we-do/climate-action-note/state-of-climate.html.

81 Climate Litigation in the Global South: Mapping Report Climate Litigation in the Global South: Mapping Report, pp. 34–35.

82 *Trustees for the Time Being of GroundWork v Minister of Environmental Affairs, ACWA Power Khanyisa Thermal Power Station RF (Pty) Ltd, and Others*. [Accessed 5 September

for the Time Being of GroundWork v Minister of Environmental Affairs, ACWA Power Khanyisa Thermal Power Station RF (Pty) Ltd, and Others), the environmental organisation GroundWork filed a lawsuit requesting that the Supreme Court of South Africa review and annul the Department of Environmental Affairs' authorisation to develop a 600 MW coal-fired industry, the "Khanyisa Project", without first considering the impacts of the industry on climate change.

The Court held that the climate change impacts of a coal industry must be assessed and considered comprehensively as part of an environmental impact assessment under the National Environmental Management Act (107 of 1998) before an authorisation decision. The Court further recognised that South Africa's commitment under the Paris Agreement is one of the reasons why climate change is a relevant consideration for the environmental review of a coal-fired industry.

Another relevant case for what is discussed in this text is 3491/2021 (*Sustaining the Wild Coast NPC and Others v Minister of Mineral Resources and Energy and Others*) in which four environmental and human rights organisations (Sustaining the Wild Coast NPC, Mashona Dlamini, Dwesa-Cwebe Communal Property Association, and four others) filed a lawsuit in the High Court of South Africa (Eastern Cape Division, Grahamstown) against the Minister of Mineral Resources and Energy, Minister of Environment, Forests and Fisheries, Shell, and Impact Africa, requesting the annulment of the decision that ordered the seismic survey to be carried out on the east coast of South Africa.

The Court annulled the decision on the grounds that the operating authorisation had been granted without taking into account the applicants' right to information and participation. It further agreed that there is reasonable apprehension of irreparable harm and imminent harm to the law, as seismic research involving the extraction of fossil fuels could have adverse effects on the climate, the cultural practices of the requesting communities, the conservation of the oceans, and the spiritual and sustainable use of the ocean for healing and fishing purposes. It acknowledged the concern of communities that seismic research will lead to exploration without a climate impact assessment, which appears to be inconsistent with the commitments made at COP 26 on climate.[83]

9.3.2 *Kenya*

The Constitution of the Republic of Kenya enshrines the right to the environment in Article 42, which associates a right of popular action for its defence,

2024]. Available from: 20170905_Case-no.-6156117_petition.pdf (climatecasechart.com).

83 COP 26. [Accessed 5 September 2024]. Available from: 20220901_Case-No.-34912021_judgment-1.pdf (climatecasechart.com).

regardless of whether the perpetrator is a victim, in the terms that are transcribed below:

Article 70.

1. *If a person alleges that a right to a clean and healthy environment recognised and protected under Article 42 has been, is being or is likely to be, denied, violated, infringed or threatened, the person may apply to a court for redress in addition to any other legal remedies that are available in respect to the same matter.*
2. *On application under clause (1), the court may make any order, or give any directions, it considers appropriate:* to *prevent, stop or discontinue any act or omission that is harmful to the environment;* to *compel any public officer to take measures to prevent or discontinue any act or omission that is harmful to the environment;* or *to provide compensation for any victim of a violation of the right to a clean and healthy environment.*
3. *For the purposes of this Article, an applicant does not have to demonstrate that any person has incurred loss or suffered injury.*

In more precise terms, the Climate Change Act of 2016, revised in 2023,[84] provides in paragraph 1 of Article 23 that "A person may, pursuant to Article 70 of the Constitution, apply to the Environment and Land Court alleging that a person has acted in a manner that has or is likely to adversely affect efforts towards mitigation and adaptation to the effects of climate change". In Article 23(2), the Law reproduces Article 70(2) of the Constitution transcribed above. The Sabin Center has registered two climate litigation cases in Kenya, one in 2016 (decided) and another in 2022 (pending).

In the 2016 case, an NGO challenged the environmental license issued by the National Environmental Management Authority on the grounds that the Environmental Impact Assessment that supported its issuance did not take into account all likely damages, mitigation measures were insufficient, and the EIA process did not adequately involve the participation of local communities. In 2019, the National Court for the Environment and Land issued a decision in favour of the NGO, annulling the environmental license and forcing a new procedure to be carried out in which climate change must be considered, among other issues, under the terms provided for in the Climate Law.[85] In the second case, the plaintiffs allege that the flooding in Lake Baringo caused by climate change has caused displacement, loss of human life, and property damage, which constitutes both a violation of their human rights and of the duties of the State under the Constitution and the Climate

84 Act No. 9 of 2023 [Accessed 5 September 2024]. Available from: ClimateChangeAct11of2016.pdf (kenyalaw.org).

85 *Save Lamu & 5 others v National Environmental Management Authority (NEMA) & another*, 2019, eKLR. Available from: http://kenyalaw.org/caselaw/cases/export/176697/pdf.

Change Act of 2016. Therefore, they demand compensation from the State for damages.[86] In spite of reports concerning the scheduling of the final hearing for 2024,[87] there have been no developments in the case.

9.3.3 *Namibia*

In Namibia, the only case registered by the Sabin Center refers to the action brought by the Ncumcara Community Forest Management Association against the Environmental Commissioner in the High Court of Namibia, challenging the issuance of a permit granted to Reconnaissance Energy Africa, a Canadian oil and gas exploration company, for oil drilling in the Okavango Delta. The plaintiffs claimed that their human rights were being violated by allowing drilling on community-managed land, arguing that the land was already threatened due to climate change and that communities had not been properly consulted.

On the main grounds that the competent administrative body, *in casu*, the Minister, had not upheld the claimants' complaint in the case, the Court declared itself incompetent insofar as the Environmental Management Law[88] reserves the right to decide on complaints to the Minister, considering that it would be competent only if the Minister refused to take any decision. Thus, it rejected the preliminary injunction authorising the company to continue the work.[89]

86 Environment and Land Court (ELC) of Iten, *Legal Advice Centre T/A Kituo cha Sheria & Anor v Attorney General and 7 Others*, Petition No. 007 of 2022.

87 See "In Kenya, Flooding Lakes Have Displaced Thousands. A Novel Lawsuit Blames Climate Change". Science. Available from: https://www.science.org/content/article/kenya-flooding-lakes-have-displaced-thousands-novel-lawsuit-blames-climate-change.

88 Environmental Management Act 7 of 2007 (50) "(1) Any person aggrieved by a decision of the Environmental Commissioner in the exercise of any power in terms of this Act may appeal to the Minister against that decision. (2) An appeal made under subsection (1), must be noted and must be dealt with in the prescribed form and manner. (3) The Minister may consider and determine the appeal or may appoint an appeal panel consisting of persons who have knowledge of, and are experienced, in environmental matters to advise the Minister on the appeal. [The comma after the word "experienced" should appear after the phrase "experienced in".] (4) The Minister must consider the appeal made under subsection (1), and may confirm, set aside or vary the order or the decision or make any other appropriate order including an order that the prescribed fee paid by the appellant, or any part thereof, be refunded. (5) Any expenditure resulting from the performance of duties by the appeal panel in terms of subsection (3) must be paid from the State Revenue Fund from moneys appropriated by Parliament for that purpose. (6) An appeal made under subsection (1) does not suspend the operation or execution of the decision pending the decision of the Minister, unless the Minster, on the application of a party, directs otherwise".

89 High Court of Namibia, Main Division, Windhoek Judgment Case No.: HC-MD-CIV-MOT-GEN-2022/00289. *Ncumcara Community Forest Management Association v The Environmental Commissioner* (HC-MD-CIV-MOT-GEN-2022-00289), 2022. NAHCMD 380 (29 July 2022). Available from: climatecasechart.com.

9.3.4 Nigeria

In Nigeria, the Fundamental Rights Enforcement Procedure Rules of 2009 confers a right of access to justice for the defence of human rights, including those contained in the African Charter on Human and Peoples' Rights. According to the Sabin Center, climate litigation cases in Nigeria can be grouped into two categories: (i) impacts of energy-related projects (gas flaring and liquefied natural gas [LNG] projects) and (ii) impacts of oil spills.

Among the cases recorded, the case of *Gbemre v Shell Petroleum Development Company Nigeria Ltd. and Others* in 2005 stands out, in which the plaintiff alleged that the flaring of gas by oil and gas companies violated the rights to life and dignity, and also reported significant impacts on the climate and health of communities. The Federal Supreme Court, recognising the right to the environment and the need for environmental and social impact assessment with a strong involvement of local communities, ordered the company to suspend its activity in the community and the Federal Government to take measures to prohibit gas flaring.[90]

Although the country has legislation on climate change (The Climate Change Act 2021) and political-strategic documents, namely, the National Adaptation Strategy and the National Plan on Climate Change, some authors have criticised the regime, especially with regard to legal costs, the issue of delimiting legitimacy and assigning the burden of proof as obstacles to climate litigation in the country.[91]

9.3.5 Uganda

The National Climate Change Act of 2021, like Kenya's counterpart legislation, enshrines the right of popular action on climate matters, providing, in article 26, that:

(l) A person may apply to the High Court for relief against the Government, an individual or a private entity whose action or omission threatens or is likely to threaten efforts towards adaptation to or mitigation of climate change. (2) The High Court may, in addition to any other orders it may deem appropriate, make orders to: (a) prevent" stop or discontinue the act or omission that is the subject of the application; (b) compel the Department, lead agency or any person to take measures to reverse the act or perform the act that was omitted; or (c) provide compensation to a person that has suffered loss or damage as a result of the act or omission. (3) A person may apply to the High Court under subsection (l) notwithstanding that that person cannot prove that the act or omission of the Department, lead agency, individual or

90 *Gbemre v Shell Petroleum Development Company of Nigeria Ltd. and Others*, Unreported, Suit No.: FHC/B/CS/53/05, 14 November 2005.

91 Jegede AO, (n 1) pp. 55–67.

private entity has caused or is likely to cause personal harm or injury to that person or any other person.

The climate litigation cases registered in the country concern the Government's failures to consider climate-related mitigation and adaptation measures. In *Mbabazi and Others v The Attorney General and National Environmental Management Authority (2012)*, the plaintiffs, on behalf of four minors, alleged that the Government had failed to take adequate measures to mitigate loss and damage caused by extreme weather events. Furthermore, they interpret the Government's inaction as a violation of the constitutional duty to preserve natural resources for the benefit of present and future generations.

In the case of *Tsama William and Others v Uganda's Attorney General and Others (2020)*, victims of a recurring landslide in the Bududa district denounced to the court the Government's inaction in adopting adaptation measures to deal with the landslide, caused by climate change. Not only do they allege the urgent need to be resettled, but they demand compensation for loss of human life, damage to property, etc. Government officials dispute the accusations, arguing that local communities contributed to the landslides due to poor agricultural practices, deforestation, and poor cultivation. It should be noted that both cases are awaiting a final decision.

9.4 Concluding Considerations

We define as the object of this text, the analysis of the possibilities, limits, and obstacles to climate litigation in the African Human and Peoples' Rights System. Having analysed the three levels, regional, sub-regional, and national, that make up this system, we are able to conclude the following:

Article 24 of the African Charter on Human and Peoples' Rights entrusts public authorities with the duty to promote and protect the environment, and citizens have a right to a healthy and conducive environment. Due to the meaning and scope that the doctrine and jurisprudence of the Commission, the sub-regional and domestic courts attribute to it, it can be invoked not only to claim a right to "climate balance" but also to demand active and passive conduct for the prevention and reparation of the impacts of climate change on human rights;

Although in the African System, the status of victim is not necessary for access to regional bodies (Commission and Court) for the protection of human rights, the nature of the AU and the role of States in the architecture of the organisation, or through the Conference of Heads of State and Government, which exercises strong political control over the Commission, or through the decisive role they play in the access of individuals and non-State organisations to protection agencies, it greatly limits environmental activism at the regional level;

At the sub-regional level, the mandatory jurisdiction of the ECOWAS and EAC courts, and the possibility for individuals and organisations to access the courts without the consent of the State, and even without the exhaustion of domestic remedies, is an "open door" for these bodies to hear and judge cases of climate litigation in the future;

Despite the minor contribution of African States to the climate scenario that the world is experiencing, climate litigation in African domestic jurisdictions, as in other geographies, refers not only to the fulfilment of the goals but also to the protection of human rights in the climate context. Despite the challenges of enforcing decisions, there are good prospects for the evolution of climate litigation in domestic and sub-regional jurisdictions;

Without the paradigm shift of African Union Law, regional instances for the promotion and protection of human rights will not be the privileged stage for climate litigation cases. The African Convention on the Protection of Nature and Natural Resources, in the wake of the Aarhus Convention and the Escazú Agreement, establishes procedural and process rights in environmental matters by providing in Article 16(1) that the Contracting Parties shall adopt necessary legislative and regulatory measures to ensure access to environmental information, public participation in decision-making, and access to justice for the protection of the environment. However, if we combine the low level of ratification of this Convention combined with the fact that States continue to be subjects of reference in the African human rights system, we can conclude that there is still a long way to go, as far as access to justice for climate protection is concerned, in the African System of Human and Peoples' Rights.

References

African Commission on Human and Peoples' Rights. Explanatory note on the reporting guidelines on articles 21 to 24 of the ACHPR regarding mining operations [Internet]. [Accessed 2024 Aug 25]. Avaliable from: state-reporting-guidelines-and-principles-articles-21-and-24fre.pdf.

African Commission on Human and Peoples' Rights. Study on the impact of climate change on human and peoples' rights in Africa [Internet]. [Accessed 2024 Aug 25]. Available from: au.int.

Amado Gomes C, Minassa PS. As alterações climáticas: Em breve num tribunal constitucional perto de si. Revista do Ministério Público. 2021 out-dez;42(168):15.

Baldé A. O sistema africano de direitos humanos e a experiência dos países africanos de língua oficial portuguesa. UCE Editora; 2017. p. 167.

Bilgho PTR. The protection of the right to a healthy environment before the ECOWAS Court of Justice. Revue Africaine de Droit de l'Environnement. 2020;5:87–96.

Boshoff E. The prospects and challenges of litigating climate change before African regional human rights bodies. In: Climate litigation and justice in Africa. Bristol, UK: Bristol University Press; 2024. p. 125–8.

Bouwer K. The emergence of climate litigation in Africa. Carbon Clim Law Rev. 2021;15:123 ff.

Burger M, Tigre MA. Global climate litigation report: 2023 status review. Sabin Center for Climate Change Law, Columbia Law School & United Nations Environment Programme; 2023 [Accessed 2024 Sep 5]. Available from: columbia.edu.

Burger M, Wentz J, Metzger DJ. Climate science and human rights: using attribution science to frame government mitigation and adaptation obligations. In: Rodríguez-Garavito C, editor. Litigating the climate emergency: how human rights, courts, and legal mobilization can bolster climate action. Globalization and Human Rights. Cambridge University Press; 2022. p. 224–30.

Clarke KM, Jalloh CC, Nmehielle VO. Introduction: origins and issues of the African court of justice and human and peoples' rights. In: Jalloh CC, Clarke KM, Nmehielle VO, editors. The African court of justice and human and peoples' rights in context: development and challenges. Cambridge University Press; 2019. p. 1–54.

Gomes CA. Comentário ao artigo 24° da Carta Africana dos Direitos do Homem e dos Povos. In: Jerónimo P, et al., coordinators. Comentário lusófono à Carta Africana dos Direitos do Homem e dos Povos. Lusophone Observatory of Human Rights of the University of Minho and Human Rights - Interdisciplinary Research Center; 2018. p. 255.

Intergovernmental Panel on Climate Change (IPCC). Climate change 2023: synthesis report [Internet]. [Accessed 2024 Aug 25]. Available from: IPCC_AR6_SYR _LongerReport.pdf.

Jegede AO. Should a human right to a safe climate be recognized under the AU human rights system?. In: Addaney M, Jegede AO, editors. Human rights and the environment under African Union law. Springer Nature; 2020. p. 55 ff.

Jegede AO. State duty to "protect" rights and legal obstacles to climate litigation. In: Climate litigation and justice in Africa. Bristol, UK: Bristol University Press; 2024. p. 43.

Kabaseke C, Odaghara CT, Ashukem JCN. The interface between loss and damage, vulnerability and human rights in Africa. Afr J Clim Law Justice. 2024;1:76–7.

KlimaSeniorinnen v Switzerland (ECtHR) [Internet]. [Accessed 2024 Sep 5]. Available from: coe.int.

Loureiro Bastos F. A União Europeia e a União Africana: Pode um puzzle de que não se conhece a imagem final servir de modelo à integração do continente africano?. In: Legal and economic studies in honour of Professor António de Sousa Franco. Lisbon: Faculdade de Direito da Universidade de Lisboa; 2006. Vol. 1. p. 1038 ff.

Lumina M. The right to a clean, safe and healthy environment under the African human rights system. In: Addaney M, Jegede AO, editors. Human rights and the environment under African Union law. Springer Nature; 2020. p. 26.

Martorana CS. The new African Union: will it promote enforcement of the decisions of the African court of human and peoples' rights?. George Washington Int Rev. 2008;40:597.

Mativo J. Climate change displacement litigation in Africa: a human rights and refugee law-based approach. In: Kim Bouwer, Uzuazo Etemire, Tracy-Lynn Field, Ademola Oluborode, editors. Climate litigation and justice in Africa. Bristol, UK: Bristol University Press; 2024. p. 157–8.

Mo Ibrahim Foundation. The road to COP27: making Africa's case in the global climate debate. Forum Report 12; 2022 [Accessed 2024 Oct 28]. Available from: 2022-Ibrahim-Forum_Facts-Figures.pdf.

Moumouni I. The slow evolution of the international status of the individual in Africa. Rev Droit Public. 2020 Jan/Feb;136(1):299–302.

Murray R. The human rights jurisdiction of the African court of justice and human and peoples´ rights. In: Jalloh CC, Clarke KM, Nmehielle VO, editors. The African court of justice and human and peoples' rights in context: development and challenges. Cambridge University Press; 2019. p. 33 ff.

Obani P. Climate litigation in South Africa and Nigeria: legal opportunities and gender perspectives. In: Climate litigation and justice in Africa. Bristol, UK: Bristol University Press; 2024. p. 295 ff. For further details, see: United Nations Environment Programme. Climate Action Note | Data you need to know [Internet]. [Accessed 2024 Sep 5]. Available from: https://www.unep.org/explore-topics/climate-action/what-we-do/climate-action-note/state-of-climate.html.

Rocha A, Oliveira H. Human rights and fundamental rights. Lisbon Public Law Working Paper Series. 2024;No. 2024-1:12–13 [Accessed 2024 Sep 5]. Available from: https://papers.ssrn.com/sol3/papers.cfm?abstract_id=4714724.

Setzer J, Higham C. Global trends in climate change litigation: 2024 snapshot. London: Grantham Research Institute on Climate Change and the Environment, London School of Economics and Political Science; 2024 [Accessed 2024 Sep 30]. Available from: Global-trends-in-climate-change-litigation-2024-snapshot.pdf.

Suedi Y, Fall M. Climate change litigation before the African human rights system: prospects and pitfalls. J Hum Rights Pract. 2024 Feb;16(1):147.

Tigre MA. Climate litigation in the Global South: mapping report [Internet]. June 2024 [Accessed 2024 Aug 25]. Available from: https://climate.law.columbia.edu/content/climate-litigation-global-south-mapping-report.

United Nations Environment Programme. Global climate litigation report: 2023 status review. Nairobi: United Nations Environment Programme.

Vljoen F. A human rights court for Africa and Africans. Brook J Int Law. 2004;9:1–66.

10 Environmental Litigation and the CJEU

Overcoming Barriers to Standing?

Niels Hoek and Arianna Crosera

10.1 Introduction

Climate change and biodiversity loss are pressing issues that warrant immediate action. It will be necessary to adapt to a changing world and to mitigate any damage to ecosystems and human livelihood to remain in a safe operating space.[1] With scientific reports from the International Panel on Climate Change (IPCC) and the International Panel on Biodiversity and Ecosystem Services (IPBES) in hand, non-governmental organisations (NGOs) have increasingly argued for such (positive) action.[2] In doing so, they have challenged lacklustre policies. Success stories in the courtroom with respect to climate change have been noted across the world, from the Netherlands to Germany, Switzerland, and Brazil.[3]

However, to achieve these successes, one key precondition is needed – standing before the Court. It is, by analogy, the key that opens the door to justice. *Locus standi* or standing, is a condition where the party has the right or capacity to bring a legal action to court or to appear in court. This formal requirement has been generally found to be controversial in several instances related to climate change and environmental case law. Among others, it can exclude nature from holding any legal subjectivity in most jurisdictions (a tree cannot protest its own destruction).[4] It can also erect barriers

1 Johan R et al. A safe operating space for humanity. Nature. 2009;41(1):472–475.

2 Scientific outcome of the IPBES-IPCC co-sponsored workshop on biodiversity and climate change; IPBES secretariat, Bonn, Germany, DOI:10.5281/zenodo.4659158. IPBES. (2019). Global assessment report on biodiversity and ecosystem services of the Intergovernmental Science-Policy Platform on Biodiversity and Ecosystem Services (Version 1). p. 215. IPCC, 2019: Summary for Policymakers. In: Climate Change and Land: an IPCC Special Report on Climate Change, Desertification, Land Degradation, Sustainable Land Management, Food Security, and Greenhouse Gas Fluxes in Terrestrial Ecosystems.

3 See for example *Urgenda Foundation v State of the Netherlands* (2019), *Neubauer v Germany* (2020), *PSB and others v Brazil* (2020) and *Verein KlimaSeniorinnen Schweiz and others v Switzerland* (2024) at the European Court of Human Rights (ECHR).

4 Stone CD. Should Trees Have Standing? Toward Legal Rights for Natural Objects. Stanford Law Review. 1974;26:450. See for more examples of how standing requirements have failed environmental protection in the EU: Hoek N, et al. Implementing Rights of Nature: An

DOI: 10.4324/9781003540977-13

for individuals and NGOs who seek to challenge a wrongful policy as they, or the policy itself, are deemed to be "too far removed"[5] from global issues such as biodiversity loss and climate change. After all: how does one prove to be personally affected, or harmed, by these inherently widespread issues, which pose undifferentiated harm to numerous fringes of people (from senior citizens to youth, women, and the economically disadvantaged)?

This challenge is particularly acute within the European Union (EU) legal order, where NGOs and individuals have repeatedly faced obstacles when bringing cases before the Court of Justice of the European Union (CJEU). Considering that the CJEU has been restrictive in its climate litigation, striking down,among others, both *Carvalho* (People's Climate Case) and *Sabo* based on a lack of standing, this chapter asks: are such failed climate cases truly the end of climate litigation at the Court of Justice?[6] Here, the chapter is critical of the so-called complete system of remedies as offered by the EU when it comes to climate litigation,[7] and argues that further reform on standing before the CJEU is needed. At the same time, we argue that recent amendments to the Aarhus Regulation and the preliminary reference procedure present opportunities to engage the CJEU in its role as the supreme court within the EU legal framework, [8] when that reform is not yet available.

It is worth specifying that the CJEU has previously judged on the merits of climate cases, a more complete analysis of which can be found in Chapter 4, Part A of this volume.[9] These cases highlight how climate litigation in the broad sense can be initiated by several different actors, each with peculiar

---

EU Natureship to Address Anthropocentrism in Environmental Law. Utrecht Law Review. 2023;19:72.

5 After all, it is difficult to prove to be *distinctly* affected by issues which affect all human and non-human animals so innately (such as climate change). The reasons behind such barriers, *prima facie*, is to maintain a reasonable workflow for the courts. The line of thinking is that, if all persons were to be able to challenge every decision (in the form of an *actio popularis*) courts would see a floodgate of cases. Whether this is the case is highly contested due to the high-bar entry costs.

6 Case T-330/18 *Armando Carvalho and Others v European Parliament and Council of the European Union* (2019).

7 Several EU Institutions, from the Court to the EU Commission, have prided themselves with the EU's complete system of remedies, meaning all EU acts can sufficiently challenge through one means or another.

8 Particularly in light of the recent climate case brought under the Aarhus Regulation.

9 Since the beginning of the 2000s, several cases have been brought before the CJEU by – among others – private companies and cooperatives or associations challenging the application of EU climate legislation. See for instance Case C-343/09 *Afton Chemical Limited v Secretary of State for Transport* (2010), Case C-366/10 *Air Transport Association of America and Others v Secretary of State for Energy and Climate Change* (2011), Case C-573/12 *Ålands vindkraft AB v Energimyndigheten* (2014). The European Commission also initiated several infringement procedures against member states for failure to correctly implement EU climate legislation. See, for instance, Case C-159/06 *Commission v Finland* (2006), Case C-371/04 *Commission of the European Communities v Italian Republic* (2006).

challenges and concerns. In this chapter we specifically focus on climate cases brought by NGOs and individuals, for two main reasons. First, cases filed by applicants other than NGOs and individuals have been filed by privileged applicants in the meaning of Article 263 TFEU and, therefore, raise no significant questions on standing, which is the central topic of this chapter.[10] Second, NGOs and individuals are actors that represent a driving force in filing climate change litigation in the world, whilst at the same time being significantly restricted in their access to the CJEU. Indeed, as pointed out by the London School of Economics's 2024 Snapshot on Climate Litigation, 70% of all climate litigation cases globally were filed by NGOs or individuals.[11] In sum, the chapter focuses on these actors because of the significant barriers affecting them in seeking climate justice and their respective influence.

The structure of this chapter is as follows. Section 2 outlines the strict approach taken to standing within the infamous *Plaumann* requirements, which guide standing requirements before the CJEU. It seeks to elucidate the doctrine which has, so far, successfully tamed climate litigation at the EU level. Section 3 takes a forward-looking approach and introduces avenues for acquiring standing before the CJEU in (future) mobilisation efforts. Section 3.1 uncovers the opportunities arising outside the recent amendments to the Aarhus Regulation, detailing the substantive changes brought on by the new Regulation. Section 3.2 reviews additional lessons from the European Court of Human Rights (ECHR), which is connected to the EU's own Charter of Fundamental Rights (CFR). Next, section 3.3 touches on the preliminary reference procedure as a way forward for climate litigation under the CJEU, highlighting the opportunities and drawbacks of this approach. Section 4 sums up these avenues to acquire legal standing for NGOs within the EU system in a concise table, highlighting their respective benefits and drawbacks. A conclusion follows last.

10.2 The *Plaumann* Doctrine and the "Failed" Annulment Procedures

Despite courts all across Europe being increasingly presented with cases that can be referred to as climate litigation, the CJEU, at a first glance, seems to have remained immune to this wave of complaints.[12] In this section we will

10 A core argument of the chapter is that the bar on standing set by *Plaumann* constitutes a barrier for effective climate change litigation, and such a barrier is seen to be particularly problematic for climate cases brought by NGOs and individuals.

11 Setzer J, Higham C. Global Trends in Climate Change Litigation: 2024 Snapshot. Grantham Research Institute on Climate Change and the Environment, London School of Economics and Political Science; 2024.

12 This chapter will deal with issues before the Court only in relation to standing. It should, therefore, be read in conjunction with introductory chapters, which define climate litigation, and engage with the merits of climate litigation under the CJEU more specifically.

analyse why that is, with two of the latest climate cases brought before the CJEU, both of which have been rejected by the Court on the basis of a lack of standing according to the *Plaumann* doctrine. The aim, in this sense, is to highlight the rigidity of the Court in its application of this doctrine.

Applicants in climate and environmental cases in the EU have, in theory, several opportunities to seek justice. The CJEU and the Commission often refer to the "complete system of remedies" set out in the Treaty on the Functioning of the European Union (TFEU), which includes Article 263 TFEU (direct access to the CJEU), and Article 267 TFEU (preliminary reference procedure) and Article 277 TFEU (plea of illegality). This complete system should, in principle, allow both direct and indirect access to justice against EU acts which may infringe environmental law and higher fundamental rights.[13]

In case of direct access to the CJEU, Article 263 TFEU sets out the criteria that applicants need to satisfy to be granted standing before the Court. EU Member States and EU institutions, the Court of Auditors, the European Central Bank (ECB), and the Committee of Regions are privileged and partially privileged applicants, and they can bring cases in several instances. Individuals and NGOs can also bring actions before the Court against an act, asking for its annulment – if that act is (a) addressed to them, (b) of direct and individual concern to them, and (c) against a regulatory act which is of direct concern to them and does not entail implementing measures.[14] These criteria, however, are not self-evident and have to be interpreted by the Court. Most notably, the concept of "direct and individual concern" has been further defined in the case law of the CJEU, famously through its *Plaumann v Commission* case (1963).[15] In what later become defined as the "*Plaumann* test" or "*Plaumann* doctrine", the Court affirmed that an individual or a legal person such as an NGO may have standing before the Court only if the EU measure affects them "by reason of certain attributes which are *peculiar to them* or by reason of circumstances in which they are *differentiated from all other persons* and by virtue of these factors distinguishes them *individually*".[16]

13 For an introduction to the institutional role of the European Court of Justice in the European Union, see Moorhead T. The Legal Order of the European Union: The Institutional Role of the Court of Justice. Routledge; 2014. For a more thorough analyse on access to justice at the EU level on higher fundamental rights, see de Búrca G. After the EU Charter of Fundamental Rights: The Court of Justice as a Human Rights Adjudicator? Maastricht Journal of European and Comparative Law. 2013;20:168. On the intersection between fundamental rights and environmental case law, see Krommendijk J, Sanderink D. The Role of Fundamental Rights in the Environmental Case Law of the CJEU. European law open. 2023;2:616.

14 Consolidated version of the Treaty on the Functioning of the European Union (2012) OJ C326, Article 263.

15 Case 25-62 *Plaumann & Co. v Commission of the European Economic Community* (1963).

16 *Ibid.*

Scholars have repeatedly characterised the test as particularly difficult to attain in climate and environmental litigation, "effectively preventing most direct actions by private parties against EU institutions".[17] In climate litigation especially, this is mainly due to the challenge of establishing a causality nexus between the applicants and the harm caused by climate change as a result of poor climate policies. NGOs and individuals have repeatedly tried to break free of the *Plaumann* test by presenting the Court with different arguments, in a progressive evolution since the first cases at the end of the 1990s and the beginning of the 2000s.[18] Recent examples of the Court's restrictive use of *Plaumann* in climate litigation are *Armando Carvalho and others* (People's Climate case)[19] and *Peter Sabo and others*,[20] both containing actions for annulment of different EU legislative acts. In the two cases, the arguments of applicants for claiming standing in an annulment action significantly ranged, and they can be summarised as follows:

a) Individual concern of the applicants based on the distinct nature of the impact of climate change on them;
b) Right to an effective remedy and fair trial based on the European Charter of Human Rights;
c) Infringement of various fundamental rights of the applicants;
d) The application of the Aarhus Convention's Article 9(3), which will be further discussed in Section 3.1. of this chapter.[21]

The first case, *Carvalho and others,* was brought before the General Court by 36 individuals from across the EU, Kenya, and Fiji, and a Swedish NGO representing Sami youth – the Sáminuorra. The applicants were seeking the partial annulment of fundamental pieces of EU climate legislation – Directive 2018/410, Regulation 2018/842, and Regulation 2018/841 – and the adoption of stricter emission targets by 2030 (of at least 50% to 60%, compared to 1990 levels).[22] In May 2019, the General Court ruled on the inadmissibility of the case and refused the applicants standing under Article 263 TFEU by relying on a strict interpretation of the *Plaumann* doctrine. In its

17 See, for instance, Krężel A. Access to Justice and Strategic Climate Litigation in the EU: Curing the Incurable?. ELJ. 2023;29:265; Pagano M. Overcoming Plaumann in EU Environmental Litigation – An Analysis of ENGOs Legal Arguments in Actions for Annulment. Diritto e Processo. 2019;311:315.

18 *Ibid*; Pagano M, (n 17).

19 Case T-330/18 *Armando Carvalho and Others v European Parliament and Council of the European Union* (2019).

20 Case C-297/20 *Peter Sabo and Others v European Parliament and Council of the European Union* (2021).

21 See the crucial analysis of Hadjiyianni I. Webinar 8.6. Revising the Aarhus Regulation: Securing Adequate Legal Protection for Climate Action? University of Helsinki. 8 June 2021.

22 Case T-330/18, para. 15.

judgment – upheld by the Appellate Court – the General Court considered various scenarios that would grant standing to the applicants. In the beginning, it examined the first scenario under Article 263, meaning whether the acts were addressed to the applicants and concluded that, in fact, they were not,[23] and that the challenged acts were legislative acts (therefore also inadmissible under the third scenario).[24] It then considered the second scenario under Article 263 and thus whether applicants were *directly* and *individually* concerned by the legislative package. It concluded that even though EU law must respect "higher-ranking rules of law – including fundamental rights" the infringement of these rights [in this case, through the consequences of climate change] does not distinguish applicants individually. In the Court's opinion, if we would apply this broad doctrine, the criterion of individual concern would be rendered void.[25] The Court also stated that respect of Article 47 of the Charter of Fundamental Rights, which guarantees the right to an effective remedy and a fair trial, does not mean that applicants can enjoy an "unconditional right to have an action for annulment before the Court".[26] This reasoning was both applied to the natural persons and the Sáminuorra, a legal person in the context of Article 263. On the same grounds, the request for an injunction directed at higher emission reduction targets was rejected.

The second climate case, *Sabo and others*, was adjudicated by the Court shortly thereafter. The case was brought by several individuals and environmental non-governmental organisations (ENGOs) from EU Member States and the United States. Applicants were seeking the annulment of a provision of Directive (EU) 2018/2001 on the promotion of the use of energy from renewable sources,[27] which classifies forest biomass as a renewable energy source. They contested that the measure infringed Article 191 TFEU, the fundamental rights of applicants according to the EU Charter of Fundamental Rights, and the goal of the directive itself, "owing to the amount of carbon discharged by burning wood and to the increase in industrial logging".[28] In its ruling on the admissibility of the annulment action, the Court reiterated the *Plaumann* doctrine and affirmed that no individual concern could be claimed in this case as the Directive is an act of general application and the protection and regulation of the environment "affects everyone in both future and current generations".[29] This in itself, in the Court's opinion, "militates against

23 Case T-330/18, para. 35.
24 *Ibid*, paras. 37–41.
25 *Ibid*, para. 48.
26 *Ibid*, para. 52.
27 Directive (EU) 2018/2001 of the European Parliament and of the Council of 11 December 2018 on the promotion of the use of energy from renewable sources (recast) [2018] OJ 2018 L 328.
28 Case T-141/19, para. 19.
29 *Ibid*, para. 30.

the notion of individual concern" required by *Plaumann*.[30] The action was rejected on these grounds, with once again the result that applicants, it seems, were denied protection on the basis that the Court would then have to offer it to anyone asking.

The cases above and the variety of arguments presented to the Court in those instances show how the strict application of the *Plaumann* doctrine by the CJEU significantly impairs individuals and NGOs in their access to annulment procedures of EU legislative acts before the Court. In a broader view, the strict application of *Plaumann* in these two cases (and in several others before them) reflects a conservative approach to standing which, Garben notes, seems to be in sharp contrast with the generally strict approach towards conservation that we find in the case law tradition of the CJEU.[31] Her explanation to this phenomenon, whose opinion we share, may lie in the Court wanting to protect EU authority and EU legislation, which makes it adopt a "constructivist" approach under which the Court is a driver of "integration through law".[32] However, for climate cases specifically, we are increasingly convinced that this approach may undermine the very function of judicial review for EU legislative acts, for several reasons, also exposed by recent scholarship on the matter: (a) precisely because of the nature of climate change as a "common and shared" concern, environmental acts are often of general application, which makes it unlikely to satisfy the requirements imposed by *Plaumann*[33]; (b) judicial review in this area, and granting standing to NGOs and individuals, is particularly important due to the "structurally underrepresented nature [of environmental interests] in the decision making process"[34]; and (c) extending the reasoning of the Court, we are increasingly approaching a paradoxical situation where "the more widespread the damaging effects of a nature, the more restrictive the access to courts will be".[35] In sum, climate and environmental litigation requires a different approach to standing, one that challenges the *status quo* and responds to the necessity of justice in these times of climate emergency. While we wait for that different approach from the CJEU, these next sections of the chapter outline alternative *present* avenues for standing in climate and environmental litigation at the EU level.

30 *Ibid.*

31 The ECJ has, in numerous cases, reaffirmed itself as a Court adopting a protective approach to the application of EU environmental law, often closely scrutinising Member State implementation in this area and favouring an approach rooted in the precautionary principle. For examples in case law, see Garben S. The CJEU and Climate (In)activism?. In: Dawson M, de Witte B, Muir E, eds. Revisiting Judicial Politics in the European Union. Edward Elgar Publishing; 2024. p. 262.

32 *Ibid*, p. 263.

33 Pagano M, (n 17) p. 315.

34 Garben S, (n 31) p. 251.

35 Pagano M, (n 17) p. 315.

10.3 Alternative Avenues for Climate and Environmental Litigation in the EU

The previous section set out the main issues with the *Plauman* doctrine, showing how it has hindered climate change litigation at the EU level. Noting the importance of institutional scrutiny (of EU environmental decisions and acts) going forward, this section discusses several avenues for legal mobilisation on climate change and biodiversity litigation before the CJEU, starting with the Aarhus Convention.

10.3.1 The EU Implementation of the Aarhus Convention: An Amended Aarhus Regulation

The first potential avenue to be discussed arises from the Aarhus Convention, and subsequently, its implementation within the EU Aarhus Regulation.[36] The Aarhus Convention deals with access to information, public participation, and access to justice in environmental matters. The most relevant provision to be discussed here is Article 9(3) of the Aarhus Convention, which provides that Contracting States should provide access to administrative or judicial procedures to challenge acts (and omissions), which contravene provisions of its national law relating to the environment.[37] This is a crucial pillar within the Convention, as it secures "state-public partnership and dialogue".[38] To achieve such a dialogue in a successful manner, Article 9(4) of the Convention requires that these remedies be adequate, effective, equitable, not too expensive, and timely.[39]

It is worth noting that the EU is a Contracting Party to the Aarhus Convention. Within the EU legal order, the Convention has been implemented through the Aarhus Regulation.[40] This implementation, however, did not overcome the rigid *Plaumann* requirements on standing, and NGOs

36 Convention on Access to Information, Public Participation in Decision-Making and Access to Justice in Environmental Matters, Aarhus, Denmark, (1998), Regulation (EC) No 1367/2006 of the European Parliament and of the Council of 6 September 2006 on the application of the provisions of the Aarhus Convention on Access to Information, Public Participation in Decision-making and Access to Justice in Environmental Matters to Community Institutions and Bodies. OJ L 264, 25.9.2006, pp. 13–19.

37 Aarhus Convention, Article 9(3).

38 Weaver D. The Aarhus Convention: Towards Environmental Solidarisation. Ipswich: Springer Nature; 2024.

39 Aarhus Convention, Article 9(4). As noted by Barritt, while the Aarhus Convention mainly guarantees procedural rights, it also underpins a general *stewardship*, spanning right through substantive environmental rights. Barritt E. The Foundations of the Aarhus Convention: Environmental Democracy, Rights and Stewardship. 1st ed. Hart Publishing; 2022.

40 Regulation (EC) No 1367/2006 of the European Parliament and of the Council of 6 September 2006 on the application of the provisions of the Aarhus Convention on Access to Information, Public Participation in Decision-making and Access to Justice in Environmental Matters to Community Institutions and Bodies OJ L 264, 25.9.2006, pp. 13–19.

can instigate proceedings only "in accordance with the relevant provisions of the Treaties".[41] However, in line with the Aarhus Convention, ENGOs can utilise the Aarhus Regulation to challenge relevant *EU Non-Legislative Regulatory Acts*.[42] This is the most prominent change: examples of such acts range from the EU Decision to allow glyphosate on the internal market, to the adoption of allowable catches under the fisheries policy.[43] These acts are highly relevant for climate change mitigation and biodiversity restoration and are thus in need of scrutiny by civil society.

The question then becomes *how* these Regulatory Acts can be challenged, and to which degree NGOs have standing before the Court on these matters. In this respect, we ought to turn our attention to Article 10 (1) of the Regulation, which establishes the Internal Review Procedure.[44] The provision specifies that NGOs and organisations meeting the criteria under Article 11 are entitled to submit a request for internal review of an EU Administrative Act. At face value, this procedure is a critical avenue for potential climate and biodiversity litigation. However, at its conception, it was extremely limited.[45] The Aarhus Regulation made it so that only regulatory administrative acts of *individual scope*, i.e., those with a specific addressee, could be challenged by NGOs.[46] Indeed, most relevant acts are of *general scope*: addressed either to an entire nation or to the whole of the EU. In short, this amounted to a substantial gap in the EU's system of remedies.[47] Other complains ranged

41 Secondary law cannot overrule the TFEU, in light of the EU hierarchy of norms. Eurlex. Hierarchy of EU Norms. [Accessed 28 August 2024]. Available from: https://eur-lex.europa.eu/EN/legal-content/glossary/eu-hierarchy-of-norms.html.

42 See Article 289 of the Treaty on the Functioning of the European Union. These are decisions to be adopted to enable delegation (delegated acts) or in order to implement a legislative act (implementing acts). Administrative acts, according to the Amendment Aarhus fall under this, "as a non-legislative act adopted by an EU institution, which has legal and external effects that contain provisions which may contravene environmental law".

43 Leonelli GC. Access to the EU Courts in Environmental and Public Health Cases and the Reform of the Aarhus Regulation: Systemic Vision, Pragmatism, and a Happy Ending. Yearbook of European Law. 2021;40:230. See, for the examples given in the paragraph, 96/281/EC: Commission Decision of 3 April 1996 concerning the placing on the market of genetically modified soybeans (Glycine max L.) with increased tolerance to the herbicide glyphosate, pursuant to Council Directive 90/220/EEC (Text with EEA relevance), OJ L 107, 30.4.1996, pp. 10–11; Council Decision (EU) 2023/2900 of 11 December 2023 on behalf of the European Union in the North-East Atlantic Fisheries Commission and repealing Decision (EU) 2019/86.

44 Article 10 of the Aarhus Regulation.

45 Crossen T, Niessen V. NGO Standing in the European Court of Justice – Does the Aarhus Regulation Open the Door? Review of European Community & International Environmental Law. 2008.

46 T-241/04, *EEB and Stichting Natuur and Milieu v Commission* (2005) ECLI:EU:T:2005:426; T-91/07; Pagano M, (n 25). As a result, the procedure was widely critiqued: https://www-ceeol-com.eu1.proxy.openathens.net/search/viewpdf?id=1019473.

47 *Ibid.* As a result, NGOs had to indirectly rely on the preliminary reference procedure, to be discussed in section 3.4, to challenge EU Regulatory Acts. Wolf S. Access to EU Environ-

from the lack of impartiality in the procedure, as the review would be done by the EU body itself, and concerns were also voiced with respect to the fact that members of the public were excluded from this.[48]

Perhaps unsurprisingly, this gap caused frictions with the access to justice requirements as formulated by the Aarhus Convention. In the end, the Aarhus Compliance Committee (ACC) concluded that, due to the (i) extremely limited internal review procedure and (ii) the constraints set out by the *Plaumann* doctrine, the EU was in *direct violation* of the rights guaranteed under the Convention.[49] In response to this, the Commission proposed a revision to the Aarhus Regulation, which, after a long and drawn-out process, was adopted by the other EU institutions.[50] The most crucial change in this respect is that the updated Regulation significantly increased the range of EU regulatory acts which fall under the internal review procedure, including administrative acts of *general scope*. Leonelli puts it crisply, stating that these changes "fill a vacuum, and solve the main problem which lay at the heart of the EU system of access to justice in environmental public interest cases".[51] ENGOs have basked on the opportunities provided: since 2021, the EU Commission alone has received a total of 43 requests for internal reviews.[52] However, it is important to note that many scholars such as Kręźel, de Lucia, and Leonelli have also been critical of whether this change might lead to substantive results.[53]

In our view, there is merit to this critique. This is because the review is (still) completed by the EU institution that adopted the act and not by the

mental Information: EU Compliance with Aarhus Convention. ERA Forum. 2013;14:475. Available from: https://doi.org/10.1007/s12027-013-0327-7.

48 De Lucia L. The New Aarhus Regulation and the Defensive Behaviour of the European Legislator. Review of European Administrative Law. 2022:15(2).

49 Pirker B. Implementation of the Aarhus Convention by the EU – An Inconvenient Truth from the Compliance Committee. European Law Blog; 24 April 2017. [accessed 28 August 2024]. Available from: https://europeanlawblog.eu/2017/04/24/implementation-of-the-aarhus-convention-by-the-eu-an-inconvenient-truth-from-the-compliance-committee/. Pánovics A. Requests for Internal Review and the Revised Aarhus Regulation. Essays of Faculty of Law University of Pécs. 2023;1. Available from: https://doi.org/10.15170/studia.2023.01.08. Aarhus Convention Compliance Committee. Findings and Recommendations with Regard to Communication ACCC/C/2008/32 (Part II) Concerning Compliance by the European Union. Advance unedited version, 17 March 2017.

50 Regulation (EU) 2021/1767 of the European Parliament and of the Council of 6 October 2021 amending Regulation (EC) No 1367/2006 on the application of the provisions of the Aarhus Convention on Access to Information, Public Participation in Decision-making and Access to Justice in Environmental Matters to Community Institutions and Bodies PE/63/2021/REV/1 OJ L 356, 8.10.2021, pp. 1–71.

51 Leonelli GC, (n 43).

52 Pagano M. Climate Legal Mobilisation under the New Aarhus Regulation. Special Issue on the Aarhus Regulation of the German Law Journal. Preprint; 2024.

53 De Lucia L, (n 48).

Court itself.[54] Moreover, when the matter does reach the Court, it pertains, primarily, to the refusal to grant an internal review, which does not equate amending or appealing the regulatory act in question. A successful annulment starts a procedure, rather than ending one. Additionally, the burden of proof is quite high, as noted by Leonelli, and successful escalation to the CJEU requires a "manifest error of assessment".[55] On a more substantive note, as pointed out by Eliantonio, it is problematic that the review procedure excludes non-binding (soft) law.[56] For example, a future guidance document by the Commission on implementation of the Nature Restoration Law may have a serious impact on how the term "good condition" of ecosystems is interpreted, impacting the baseline level for restoration measures within the Regulation.[57] Another example may lie in how projects of "common interests" are defined on transnational energy infrastructure projects.[58] Both of these examples may be of general scope, but they remain outside of the reach of environmental litigants due to their soft law character.[59] Additionally, under the current exceptions granted by the Aarhus Regulation, there is still no route to challenge EU decisions on State aid (which has been exempted).[60] These EU Regulatory Acts are equally relevant for climate and biodiversity litigation, and pertain, for example, to the balance between renewable versus fossil energies versus fossil fuel subsidies.[61] For these reasons, combined with the rigidity of the *Plaumann* doctrine – which remains upheld – one can remain highly sceptical of whether the so-called complete system of remedies, as coined by the Treaties, has been achieved to this day.[62]

54 Krężel A. Aarhus Regulation Administrative (self-)Review Mechanism: The Inevitable Failure to Contribute to Access to Justice in the EU?. European Energy and Environmental Law Review. 2023;31(3):136.; De Lucia L, (n 48).

55 Leonelli GC, (n 43).

56 See Eliantonio M. Webinar 8.6. Revising the Aarhus Regulation: Securing Adequate Legal Protection for Climate Action? University of Helsinki. 8 June 2021.

57 Hoek N. A Critical Analysis of the Proposed EU Regulation on Nature Restoration: Have the Problems Been Resolved?. European Energy and Environmental Law Review. 2022;10(1).

58 Example credited to Eliantonio M, (n 56).

59 It is relevant that the word "binding" has been removed from the definition of an administrative act under the Amended Aarhus Regulation. This may open up a focus on substantive content rather than legislative character. See Pagano M, (n 44).

60 See for an analysis on this matter, Client Earth. The Amended EU Aarhus Regulation One Year In: New Requests in Review" [Accessed 20 August 2023]. Available from: https://www.clientearth.org/projects/access-to-justice-for-a-greener-europe/updates-annual-newsletters/the-amended-eu-aarhus.

61 Examples should be credited to Friel A. Webinar 8.6. Revising the Aarhus Regulation: Securing Adequate Legal Protection for Climate Action? University of Helsinki. 8 June 2021.

62 The complete system of remedies is cited in Article 263 TFEU.

10.3.2 Critical Lessons from the ECtHR on Standing

In the previous section, we have discussed how the Aarhus Regulation gives rise to new legal opportunities: NGOs can now challenge acts that they were not able to challenge before. However, whilst legislators have opened these avenues through revising existing law, the role of Courts *themselves* in shifting doctrine should not be overlooked. Of relevance is the recent case *KlimaSeniorinnen v Verein* by the European Court of Human Rights (ECtHR), which loosened standing requirements for NGOs in environmental cases.[63]Although the ECtHR is not an EU court, it is highly relevant in the context of EU litigation before the CJEU for two reasons. First, because the EU seeks to, in due time, become a Member State to this convention (meaning it would have to adhere to its rulings).[64] Second, the CJEU uses the ECHR as an interpretative tool, particularly in the context of the EU's own Charter of Fundamental Rights.[65] In particular, the ECtHR's approach in *KlimaSeniorinnen v Verein* may contribute to a form of cross-fertilization, influencing the CJEU to consider similar adjustments to standing requirements in environmental cases, thereby further aligning EU litigation practices with evolving standards under the ECHR.[66] In other words, what unfolds at the ECtHR does not happen in isolation and may give weight to (similar) future claims before the CJEU.

In this context, we must consider the recent *KlimaSeniorinnen* case from the ECtHR and its potential implications. The applicants in *KlimaSeniorinnen* – a group of elderly women – argued that they had standing before the Court to challenge what they perceived as inadequate climate policies by the Swiss government. The case bears notable similarities to the *Carvalho* case previously discussed in relation to the CJEU. As Pagano observes, both Courts grappled with the same fundamental question: "how should courts protect citizens' human rights from public authorities' omissions on climate change?".[67]

63 *Verein KlimaSeniorinnen Schweiz and Others v Switzerland* of 9 April 2024.

64 Charter of Fundamental Rights of the European Union OJ C 326, 26.10.2012, pp. 391–407, EU accession to the ECHR is legally required under Article 6(2) of the Treaty of Lisbon. However, it is noteworthy that this may create tension within the EU primary law, and there is great uncertainty in this respect. Opinion pursuant to Article 218(11) TFEU (Opinion 2/13) EU:C:2014:2454, para. 258.

65 Charter of Fundamental Rights of the European Union [2012] OJ C326/391, Articles 52(3) and 53.

66 The ECJ does cite and cross-reference judgments from the ECtHR, showcasing the inherent link between the two regimes. Although, to be noted, the cross-reference is less than expected. Frese A, Olsen H. Spelling It Out – Convergence and Divergence in the Judicial Dialogue between CJEU and ECtHR". Nordic Journal of International Law. 2019;88(3):429–458. Available from: https://doi.org/10.1163/15718107-08803001.

67 Pagano M. Legal Standing in Climate Litigation before the ECtHR and the CJEU. EU Law Live; 28 May 2024. Available from: https://eulawlive.com/op-ed-legal-standing-in-climate-litigation.

Similar to the CJEU, the ECtHR has been quick to dismiss *actio popularis* claims, emphasising that to attain victim status, applicants must demonstrate a need for protection more urgent than that of the general public. This requirement presents a significant hurdle, particularly in the context of climate change, which impacts society as a whole.[68] While the victim status criterion under the ECtHR differs from the *Plaumann* test – specifically, it does not necessarily require that the applicant is personally targeted by the act or omission – this distinction does not make the test less challenging.[69] Applicants still face similar obstacles to those encountered under the *Plaumann* test, including difficulties in establishing causality and demonstrating individualised harm.[70]

However, in *KlimaSeniorinnen*, the Court took a crucial shift on standing for NGOs that warrants attention. Previously, individual members of NGOs had to showcase that they held an individual victim status. In *KlimaSeniorinnen*, the Court rolled this back. To summarise this shift, the standing requirements for NGOs were watered down to include mere requirements on the NGO's (i) lawfulness, on its (ii) dedicated purpose and, finally, with respect to (iii) their relevant qualifications to be able to represent a possible victim group. In other words, granting standing to NGOs in climate litigation requires an "actual and sufficiently close connection to the matter complained of and to the individuals seeking protection against the adverse effects of climate change on their lives".[71] This provides significant leeway for what otherwise may have been a near-impossible causality test to overcome. In summary, while the Court did close the door on the *actio popularis* for individuals, NGOs now benefit from a much more flexible approach to standing before the ECtHR in future climate litigation.[72]

This shift, in the end, may have profound implications for climate litigation at the CJEU. For example, the test developed in *KlimaSeniorinnen* could be brought forward as an argument in the context of litigation at the CJEU, whereby the Court could use it as an interpretative tool to overcome the rigidity of *Plaumann*.[73] Here, it should be granted that the CJEU places a heavy emphasis on the autonomy of the EU legal order. However, two important points ought to be considered. First, the conclusion, for now, is that as long

68 See *KlimaSeniorinnen*, para. 487.

69 Pagano M, (n 67).

70 Brucher A, De Spiegeleir A. *Verein KlimaSeniorinnen Schweiz v Switzerland* and Article 6(1) of the ECHR: Of Climate Change and Craftsmanship. EU Law Live.

71 See *KlimaSeniorinnen* para. 621. Burcher and Spiegeleir, (n 70).

72 *Ibid.*

73 Also see the analysis of Piet Eeckhout, who notes: "Given that the EU Charter must be interpreted in light of the ECHR, the CJEU should find [NGOs] [...] directly and individually concerned by EU climate policy". Eeckhout P. From Strasbourg to Luxembourg? The KlimaSeniorinnen judgment and EU remedies. [Accessed 23 September 2024]. Available from: https://verfassungsblog.de/from-strasbourg-to-luxembourg/.

as *Plaumann* lives, the EU will be in a potential breach of the ECHR.[74] And second, if an EU accession to the ECHR does proceed, as codified in Article 6 (2) of the TFEU, *Plaumann* may have an (undefined) expiration date. Framed more positively, the *KlimaSeniorinnen* standing solution offers a potential way for the CJEU to address its rigid *Plaumann* approach, aligning with Aarhus Convention obligations without fully opening the gates, as the pressure to revise this closed system continues to grow.

10.3.3 Article 267 TFEU and the Preliminary Reference

In the previous section, we have analysed the possible effect that the ECtHR's loosening of its standing requirements for climate cases could have on the CJEU's approach to standing. In this section, we will describe a (yet) unexplored avenue to overcome the *Plaumann* impasse: the use of the preliminary reference procedure in accordance with Article 267 TFEU. Together with direct access to the CJEU Article 263 TFEU, this indirect procedure forms, in the eyes of the Court, a complete system of remedies to ensure judicial review of the legality of acts of EU institutions.[75] In what seemed like a promising development, the procedure was mentioned by the General Court itself in *Carvalho*. Reaffirming that the treaties have established "a complete system of legal remedies and procedures", the Court states, at paragraph 53, that where standing is not possible before the CJEU, an indirect plea of invalidity [of an EU act] can be referred to the Court by national courts through a preliminary ruling.[76]

In theory, this avenue is thus one of the most promising, as it allows NGOs and individuals to take a stand against EU climate and environmental measures. A hypothetical scenario for the use of a preliminary reference procedure would entail an action questioning the validity of an EU environmental or climate legislation being brought in front of a "court or tribunal" of a Member State for the purposes of Article 267 TFEU.[77] That court would then have to submit the question to the CJEU if it would consider the answer necessary to provide a judgment in the case at hand.[78] Courts of last instance and courts which are considering declaring an EU measure invalid may be considered as

74 One counter argument to this may be the *bosphorus* assumption, which notes that provided the EU would provide equal human rights protection and can guarantee "equivalence", no breach incurs. However, given the disparity between the standing requirement between the two institutions, in our view, these two systems are no longer "comparable". See Pagano M. Overcoming Plaumann: Environmental NGOs and Access to Justice before the CJEU. Florence: European University Institute; 2023. p. 179.

75 See *Carvalho* (n 19), para. 53.

76 *Ibid.*

77 The criteria for the definition of court or tribunal are set out in – among others – Case C-407/98, *Katarina Abrahamsson and Leif Anderson v Elisabet Fogelqvist* (2000).

78 TFEU, (n 14), Article 267.

having an obligation to refer a preliminary reference question to the CJEU[79] – especially considering that case law has not definitively settled this matter.[80] These obligations and the fact that this avenue was suggested by the Court itself leads to a certain hope that the preliminary reference is a viable path to bypass *Plaumann*. However, our opinion is that this option has its own challenges.

A first set of challenges lies in the fact that the preliminary ruling procedure is in its origin a national procedure. This origin implies that different judicial conditions in Member States may affect whether the preliminary question may reach the CJEU in the first place.[81] In accordance with the principle of procedural autonomy, EU Member States have retained their own procedural laws – provided they effectively[82] and equivalently[83] safeguard the rights derived from EU law – which is often translated in differences between Member States on access to national courts. This may constitute a first barrier in the case that national law is particularly restrictive in its access requirements. A second relevant barrier lies in whether the preliminary ruling procedure is commonly used among the national judiciary. Here, a certain imbalance between Member States is confirmed by the statistics of the CJEU itself: by far, the majority of preliminary reference procedures from 2019 to 2023 were sent to the Court by judicial bodies in Germany, Bulgaria, Poland, Italy, Romania, Spain, and Belgium.[84] It follows that applicants in other countries may face more difficulties in having a court refer a question to the CJEU. It is to be noted that this issue is, of course, resolved – in principle – when the court has the obligation to refer the case to the CJEU, either because it is a court of last instance or because it is considering the validity of EU law. However, here the fact that only the court of last instance has the obligation to refer a preliminary question to the CJEU adds a disproportionate economic burden and lengthens the proceedings for applicants to reach that Court.

A second set of challenges relates to the question of competences concerning environmental and climate policies at the EU level. Legislative measures on climate and the environment such as the ones contested in *Sabo* and

79 Case 314/85, *Foto-Frost v Hauptzollamt Lübeck-Ost* (1987) para. 15.

80 See Case 283/81, *Srl CILFIT and Lanificio di Gavardo SpA v Ministry of Health* (1982).

81 These are the main points highlighted by scholars such as Kręźel and Garben, who note that the use of a preliminary reference depends on the discretion of national courts. See, for instance, (n 17).

82 Case C-425/16, *Hansruedi Raimund v Michaela Aigner* (2017) para. 40.

83 The principle of equivalence limits procedural autonomy in that it implies that national procedural rules must apply without distinction to actions alleging infringements of EU law, as much as to actions alleging infringements of national law. See Case C-231/96, *Edilizia Industriale Siderurgica Srl (Edis) v Ministero delle Finanze* (1998) para. 36.

84 CJEU. Press Release No 59/24 Luxemburg; 22 March 2024. [Accessed 29 August 2024]. Available from: https://curia.europa.eu/jcms/upload/docs/application/pdf/2024-03/cp240059en.pdf.

Carvalho are normally adopted under title 191(2) TFEU, this legal basis, in principle, allows Member States to set higher standards for themselves. In the case of climate targets then, the court could decide that it would ultimately be the Member States' responsibility (and, consequently, liability) to draft a more ambitious legislation, which is often the request made in cases of annulment. As explained by Garben, in that case, the validity of EU legislation would ultimately not be in question.[85]

Finally, we want to highlight once again the fact that – especially in light of the challenges outlined above – indirect access to the Court through a preliminary procedure is inadequate if used as the sole mechanism to ensure accountability in EU climate and environmental legislation. This is perhaps the main risk in relying on the preliminary procedure as a main avenue for climate litigation, a risk that was exposed before by the Aarhus Convention Compliance Committee (ACCC). In its findings and recommendations on the EU's compliance with the Convention, the ACCC observed that the procedure did not compensate for the lack of standing before the EU courts caused by *Plaumann* and the fact that that lack of standing was incompatible with the EU's commitments under Aarhus.[86]

10.4 Benefits and Drawbacks of Avenues for Standing Reform in the EU

This section summarises the findings from the previous sections, drawing out the common red thread. It is clear that currently, the complete system of remedies envisioned by the TFEU has not been realised in full. The table below speaks to these gaps, but, crucially, it also touches on the opportunities for litigation on climate change and biodiversity loss at the CJEU.

10.5 Concluding Remarks

This chapter has explored the potential for advancing climate change litigation before the CJEU, highlighting three key avenues: the Amended Aarhus Regulation, the co-synergies between the CJEU and the European Court of Human Rights (ECtHR), and the preliminary reference procedure. It is our view that the rigidity of the CJEU in the interpretation of the *Plaumann* doctrine remains the main obstacle to successful environmental and climate litigation at the EU level. Moving forward, two interventions could significantly improve the present situation: either a *bold* treaty change aimed at modifying the conditions for standing under Article 263 or a *bold* decision

85 See Garben S, (n 31) p. 255.

86 Aarhus Convention Compliance Committee (ACCC), ACCC/M/2017/3 – "Advice by the Aarhus Convention Compliance Committee to the European Union concerning the implementation of request ACCC/M/2017/3" (2017), para. 34(90).

Table 10.1 Avenues for Standing Reform in EU Climate and Environmental Litigation

Intervention or procedure	*Opportunities*	*Drawbacks*
An annulment procedure (Article 263 TFEU)	Directly challenge any EU measure producing legally binding effects on third parties, including legislation, on its legality before the CJEU.	(i) *Plaumann* requirements serve as a significant barrier to environmental litigation by NGOs. This procedure failed on numerous accounts and many arguments to overturn *Plaumann* – from the distinct effect of climate change on applications, to an infringement of their fundamental rights – have been rejected by the Court.[a]
Amended Aarhus Regulation	The Internal Review Procedure in the EU has been widely expanded in the Amended Aarhus Regulation.	(i) Only applies to non-legislative decisions, (ii) judicial review is limited, as the first reading relies on internal scrutiny of the relevant EU institution (iii) significant limitations remain in the administrative acts which can be challenged, particularly with respect to state aid and soft law, which are currently excluded.
Reference to the case law of the European Court of Human Rights (ECHR)	*KlimaSeniorinnen* can influence the CJEU, providing fruitful ground for similar cases at the CJEU (gnawing at the borders of the *Plaumann* doctrine).	(i) the EU is not part of the ECHR (yet) with no end to the stalemate in sight and, (ii) the CJEU has stuck to autonomy of EU law, highlighting a reluctance to cross-reference on sensitive matters.[b]
Preliminary Reference Procedure (Article 267 TFEU)	Through a preliminary reference on the validity of EU legislation, NGOs and individuals may have the (indirect) ability to challenge EU legislation and decisions that contravene EU Environmental Law. It remains a critical avenue for potential climate litigation at the EU level.	(i) Standing requirements differ amongst Member States due to the EU principle of procedural autonomy (ii) differences among Member States in the frequency of use of the procedure, (iii) different cost of legal aid based on the state, and thus (iv) the procedure is inadequate as the *only* option for climate litigation: there is an overreliance on the procedure due to limited alternatives (to challenge legislative acts).
Revising the treaty on Article 263 (3) by expanding the standing criteria for NGO in environmental matters	Direct ability to overturn *Plaumann* and guarantee, a "complete system of remedies".	(i) Requires wide Member State support, which is a significant challenge. However, the EU Parliament has called for citizens to obtain more participatory mechanisms alongside subsequent treaty reform, meaning there is reason for (timid) optimism.[c]

[a] Examples cited from Ioanna Hadjiyianni, (n 14).[b] Particularly in light of the fundamental principle of autonomy of EU law.[c] See Europarl. [Accessed 28 August 2024]. Available from https://www.europarl.europa.eu/news/en/press-room/20231117IPR12217/future-of-the-eu-parliament-s-proposals-to-amend-the-treaties. For example, while petitions to the EU Commission are a welcome tool for participation, they need a high threshold for success, and the EU Commission has complete discretion whether to proceed with amendments to environmental laws (or new proposals). Additionally, while the European ombudsman holds power to investigate complaints about poor administration, this again is a soft tool which does not force EU institutions to resolve infringements of environmental law. Judicial review, in this sense, is a more coercive method to achieve climate targets. While such a comparative discussion goes beyond the scope of this chapter, it is noteworthy that soft participatory methods on their own alone are not sufficient – and addressing the EU's system of remedies (as flagged in this chapter) is required to close this gap.

from the CJEU overturning *Plaumann*. In both cases, political actors and judicial actors alike have held back on such changes. Yet, compared to a few years ago, we can conclude that there is indeed a "better climate" for climate cases at the EU level. In this landscape, our hope mainly resides in the possibility for the CJEU to consider the reasonings of other courts – such as the ECtHR – which have interpreted their standing requirements for ENGOs more loosely, based on the peculiar nature of climate cases. Until then, the EU's complete system of remedies for environmental cases remains elusive.[87]

Reference List

Antoniolli L. Climate change litigation and the rule of law in the European Union. In: Antoniolli L, Ruzza C, editors. The rule of law in the EU. Springer; 2024.

Barritt E. The foundations of the Aarhus convention: environmental democracy, rights and stewardship. 1st ed. Hart Publishing; 2022.

Brown C. The Plaumann problem: how the people's climate case widened the gap to judicial review of the EU's inadequate climate policy student articles & comments. Denver J Int Law Policy. 2021;50:197.

Brucher A, De Spiegeleir A. 'Verein KlimaSeniorinnen Schweiz v Switzerland and Article 6(1) of the ECHR: Of Climate Change and Craftsmanship' (EU Law Live, 9 April 2024).

Crossen T, Niessen V. NGO standing in the European court of justice – Does the Aarhus regulation open the door?. Rev Eur Community Int Environ Law. 2008, 333.

de Búrca G. After the EU charter of fundamental rights: the court of justice as a human rights adjudicator?. Maastricht J Eur Comp Law. 2013;20:13–51.

De Lucia L. The new Aarhus regulation and the defensive behaviour of the European legislator. Rev Eur Admin Law. 2022;15(2):7.

Eeckhout P. *From Strasbourg to Luxembourg? The KlimaSeniorinnen judgment and EU remedies* [Internet]. Verfassungsblog; [Accessed 2024 Sep 23]. Available from: https://verfassungsblog.de/from-strasbourg-to-luxembourg/.

Eliantonio M. *Revising the Aarhus regulation: securing adequate legal protection for climate action?* [webinar]. University of Helsinki; 2021 Jun 8.

Eurlex. Hierarchy of EU norms [Internet]. Available from: https://eur-lex.europa.eu/EN/legal-content/glossary/eu-hierarchy-of-norms.html.

Frese A, Olsen H. Spelling it out – Convergence and divergence in the judicial dialogue between CJEU and ECtHR. Nordic J Int Law. 2019;88(3). https://doi.org/10.1163/15718107-08803001.

Friel A. *Revising the Aarhus regulation: securing adequate legal protection for climate action?* [webinar]. University of Helsinki; 2021 Jun 8.

Garben S. The CJEU and climate (in)activism?. In: Dawson M, de Witte B, Muir E, editors. Revisiting judicial politics in the European Union. Edward Elgar Publishing; 2024.

Hoek N. A critical analysis of the proposed EU regulation on nature restoration: have the problems been resolved?. Eur Energy Environ Law Rev. 2022;10(1):320–333.

Hoek N, Kaststeen I, van Gils S, Janssen E, van Gils M. Implementing rights of nature: an EU natureship to address anthropocentrism in environmental law. Utrecht Law Rev. 2023;19:72–86.

87 Eliantonio M, (n 56).

IPBES. Global assessment report on biodiversity and ecosystem services *of the* intergovernmental science-policy platform *on* biodiversity *and* ecosystem *services.* IPBES Secretariat; 2019.

IPCC. Climate change and land: an IPCC special report on climate change, desertification, land degradation, sustainable land management, food security, and greenhouse gas fluxes in terrestrial ecosystems. IPCC; 2019.

Krommendijk J, Sanderink D. The role of fundamental rights in the environmental case law of the CJEU. Eur Law Open. 2023;2:616–635.

Krężel A. Aarhus regulation administrative (self-) review mechanism: the inevitable failure to contribute to access to justice in the EU?. Eur Energy Environ Law Rev. 2023;31(3):136–144.

Leonelli GC. Access to the EU courts in environmental and public health cases and the reform of the Aarhus regulation: systemic vision, pragmatism, and a happy ending. Yearb Eur Law. 2021;40:230–264.

Moorhead T. The legal order of the European Union: the institutional role of the court of justice. Routledge; 2014.

Pagano M. Climate legal mobilisation under the new Aarhus regulation. Ger Law J. Special issue on the Aarhus Regulation. Preprint; 2024;1.

Pagano M. Overcoming plaumann in EU environmental litigation – An analysis of ENGOs legal arguments in actions for annulment. Diritto e Processo. 2019;311–360.

Pánovics A. Requests for internal review and the revised Aarhus regulation. Essays Fac Law Univ Pécs. 2023;1. https://doi.org/10.15170/studia.2023.01.08.

Pirker B. Implementation of the Aarhus convention by the EU – An inconvenient truth from the compliance committee. Eur Law Blog. 2017 Apr 24 [Accessed 2024 Aug 28]. Available from: https://europeanlawblog.eu/2017/04/24/implementation-of-the-aarhus-convention-by-the-eu-an-inconvenient-truth-from-the-compliance-committee/.

Rockström J, Steffen W, Noone K, Persson Å, Chapin III FS, Lambin EF, Lenton TM, Scheffer M, Folke C, Schellnhuber HJ, Nykvist B, de Wit CA, Hughes T, van der Leeuw S, Rodhe H, Sörlin S, Snyder PK, Costanza R, Svedin U, Falkenmark M, Karlberg L, Corell RW, Fabry VJ, Hansen J, Walker B, Liverman D, Richardson K, Crutzen P, Foley JA. A safe operating space for humanity. Nature. 2009;41(1):427.

Setzer J, Higham C. *Global trends in climate change litigation: 2024 snapshot.* Grantham Research Institute on Climate Change and the Environment, London School of Economics and Political Science; 2024.

Stone CD. Should trees have standing? Toward legal rights for natural objects. Stanford Law Rev. 1974;26:450.

Verein KlimaSeniorinnen Schweiz and Others v Switzerland (2024), the European Court of Human Rights (ECHR).

Weaver D. The Aarhus convention: towards environmental solidarisation. Springer Nature; 2024.

Wolf S. Access to EU environmental information: EU compliance with Aarhus convention. ERA Forum. 2013;14:475. https://doi.org/10.1007/s12027-013-0327-7.

11 Climate Litigation before International Courts

Conclusive Remarks on a Comparative Study

Carla Amado Gomes, Heloísa Oliveira, Armando Rocha, and Matteo Fermeglia

11.1 Introduction

The institutional and substantive fragmentation of international law requires a particularly challenging synthesis effort in a comparative study on international climate cases. These concluding remarks present a non-exhaustive overview of common features and distinctive particularities of the legal systems examined in the preceding chapters. As noted in the introduction, the label "UN system" was used to aggregate institutions and treaties adopted under the aegis of the United Nations ("UN") to provide insight into coordination efforts or particularities.

11.2 The Agents of Climate Cases: A Consequence of Access Rules

Whilst access to the International Court of Justice ("ICJ") and the International Tribunal for the Law of the Sea ("ITLOS") is limited to States, access to UN human rights treaty-based bodies is open to both States and individuals, and access to the International Criminal Court ("ICC") is restricted to individuals. Both chapters on the UN system observed the challenges of using the ICC (despite recent developments and initiatives) but also identified a common trend across the ICJ, ITLOS, and human rights bodies: States refrain from instituting climate change–related proceedings against other States. Accordingly, there is no contentious dispute pending before the ICJ or ITLOS, but this has not prevented advocacy groups and concerned States from considering the ICJ's and ITLOS's advisory jurisdiction – being less intrusive and producing non-binding opinions – as an opportunity to request clarification on States' obligations regarding climate change.

In contrast, individuals do not share the same concerns regarding the use of adversarial proceedings. There is thus a clear trend in individuals resorting to treaty-based human rights bodies (such as the Human Rights Committee or the Committee on the Rights of the Child) to request a non-binding assessment of whether a State has violated its human rights obligations in relation to the complainant. Although the current jurisprudence is limited to these bodies, others, such as the Committee on Economic, Social, and Cultural Rights, may also be used in the near future.

DOI: 10.4324/9781003540977-14

This shift towards rights-based claims has also placed regional human rights enforcement systems under the spotlight in climate cases. Unlike the UN system, the African Charter of Human and Peoples' Rights explicitly recognises a right to a healthy environment, both as a collective right and as an individual right. Climate change would therefore fall under this right. Additionally, access to regional bodies in the African system does not require victim status, and the notion of victimhood appears more flexible than in other systems. Victims include not only those who, individually or collectively, suffer harm – whether physical or psychological – but also direct family members, dependents, and those harmed while assisting victims or preventing harm.

These features would make the African system a prominent battleground in international climate litigation. However, the nature of the African Union and the role of States in its institutional architecture – whether through the Conference of Heads of State and Government, which exercises strong political control over the Commission, or through their decisive role in determining access for individuals and non-State organisations to protection mechanisms – significantly limit environmental activism at the regional level.

Conversely, the European system imposes stricter conditions on court access. The European Convention on Human Rights ("ECHR") does not allow for *actio popularis* and restricts standing to those who can demonstrate victim status and *locus standi*. As the ECHR was originally designed for individual complaints, non-governmental organisations ("NGOs") and collective entities were not initially included in its standing provisions. However, the Court has progressively extended standing to collective entities acting on behalf of individuals, adopting a flexible and evolving approach in response to societal conditions.

However, unlike the African system, victim status in the European system requires a direct and personal impact of the challenged action or omission by the State on the applicant. Hypothetical violations are not admissible, and claims based on potential future violations of the Convention are rarely accepted. The issue of standing in climate cases was particularly examined in *KlimaSeniorinnen v Switzerland*, where the Court held that victim status depends on the severity of climate change exposure in relation to the State's alleged action or inaction, as well as the existence or absence of effective harm mitigation measures. The Court yet granted NGO standing in litigation on behalf of individuals, based on an evolving interpretation of victim status and the Aarhus Convention.

The rules governing direct access for individuals and NGOs to the Court of Justice of the European Union ("CJEU") further confirm that strict assessments of standing are a defining characteristic of European legal systems, extending beyond human rights courts. Despite the unique features of EU law – where a significant portion of legislation is directly applicable to companies and citizens – the CJEU has consistently applied the demanding *Plaumann* test, which requires a differentiated position based on individual factors. As a result, many climate cases have been deemed inadmissible when brought directly by non-privileged applicants, including NGOs, citizens, and companies. It is also worth noting that, unlike other international courts, EU Member States play an active role in CJEU climate litigation due to the special nature of EU law.

Companies have been particularly active in EU climate litigation, either challenging regulatory measures or, more frequently, disputing technical or procedural aspects of climate laws. However, civil society involvement has been growing rapidly, making NGOs key actors in EU climate cases. The *Carvalho* (2018) and *Sabo* (2019) cases marked important milestones for civil society litigation, despite their early dismissal on admissibility grounds. In response to these setbacks, more recent cases have followed an internal review procedure under the Aarhus Regulation before being brought before the Court.

In sharp contrast with the European context, even a brief analysis highlights the Inter-American Court of Human Rights ("IACtHR") as the most progressive of all regional human rights courts. Similar to the African system, although quite different from a formal standpoint, the right to a healthy environment in the Inter-American system is recognised as both an individual and a collective right, particularly in cases concerning Indigenous peoples. This directly impacts standing requirements, as the intrinsic connection between individuals and their land broadens access to justice.

However, the most distinctive feature of the Inter-American system is its recognition of extraterritorial jurisdiction, grounded in control over domestic activities with extraterritorial effects, as established in Advisory Opinion 23/17 and reinforced in Advisory Opinion 32/25. This principle was further reinforced by Resolution 3/21 of the Inter-American Commission of Human Rights ("IACmHR") and has already influenced other entities, such as the UN Committee on the Rights of the Child (in *Sacchi v Argentina*, 2021), strongly diverging from the strictly restrictive stance of the European Court of Human Rights ("ECtHR") on extraterritorial obligations, as reaffirmed in *Duarte Agostinho and Others v Portugal and 32 Others* (2024). The causality test applied in climate cases has a significant impact not only on jurisdiction but also on standing, as its strict or expansive interpretation can shape the admissibility of cases.

It is, therefore, evident that legal culture plays a fundamental role in the interpretation of legal texts and the enforcement of norms, shaping divergent climate litigation frameworks across regions.

11.3 Between Fragmentation and Cross-Regime Interpretation: Legal Grounds in Climate Cases

Legal grounds in climate cases depend on the legal acts falling under the jurisdiction of each court or body. At first glance, the most obvious source of a legal obligation to mitigate or adapt to climate change appears in the United

Nations Framework Convention on Climate Change ("UNFCCC") or the Paris Agreement. However, Articles 14 and 24 of these treaties condition the initiation of proceedings on a State's explicit declaration of consent to the jurisdiction of the ICJ or an arbitral tribunal. As most States have refrained from granting such consent, litigation under these bodies is effectively precluded. Resorting to the ICJ's jurisdiction under Article 36 of the ICJ Statute remains possible but uncertain. This suggests that arguments invoking the UNFCCC or the Paris Agreement can primarily be raised in advisory proceedings. Unsurprisingly, therefore, the issue of States' responsibilities has been raised before the ICJ under the advisory opinion procedure upon the United Nations General Assembly's resolution (A/77/L.58) in 2023.

However, the UNFCCC and the Paris Agreement do not operate in isolation. A broad set of alternative international legal grounds applies in climate cases, including general international law principles (e.g., State sovereignty, territorial integrity, and self-determination), general environmental law (e.g., the no-harm principle, precaution, and prevention), the law of the sea (e.g., obligations to protect, preserve, and improve the marine environment), and general human rights law. As a universal court with broad jurisdiction, the ICJ can interpret and apply all these legal norms, including those enshrined in the UNFCCC, the Paris Agreement, and the law of the sea. The only exception concerns treaties that explicitly grant exclusive jurisdiction to another international court.

By contrast, ITLOS operates as a specialised tribunal with jurisdiction limited to the law of the sea. As such, it can interpret and enforce only the United Nations Convention on the Law of the Sea ("UNCLOS") and related treaties, including climate obligations linked to law of the sea. Nevertheless, UNCLOS provisions often require interpretation in light of broader international law principles, following the principle of systemic integration. This explains why in the Commission of Small Island States ("COSIS") Advisory Opinion, ITLOS exclusively referenced States' obligations under UNCLOS but extensively cited the Paris Agreement to contextualise these obligations in relation to GHG emissions and climate adaptation. The COSIS Opinion thus exemplifies how cross-regime interpretation helps prevent inconsistent rulings across international courts and tribunals concerning States' climate obligations.

Conversely, human rights bodies exercise a more specialised jurisdiction, as they are restricted to interpreting and enforcing their constitutive treaties. For example, while the Human Rights Committee evaluates compliance with the International Covenant on Civil and Political Rights ("ICCPR"), the Committee on the Rights of the Child assesses States' obligations under the UN Convention on the Rights of a Child ("UNCRC"), and the Committee on Economic, Social, and Cultural Rights does the same for the International Covenant on Economic, Social and Cultural Rights ("ICESCR").

Unsurprisingly, decisions in cases such as *Billy*, *Teitiota*, and *Sacchi* were limited to examining potential infringements of rights explicitly protected by these treaties. Although, in theory, a wide range of human rights may be invoked in climate cases, complainants most frequently rely on rights to life, physical integrity, health, privacy, family life, equality, non-discrimination, cultural rights, and self-determination. While the right to a healthy environment was recognised by the UN General Assembly, it is not yet guaranteed under universal human rights treaties.

However, since human rights norms are inherently broad and subject to systemic interpretation, human rights bodies inevitably reference other international legal instruments to clarify States' obligations in climate-related complaints. Thus, while these bodies lack jurisdiction over the UNFCCC or the Paris Agreement, they frequently cite these treaties to interpret the scope of human rights obligations in the context of climate change. As with ITLOS, systemic integration facilitates coherence between international legal frameworks and reduces inconsistencies across climate jurisprudence.

In regional human rights systems, climate cases remain rare. However, an analysis of existing environmental jurisprudence provides insight into potential future regional approaches.

In the African system, no climate cases are currently pending before the African Court, primarily due to strict admissibility requirements, particularly the exhaustion of domestic remedies. However, a recent initiative seeks to bring climate change before the African Court through a request for an advisory opinion under Article 4(1) of the 1998 Protocol.

Climate protection may be inferred from various legal instruments operating within and beyond the African Charter on Human and Peoples' Rights ("ACHPR") framework, such as the Maputo Protocol on Women's Rights in Africa, the African Charter on the Rights and Welfare of the Child, the Kampala Convention on Internally Displaced Persons, and the Revised African Convention on the Conservation of Nature and Natural Resources. Nevertheless, Article 24 of the ACHPR remains the primary legal basis for climate claims.

Sub-regional courts, such as the Economic Community of West African States ("ECOWAS") Court of Justice, have increasingly framed climate change and GHG emissions as environmental issues within the scope of Article 24. The right to a general satisfactory environment is framed as a peoples' right. This is rooted in the African cosmovision and understanding of a just world order, where life is understood as being established in connection with Nature and in a shared and communal manner. This, however, does not exclude the framing of Article 24 as also an individual right.

Moreover, African case law has linked Article 24 to the right to development (Article 22), requiring a case-by-case balancing of these rights without establishing a fixed hierarchy. The ECOWAS Court and the Commission have interpreted Article 24 as imposing three core duties on States: to respect, protect, and fulfil environmental rights. These obligations include taking reasonable measures to prevent pollution and ecological degradation, promoting conservation, and ensuring ecologically sustainable development and use of resources. Implied in this framework is an obligation of due diligence, subject to oversight by the African Court and Commission. In addition, the ECOWAS Court of Justice established that Article 24 ACHPR includes not only obligations of means, but also obligations of results. We can conclude that the African judicial system emphasis is placed on the effectiveness of State's actions against climate change in terms of implementation of mitigation action and policies.

Environmental cases in the African system have also arisen beyond the scope of Article 24 by linking environmental protection to the effective enjoyment of economic, social, and cultural rights. In this context, the rights to health (Article 16), education (Article 17), housing (Article 14), food (Articles 4 and 16), and water (Article 4) could also play a role in future climate cases. Additionally, African courts have recognised the intrinsic connection between traditional and cultural practices and the environment, emphasising their fundamental link to the right to a healthy environment.

In contrast, the ECtHR has issued numerous environmental rulings, despite the absence of an explicit right to a healthy environment in the ECHR. Instead, environmental obligations are derived from other human rights provisions, particularly the rights to life (Article 2) and respect for private and family life and home (Article 8), along with rights to a fair trial (Article 6), freedom of expression (Article 10), freedom of assembly and association (Article 11), effective remedies (Article 13), and property (Article 1 of Protocol No. 1). This extensive body of environmental jurisprudence provides multiple legal pathways for climate cases.

However, the key challenge in climate litigation before the ECtHR remains causation, which is essential for establishing positive obligations under the Convention. This issue was central in the *KlimaSeniorinnen* judgment, where the Court examined causation from two perspectives: scientific evidence (factual causation) and the actual impact of climate change on the enjoyment of protected human rights. While the Court recognised factual causation, it ultimately did not apply the causality test, dismissing individual claims due to a lack of victim status and addressing the NGO's complaint only in abstract terms, due to the lack of demonstrable concrete individual harm. Nonetheless, the judgment introduced two important principles for assessing State responsibility: discretion and proportionality.

Establishing causation is inherently difficult in climate cases, as climate change is a diffuse, multi-source, global, and intertemporal phenomenon. This complexity presents a unique challenge in the European legal framework, which is inherently centred on individual rights and claims. Unlike other systems, the European approach struggles to accommodate collective and global interests in climate litigation.

The American system has also dealt with numerous environmental cases. Both the IACmHR and the IACtHR have played a decisive role in shaping international environmental and climate principles and rights in Latin America. The express recognition of a right to a healthy environment dates to 1988 (Article 11 San Salvador Protocol), probably influenced by the explicit enshrinement in the African system in 1982. However, in spite of the earlier recognition in the African Charter, the potentialities of the right to a healthy environment have been far more developed in the Inter-American system.

Although the Inter-American human rights system shares some similarities with the European system – a significant set of environmental cases – it mostly exhibits notable differences. Recent jurisprudence has confirmed that the right to a healthy environment results not only from the San Salvador Protocol, but it is also rooted in the "progressive development" clause of the American Convention on Human Rights ("ACHR") itself (Article 26). The longstanding "green jurisprudence" of the IACtHR, shaped through binding judgments and advisory opinions – most notably Advisory Opinion 23/17 and recently Advisory Opinion 32/25 – demonstrates this significant evolution. Beyond the right to a healthy environment, this case law has addressed key human rights related to climate change, including the right to life (Article 4), personal integrity (Article 5), health (Article 10 of the San Salvador Protocol), communal property and participatory rights (Article 21), adequate nutrition (Article 12 of the San Salvador Protocol), and access to water (Article 26). Any of these rights could serve as the legal foundation for future climate litigation within the Inter-American system. However, the critical question is how the IACtHR will address climate litigation in cases that explicitly engage with the unique complexities of climate change.

In Advisory Opinion 23/17, the IACtHR (re)centred the right to a healthy environment, emphasising the strict relationship between environmental protection and human rights realisation and signalling an unquestionable duty of States to promote environmental justice through the reduction of human-made environmental impacts. This approach culminated in the *Lhaka Honhat v Argentina* (2020) case, where the Court for the first time applied the right to a healthy environment as an autonomous right under Article 26 of the ACHR, extending its scope to the protection of natural ecosystems, such as forests, rivers, and seas. This ecocentric perspective was further reinforced in *La Oroya v Peru* (2023), where the Court ruled that environmental protection applies even in the absence of concrete evidence of harm or risk to individuals.

By combining an ecocentric approach with the recognition of collective environmental rights and a broader acceptance of extraterritorial jurisdiction over GHG emissions, the Inter-American system presents promising prospects for future climate litigation. The landmark *Inuit* case (2005) was one of the earliest attempts to articulate "climate rights" for vulnerable communities based on personal and property rights. Currently, two additional cases are pending before the Inter-American system that invoke similar arguments. A key milestone in the system's evolution was Resolution 3/21, which consolidated two decades of case law and established positive State obligations regarding climate change. This resolution outlines multiple legal avenues through which climate cases can be brought before the Inter-American human rights system. The forthcoming advisory opinion on climate change is expected to reaffirm the Court's progressive stance and further refine its climate jurisprudence. The

Advisory Opinion 32/25 reaffirmed the Court's progressive stance and further refined its climate jurisprudence by recognizing, *inter alia*, a *jus cogens* norm prohibiting irreversible environmental harm and a duty to mitigate GHG emissions resulting from the human right to a healthy environment.

The landscape of climate litigation in EU law differs significantly from other international legal systems, in terms of both quantity and quality. This is largely due to the fact that the EU has adopted and implemented a substantial body of legislative acts addressing climate change, resulting in nearly 200 climate-related cases. As a consequence, most EU climate litigation does not focus on the absence of mitigation or adaptation measures but rather on challenges related to their implementation.

The core areas of EU climate litigation concern the reduction of GHG emissions, particularly within the framework of the EU Emissions Trading System, and energy production. The legal grounds invoked in these cases are diverse, often involving issues of competence, legal interpretation, validity challenges, and conflicts or overlaps with other areas of EU law, such as freedom of movement, state aid, public procurement, and tax law. Given the continuous adoption of new EU climate laws, litigation is expected to increase, with new legal grounds emerging over time.

However, a notable shift is occurring in recent cases, as claimants increasingly challenge the predominantly economic nature of climate litigation before the CJEU. While many cases still focus on GHG emissions and energy production, new claims are raising complex legal questions about balancing social cohesion with environmental goals and addressing the intersectional dimensions of sustainability.

To date, fundamental rights have played only a marginal role in CJEU climate litigation. Nonetheless, the Court may soon move closer to the issues addressed by human rights tribunals, as a growing number of pending cases invoke fundamental and participatory rights violations. These cases focus on both mitigation measures and just transition claims, signalling a possible evolution in the Court's approach to climate litigation.

11.4 A Final Note: The Relevance of the Cultural Background

A cross-cutting conclusion emerges from the preceding chapters and these conclusive remarks: while formal legal fragmentation plays a crucial role in shaping the procedural and substantive aspects of climate litigation, the social and legal environments underlying judicial decisions are equally significant.

The progressive, ecocentric case law of the Inter-American human rights system cannot be fully understood without considering the broader Latin American movement of transformative constitutionalism, as well as the growing domestic recognition of the rights of nature. Similarly, African and Latin American legal traditions share sociocultural perspectives on vulnerability and collective rights, which explains why both systems provide space for climate rights, albeit recognised under different subjects – whether individuals, peoples, or communities.

In contrast, despite the distinct characteristics of EU law and human rights law, a common thread can be found in the European legal tradition: a legal culture centred on individual rights and claims, with strict notions of causality and jurisdiction. This individual-centric approach influences standing rules, the definition of substantive obligations, and the broader capacity of European courts to engage with climate-related claims. As a result, it presents significant limitations when addressing environmental issues, which are inherently collective and transboundary. This challenge becomes even more pronounced in the context of climate change, a global and intergenerational problem.

The UN system, which integrates diverse legal cultures, reflects apparent contradictions in its approach to climate litigation. On the one hand, universal human rights treaties do not explicitly recognise an autonomous right to a healthy environment and instead rely on an indirect, duty-based protection framework similar to that of the European system. On the other hand, the UN Committee on the Rights of the Child has recognised extraterritorial jurisdiction in climate cases, aligning with the American system and contradicting the restrictive approach of the ECtHR.

A key takeaway from this book is that despite the procedural and substantive hurdles imposed by formal legal fragmentation, the fundamental factors shaping the outcomes of climate cases stem from deep-rooted legal and cultural divergences across regions. The upcoming ICJ advisory opinion on States' obligations in relation to climate change will be a critical moment in determining how these contrasting worldviews will be reconciled on a global scale.

Index

1998 Protocol 106, 108–109, 230, 233, 270

Aarhus Convention 148, 151, 215–218, 224, 250–253, 256–271
actio popularis 92, 207, 209, 211–212, 218–219, 250, 270
action (individual or joint) 9–10, 22, 25, 34–35, 37, 43–44, 50, 54, 56, 58, 63–64, 68, 70, 78, 81, 91, 93–94, 112, 117, 120, 123, 128, 135–137, 139–144, 147–152, 154–155, 168, 173, 179–181, 187–189, 192–193, 196, 198, 201, 209–212, 215, 217–222, 225, 228–229, 232–233, 237–238, 241–242, 247, 250–253, 257, 260–261, 267, 271
action for annulment 131–132, 137, 147, 149, 252–255, 267
action for damages 131–132, 137
action for failure to fulfil obligations 137
admissibility (decided on) 90–94, 129, 131–132, 137–141, 144–149, 211, 270–271
Adou Kouame 116
advisory jurisdiction (generally) 9, 10, 20, 54, 58, 108–109, 170–171, 269; and African Court on Human and Peoples' Rights 106, 108–110, 117–123, 231–238, 273–274; European Court of Human Rights (ECtHR) 44, 60, 75–83, 86, 94–96, 100, 102–105, 180, 206–229, 247, 249, 258–264, 271; Inter-American Court of Human Rights (IACtHR) 10, 27, 41–47, 51–70, 105, 115, 180, 187–204, 226–227, 268, 271–272; International Court of Justice (ICJ) 6, 10–14, 16–19, 31, 33, 37–38, 161–174, 181–183, 266–269, 274; International Tribunal for the Law of the Sea (ITLOS) 6, 9–10, 15–23, 37–38, 118, 161, 167–174, 182–183, 266, 269–270
Advisory Opinion 8–11, 16, 18, 20, 26, 28, 33, 38–40, 42, 44–45, 51–55, 58–61, 63, 68–70, 105, 109–110, 127, 163–164, 166–173, 181–187, 190, 194–201, 227, 266, 268–269, 272, 274
African Adaptation Initiative 120
African Charter on Human and Peoples' Rights (AfrCHPR, African Charter) 31, 35, 106–107, 109–110, 113, 115–116, 118, 122, 123, 226–237; and Article 24 106–107, 112–121
African Charter on the Rights and Welfare of the Child 112, 227, 270
African Commission on Human and Peoples' Rights (AfrCmHPR, African Commission, ACHPR) 26, 33, 105–123, 224–225, 228, 230–232, 244
African Convention on the Conservation of Nature and Natural Resources 112, 227, 270
African Union Climate Change and Resilient Development Strategy and Action Plan 134
Alliance of Small Island States (AOSIS) 168
allowance allocation 134, 141, 143, 153, 154
American Convention on Human Rights (ACHR) 23, 31, 35, 42, 51–54, 58, 61, 63, 188–199, 202, 226, 227, 272; and Article 4 51–52, 195; Article 5 195; Article 8 195; Article 13 195; Article 25 195; Article 26 35, 51–55, 188–189, 227, 272

Amicus curiae 168, 171, 187, 199–201
anti-climate litigation 141–142, 149, 155
arbitration 7, 14, 16–17, 164–165, 177
Arctic Athabaskan Councils Petition 47, 60
attribution 46, 167, 174, 229
authoritativeness (of a court, judgment, or opinion) 7, 18, 38

best available science 12, 56
Billy, Daniel 15, 24, 105, 178
burden-sharing 75, 79, 93, 98, 215, 220
business operators *see* corporations

carbon border adjustment mechanism 136
carbon budget 98, 228
carbon neutrality 98–99
Carême 75, 209, 211, 213
causation 76–90, 95–97, 99–104, 115, 181, 271
Centre For Legal Resources on Behalf of Valentin Câmpeanu 207, 209
Charter Of Fundamental Rights of the European Union (CFREU) 136, 148, 150–151, 153, 252, 258, 264
Charter of the Organisation of American States (OAS) 53, 188–189, 192, 194, 206
child(ren) 24–25, 30–31, 35–36, 48–49, 52–53, 60–61, 111–112, 152, 174–180, 227, 266, 268–270, 274
Children of Cité Soleil's Petition 48
choice of means *see* margin of appreciation or discretion
climate displaced persons 12, 43, 57, 85, 112, 122, 183, 252
climate migration *see* climate displaced persons
climate refugees *see* climate displaced persons
climate science 167, 224, 229
collective rights 115, 218, 267–268, 273
Commission of Small Island States (COSIS) on Climate Change and International Law 8, 12, 15–22, 118, 167, 171–174, 183, 269
common but differentiated responsibilities principle 22, 59, 111, 168, 198
compensation for harm (or reparation for damages) 25, 50, 55–56, 115–116, 131–132, 134, 137, 142, 197–198, 240–241, 243
conciliation 169, 177
Conference of the Parties (COP) to the UNFCCC and/or the Paris Agreement 5
corporations 25, 62, 141–142, 214
consent to jurisdiction 6–7, 19, 162–163, 167–169, 269
corporate litigation 25, 141–142
COSIS Agreement 20, 172
COSIS Opinion 8, 12–22, 118, 172–174, 183, 269
cross-fertilization (among international courts) 258
cross-regime interpretation and/or integration 51, 268–273

Declaration on the Rights and Duties of Man(or Declaration of the Rights and Duties of Man) 31, 53, 188, 191, 193–194
deforestation 37, 43, 44, 65, 194, 203, 243
desertification 13, 30, 225, 247
diagonal human rights claims 58, 63
dispute jurisdiction (generally) 6–11, 18–20, 65, 109, 127, 134, 161–171, 176–177, 192, 195, 201, 218–221, 234, 266; and African Court on Human and Peoples' Rights 6, 109, 230, 233, 236; European Court of Human Rights 44, 60, 75, 83, 86, 90, 94–96, 100, 102–105, 180, 206–207, 209, 211, 213–215, 217–219, 221–222, 226, 228, 247, 249, 258, 262–263, 268; Inter-american Court Of Human Rights 10, 27, 41–42, 46, 51–52, 54–55, 58, 60–61, 70, 105, 180, 187, 189, 192, 193, 200, 202, 204, 227, 268; International Court of Justice 6, 10, 161–166, 171, 181, 266; International Tribunal for the Law of the Sea 6, 18–19, 161, 167, 169, 171, 266
Draft Continental Strategy 120
drop in the ocean argument 89–90
due diligence obligations 12, 16–17, 22, 27, 45, 50–51, 56–62, 117, 123, 181, 183, 270

East African Community (EAC) Court of Justice 108, 230, 237

Economic Community of West African States (ECOWAS) Court of Justice 105, 108, 113–123, 236, 270, 271
Endorois 115, 121
energy law 135
Environmental Impact Assessment 22, 67, 147, 240
Escazú Agreement 43, 58, 68, 244
European Convention On Human Rights (ECHR) 23, 31, 75–76, 78, 80–81, 83–84, 86–87, 89, 91–96, 98, 100, 103–104, 153, 206–222, 226, 228, 260, 267, 271; and article 2 95, 214; article 6 76, 214, 219; article 8 75–77, 86–87, 92, 98, 209, 214, 228; article 34 23, 75, 206–207, 210, 214, 222: article 46 100
European Union Emissions Trading System (ETS) 129–136, 139, 141–145, 153–155
exhaustion of domestic remedies 180, 235, 244, 270
extraterritorial obligations 60–61, 69
extreme weather events 123, 194, 243

food access and/or security 23, 43, 48, 53, 122, 200, 203
fossil fuel (extraction, phase out) 43–44, 239
fragmentation of international law 1, 266
fundamental rights litigation 136, 148, 152–153, 155, 190, 242, 249, 251, 273
future generations 30, 47, 53, 65, 120, 142, 167, 180, 195, 217, 243, 252

general environmental law (and principles of) 68, 269
global warming 18, 23, 45–47, 49, 122, 193, 210–211, 217, 224, 238
greenhouse gas(es) (GHG) 5, 43, 59, 92, 105, 133–134, 145, 151, 154, 172, 178–179, 193, 198, 210, 225, 247; and concentration 5, 225; emissions 5, 12, 15, 17–19, 21–25, 37, 43, 46–47, 50, 54–63, 79–80, 82–89, 92, 97, 99, 105, 113, 115, 117–119, 129–135, 141–147, 150–155, 167, 172–173, 178–180, 193, 197, 210, 216–217, 219, 225, 269–270, 272–273; sinks and reservoirs 172
Greenpeace International 148, 211, 214

hearing on climate change 49, 240–241
highest possible ambition 12–13, 39, 56
human rights obligations (to mitigate and/or adapt) 15, 36, 42, 44–45, 50–51, 56, 66, 68–69, 81, 91–92, 103–104, 174, 198, 266, 270

indigenous groups 25, 29–36, 42, 44–47, 49–56, 62–63, 66, 68–69, 81, 91–92, 103–104, 115, 121–122, 168, 178–179, 190, 193–199, 203, 226, 268
individuals (concerned) 26, 36, 68, 80, 91–95, 116–117, 121–123, 175–176, 193–194, 204–222, 229, 234–237, 248–251, 259–260, 263, 266–269
inter-americanization 42, 64, 69–70
Intergovernmental Panel on Climate Change (IPCC) 5, 13, 15, 18, 28, 36, 39, 43, 84–85, 106, 123, 168, 224, 247
internal review procedure 148–149, 255, 256, 263, 268
International Covenant on Civil and Political Rights (ICCPR) 24, 27–33, 36, 167, 175, 177–178, 183, 268, 269
International Covenant on Economic, Social and Cultural Rights 24, 29, 174, 269
International Law Commission 169
internationally wrongful act 167
International Union for Conservation of Nature and Natural Resources (IUCN) 11, 26, 168
Inuit Petition 45–49, 69, 193

judicial clarification and/or development of the law 44, 46, 109, 180
judicial dialogue 64–69, 254, 258, 264
judicial restraint 128
jurisdiction (of States) 1, 7, 9, 13, 19–20, 22, 25, 58–63, 108, 161–171, 180–183, 210, 229, 231, 235–236, 238, 244; and extraterritorial jurisdiction 25, 45, 60–61, 70, 196, 210, 268, 272, 274

Kampala Convention for the Protection and Assistance of Internally Displaced Persons 112, 127, 270
Kichwa Indigenous People of Sarayaku 194, 203
Kyoto Protocol 5, 15, 144, 164

La Oroya 45, 51, 55–58, 61–62, 70, 197, 272
Lhaka Honhat 45, 51, 54–56, 58–59, 62, 65–66, 115, 197, 200, 272
local authorities 150, 219
local Communities 242–243
locus standi see standing
loss and damage 9, 11, 25, 62, 225, 243

Maputo Protocol to the ACHPR on the Rights of Women in Africa 35, 111, 227, 270
margin of appreciation or discretion (of domestic authorities) 22, 95–96, 98, 154
marine environment 15–22, 172–173, 269; and obligation to protect and preserve 228; pollution 15, 17–22
market stability reserve 134, 145, 153, 154
Mayagna (Sumo) Awas Tingni 29, 51–52
merits (decided on) 14, 24, 26, 28–30, 33, 51, 54–55, 77–79, 90, 94, 100, 102, 115, 129, 131–132, 137–139, 142, 163, 191, 211–212, 218, 221, 238, 248–249
migration *see* climate refugees displaced persons
Müllner 213

Nairobi Declaration on the African Process for Combating Climate Change 120, 225
national allocation plans 133–134, 143–144, 148, 153
nationally determined contribution (NDC) 12, 110–111, 198
Neubauer 28, 247
no-harm principle 58, 60, 90, 152, 196, 269
non-discrimination 33–34, 122, 150, 270
non-governmental organizations (NGOs, civil society organizations) 39, 46, 49, 70, 75, 110, 130–131, 135, 140, 151–152, 165, 189–192, 200, 206–207, 214–219, 222, 229–230, 233–235, 240–241, 247–260, 263, 267–268, 271

obligation 5, 8–13, 15–22, 24, 26–30, 32–34, 36, 38–39, 42, 44–45, 48, 50–51, 54, 56–63, 65–69, 75–83, 85–106, 109–114, 117–119, 121–123, 128, 131–132, 137, 151, 164, 167–169, 171–174, 177–178, 181–183, 189, 195–201, 227–229, 234, 237, 260–261, 266, 268–271, 274; and of adaptation 11, 35–36, 50, 58–59, 62, 85, 87–88, 109, 114–115, 117, 149, 179, 181, 229, 240, 242, 268–269; of cooperation 21, 63, 107, 154, 155, 204; to implement a regulatory framework 22, 62, 95–96, 105–106, 119; of means 271; of mitigation 12, 15, 22, 35–36, 39, 50, 57, 60–63, 79, 85, 94, 98, 101, 105, 109–118, 181, 198, 210–211, 242–247, 268, 273; of negotiation 22; to prevent transboundary harm *see* no-harm principle; to regulate 19, 54, 56–59, 62, 86, 118, 119; of result 12, 118, 271; to supervise and monitor 54, 56–59
OC-22/16 194
OC-23/17 26, 28, 35, 52, 55, 59–60, 68, 190, 191, 196–197, 201, 227
OC-32/25 61–64, 69–70, 268, 272, 273
Ogiek 121
Organization Of American States (OAS) 48, 53, 63, 188–189, 191–192, 194, 198, 226

Pacific Islands Forum 168
Paris Agreement 5–8, 11–12, 14–15, 17, 19, 21–23, 39, 50, 56, 60, 63, 110–111, 120, 152, 154, 164–165, 167, 172, 198, 226, 234, 239, 269–270
people's rights 2, 23, 26, 30–35, 46, 55, 105–106, 108–110, 113–117, 120–123, 225–226, 228, 230–234, 236, 244, 267
Plaumann Doctrine 249–267
polluter-pays principle 56, 147
positive obligations 26–27, 36, 38, 50, 59, 75–104, 123, 228, 271
precaution principle or approach 50
precedent 7, 19, 53, 69, 80, 203
preliminary reference procedure 248, 255, 260–263
prevention principle 16–17, 59, 65
principle of legal certainty 14, 149
principle of proportionality 84, 92, 96–97, 150, 154, 271
principle of sincere cooperation 154
principle of transparency 58, 62–63, 67–69, 154, 217

Principles and Guidelines on the Implementation of Economic, Social and Cultural Rights in the African Charter on Human and Peoples' Rights 115, 122
procedural measures 95–97
Protocol of Buenos Aires 188
provisional measures 169, 188, 201–203

quantitative emission reduction targets 100, 152, 252

resilience building 119
Resolution 3/21 on the Climate Emergency 45, 50, 60, 68, 268, 272
Revised African Convention on the Conservation of Nature and Natural Resources 112
right of access to justice in environmental matters219, 230, 242
right to a healthy environment (RHE) 42, 45, 48, 51–55, 57, 61, 70, 113–114, 116, 119, 153, 188–190, 193, 195, 197, 226–228, 233, 236, 244, 267, 270–274
right to cultural identity 25, 29–30, 47
right to development 29, 270
right to enjoy one's home and family life 25
right to food 122
right to health 35, 112–114, 117, 121, 122, 180, 227, 270, 272
right to housing 35, 111, 122, 217
right to information in environmental matters 237
right to life 24–28, 51–53, 61, 123, 148, 152, 177–178, 180, 183, 195–196, 206, 210, 212, 214, 220, 226, 237, 270, 272
right to participation in environmental matters 58, 190, 215, 227, 244, 254
right to personal integrity 195, 203, 227, 272
right to property 23, 45–47, 51, 54, 148, 152, 195, 237, 272
right to sanitation 35, 112, 122
right to self-determination 28–33, 122, 183, 269–270
right to water 122

Sacchi 24–25, 35, 60, 179–180, 268, 269
San Salvador Protocol 51, 52, 188, 191, 193, 195, 226, 271, 272; and Article 10 272; Article 12 272
Saramaka 30, 194, 196
scientific evidence and knowledge 12, 14, 80, 83, 97, 100, 271
sea level rise 13, 14, 24, 39, 119, 178, 224
Social and Economic Rights Action Center (SERAC) 113, 114, 116, 117, 119, 122, 123, 232, 233
Socio-economic Rights and Accountability Project (SERAP) 110, 113, 115, 116, 118, 123, 228, 237
Small Island Developing States (SIDS) 9, 167
Small Island States 8, 9, 20, 43, 167, 168, 171, 172, 269
standing (issues of) 92, 93, 99, 139, 147–149, 152, 155, 162, 165, 167, 172, 182, 187–190, 192–193, 195, 202–203, 206–222, 247–255, 259–264, 267–268, 274
State responsibility 18, 23, 38, 39, 55, 62, 63, 80–82, 84, 102, 103, 167, 173, 271
State's fair share 59
Stockholm Declaration 16
strategic litigation 140–142, 151, 156
Sub-Regional Fisheries Commission (SRFC) Opinion 20, 22, 171
substantive measures 95
systemic interpretation *see* cross-regime interpretation

taxonomy regulation 132, 135, 138, 140, 148, 149, 152
technical assistance 21
transboundary environmental damage 58, 60, 196
Treaty on the Functioning of the European Union (TFEU) 139, 145, 147, 150, 154, 249–252, 255, 257–258, 260, 262–263; and Article 191 147, 150, 252, 262; Article 194 154; Article 263 139, 249–252, 257, 260, 262–263; Article 267 250, 260, 267; Article 277 250

UN Charter 10, 13, 28, 136, 161–162, 164, 232, 234, 251, 267
UN Committee on the Rights of the Child 24–25, 178–180, 266, 268–269, 274
UN General Assembly (UNGA) 10, 29, 31, 163–167, 174, 181–182, 269–270

UN Guiding Principles on Business and Human Rights 57, 62
UN Human Rights Committee (HRC) 24–38, 105, 174–175, 177–178, 183, 224, 266, 269
UN Human Rights Council 23, 25, 44, 174, 183, 224
UN Security Council 10, 33, 163
United Nations Convention on the Law of the Sea (UNCLOS) 10–11, 14, 17–23, 167, 169–174, 269
United Nations Framework Convention on Climate Change (UNFCCC) 5–8, 11–17, 19, 21–23, 38, 57, 89, 110, 120, 152, 164–165, 172, 181, 226, 268–270
UNGA Res 77/276 5, 10, 182
Urgenda 28, 59, 247

Verein KlimaSeniorinnen 8, 75–80, 83–105, 118, 152, 209, 211–213, 215–222, 228, 247, 258–260, 263–264, 267, 271
victim status 75, 77, 79, 90–92, 94, 102, 201, 206–208, 210–215, 217, 220–222, 230, 259, 267, 271
Vienna Convention on the Law of Treaties (VCLT) 19, 162
vulnerability (increased) 106, 196, 204
vulnerable groups and communities 51, 120, 180, 190, 272
vulnerable States 38

water (access and/or security) 23, 30–31, 35, 43, 48, 53, 55–56, 119, 122, 144, 197, 200, 203, 225, 259, 271, 272
women 26, 34–35, 49, 111, 122, 174–175, 177, 191, 211, 213, 227, 248, 258, 270
World Meteorological Organization 166

Yakye Axa Indigenous Community 29, 51–52, 62, 196
Yanomami 203
youth 37, 48, 180, 248, 251

Zero Draft Report 120

FSC
www.fsc.org
MIX
Papier | Fördert gute Waldnutzung
FSC® C083411

Kolibri 360 GmbH
Ferdinand-Jühlke-Straße 7
99095 Erfurt, Deutschland
produktsicherheit@kolibri360.de